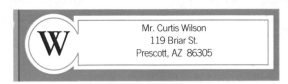

Now, That's a Good Question!

D0956995

R.C. SPROUL

Now, That's a Good Question!

TYNDALE HOUSE PUBLISHERS, INC.
WHEATON, ILLINOIS

Library of Congress Cataloging-in-Publication Data

Sproul, R. C. (Robert Charles), date
    Now, that's a good question! / R. C. Sproul.
      p. cm.
    Includes bibliographical references and index.
    ISBN 0-8423-4711-9 (alk. paper)
    1. Theology, Doctrinal—Popular works. 2. Theology, Doctrinal—Miscellanea.
    3. Evangelicalism—Miscellanea. I. Title.
    BT77.S7185   1996
    230—dc20   95-26112

Printed in the United States of America

10 09 08 07 06 05
17 16 15 14 13 12

CONTENTS

PREFACE

The theologian often suffers under the same burden as the quick-draw shooter in the Old West. Just as young gunslingers sought out famous veterans in order to give a challenge and win a reputation, so some people (especially students!) take almost diabolical glee in finding that one theological stumper. No doubt the great medieval scholastic debate on how many angels could dance on the head of a pin had as its root a question posed by a mischievous student.

Nearly ten years ago I set myself up for a plethora of challenges. At Ligonier Ministries in the mid-1980s we invited interested friends to join us in a recording studio to ask whatever theological questions they wished. I did not hear or read the questions in advance but had to try to answer them in the space of four minutes each. The questions and answers were recorded and broadcast on assorted radio stations. The program was called simply *Ask R. C.* Three hundred or so of those questions and answers are now together in this book, nicely cleaned up and missing assorted "uh's" and "um's."

Perhaps the first good question we should ask is why I would subject myself to such an ordeal. Unlike so many of the questions in this book, this is an easy one to answer. People have real, important, difficult questions. While answering insincere questions is a bane of my profession, answering sincere ones is a joy.

Confusion in any endeavor can be debilitating. When we begin to ask questions of great importance and when those questions lead us to the character of God, confusion is natural. We should almost expect it. God, after all, is infinite, while we are quite finite. Our confusion often flows from this fundamental truth—the finite cannot grasp the infinite.

God, however, does not leave us in this precarious spot. In his mercy and tenderness he has condescended to speak with us, to teach us through his creation and his Word. What an honor, then, to be of the profession that seeks to help people learn what God has revealed. What I hope you will find in this book is not R. C. Sproul's thought on assorted thorny questions, but God's wisdom.

The real danger in taking up the challenge of answering the questions of others is not that there might be questions for which I have no answers. The true danger is that I might give answers that aren't true—that I might teach error. This is the danger Scripture warns about when it promises a strong judgment awaiting teachers who lead others astray. My problem then is not only that I am finite but that I am fallible. As a human being I do err; it's possible that I have erred even as I have answered the questions included in this book.

You, though, can help alleviate my fear. As you read through this book looking for answers, please do so with the spirit of the Bereans. *Please check the Scripture, for it alone is our ultimate authority.* It alone is infallible in all that it teaches. It is our guide and our light. When we have a question, we can always say of Scripture, "Now, that's a good answer."

I

Knowing God

———

"Let not the wise man glory in his wisdom,
Let not the mighty man glory in his might,
Nor let the rich man glory in his riches;
But let him who glories glory in this,
That he understands and knows Me,
That I am the Lord, exercising lovingkindness,
judgment, and righteousness in the earth.
For in these I delight," says the Lord.

JEREMIAH 9:23-24

Questions in This Section:

Why does God love us so much?

What are the attributes of God?

What is the average Christian's understanding of God?

Why does God remain invisible?

What is the "providence of God"?

What does it mean for us to call God our Father?

What are the characteristics of the Christian God that differentiate him from other gods?

Among the other world religions, are there any that share the Christian concept of the holiness of God?

Throughout the Bible we are told to fear God. What does that mean?

I'm told that the Bible says God makes himself known to all people through his created world. In what way could the average person see God and his attributes through nature?

Why did God need to send angels down to check out the evil of Sodom and Gomorrah? Wouldn't he know these things already?

What is a miracle, and do you think God still performs them today?

Do you believe that God has audibly spoken to anyone since the apostolic age?

How would you define the sovereignty of God?

How do we reconcile the fact that God is sovereign with the fact that he has given us free will as persons?

In reference to John 6:44, does God compel people to come to him?

What is predestination?

Why does God allow random shootings, fatal accidents, and other horrible things to occur?

In the Old Testament God brought judgment against Israel and other nations through catastrophic events. Does this still happen?

Why does God love us so much?

That's one of the most difficult questions to answer if we think of it from God's perspective.

Here we are, his creatures who have been made in his image with the responsibility of mirroring and reflecting his glory and his righteousness to the whole world. We have disobeyed him countless times in every place and in every way. In so doing we have misrepresented his character to the whole universe. The Bible tells us that nature itself groans in travail, waiting for the day of the redemption of mankind, because nature suffers under our unrighteousness (Rom. 8:22).

When we think of how disobedient and hostile we've been toward God, we wonder what it is that would provoke him to love us so much. In Romans 5:7, when Paul is astonished by the love of Christ that was manifested in his death, he says, "Scarcely for a righteous man will one lay down his life, but imagine one who is perfect laying down his life for those who are not perfect and praying for those who are in the very act of killing him." That's the kind of love that transcends anything we have been able to experience in this world. I guess the only thing I can conclude is that it is the nature of God to be loving. This is part of his internal and eternal character.

The New Testament says that God is love. That can be one of the most misunderstood verses in the Scripture. We remember a few years ago when it was fashionable to say that "happiness is a warm puppy." We had these brief definitions of what happiness was, and the same thing was applied to love—"Love means never having to say you're sorry," etc.—and we're all very interested in what is involved in the whole act of loving.

But when the Bible says God is love, that statement is not what we would call an analytical statement whereby we can reverse the subject and predicate, and say that therefore love is God. That's not what the Bible means. Rather, what the Jewish form of expression says here is that God is so loving and his love is so consistent, so profound, so deep, so transcendent, and such an integral part of his character that to express it in the maximum way possible, we say that he is love. That is simply saying that God is the ultimate standard of love.

What are the attributes of God?

When we talk about the attributes of God, we're referring to those characteristics that describe God's being. He is one. He is holy. He is omniscient. He's omnipresent. He's omnipotent.

Those are some of the different words that we use to describe the nature and character of God; these are characteristics we attribute to God's being. When we describe someone's attributes, we usually make a distinction between a person and his attributes. For instance, you may say your mother is patient, but you wouldn't say that your mother is *patience*. And you would say that your mother is more than a mere list of traits. In the same way, God is not just a list of attributes. But God is different from your mother in that it was God's being that defined attributes in the first place. By gaining a better understanding of God, we can learn more about what true kindness is, what truth, beauty, patience, strength are. In this sense, God *is* his attributes. It's not that he's a composite being—three pounds of omniscience and three pounds of omnipresence, and three pounds of self-existence, etc.—added together to give us a concept of God. Rather, God in his essence, in his very being, is holy, and that holiness is immutable. All of God is immutable and all of God is holy. These attributes cannot be heaped up like sand in a sandpile to give us a composite portrait of God.

By studying the individual attributes of God, however, we're not dissecting God into composite parts. We're simply focusing our attention for a moment on one dimension or one aspect of his being. This can be very helpful to our understanding of God because the only way we are able to know God is through his attributes. The more we understand them, the more we understand his being and his character, and the more we are motivated to worship and obey him.

For more information on God's attributes, I'd like to suggest a book I've written on that very subject, *The Character of God* (Servant, 1995), in which I discuss the attributes of God for study by the layperson.

What is the average Christian's understanding of God?

I don't know what the majority view of God is in the Christian world. I can only guess from the small universe in which I live and the exposure that I have to various groups of people.

I certainly encounter a view of God that is widespread in the Christian community whereby God is somewhat reduced in scope from the biblical portrait that we have of him. He is seen as a sort of celestial grandfather who is benevolent in every respect and whose chief characteristic—and sometimes only attribute—is the attribute of love. We know that the Bible certainly puts an emphasis on the love of God and even goes so far as to say that God is love.

But I think we are in grave danger of stripping God of the fullness of his character as it is revealed in Scripture. This becomes a not-so-subtle form of idolatry. For example, if we obscure the holiness of God, or the sovereignty of God, or the wrath of God, or the justice of God, and sort of pick and choose those attributes of God that we like and then deny those that frighten us or make us uncomfortable, we've exchanged the truth of God for a lie, and we are worshiping a god who is in fact an idol. It may be a sophisticated idol—it's not one made of wood or stone or brass—but, nevertheless, the concept of God we worship must be a concept that agrees with the God who is.

I've been on a crusade for years to focus attention on the doctrine of God—the character of God. Three of my books deal with the doctrine of God the Father: *The Holiness of God, Chosen by God* (which focuses on God's sovereignty), and the latest one, *The Character of God* (which deals with the attributes of God). I wrote them intentionally as a trilogy to emphasize the character of God the Father because I think we are in grave danger of his being overlooked or distorted in the contemporary Christian world. We have some idea of who Jesus is, and the charismatic renewal has brought much more attention to the Holy Spirit in recent years. But we almost systematically ignore God the Father. You also find that many Christians ignore the Old Testament. The whole history of the Old Testament is the revelation chiefly of God the Father. Everything we read of God the Son and God the Holy Spirit—so amplified in the New Testament—presupposes the knowledge of God the Father that is given to us in the Old Testament. I think it's a priority for the Christian community to develop a higher understanding of the character of God.

Why does God remain invisible?

I don't think there's anything that makes living the Christian life more difficult than the fact that the Lord we serve is invisible to us. You know the expression in our culture "Out of sight, out of mind." It's very, very difficult to live your life dedicated to someone or something you cannot see. Often you hear people say that when they can see it, taste it, touch it, or smell it, they'll believe and embrace it, but not before. This is one of the most difficult problems of the Christian life: God is rarely perceived through our physical senses.

On the other side of the coin, I would say that one of the greatest hopes set before the Christian church is the promise of what we call in theology the beatific vision, or the vision of God. We think of John's letter in which he said,

"Beloved, now we are children of God; and it has not yet been revealed what we shall be, but we know that when He is revealed, we shall be like Him, for we shall see Him as He is" (1 John 3:2). The Latin there means "as he is in himself." That is to say, that which is totally concealed from our eyes right now, namely the very substance and essence of God, we will see in all of his glory and majesty and splendor in heaven.

I've often wondered about the text that says we will be like him, for we shall see him as he is. Does the Bible teach us that we will be totally cleansed from sin, totally glorified? Is this an experience that will eliminate sin from us altogether? Will it be because we catch a direct glimpse of the majesty of God? For example, if I see him—if he becomes visible to me—is that going to be the cleansing thing that rids all sin from my life; or is my seeing him going to be a result of his first cleansing me? I suspect it's the latter.

Scriptures tell us uniformly that no person shall see God and live; this is because God is holy, and we are not (see Exod. 33:20 and 1 Tim. 6:15). Even Moses, as righteous as he was, pleaded with God on the mountain to let him have an unveiled look at God's glory. God only allowed him to catch a refracted glimpse of God's back parts, but he said to Moses, "My face shall not be seen." Ever since Adam and Eve fell and were driven from the Garden, God has been invisible to human beings, but not because God is intrinsically incapable of being seen. The problem is not with our eyes but with our hearts. In the hymn "Immortal, Invisible, God Only Wise," there is that wonderful phrase "All praise we would render: O help us to see / 'Tis only the splendor of light hideth Thee."

In the Sermon on the Mount, Jesus made the promise that someday a certain group of people would see God. Blessed are those who mourn, for they shall be comforted. Those who hunger and thirst shall be filled. *Blessed are the pure in heart, for they shall see God.* It's because we're not pure in heart that God remains invisible, and only when we're purified will we see him.

What is the "providence of God"?

The word *providence* is a simple word made up of a prefix and a root. It means "to see beforehand." We could dismiss the providence of God by saying that God sees everything that happens in this world before it happens; he is the great celestial observer of human history. But the doctrine of providence involves so much more than God as a divine onlooker.

There are basically only three ways in which we can look at the relationship between God and this world. There is the deistic view, in which God creates the world and winds it up like a watch with built-in secondary causes, and the world works like a machine. God steps out of the picture, simply observes everything that takes place in this world, and he never intervenes, never intrudes. Everything happens according to the built-in secondary causes in the universe. That view has certain advantages to it because then nobody can blame God for anything that goes wrong. We can say that we as creatures are bringing about all of the tragedies and catastrophes in this world and that God is absolved because his hands are tied.

Another viewpoint, which is an overreaction to deism, claims that there are no real secondary causes in this world. Everything that happens is a direct result of God's immediate intervention; God causes my hand to go up and to go down. If there's an automobile accident at the intersection, God directly caused that. Free will is a total illusion, and there are no such things as secondary causes. We think that we're acting as responsible people, but we're not. God does it all. That's what we would call an ethical monism, whereby God determines everything and he actually causes everything that takes place.

I believe that the biblical view, which in my judgment is the classical historical Christian view, is a rejection of both of those positions. We believe that God created the universe and gave the power of secondary causality to things and people within it so that we actually can do things by our own volition, through our decisions, our minds, our wills and activities. But at every single point of our actions and of the secondary causes that are at work, God remains sovereign. There are times he works through secondary causes to bring about his will, and there are times he works without those secondary causes. Sometimes he just intrudes into the scene as he did in the blaze of Jesus' miracles in the New Testament; other times he makes use of our decisions and our activities to bring about his sovereign will. The providence of God means that God is sovereign over everything that happens in this world.

What does it mean for us to call God our Father?

One of the most well-known statements of the Christian faith is the Lord's Prayer, which begins with the words "Our Father which art in heaven." This is part of the universal treasury of Christendom. When I hear Christians in a private gathering praying individually, almost every single person begins their prayer by addressing God as Father. There's nothing more common among us than to address God as our Father. So central is this to our Christian experience that in the nineteenth century, there were some who said the basic essence of the whole Christian religion can be reduced to two points: the universal brotherhood of man and the universal fatherhood of God. In that context I am afraid we have missed one of the most radical teachings of Jesus.

A few years ago, a German scholar was doing research in New Testament literature and discovered that in the entire history of Judaism—in all existing books of the Old Testament and all existing books of extrabiblical Jewish writings dating from the beginning of Judaism until the tenth century A.D. in Italy—there is not a single reference of a Jewish person addressing God directly in the first person as Father. There were appropriate forms of address that were used by Jewish people in the Old Testament, and the children were trained to address God in proper phrases of respect. All these titles were memorized, and the term *Father* was not among them.

The first Jewish rabbi to call God "Father" directly was Jesus of Nazareth. It was a radical departure from tradition, and in fact, in every recorded prayer we have from

the lips of Jesus save one, he calls God "Father." It was for
that reason that many of Jesus' enemies sought to destroy
him; he assumed to have this intimate, personal relationship with the sovereign God of heaven and the creator of
all things, and he dared to speak in such intimate terms
with God. What's even more radical is that Jesus says to his
people, "When you pray, you say, 'Our Father.'" He has
given to us the right and privilege to come into the presence of the majesty of God and address him as Father
because indeed he is our Father. He has adopted us into
his family and made us coheirs with his only begotten Son
(Rom. 8:17).

What are the characteristics of the Christian God that differentiate him from other gods?

Perhaps the most unique characteristic of the Christian
God is that he exists. The other ones don't. Of course, that
is a matter of profound debate, as we all know.

I would say the chief and most critical differences have to
do, ultimately, with the Christian God's character of holiness. You're going to get an argument on this from other
people who will say that their gods are holy, too. What is
unique about Christianity among all the world religions is its
central doctrine of a once-for-all atonement that is offered
to people to grant them salvation. Old Testament Judaism
had a provision for the atonement of sin, but most religions
have no provision for an atonement, basically because they
do not consider it to be a prerequisite for redemption.

My question is, Why would a world religion not consider
an atonement necessary for redemption unless, in their

view, God is less than holy? If God is perfectly just and people are not perfectly just, yet those people are trying to be in a vital relationship with God, you have a basic, overwhelming problem. How would a God who is holy and just accept in his presence unjust creatures? That's what Judaism and Christianity understand as the vital problem. Human beings who are unjust must be justified somehow to enter the presence of a holy God. That's why the whole focus of Judeo-Christianity is at the point of atonement, which brings about reconciliation. But if you don't believe that God is all that holy, there's no need for any concept of reconciliation. We can live however we want because this kind of god is a cosmic bellhop who will overlook all of our sins and do whatever we want him to do for us. I would say the holiness of God is the vital difference.

Among the other world religions, are there any that share the Christian concept of the holiness of God?

There are no other religions that have a concept of God's holiness identical to the Christian concept. However, some other religions maintain a kind of parallel and approximate view of the matter, and certainly they have a concept of the holiness of God.

Insofar as Judaism in its various forms embraces the Old Testament, it would certainly embrace the concept of holiness we find there. We know that though there's an expansion of revelation as to the nature of God's holiness in the New Testament, it's certainly not an esoteric idea in the Old Testament. In fact, some of the most vivid displays of God's majesty and holiness are found in the Old Testament.

There are two ways in which the Bible speaks of God's holiness. The most commonly understood meaning of holiness in our culture is with respect to God's purity or his moral virtue—his righteousness. Certainly the Bible does use *holy* at times to describe the righteous, moral, pure character of God, but that's the secondary meaning of holiness. The primary meaning of holiness refers to God's apartness—otherness, transcendence—that sense in which he is much more majestic in all of his being than is any creaturely being. The transcendence of God is a dominant motif in the Old Testament and is certainly a part of the creeds of classical Judaism and Islam, insofar as Islamic religion builds upon much that was taken from the Old Testament. They see Muhammad as a descendant of Ishmael. They give certain allegiance to the patriarchs, and they deal with that concept of holiness.

The great difference between Christianity and other world religions regarding God's holiness is found in the concept of atonement. Judaism's view of atonement in the Old Testament was the sacrificial system that was part of their worship. The Christian view sees atonement as the once-for-all sacrifice made by a Savior, a suffering Savior, who died for the sins of the people. That concept is absent in other world religions, and it has always distressed me. I don't see how the other world religions could be comfortable with the fact of human sinfulness and the fact of the holiness of God *without* a mediator, without a Savior. It seems that they would have to negotiate either the sinfulness of man or the holiness of God to be comfortable where they are.

Throughout the Bible we are told to fear God. What does that mean? Can you give an example?

We need to make some important distinctions about the biblical meaning of "fearing" God. These distinctions can be helpful, but they can also be a little dangerous.

When Luther struggled with that, he made this distinction, which has since become somewhat famous: He distinguished between what he called a servile fear and a filial fear. The servile fear is a kind of fear that a prisoner in a torture chamber has for his tormentor, the jailer, or the executioner. It's that kind of dreadful anxiety in which someone is frightened by the clear and present danger that is represented by another person. Or it's the kind of fear that a slave would have at the hands of a malicious master who would come with the whip and torment the slave. Servile refers to a posture of servitude toward a malevolent owner.

Luther distinguished between that and what he called filial fear, drawing from the Latin concept from which we get the idea of family. It refers to the fear that a child has for his father. In this regard, Luther is thinking of a child who has tremendous respect and love for his father or mother and who dearly wants to please them. He has a fear or an anxiety of offending the one he loves, not because he's afraid of torture or even of punishment, but rather because he's afraid of displeasing the one who is, in that child's world, the source of security and love.

I think this distinction is helpful because the basic meaning of fearing the Lord that we read about in Deuteronomy is also in the Wisdom Literature, where we're told

17

that "the fear of the Lord is the beginning of wisdom." The focus here is on a sense of awe and respect for the majesty of God. That's often lacking in contemporary evangelical Christianity. We get very flippant and cavalier with God, as if we had a casual relationship with the Father. We are invited to call him Abba, Father, and to have the personal intimacy promised to us, but still we're not to be flippant with God. We're always to maintain a healthy respect and adoration for him.

One last point: If we really have a healthy adoration for God, we still should have an element of the knowledge that God can be frightening. "It is a frightening thing to fall into the hands of the living God" (Heb. 10:31). As sinful people, we have every reason to fear God's judgment; it is part of our motivation to be reconciled with God.

I'm told that the Bible says God makes himself known to all people through his created world. In what way could the average person see God and his attributes through nature?

Romans 1 speaks plainly of this universal revelation that God makes to the world even as it's hinted at in other places, such as the psalm that tells us, "The heavens declare the glory of God, and the firmament shows his handiwork." In writing to the Romans, Paul says that ever since the creation of the world, the existence of God is not only revealed but is clearly perceived through the things that are made. He speaks of the invisible qualities of God being understood or known through the visible things of creation. In light of this revelation, the whole world is without excuse if they reject God. No one can claim ignorance of God as an excuse for refusing to honor him or to be grateful to him. That's the burden of the first chapter of Romans.

Now, how would the average person see this? I recall a conversation I heard once on a talk show in which three very sophisticated theologians debated the question of the existence of God. One was Jewish, one was Roman Catholic, and one was Protestant. They were arguing whether or not you could prove the existence of God. It was a very technical level of debate, and then they opened up the telephone lines and allowed the "average person" to get involved. A woman called in whose poor grammar indicated she wasn't very highly educated. She said, "I don't know what's wrong with you guys. Why don't you just open your eyes and look out the window?" She set these trained theologians on their ears with a very direct and straightforward appeal to nature itself as proof of the existence of God.

In theology there's a historical question of whether or not this revelation that God makes in nature is what we call *immediate* or *mediate*. In this sense, these terms don't refer to time, but to whether God reveals himself directly to you and me or makes himself known through some intermediate person or thing, respectively. For example, we see a clock, and that suggests that a clockmaker made it. This clock is an example of mediate revelation. We don't have to have a Ph.D. to recognize that a clock didn't create itself. It was produced by somebody in an intelligent way with some kind of design. I think the Bible teaches that we have both an immediate and a mediate knowledge of the existence of God.

What Paul talks about in Romans 1 is what we would

call mediate. He says that we know God through the things that are made. That does require some thinking. I see something out there that has order and harmony and organization to it, and I have to reason that there's some cause for this, and I assign this cause for all that exists out there to the great Author of creation. I think this is how the average person would make the connection.

When the Lord was talking to Abraham about Sodom and Gomorrah, he said, "I will go down and see if they have done entirely as it has been told to Me." Why does God say he needs to go down to see these cities? Wouldn't he know these things already?

God would know it without having to go down and check it out personally because God is omniscient. He knows all things; the hairs on the heads of the people of Sodom and Gomorrah were numbered. He knew everything they had ever done, every idle word they had ever spoken. He didn't need to canvass them with a new census to see how wicked they were.

There are two ways of approaching this difficult verse (Gen. 18:20). Often these conversations with God were really conversations with angelic messengers who were representing God. The angelic messengers themselves do not have the omniscience that we attribute to God. It may be in this case that the angelic visitor who was going to check out the situation was speaking for himself.

Even in Abraham's test at Mount Moriah, where he was told to offer Isaac on the altar and at the very last minute as he stretched out his arm to plunge the knife into the

chest of his son, the voice of the Angel of God stopped
him and said, "Lay not thy hand now upon your son,
Abraham, because now I know that you love me." The
suggestion is that God didn't know of Abraham's love
before this happened. It's as if God were a celestial spectator pacing back and forth, wringing his hands, hoping
that Abraham would make the right decision and do the
right thing, but he was helpless to do anything about it
until the outcome.

A lot of people think of God in those terms, as if he is
just a cosmic spectator of what's going on and he doesn't
know the end before the beginning. They make God finite,
dependent, derived, everything less than the God who is
revealed in Scripture.

The second approach to this passage takes into account
that every time the Bible describes anything about God,
whether it's in a narrative or a didactic passage, whether
it's abstract or concrete, the only language available to
the biblical writers was human language. We can't talk as
fish, we can't talk as snails, because we're not snails and
we're not fish. Nor can we talk as God. When God speaks
to us and reveals himself to us, the only language we can
understand is human language. When the Bible uses
what we call phenomenological language, or the language of appearances, the Bible speaks of God's learning.
It describes very crude images, such as God having his
feet on the couch. At the same time, the Bible tells us
that even though it uses human language, God is not a
human who can be contained or fully described by these
figures of speech.

I think that in the situation of Sodom and Gommorah,

either the angel was speaking for himself—he did have to go see what the cities were like—or this was God's way of explaining the situation to Abraham, letting Abraham know what would happen and that God was in charge.

Please define a miracle and state whether or not you think God still performs them today.

There is a tremendous difference between the popular definition of a miracle in our culture and the narrow technical definition of a miracle that theologians work with in their science. We can often have serious communication problems when people ask me whether I believe that God is doing miracles today.

If by a miracle we mean that God is alive and well and running his world by his providence, affecting the course of human events, then by all means God is doing those things. If the question is asking whether or not God is answering prayers, then I would say emphatically, yes, God is answering prayers. If people are asking whether the providence of God is bringing extraordinary things to pass today, I would say absolutely. Does God heal people in response to prayer? I would say yes to all of those questions because I'm convinced that God is alive and well and doing all of those things.

If we define a miracle as a supernatural work of God, then I would say that God certainly does supernatural works today. The rebirth of a human soul cannot be done by natural means; only God can do it through his power, and God is certainly doing that every day. If that's what people mean by a miracle, then God is doing miracles today. Some people define a miracle so broadly as to say that even the birth of a child is a miracle because it's a marvelous thing that couldn't happen apart from the power of God. So they would define a miracle as any wonderful thing that happens by the power of God. If that's the definition of miracle, then again I would say that, absolutely, God is performing them today.

However, we may be speaking of miracle in the technical sense of an action performed against the laws of nature—God circumventing the very laws he put into motion—for example, bringing life out of death or something out of nothing, such as Jesus raising Lazarus from the dead when his body was in a state of decomposition after four days in the tomb. No, I don't think that God is doing that kind of miracle today.

I certainly believe God could raise every human being in every cemetery in this world today if he wanted to. But I don't think he is performing those kinds of miracles today. The chief reason he did those things in biblical days was to certify revelation as divine—to back up what he spoke with evidence of his authority. Since we now have the Bible, other, miraculous sources of revelation are no longer necessary.

Do you believe that God has audibly spoken to anyone since the apostolic age?

I don't know for sure whether God has or not. Certainly there are abundant cases in church history where people claim to have heard voices that were the audible voice of God. Joan of Arc would be Exhibit A. That testimony has come more than once from people whom we generally recognize as being reputable saints, and so I hesitate to cast aspersions on their testimony.

On the other hand, we find that even in sacred Scripture, during a time when God was giving direct communication of divine revelation, the occurrences of an audible voice of God were extremely rare. I can only think of three times in the New Testament that there's a record of God speaking audibly, and all three of them were occasions where the Father made a public declaration about his Son, who incidentally is no longer with us on this planet in the flesh. There's no other record of anyone being talked to by God audibly, with the exception of Saul (Paul) on the road to Damascus.

Even in the Old Testament, though it happens with those who are agents of revelation, those occurrences are very rare indeed. In biblical times, even at the height of divine revelation, audible revelation direct from heaven was rare.

I don't think we are in a period of redemptive history in which we're getting special revelation from God. It would seem to me it would be even less likely that you would get that kind of audible expression from God today. Add to that a factor that many Christians don't like to consider: Hearing voices when there's no discernible source can be a manifestation of a psychosis. I'm not saying it is, but it can be. There are people who do suffer from hallucinatory experiences in which they hear voices as a result of chemical imbalances and so on. I can't think of anyone who has ever told me they actually heard the audible voice of God, but if they did, I would be concerned about their mental state. I wouldn't conclude immediately that they were crazy, but I don't think it's normal or expected in the devout Christian life to be hearing the audible voice of God.

How would you define the sovereignty of God?

I have a close friend who came to this country from England. His name is John Guest. He is an Episcopalian priest in Pittsburgh. When he first came to the United States, he visited an antiquarian in Philadelphia, and there he saw some slogans and mementoes and poster boards that actually date back to the eighteenth century, during the American Revolution. He saw signs like "Don't tread on me" and "No taxation without representation," but the one that caught his eye was the one that said in bold letters, "We serve no sovereign here." When John looked at that, as an Englishman, he said, "How can I possibly communicate the idea of the kingdom of God in a nation that has a built-in allergy to sovereignty?"

As Americans we're used to a democratic process of rule. When you're talking about sovereignty, you're talking about government and about authority. From a biblical perspective, when the Scriptures speak of God's sovereignty, they reveal God's governmental authority and power over his entire universe.

In my classes in the seminary, I raise questions like, "Is God in control of every single molecule in the universe?" When I raise that question, I say, "The answer to that question will not determine whether you are a Christian or a Moslem, a Calvinist or an Arminian, but it will determine whether you are a theist or an atheist." Sometimes the students can't see the connection. And I say to them, "Don't you realize that if there is one molecule in this universe running around loose outside the scope or the sphere of God's divine control and authority and power, then that single maverick molecule may be the grain of sand that changes the entire course of human history, that blocks God from keeping the promises he has made to his people?" It may be that one maverick molecule that will prevent Christ from the consummation of his kingdom. For if there is one maverick molecule, it would mean that God is not sovereign. If God is not sovereign, then God is not God. If there is any element of the universe that is outside of his authority, then he no longer is God over all. In other words, sovereignty belongs to deity. Sovereignty is a natural attribute of the Creator. God owns what he makes, and he rules what he owns.

How do we reconcile the fact that God is sovereign with the fact that he has given us free will as persons?

I don't see any problem in reconciling the sovereignty of God with man's free will as long as we understand the biblical concept of freedom. With respect to mankind, human beings are given the ability to make free choices, but our freedom is a limited freedom. We are not absolutely free. Remember, God said to Adam and Eve, "You may eat of all of the trees in the Garden." But then he added a restriction: "Of this tree you may not eat. If you do, you will surely die."

Now, God is a being who has the ability to make free

choices, and I am a being who has the ability to make free choices. The difference, however, is that I am not sovereign. God is sovereign. God has more authority than I do. God has the right and the power and the authority to do whatsoever he pleases. I have the power and the ability and the freedom to do those things that I can do, but my freedom can never override the power or the authority of God. My freedom is always limited by the higher freedom of God. What is a contradiction is *God's sovereignty* and *human autonomy*. *Autonomy* means that man can do whatever he wants without being worried about judgment from on high. Obviously those two are incompatible, and we do not believe that man is autonomous. We say that he is free, but his freedom is within limits, and those limits are defined by the sovereignty of God. This is a simple analogy: In my house I have more freedom than my son. We both have freedom, but mine is greater.

In reference to John 6:44, does God compel people to come to him?

That passage, of course, is very controversial. In an older translation of it, Jesus says, "No man can come to me unless the Father draws him." The dispute about that passage has to do with the meaning of the word translated "to draw." What does it mean? There are those biblical scholars and Christians who believe that it means to entice, to woo, or to seek to persuade. For them, then, what Jesus is saying is, "People, if left to themselves, are not going to seek me out; there has to be something added to their normal inclinations before they would be moved to come in my direction." Jesus is saying that God has to do something. And the old translation is that he has to draw them just as the Siren voices drew Ulysses to the sea. They tried to entice him, persuade him, and woo him to come by being as attractive as possible in granting the invitation. Some people hold the strong opinion that wooing is the very opposite of compulsion, that God doesn't compel people to come to Jesus but he does entice them and encourage them and try to woo them and show them how attractive Jesus is so that they will incline themselves to respond to Jesus.

I once had a debate on this subject with a professor of New Testament studies who was an expert in the biblical languages. I was taking the position that God does more than invite and entice and woo. I think the word here is very strong because it is the same word that is used in the book of Acts when Paul and Silas are dragged into prison. It's not like the jailer went inside the bars and tried to woo Paul and Silas, saying, "Come on, fellows, please come on in here." He compelled them to go inside that jail. I think the word there is strong, and I pointed that out to the New Testament professor. Then he surprised me somewhat because he quoted the use of the same verb that he found in some other Greek literature where the verb was used to describe the human activity of drawing water from a well. And the professor went on to say, "Now, you don't compel water to come up out of a well." And I said, "But I have to say you don't woo it either. You don't stand up there and say, 'Here, water, water, water,' and expect the water on its own power to jump up out of the well into your bucket. You have to go down with your bucket and take that water."

I think the force of that verb is to say that we are in desperate need of the assistance of God to come to Christ, and we will not come to Christ unless the Father brings us to him.

What is predestination?

When the Bible speaks of predestination, it speaks of God's sovereign involvement in certain things before they happen. He chooses in advance certain things to take place. For example, he predestined creation. Before God created the world, he decided to do it.

Usually when people think of predestination, they think about whether or not somebody was hit by an automobile on a given day because God had decided ahead of time that that should happen on that day.

Theologically, the principal issue of predestination in the Bible has to do with God selecting people for salvation beforehand. The Bible clearly does teach that somehow God chooses people for salvation before they're even born. Virtually every Christian church believes that, because this concept is so clearly taught in Scripture.

Paul refers to Jacob and Esau. Before they were even born, before they had done any good or evil, God decreed in advance that the elder would serve the younger: "Jacob have I loved; Esau have I hated." The point there is that God had chosen certain benefits for one of those two before they were even born.

The real debate is, On what basis does God predestine? We know that he predestines, but why does he predestine, and what is the basis for his choices? Many Christians believe that God knows in advance what people are going to do, what choices they're going to make, and what activities they're going to be involved in. As he looks through the corridor of time and knows what choices you will make, for example, he knows that you will hear the gospel. He knows whether you will say yes or no. If he knows that you are going to say yes, then he chooses you for salvation on the basis of his prior knowledge. I don't hold that position. I think that God does this sovereignly, not arbitrarily, not whimsically. The only basis I see for predestination in the Bible is the good pleasure of his own will. The only other reason is to honor his only begotten Son. The reason for his selection is not in me and not in you and not in some foreseen good or evil, but in his own sovereignty.

Why does God let random shootings, fatal accidents, and other horrible things occur?

Since we believe that God is the author of this planet and is sovereign over it, it's inevitable that we ask where he is when these terrible things take place.

I think the Bible answers that over and over again from different angles and in different ways. We find our first answer, of course, in the book of Genesis, in which we're told of the fall of humanity. God's immediate response to the transgression of the human race against his rule and authority was to curse the earth and human life. Death and suffering entered the world as a direct result of sin. We see the concrete manifestation of this in the realm of nature, where thorns become part of the garden and human life is now characterized by the sweat of the brow and the pain that attends even the birth of a baby. This illustrates the

THINK ABOUT That →

fact that the world in which we live is a place that is full of sorrows and tragedy.

But we must never conclude that there's a one-to-one correlation in this life between suffering and the guilt of the people on whom tragedies fall. If there were no sin in the world, there would be no suffering. There would be no fatal accidents, no random shootings. Because sin is present in the world, suffering is present in the world, but it doesn't always work out that if you have five pounds of guilt, you're going to get five pounds of suffering. That's the perception that the book of Job labors to dispel, as does Jesus' answer to the question about the man born blind (John 9:1-11).

SPECIFIC OR GENERAL?

On the other hand, the Bible makes it clear that God lets these things happen and in a certain sense ordains that they come to pass as part of the present situation that is under judgment. He has not removed death from this world. Whether it's what we would consider an untimely death or a violent death, death is part of the nature of things. The only promise is that there will come a day when suffering will cease altogether.

The disciples asked Jesus about similar instances—for example, the Galileans' blood that was mingled with the sacrifices by Pilate or the eighteen people who were killed when a temple collapsed. The disciples asked how this could be. Jesus' response was almost severe. He said, "Unless you repent, you will all likewise perish," again bringing the question back to the fact that moral wickedness makes it feasible for God to allow these kinds of dreadful things to take place in a fallen world.

In the Old Testament, God brought judgment against Israel and other nations through catastrophic events. Does this still happen?

Is God still God? Is God still the Lord of history? The difference is this: When God used a catastrophe as an arm of judgment in the Old Testament, we know that his judgment was behind the catastrophic event because we have the benefit of the written revelation telling us that this was God's hand in history. As we live out our lives and see nations suffer catastrophes and calamity strike people, we don't know exactly what the relationship is between those catastrophes and the judgment of God.

Let me construct a biblical parallel here. In the ninth chapter of John's Gospel, the Pharisees raised this question about a man born blind: Was this man born blind because he was a sinner or because his parents were sinners? Jesus' answer: It was neither one of them. He was born blind for another reason altogether. It wasn't done as a matter of course, as an expression of divine judgment. That text and the whole book of Job should restrain us in the case of individuals from ever assuming that a person's tragedy or catastrophe or calamity is a direct act of divine judgment. Now, it may be. We see countless cases in Holy Scripture where God does, in fact, bring calamity upon the house of a person who has been flagrant in disobedience toward God. The Bible is saying that if we are guilty, God may withhold judgment until later, or we may receive temporal judgment in this world right now at his hands. We never know for sure whether the calamity we experience as individuals is a direct act of judgment or not. What is true of individuals is also true of nations.

I remember hearing Billy Graham say in a sermon a few years ago, "If God does not bring judgment upon the United States of America, he's going to have to apologize to Sodom and Gomorrah." Remember, Jesus warned the cities that heard his message, Chorazin and Bethsaida, that the Day of Judgment would be more tolerable for Sodom and Gomorrah than it would be for them. While we no longer have prophetic interpretation of God's reasoning for bringing judgment, we do know that no nation is ever exempt from the judgment of God.

2

Who Is Jesus?

He was in the beginning with God.
All things were made through Him. . . .
In Him was life, and the life was the light of men.
And the light shines in the darkness,
and the darkness did not comprehend it. . . .
He came to His own, and His own did not receive Him.

JOHN 1:2-5, 11

Who Is Jesus?

Questions in This Section:

The prophecy concerning the birth of Christ comes from Isaiah 7:14: "Behold, a virgin shall conceive and bear a son, and his name shall be called Immanuel." Why was he then called Jesus?

How can a person have a divine nature and a human nature at the same time in the way that we believe Jesus Christ did?

When Paul wrote that Jesus emptied himself and became a servant and yet he was God, in what ways did he retain or not retain his powers of being God?

In the Gospel of John, Jesus says, "The Father is greater than I." What does he mean by that?

Was Christ capable of sinning?

Why did Jesus say some people wouldn't die before he came back?

What did Jesus mean when he said we would do greater work than he did?

What was God's answer to Jesus' question "My God, my God, why hast thou forsaken me?"

Did Jesus ever laugh?

The prophecy concerning the birth of Christ comes from Isaiah 7:14: "Behold, a virgin shall conceive and bear a son, and his name shall be called Immanuel." Why was he then called Jesus?

That does, on the surface, seem like a flat-out contradiction, doesn't it? The prophecy in the Old Testament is that his name will be Immanuel, and then we go to the New Testament, and they don't name him Immanuel; they name him Jesus. How do we deal with that?

First of all, let's not assume that Isaiah is radically mistaken. If we look at the full import of his prophecy, we stand in utter amazement at the detailed way in which the prophecies of Isaiah do in fact come to pass in the life of Jesus. If we go just two chapters past the "Immanuel" prophecy, we find another familiar passage that we repeat virtually every Christmas during our times of worship. Isaiah went on to say that the Messiah who would be born would be given the name "Wonderful, Counselor, Mighty God, Everlasting Father, Prince of Peace." How many names does he have? In chapter 7 he says his name is going to be Immanuel, and in chapter 9 he says it's going to be Prince of Peace, or Mighty God, or Everlasting Father. So in his own writing, Isaiah was calling attention to the fact that the Messiah would have a multitude of names. He does not reduce Jesus' titles to one, so I don't think he is using the word "name" to refer to the family name or the proper name of Jesus, but he is referring to a crucial title

39

that would be given to Jesus, and in fact it was. Immanuel is one of his titles in the New Testament—Immanuel, "God with us."

The name *Jesus* is given to him by God by means of the evangelical messenger who announced the Father's choice to name the Son, and he's called Jesus because that name means "Savior"—one who will save his people. His name indicates his mission, his ministry. I think one of the most fascinating studies is to go through the Scriptures and list the names that are attributed to Jesus.

I attended a convocation at a theological seminary once at which a Swiss theologian gave an address. At an academic occasion like that, one expects to hear a very technical, sophisticated, boring piece of theology. This professor simply got up before the assembly and began to recite the names of Jesus, saying, "Alpha and Omega, Son of Man, Lion of Judah, Lamb without Blemish, the Messiah, the Son of God, the Rose of Sharon . . ." He went on for forty-five minutes and still didn't exhaust all of the names and titles that the New Testament attributes to Jesus—Jesus, the most titled man in human history.

How can a person have a divine nature and a human nature at the same time in the way that we believe Jesus Christ did?

One of the great crises in evangelical Christianity today is a lack of understanding about the person of Christ. Almost every time I watch Christian television, I hear one of the classical creeds of the Christian faith being denied blatantly, unknowingly, unwittingly. And of course, part of the reason is that it is so difficult for us to understand how one person can have two natures. You are asking me the question "How?" I don't know *how;* I know *that* Jesus is one person with two natures. How can that be? Long before there was a human nature, there was a second person of the Trinity. Here the second person of the Trinity, very God of very God, God himself, was able to take upon himself a human nature. No human being could reverse the process and take upon himself a divine nature. I cannot add deity to my humanity. It's not as if Christ changed from deity *into* humanity. That's what I hear all the time. I hear that there was this great eternal God who suddenly stopped being God and became a man. That's not what the Bible teaches. The divine person took upon himself a human nature. We really can't understand the mystery of how this happened. But it is conceivable, certainly, that God, with his power, can add to himself a human nature and do it in such a way as to unite two natures in one person.

The most important council about this in the history of the church, whose decision has stood for centuries as the model of Christian orthodoxy and is embraced by Lutherans, Presbyterians, Methodists, Roman Catholics, Baptists—virtually every branch of Christendom—is the Council of Chalcedon. It was held in the year 451, in which the church confessed its belief about Jesus in this way: They said that we believe that Jesus is *verus homus, verus Deus*—truly man, truly God. Then they went on to set boundaries for how we're to think about the way in which these two natures relate to each other. They said that these two natures are in perfect unity, without mixture, division, confusion, or separation. When we think about the Incarnation, we don't want to get the two natures mixed up and think that Jesus had a deified human nature or a humanized divine nature. We can distinguish them, but we can't tear them apart because they exist in perfect unity.

When Paul wrote that Jesus emptied himself and became a servant and yet he was God, in what ways did he retain or not retain his powers of being God?

The concept of "emptying" was a raging controversy in the nineteenth century, and elements of it remain today. The Greek word used by Paul in the second chapter of Philippians, *kenosis,* is translated as "emptying" in most Bible versions. The question is, Of what did Jesus, in his human (incarnate) state, empty himself?

The popular view in certain circles in the nineteenth century was that at the time of the Incarnation, the eternal God, the second person of the Trinity, laid aside—emptied himself of—his divine attributes so that he could become a man. And in becoming a man in the very real sense, he stopped being God. And so there is the transformation from deity to humanity because he set aside his omniscience, his omnipotence, his self-existence, and all of those other attributes that are proper to the nature of God.

There was one orthodox theologian during the middle of that controversy who said somewhat caustically that the only emptying that theory proved was the emptying of the minds of theologians who would teach such a thing as God stopping for one second to be God. If God laid aside one of his attributes, the immutable undergoes a mutation; the infinite suddenly stops being infinite; it would be the end of the universe. God cannot stop being God and still be God. So we can't talk properly of God laying aside his deity to take humanity upon himself. That is why orthodox Christianity has always declared that Jesus was *verus homus, verus Deus*—truly man, truly God; fully man and fully God. His human nature was fully human, and his divine nature always and everywhere was fully divine.

Nevertheless, the apostle Paul does speak of Christ emptying himself of something. I think the context of Philippians 2 makes it very clear that what he emptied himself of was not his deity, not his divine attributes, but his prerogatives—his glory and his privileges. He willingly cloaked his glory under the veil of this human nature that he took upon himself. It's not that the divine nature stops being divine in order to become human. In the Transfiguration, for example (Matt. 17:1-13), we see the invisible divine nature break through and become visible, and Jesus is transfigured before the eyes of his disciples. But for the most part, Jesus concealed that glory. I think Paul is saying in Philippians 2 that we're to imitate a willingness to relinquish our own glory and our own privileges and prerogatives.

In the Gospel of John, Jesus says, "The Father is greater than I." What does he mean by that?

Sometimes when Jesus makes straightforward statements that appear to mean one thing on the surface, they require that we go a bit beneath the surface to resolve the apparent difficulty. In this case, that kind of extra labor is not required. Jesus meant exactly what he said: "The Father is

greater than I." That's somewhat distressing for Christians
because we have this sacred doctrine of the Trinity that
describes the unity of the three persons of the Trinity—
Father, Son, and Holy Spirit. Here the Son of God is saying
that the Father is greater than he is. This is one of the reasons the church has always confessed a doctrine called the
subordination of Christ. Notice that it's not called the inferiority of Christ. I stress that because in our culture some
people conclude that subordination necessarily implies
inferiority.

The reason Christian theology contains a doctrine about
the subordination of Christ is that even though the second
person of the Trinity is coessential with the Father (he's of
the same essence, "very God of very God," eternal in his
being) there is a distinction among the persons of the Godhead. In the economy of redemption and even of creation,
we see certain works attributed to the Father, others to the
Son, and others to the Holy Spirit.

The traditional view is that the Son is begotten of the
Father—not created, but eternally begotten. The Father is
not begotten of the Son. The Son is sent into the world by
the Father; the Son does not send the Father. Jesus said,
"I do nothing on My own authority, only that which the
Father tells me to do." His meat and his drink were to do
the will of the Father. He was commissioned by the Father
to come into the world for the work of redemption. In that
plan of redemption in the Godhead itself, one sends the
other, and the one who sends is said to be greater than the
one who is sent in terms of the economic distinctions and
the structure by which the Godhead works.

By the same token, the church historically, except for

the *filioque* dissenters, has stated that, as the Father sends the Son, so the Holy Spirit is sent by both the Father and the Son. As the Son is subordinate to the Father in the work of redemption, so the Spirit is subordinate to both the Father and the Son. But again, that does not mean an inequality of being or dignity or divine attributes. The second person of the Trinity is fully God; the third person of the Trinity is fully God. In that work of redemption we see the expression of superordination and subordination.

Was Christ capable of sinning?

Did Jesus have the ability to sin? The problem hidden in that question is that if Jesus did have the ability to sin, does that mean he had original sin and participated in a fallen nature? If that were the case, he wouldn't even be qualified to save himself, let alone us. If he did not have the ability to sin, was his temptation (so central to God's giving him the crown of glory for his obedience) just a charade—was he really not subjected to real temptation?

The New Testament tells us that Jesus was like us at every point save one: He was without sin. It tells us that Jesus became incarnate and took upon himself human nature. It also tells us that he is the second Adam. Generally, classical Christology teaches that when Jesus was incarnate and became the new Adam, he came born with the same nature that Adam had before the Fall. Adam didn't have original sin when he was created. So Jesus did not have *original sin.* So we would ask the same question: Was Adam capable of sinning? Yes, he was. Christ, the second Adam, was also capable of sinning in the sense that he had all of the faculties and all of the equipment necessary to sin if that's what he chose to do.

Could Jesus have sinned if he had wanted to? Absolutely. Of course, he didn't want to. So if you ask it a different way, could Jesus sin if he didn't want to? No, he couldn't sin if he didn't want to any more than God could sin because God doesn't want to sin. Wanting to sin is a prerequisite for sinning. THINK ABOUT THAT

But then we have to push it one step further: Could Jesus have wanted to sin? Theologians are divided on this point. I would say yes, I think he could have. I think that's part of being made after the likeness of Adam. When we're in heaven and are totally glorified, then we will no longer have the power and ability to sin. That's what we look forward to; that's what Jesus earned for himself and for us through his perfect obedience. Christ's perfect obedience was not a charade. He actually was victorious over every conceivable temptation that was thrown his way.

Why did Jesus say some people wouldn't die before he came back?

This question had a dramatic influence on Albert Schweitzer when he was studying New Testament theology. Jesus said, "This generation will not pass away until all of these things come to pass. . . . You will not go over all the cities of Israel until all of these things come to pass. . . . Some of you will not taste death until all of these things come to pass."

Schweitzer looked at those passages, and he thought of them as obvious cases where Jesus blew it, where Jesus expected his return in the first century. Schweitzer saw this expectation of the early return of Jesus in early writings of Paul. Then there was an adjustment in the later writings of the Bible to account for the great disappointment that Jesus didn't show up in that first generation. That's been a matter of great consternation for many people.

Jesus didn't say, "Some of you aren't going to die until I come back." He said, "Some of you will not taste death until all of these things come to pass." The difficulty lies in the structure of the language. The disciples are asking Jesus about the establishment of the kingdom. Jesus talks about two distinct issues. He talks about what obviously involved the destruction of Jerusalem when he said that the temple would be destroyed. Then at the end of the Olivet discourse, he talks about his return on clouds of glory.

Some of the best New Testament scholarship that I've seen is on the meaning of the Greek words translated "all of these things." An excellent case can be made that when Jesus used that phrase, "these things" of which he was speaking pertained to the destruction of the temple and of Jerusalem. It's amazing that Jesus of Nazareth clearly and undeniably predicted one of the most important historical events in Jewish history before it took place. This wasn't just a vague Nostradamus or Oracle of Delphi type of future prediction; Jesus vividly predicted the fall of Jerusalem and the destruction of the temple, which indeed took place in A.D. 70, while many of his disciples were still alive. It was also before the missionary outreach had reached all of the cities of Israel and before that generation had, in fact, passed away. Those cataclysmic events that Jesus had predicted on the Mount of Olives did, indeed, take place in the first century.

What did Jesus mean when he said we would do greater work than he did?

First of all, he said that to his disciples and only to us indirectly, if at all. He is speaking to the first-century church, and he makes the statement that the works they do will be greater than the works that he performed.

Let me tell you what I don't think it means. There are many today who believe that there are people running around this world right now who are performing greater miracles, performing miracles in greater abundance, and actually doing more incredible acts of divine healing than Jesus himself did. I can't think of any more serious delusion than that, that somebody would actually think they have exceeded Jesus in terms of the works he has done. There's nobody who comes close to the work that Jesus did. Some say that perhaps we can't do greater works than Jesus individually but that corporately we are able to exceed in power the things that Jesus did.

We see amazing things happening in the first-century church through the power that Christ gave to his apostles. We see people raised from the dead through Peter and Paul. But at the same time I would challenge people by telling them to add up all of the miracles that, according to New Testament records, were wrought through the hands of Paul, Peter, and the rest of the disciples corporately, put them all together, and see if they measure a greater degree than those which our Lord performed.

If Jesus meant that people would do greater miracles than he performed in the sense of displaying more power and more astonishing things than he did, then obviously

one of the works that Jesus failed to perform was sound
prophecy, because that just didn't happen. Nobody
exceeded Jesus' works. That's what leads me to believe
that's not what he meant.

I think he's using the term "greater" in a different way.
I heard a church historian say that he was convinced that
when Jesus made the statement "Greater works than these
will you do," he was referring to the whole scope of the
impact of Christ's people and his church on the world
throughout history.

I know a lot of people look at the history of Western civilization and say that the bulk of the church's influence has
been negative—the black eye of the Crusades, the Galileo
episode, and holy wars, etc. If you look at the record, you
will see that it was the Christian church that spearheaded
the abolition of slavery, the end of the Roman arena, the
whole concept of education, the concept of charitable hospitals and orphanages, and a host of other humanitarian
activities. I think, personally, that that's what Jesus meant
when he talked about greater works.

What was God's answer to Jesus' question "My God, my God, why hast thou forsaken me?"

We can look at this in two ways. On the one hand, there
was no answer. Jesus screamed that question to heaven. He
screamed it audibly, and there was no audible reply. As far
as the New Testament indicates, there are only three occasions on which God speaks audibly, and this was not one of
them. The Son of God was screaming in agony, and the
Father remained silent.

On the other hand, we could say that three days later God screamed an answer with the empty tomb, bringing forth the Holy One. I think that plaintive cry from Jesus on the cross is one of the most important and misunderstood verses in all of sacred Scripture. The explanations for it have run the gamut. Albert Schweitzer was filled with consternation and saw in it a clue that Jesus died in a spirit of bitter disillusionment, that he had spent his ministry expecting God to bring the kingdom of God dramatically through Jesus' ministry—and God did not do it. Schweitzer believed that Jesus allowed himself to be arrested and led right to Golgotha, expecting that God was going to rescue him at the last moment from the cross. Suddenly, when Jesus realized that there was not going to be a rescue, he screamed in bitter disillusionment and died a heroic death, but with an embittered spirit nevertheless. That was Schweitzer's view, but others have taken a different one.

We realize that the words Jesus cried on the cross are an exact quotation of what David penned in Psalm 22. Some people say that here in his agony Jesus fell back on his knowledge of Scripture by reciting it. I don't think Jesus was just quoting Bible verses on the cross, but it certainly would have been appropriate for him to use a statement of Scripture to express the depth of his agony.

When I was ordained, I was given the opportunity to choose my own ordination hymn. I chose "'Tis Midnight; and on Olive's Brow." There's a verse in that hymn that says that the Son of Man was not forsaken by his God. As much as I love the hymn, I hate that verse because it's not right. Jesus didn't just *feel* forsaken on the cross; he *was* totally forsaken by God while he hung on the cross because that's exactly what the penalty for sin is. As the apostle Paul elaborates, sin cuts us off from the presence and benefits of God. Christ screamed, "Why have I been forsaken?" It wasn't just a question; it was a cry of agony. Christ knew the answer. The answer was given to him the night before, in Gethsemane, when the Father made it clear that it was necessary for him to drink that cup.

Did Jesus ever laugh? What do the Scriptures tell us about his character and sense of humor?

I've heard some people answer this question in the negative by saying that laughter is always a sign of frivolity and a thinly veiled attempt to make light of things that are sober. They say life is a sober matter; Jesus is described as a man of sorrows. He's described as one who was acquainted with grief. He walked around with enormous burdens upon him. Add to that the fact that there's not a single text in the New Testament that explicitly says Jesus laughed. There are texts, of course, that tell us he cried. For example, John 13 tells us that in the upper room Jesus was deeply troubled in his spirit. We know that he experienced those emotions, and yet it's strange that nowhere does it tell us that he actually laughed.

You also asked if he had a sense of humor. When we translate any language into another, we will often miss subtle nuances of speech. If we don't have a knowledge of the original language and its idioms, we might miss the humor. Also, different cultures have different ways of being humorous. Jesus used one form of humor we call sarcasm. In his responses to Herod, for example, he called him a fox and made other statements that I think had a touch of oriental humor to them. It's purely speculative whether or not Jesus laughed, but I can't imagine that he didn't laugh for this reason: He was fully human, and he was perfect. We certainly wouldn't attribute to Jesus any sinful emotions or forms of behavior, and it would seem to me the only reason to think he didn't laugh would be if we first came to the conclusion that laughter is evil.

The Bible does say that God laughs. In the Psalms it's a derisive laugh. When the kings of the world set themselves against God and take counsel against God, it says that he who sits in the heavens shall laugh. God will hold them in derision. It's sort of a "huh!" kind of laughter. It's not a jovial response of happiness, but nevertheless it's laughter.

In the Wisdom Literature of the Old Testament—for example, in Ecclesiastes—we're told that certain things are appropriate at certain times. There's a time to plant, a time to reap, a time to build, a time to tear down; there's a time to dance, a time to sing, a time to laugh, a time to cry. Since God has, in his seasons, appointed appropriate times for laughter, and Jesus always did what was appropriate, it would seem to me that when it was time to laugh, he laughed.

3

The Work of the Holy Spirit

It is to your advantage that I go away;
for if I do not go away, the Helper will not come to you;
but if I depart, I will send Him to you.
And when He has come, He will convict the world of sin,
and of righteousness, and of judgment.

JOHN 16:7-8

Questions in This Section:

Does every human being have the potential to receive the Holy Spirit?

What was the role of the Holy Spirit in the Old Testament?

Is there a difference between being baptized with the Holy Spirit and being filled with the Holy Spirit?

Is there a difference between the Holy Spirit being with someone and in someone?

Could you explain the baptism of the Holy Spirit that came upon the hundred and twenty in the upper room after the ascension of Christ?

In Galatians 5, Paul makes the statement "Walk by the Spirit, and you will not carry out the desire of the flesh." What does this mean?

What does the Bible mean when it talks about quenching the Holy Spirit?

Does the Spirit ever lead in a way that's contrary to biblically revealed ethics?

Scripture says that Christ stated the unforgivable sin as being blasphemy against the Holy Spirit. Can you expand on that? How should I pray for someone committing that sin?

Acts 13:52 says, "And the disciples were continually filled with joy and with the Holy Spirit." Why is it that most Christians today aren't "continually" in this state?

Does every human being have the potential to receive the Holy Spirit?

There is a certain sense in which every human being already has the Holy Spirit. Not in the redemptive sense—the sense in which Christians normally speak about having the Holy Spirit—but in the sense that they are alive. The Bible tells us that the power for life itself is grounded in the Holy Spirit. Paul said to those philosophers at Mars Hill, "In him we live and move and have our being." In the history of Christian theology it's been a virtually universal idea that the life principle in the world is the Holy Spirit, and no one can even be alive without at least having the life source of God, the Holy Spirit. But that's not the redemptive sense in which we talk about having the Spirit by conversion or regeneration or being indwelt with the Holy Spirit or baptized in the Holy Spirit—these are distinguishable works of God the Holy Spirit.

You ask, "Does every human being have the potential to receive the Holy Spirit?" Let's talk about the Holy Spirit in terms of his entering into a life to regenerate—to convert a person and to dwell in that person in a saving way. Does every human being have the potential to receive the Spirit in that regard? Well, now let me sound like a confused modern theologian by saying yes and no.

Yes, in the sense that every human being has the potential to receive the Holy Spirit insofar as human beings are made in the image of God. Even though we're fallen, every human being has the capacity to be a receptacle of the indwelling Holy Spirit. There's nothing about one person or one group of people or one race or one sex that makes them lack the potential to be visited by the Holy Spirit. God the Holy Spirit can come and regenerate and dwell within any human being he so desires.

Yes, there is this innate or intrinsic potential for every human being to be filled with the Holy Spirit or regenerated by the Holy Spirit. But the Holy Spirit goes where he wills and where the Father sends him and where the Son sends him, and I don't believe that God sends the Holy Spirit to regenerate everybody. They will not be regenerated whom the Holy Spirit is not sent to regenerate. And so if God does not choose to indwell a person by the Holy Spirit, that person will not be indwelt by the Holy Spirit.

What was the role of the Holy Spirit in the Old Testament?

The role of the Holy Spirit in the Old Testament was not principally different from the role of the Holy Spirit in the New Testament. While there are some differences, there's an essential unity between the two Testaments.

The Holy Spirit was active in many ways in Old Testament times. First and foremost was the Trinity's part of the work of creation. In the act of creation itself, the Father, the Son, and the Spirit were all involved. The Spirit brooded over the water and brought order and structure out of the yet unordered universe that we find in the opening chapters of Genesis. People were regenerated in the Old Testament just as they are regenerated in the New Testament, and one cannot be regenerated except through the influence of God the Holy Spirit. David needed the regenerating power of God just as much as the apostle Paul needed it in the New Testament.

We also know that the Spirit was very active charismatically; that is, by gifting certain people in the Old Testament and equipping them for specific tasks. For example, the king of Israel was anointed with oil, symbolizing his being anointed by the Holy Spirit to be empowered to carry out his vocation in a godly way. The same was true of priests. The prophets of Israel, who were agents of revelation, were inspired by God the Holy Spirit and equipped to be the messengers of God to the people and to give us sacred Scripture in the same basic manner that the apostles in the New Testament were so endowed and superintended by the Holy Spirit. So we see that the Spirit was active—regenerating, sanctifying, preserving, interceding for—doing all of those things in the Old Testament that he does in the New Testament.

What's the difference? In the Old Testament book of Numbers, when Moses was complaining because the burden of leading all the people had become so weighty it was about to crush him, he pled for relief from God. God told him to gather seventy of the elders of Israel in order to take from the Spirit that was upon Moses and distribute it to the seventy so they could help him lead the people of Israel. That's exactly what the text said happened. God then gave this charismatic empowering, this special gift, to seventy other people, not just Moses, so that they could all participate in ministry. That was not regeneration or sanctification, it was an empowering for ministry given only to select individuals. Moses' prayer was, "Oh, that all the

Lord's people were prophets and that the Lord would put His Spirit upon them!" (Num. 11:29). What Moses prayed for became a prophecy in the pen of the prophet Joel, who said that in the latter days that's exactly what would happen. And on the Day of Pentecost it did happen. The apostle Peter said that it was about this that Joel was writing, that now the Spirit to empower the church for ministry is given to everybody, not just to the leaders.

Is there a difference between being baptized with the Holy Spirit and being filled with the Holy Spirit? If so, what is that difference?

At times when we read the New Testament record of those who are baptized in the Spirit or filled with the Spirit, it seems that these terms are used interchangeably, that they refer to the same phenomenon. At other times there's a little distinction that is not altogether clear in the text. Sometimes it seems that to discern the difference requires a knife sharper than the one I own.

Let's just go back and ask this question: What does the Bible mean by the term "baptized in the Holy Spirit"? In the New Testament there's a distinction between being born of the Spirit—which is the work of the Holy Spirit to regenerate us, to change the disposition of our hearts and make us alive spiritually—and to baptize us in the Holy Spirit. We read about the baptism of the Holy Spirit principally on the Day of Pentecost and subsequent events similar to the Day of Pentecost in which those who were gathered were baptized in the Holy Spirit. We understand that the people who were baptized in the Holy Spirit were already believers and they were already regenerated. So we must distinguish between the Spirit's work in making us spiritually alive and the Spirit's work in baptizing us, whatever baptizing means. Most churches would affirm that the primary meaning of the concept of baptism in the Holy Spirit is the work of the Spirit upon a human being to endow that person with the power necessary to carry out their mission and vocation as a Christian.

In the Old Testament that *charisma,* the gift of the empowering of the Holy Spirit, was limited to certain individuals such as priests and prophets and mediators like Moses. But the point of the New Testament is that the whole body of the people of God is now being equipped and empowered from on high to carry out its task. Notice that Pentecost is tied very closely to the great commission. Jesus said, "Go into Jerusalem, Judea, Samaria, and the outermost parts of the earth, but before you go, tarry in Jerusalem. After the Holy Spirit comes upon you, then you can go and carry out this mandate."

The "baptism of the Spirit" refers to being equipped or empowered by God's Spirit to carry out the task that Jesus has given the church. When the Spirit equips us or baptizes us, we are immersed, as it were, in the Holy Spirit; sometimes the Scriptures refer to this as being filled with the Holy Spirit. Other times the term "being filled with the Holy Spirit" is used in the same way as being filled with love or filled with joy—there's this sensation of superabundance of the presence of God. I think that sometimes the Scripture is speaking of something more than simply being equipped for ministry, but having an awareness, a keen awareness and consciousness, of the powerful presence of the Spirit.

Is there a difference between the Holy Spirit being with someone and in someone?

There is a difference, but I want to be careful about how I explain it for this reason: I think too many people make far too much out of the difference in the preposition. The Bible is not precise enough to give us a whole doctrine that is to be developed on the basis of "with" and "in."

The Holy Spirit can be said to be with a person who is not regenerate; that is, he's not born of the Spirit, but the Spirit can work with that person or be in that person's presence for a season—just as he used Cyrus in the Old Testament, who was presumably not a believer. The Holy Spirit can come and assist people in a common grace way in many forms and functions in this world without indwelling them as part of his permanent residency.

When we talk about the indwelling of the Holy Spirit, we're talking about his actually coming into the very being of a Christian in a salvific way that is a result of spiritual rebirth.

However—and this may confuse everybody—in a certain sense the Holy Spirit is in everybody. The Holy Spirit is not only the Spirit of God dwelling in us for the purpose of sanctification and redemption, but the Holy Spirit is also ultimately the power source of *all* life. Without a certain participation in the power and presence of the Spirit of God, nothing in this world would exist. The world hangs together through the power of the Spirit of God. If God were to withdraw his Holy Spirit totally, everything would die—believers and unbelievers alike.

Insofar as the Holy Spirit is the power supply or the

source of life itself, he's in everybody. We're making a distinction here between creation and redemption. He's not working in people who are unregenerate in a spiritual way to bring about their sanctification and their consequent ultimate redemption; these activities happen only in those whom he has regenerated. This is the basic difference.

Could you explain the baptism of the Holy Spirit that came upon the hundred and twenty in the upper room after the ascension of Christ?

To do that briefly would be to do a severe injustice to a very important concept in the New Testament, but I will try to give an adequate summary.

The New Testament interpreted that experience through Peter's speech. The people asked what was going on when they saw and heard the tongues of fire, the sound of the mighty rushing wind, and the people preaching the gospel in their own languages. Some people thought they were witnessing a mass experience of drunkenness. Peter responded by saying, "These are not drunk as you suppose. This is that of which the prophet Joel spoke." Then he referred them back to a prophecy in the Old Testament that was written by the prophet Joel, in which he stated that in the latter days God would pour out his Spirit upon all flesh.

We have to understand this experience also in light of Jesus' preparatory remarks before his ascension as he commissioned his disciples to go into the world and preach the gospel to every living creature, to go "first to Jerusalem, then to Judea, Samaria, and to the outermost parts of the earth." He told them, however, that before they embarked on that task, they should tarry in Jerusalem to await the outpouring of the Holy Spirit. He said, "You shall receive power after the Holy Spirit has come upon you."

Historically every Christian denomination has had some doctrine of the meaning of the baptism of the Holy Spirit. For the most part, the different churches agree that the significance of the baptism of the Holy Spirit is an empowering of the people of God to perform the ministry that Christ has assigned to his church.

In the Old Testament the Spirit was given only to a handful of people, namely the priests and prophets. The rank and file did not participate. Even in the case of Moses, as we read in Numbers 11, God came to Moses and took of the Spirit that was upon Moses and distributed it to seventy other people. He gave it to the seventy elders so that they could participate in the power to perform the ministry that was necessary. At that time Moses uttered a prayer. He said, "Would to God that all of the Lord's people were prophets and that the Lord would put His Spirit upon them." That prayer became a prophecy in Joel, and I think the book of Acts interprets that event, saying that God has kept his promise. He has not just poured out his Spirit upon the clergy, the priests, the prophets, or the kings, but he has given his Spirit and gifted all one hundred and twenty. All of the people of God now receive the Holy Spirit not only in regeneration, in rebirth, and in indwelling but also in the gift of the ability to participate and function in the body of Christ in Christ's ministry.

In Galatians 5, Paul makes the statement "Walk by the Spirit, and you will not carry out the desire of the flesh." It sounds so simple, but what does it actually mean?

Whenever you see spirit and flesh set side by side in a passage ("the spirit is willing, but the flesh is weak" or "the spirit wars against the flesh," as Paul says here), we're talking about, not the warfare between the physical body of man and his internal, mental, or spiritual inclinations, but rather the conflict that every Christian experiences between his old nature—his fallen nature, which is corrupt and is filled with desires that are not pleasing to God—and the new nature within him that has been brought to pass by the indwelling power of the Holy Spirit.

Now, life becomes complicated once we are renewed by the Holy Spirit (when we become a Christian); now we have two principles at war within ourselves: the old inclinations and the new inclinations. The old inclination is against God, and the new inclination is to obey God and to do that which is pleasing to him. In this Galatians passage, Paul discusses the ongoing battle that all Christians experience. He admonishes us at one point and says, "Follow the new principle; follow the new spirit, not the old pattern that was characteristic of your original state of fallenness." He's not saying that your physical body is at war with your soul, but that your natural inclinations are at war with the transformation toward which the Holy Spirit is constantly moving you as a child of God. And that does involve a decision and an act of the will.

What does the Bible mean when it talks about quenching the Holy Spirit?

I think, first of all, we need to understand that the term *to quench* in the New Testament is a metaphor; it involves a figurative use of language. So often, the Spirit is conveyed with the image of the burning, consuming flame of fire. We know that the Holy Spirit is not fire. He is the third person of the Holy Trinity and is not to be identified ultimately with fire itself. We don't worship fire. But the New Testament uses this imagery to describe the Spirit coming upon us and indwelling us as Christian people. We are to be, as it were, set aflame with a holy passion for the things of God. Whatever it is that hinders or stifles our internal cooperation with the indwelling Spirit of God is a kind of quenching of the Spirit. Just as we would take a garden hose to put out a fire in the backyard, we quench the flames by smothering them under that water.

When the Holy Spirit initially comes upon us—when we are born of the Spirit—I'm convinced that the first act of the Holy Spirit is to come into our lives in a sovereign, instantaneous, effective moment by which the Spirit brings us to spiritual life. We don't cooperate with it. We are as passive in it as we were when we were conceived and born biologically. I'm convinced that this work of life by which we are born of the Spirit (which the New Testament calls quickening) is the sovereign work of God.

I once had the marvelous experience of meeting with Billy Graham. We talked about many things in that meeting. Billy told me how he came to Christ the first time. Here's the greatest evangelist probably in the history of the world—at least in terms of the number of people he's reached—telling his conversion story to me with the same excitement as if it had happened yesterday afternoon. When he explained how God began to work in his life and move in his heart, when he talked about being brought from the kingdom of darkness into the kingdom of light, his final words were these: "The Holy Spirit did it all." I couldn't agree more.

After that moment of being quickened to new life, of regeneration, the rest of the Christian life is a cooperative venture between the new person in Christ and the power of the Holy Spirit, who dwells inside him or her. The more we cooperate with the Spirit, the more we grow in grace, but we can retard and hinder that growth by doing those things that would put out the fire.

Does the Spirit ever lead in a way that's contrary to biblically revealed ethics?

No, of course not. The Holy Spirit couldn't possibly lead somebody to disobey the Holy Spirit's teaching. That would be God acting against himself. I would think it would be elementary and manifestly obvious to every Christian that God the Holy Spirit will not give you as an individual a leading to act in defiance of the written Word of God.

I speak so strongly about this precisely because I run into people all the time who tell me that God has given them an inclination or a private leading that excuses them from the moral obligations God has set forth. I've had people tell me that they prayed about committing adultery and that God the Holy Spirit gave them peace about it. How much lower can you go? That's not blasphemy against the Holy Spirit, but that certainly grieves the Holy Spirit. It also comes perilously close to blasphemy against the Holy Spirit to not only refuse to repent of sin but to attribute the motivation and the license for it to God himself. This is the propensity we have, to call good evil and evil good.

I've seen otherwise devout and earnest Christians talk in this manner. I've had biblical scholars look me straight in the eye and tell me that the Holy Spirit gave them permission to do something that God clearly prohibits in his Word. This is one of the reasons the Scriptures tell us to test the spirits to see if they are from God. How do we test a spirit? How do I know if I have the leading of the Holy Spirit? That can be a very whimsical and subjective type of thing. I do believe that God the Spirit inclines our hearts in certain directions and will help to lead us in the living of this life, but we have to be very careful lest we confuse the leading of the Spirit with indigestion or, what's worse, the leading of the anti-Spirit, the leading of the enemy himself, who would seek to lead us astray. Remember that Satan disguises himself as an angel of light.

If you believe that the Scriptures come through the inspiration of God the Holy Spirit and that he is the Spirit of truth and it is that truth that is embodied in the sacred Scripture, then the easiest way to test any private inclination or group leaning that you get from other people is with the written Word of God. I'm confident that there we have the leading of the Spirit. There the Spirit is inspired.

The Spirit of truth has set forth for us in the propositions of Scripture what is pleasing to God and in keeping with his perfect will. I can't conceive of God the Spirit telling me to disobey what God has spoken.

Scripture says that Christ stated the unforgivable sin as being blasphemy against the Holy Spirit. Can you expand on that, and how should I pray for someone committing that sin?

There's a lot of confusion over the sin that Jesus says cannot be forgiven either in this world or in the world to come. Some people think that the unforgivable sin is murder because the Old Testament gives us such strong sanctions against murder and says that if a person has committed murder, even if he repents, he is still to be executed. Others believe that it's adultery because adultery violates the union of two people. As gross as these sins may be, I don't think they fit the description here because we see that King David, for example, who is guilty of both adultery and murder, is forgiven.

I think Jesus is clear. He does identify it. He says that the sin is blasphemy against the Holy Spirit. What does that mean? First of all, let's understand that blasphemy is a sin that can only be done with words. It's a sin that you commit with your mouth or with your pen—it's a verbal sin. It has to do with saying something against the Holy Spirit. You remember that the religious leaders—the clergy, the Pharisees, and the Sadducees—were the ones who were constantly being hostile toward Jesus and stirring up a conspiracy to do him in. They plotted to kill

Jesus, and they were constantly attacking him and charging him with this and that. On one occasion they said that Jesus was casting out Satan by the power of Satan. It's almost as if Jesus said, "Hold it right there, guys. I've been patient with you, I've been tolerant with you, I've been long-suffering, but you are coming perilously close now to making an accusation against me that's going to wipe you out now and forever." He said that any sin against the Son of Man can be forgiven, but if you blaspheme against the Holy Spirit (to ascribe the work of the Holy Spirit to Satan, or to equate them), you've had it. Notice also that when Jesus is on the cross, he prays for those very men who have put him there: "Father, forgive them—" Why? "—for they know not what they have done." And on the Day of Pentecost when Peter gave his ripsnorting sermon, he talks about those who killed Jesus, that they would not have done it had they known. After the Resurrection, the Holy Spirit raised Jesus up and declared him to be the Christ with power. If you read the book of Hebrews, you'll see that the distinction between blaspheming Christ and blaspheming the Holy Spirit falls away.

As for those who have committed "the sin unto death," the Bible says that we are not required to pray for those people. We are to pray for people who are committing any other sin, but if we see a person committing the sin unto death, we are not required to pray for them. The Bible doesn't say we are not allowed to pray for them, but we're not required to, and I would think that would apply to this sin.

Acts 13:52 says, "And the disciples were continually filled with joy and with the Holy Spirit." Why is it that most Christians today aren't "continually" in this state?

First of all, when we read a statement like that in the book of Acts, it describes the attitude and posture of the disciples at a particular time in redemptive history. I think we would be remiss if we actually thought that the book of Acts was trying to tell us that throughout their entire lives, under all circumstances, in every moment, the early church Christians were always constantly bubbling over with joy. We read the letters of the apostle Paul in which he is expressing profound anguish and sorrow and grief at different points in his ministry. He talks about the fact that he has learned how to be content in whatever state he's in and that there is an undercurrent, a supporting system, of joy that is basic to his whole Christian life. However, that joy regularly suffers the intrusions of sorrow, disappointment, and frustration. In fact, he says that he is at times perplexed but not in despair, he is cast down but not destroyed, he has to struggle just as you and I have to struggle.

One particular short period of time in the early church when there was much about which to be happy and to rejoice occurred when the Holy Spirit was being poured out and there was one triumph after another of the outpouring of God's Spirit. Of course, this was a time of celebration, a time of jubilation as the Spirit was being poured out on the church and the church was seeing the remarkable expansion of growth and development that went with its early years.

It may be that in general Christians today are not as happy or as joyful as they were in the first century. I'm not sure that's the case, but if it is, I think it's something we could normally expect after two thousand years of being removed from the immediate presence of the ministry of Jesus. The early church did have the advantage of being eyewitnesses to Jesus, which is why he said, "More blessed are those who believe having not seen" than those who enjoyed the privilege of being part of the original church. Obviously, if people in the Christian church today had the same experiences as those had by the fathers and mothers of our Christian church in the first century, I think we would see a deeper level of zeal and commitment and joy.

We must be careful not to idealize the early Christian community described in Acts because at times it was not pure. There were lots of problems, and in his letters Paul addresses many problems and struggles that were going on in the early church. But there was a spirit there that we need to have infect the church today, a spirit of joy and a sense of power in the presence of the Spirit of God.

4

The Book of Books

All Scripture is given by inspiration of God,
and is profitable for doctrine, for reproof, for correction,
for instruction in righteousness, that the man of God
may be complete, thoroughly equipped for every good work.

2 TIMOTHY 3:16-17

Questions in This Section:

How do you know the Bible is true?

How were the books of the Bible selected and compiled?

What was the process the church councils went through in deciding what manuscripts would be included in the Bible? What criteria did they use in deciding which books to put into the Canon?

We talk of the Bible as being the inspired Word of God. Would the men who chose the books to be included in the Bible also have been inspired by God?

How does the resurrection of Jesus validate the authority of the New Testament Scriptures?

How can we know that the Bible is the true Word of God after so many interpretations?

Why do Christians—people filled with the Spirit of truth—disagree about what the Bible says?

There are so many different interpretations of what the Bible is saying. How do I know which one is right?

When I discuss biblical concepts with my friends, I'm often met with the reply "That's your interpretation." How should I respond?

I recently obtained a Living Bible arranged for daily Bible readings. Do we need to be wary of this version?

Does the Bible claim authority over the life of a believer?

Does the Bible claim authority over the life of an unbeliever?

What can a Christian learn from the Old Testament? Is it as pertinent to my growth as the New Testament is?

How does the Old Testament apply to Christians today?

What should Christians think about evolution?

Does the Bible tell us how old the earth is?

As a Christian educator, what are some of your frustrations in your efforts to teach the Word?

How do you know the Bible is true?

That's an excellent question because so much is at stake in the Christian faith in terms of the truthfulness of Scripture. The Bible is our primary source of information about Jesus and about all of those things we embrace as elements of our faith. Of course, if the Bible isn't true, then professing Christians are in serious trouble. I believe the Bible is true. I believe it is the Word of God. As Jesus himself declared of the Scripture, "Your word is truth." But why am I persuaded that the Bible is the truth?

We need to ask a broader question first. How do we know that anything is true? We're asking a technical question in epistemology. How do we test claims of truth? There is a certain kind of truth that we test through observation, experimentation, eyewitness, examination, and scientific evidence. As far as the history of Jesus is concerned, as far as we know any history, we want to check the stories of Scripture using those means by which historical evidence can be tested—through archaeology, for example. There are certain elements of the Scripture, such as historical claims, that are to be measured by the common standards of historiography. I invite people to do that—to check it out.

Second, we want to test the claims of truth through the test of rationality. Is it logically consistent, or does it speak with a "forked tongue"? We examine the content of Scripture to see if it is coherent. That's another test of truth. One of the most astonishing things, of course, is that the

Bible has literally thousands of testable historical prophecies, cases in which events were clearly foretold, and both the foretelling and the fulfillment are a matter of historical record. The very dimension of the sheer fulfillment of prophecy of the Old Testament Scriptures should be enough to convince anyone that we are dealing with a supernatural piece of literature.

Of course, some theologians have said that with all of the evidence there is that Scripture is true, we can truly embrace it only with the Holy Spirit working in us to overcome our biases and prejudices against Scripture, against God. In theology, this is called the internal testimony of the Holy Spirit. I want to stress at this point that when the Holy Spirit helps me to see the truth of Scripture and to embrace the truth of Scripture, it's not because the Holy Spirit is giving me some special insight that he doesn't give to somebody else or is giving me special information that nobody else can have. All the Holy Spirit does is change my heart, change my disposition toward the evidence that is already there. I think that God himself has planted within the Scriptures an internal consistency that bears witness that this is his Word.

How were the books of the Bible selected and compiled, and how were the decisions made as to what would be distributed as the Word of God?

Even though we think of the Bible as being one book, it's actually a collection of sixty-six books, and we realize that there was a historical process by which those particular books were gathered together and placed in one volume that we now know as the Bible. In fact, we call the Bible the canon of sacred Scripture. *Canon* is taken from the Greek word *canon,* which means "measuring rod." That means it is the standard of truth by which all other truth is to be judged in the Christian life.

There have been many different theories set forth over the history of the church as to exactly how God's hand was involved in this selection process. Skeptics have pointed out that over three thousand books were candidates for inclusion in the New Testament canon alone, and only a handful (twenty-some books) were selected. Doesn't that raise some serious questions? Isn't it possible that certain books that are in the Bible should not be there and others that were excluded by human evaluation and human judgment should have been included? We need to keep in mind, however, that of those not included in the last analysis, there were at the most three or four that were given serious consideration. So to speak in terms of two or three thousand being boiled down to twenty-seven or something like that is a distortion of historical reality.

Some people take the position that the church is a higher authority than the Bible because the only reason the Bible has any authority is that the church declared what books the Bible would contain. Most Protestants, however, take a different view of the matter and point out that when the decision was made as to what books were canonical, they used the Latin term *recipemus,* which means "we receive." What the church said is that we receive these particular books as being canonical, as being apostolic in authority and in origin, and therefore we submit to their authority. It's one thing to make something authoritative, and it's another thing to recognize something that already is authoritative. Those human decisions did not make something that was not authoritative suddenly authoritative, but rather the church was bowing, acquiescing to that which they recognized to be sacred Scripture. We cannot avoid the reality that though God's invisible hand of providence was certainly at work in the process, there was a historical sifting process and human judgments were made that could have been mistaken. But I don't think this was the case.

What was the process the church councils went through in deciding which manuscripts would be included in the Bible?

The church met in various historic councils, in which the representatives of the church examined the documents that were up for possible inclusion. I might mention that a few of those that were not to be included involved one of the early letters of Clement of Rome, who was the bishop of Rome around A.D. 95. One of the reasons Clement's letter was not included in the Canon was that Clement, in his own writing, acknowledged the superiority of the apostles' writings.

By what criteria did the church councils evaluate those candidates for admission into the church canon? One was apostolic origin; that is, if it could be shown that a book was written by an apostle of Jesus Christ, that book was accepted into the Canon. For example, we see that the Gospel of Matthew was written by one of the twelve disciples and a member of the apostolic body, so his book was accepted as canonical from the very beginning. It didn't take until the final council at the end of the fourth century for Matthew to be included. It was there from day one. You also have books like Mark. Mark was not an apostle, but Mark was the writer for Peter, and we know that Peter's authority stood behind Mark, so Mark's Gospel was accepted very early in the Christian church. Paul's letters were accepted from the very beginning; even Peter's letters call Paul's letters "scripture."

Another criterion was a book's acceptance in the early church community. Also required was conformity with that core of books about which there was never any doubt. The handful of books that were debated went against what was already clearly established as Scripture.

We talk of the Bible as being the inspired Word of God. Would the men who chose the books to be included in the Bible also have been inspired by God?

This is one important point of dispute between historic Roman Catholic theology and classical Protestant theology. The Roman Catholic Church has gone on record, particularly at the Council of Trent in the sixteenth century, to declare that not only were the individual authors inspired in the writing of the individual books but that the church operated and functioned infallibly in the sifting and sorting process by which the canon of the New Testament, for example, was established.

To put it briefly, Rome believes that the New Testament is an infallible collection of infallible books. That's one perspective. Modern critical scholarship, which rejects the infallibility of the individual volumes of Scripture and likewise the whole of Scripture, would say that the canon of Scripture is a fallible collection of fallible books.

The historic Protestant position shared by Lutherans, Methodists, Episcopalians, Presbyterians, and so on, has been that the canon of Scripture is a fallible collection of infallible books. This is the reasoning: At the time of the Reformation, one of the most important issues in the sixteenth century was the issue of authority. We've seen the central issue of justification by faith alone, which was captured by the slogan the Reformers used: *sola fide,* "by faith alone [we are justified]." Also there was the issue of authority, and the principle that emerged among Protestants was that of *sola scriptura,* which means that Scripture alone has the authority to bind our conscience. Scripture alone is infallible because God is infallible. The church receives the Scripture as God's Word, and the church is not infallible. That is the view of all Protestant churches.

The church has a rich tradition, and we respect the church fathers and even our creed. However, we grant the possibility that they may err at various points; we don't believe in the infallibility of the church. I will say that there are some Protestants who believe that there was a special work of divine providence and a special work of the Holy Spirit that protected the Canon and the sorting process from mistakes. I don't hold that position myself. I think it's possible that wrong books could have been selected, but I don't believe for a minute that that's the case. I think that the task the church faced and did was remarkably well done and that we have every book that should be in the New Testament.

At the time who was "the church" Roman Catholic, Protestant, √ 82

Both

How does the resurrection of Jesus validate the authority of the New Testament Scriptures?

The only way that the resurrection of Jesus can validate the authority of the New Testament Scriptures is indirectly. Some New Testament authors claim that what they are writing is not composed out of their own insight, but is actually written under the supervision and superintendence of the Holy Spirit. That is a radical claim to truth that requires some form of verification for most people.

The only way the Resurrection would verify the Scriptures is this: The Resurrection validates Jesus. The Resurrection, as the New Testament claims, shows Jesus as one who does miracles and is seen to be vindicated as an agent of revelation by the very fact that God gives him the power to perform these miracles.

For example, Nicodemus came to Jesus and said, "Teacher, we know that you are a teacher sent from God or you would not be able to do these miracles." Nicodemus was thinking soundly at that point. His line of reasoning went like this: He couldn't conceive of God granting the power to perform bona fide miracles to a false prophet. The very presence of miracles indicated the authorization of what we would call the credit of the proposer. It showed God's endorsement of this particular teacher.

No higher endorsement could have been given than that Jesus was raised from the dead and vindicated and shown to be the Son of God, whom he claimed to be— fulfilling the very predictions he had made. In Acts, Paul makes the statement that God has proven Jesus to be the Christ through the Resurrection. What does that have to do with the Scripture? If indeed Christ is proven by resurrection to be the Son of God and then we discover that Christ, who is the Son of God, a prophet of God, a true teacher verified through the miracle, teaches that the Bible is the Word of God, then his verification of the Bible is what verifies the claims of the apostles.

The only way we know of the resurrection of Jesus is through the Bible. If the resurrection of Jesus proves Jesus, and Jesus proves the Bible, how do we get to the resurrection of Jesus except through the Bible? We don't have to have an inspired Bible to be persuaded of the evidence of the historical activity of the Resurrection. I don't believe in the Resurrection because an infallible Bible tells me about a resurrection. I believe that the Bible is infallible because the Resurrection authenticates Jesus as an infallible source about the Bible.

How can we know that the Bible is the true Word of God after so many interpretations?

The multiplicity and variety and even contradictory interpretations of Scripture really have little or nothing to do with the question of its origin. Let me give you an analogy.

We've seen all kinds of interpretations of the United States Constitution, but even though political parties and different judges have different views of what the Constitution says and means, and what it intended, none of that difference of opinion casts a shadow on the source of the Constitution. We know who wrote the Constitution. We know where it came from and what it is.

People get dismayed by the differences of opinion as to

what the Bible teaches. If we establish that the Bible is the Word of God, only half the battle is over. The next thing we have to figure out is, What does it say? Can we agree on what it teaches? The assumption is, if I can convince you that what I think the Bible teaches is in fact what the Bible teaches, and you agree, then you will change your view because you believe that that is the Word of God.

Many people are troubled by the fact that the Bible has been interpreted in so many ways and, as a result, have fallen into a view of relativism, which completely destroys the real significance of Scripture. It may be extremely difficult for us to find the proper interpretation, and we may be discouraged by all the disagreement about it, but part of the reason we fight so much among ourselves on matters of biblical interpretation is that we all agree that it's crucial to understand the Word of God correctly.

Why do Christians—people filled with the Spirit of truth—disagree about what the Bible says?

In an earlier book I wrote titled *Psychology of Atheism* (later released under the title *If There Is a God, Why Are There Atheists?*), I had a whole chapter about why scholars disagree. Not only do we find Christians disagreeing about what the Bible teaches, but some of the greatest minds in history disagree on some very significant points. I would say that there are three primary reasons great minds disagree on fundamental issues.

One is that we are prone to logical errors. We are given the capacity to reason, but we are not perfect in our reasoning powers. We will make illegitimate inferences. We will commit errors that violate the laws of logic. I remember when I studied the introduction to logic in college and was given examples of fallacies. The examples printed in our textbooks were not drawn from tabloid newspapers or comics but from the writings of some of the most brilliant people in history: Plato, John Stuart Mill, and David Hume. These men are universally recognized as some of the most brilliant people who ever walked the face of the earth. They made glaring logical errors that served as illustrations of how not to reason in an "Introduction to Logic" textbook. Mental errors are the first reason.

The second reason is empirical errors. Every one of us is limited in our perspective and field of experience. Not one of us has been able to survey all of the data. Sometimes our eyesight or our hearing fails us. We are limited in the senses we use to perceive reality around us. Limitations of sense perception add to making mistakes.

And the third great cause for error, whether it's in understanding the Bible or in understanding science, is bias. We're prejudiced. Sometimes we come to a problem or to a study biased against the data. We don't want to believe what the data will tell us. When we become Christians, we are not cleansed of the ability to sin. We don't always want to believe what the Bible teaches, and so we will make errors of interpretation as a result of our clouded thinking because of the hardness of our own hearts or because we don't know the tools of biblical study. We haven't learned the language sufficiently, or we have not been skilled or trained in legitimate inferences or the laws of immediate inferences, and so on.

The main reason Christians disagree on what the Bible

teaches is that we are sinners. It's a sin to misunderstand the Bible and to misinterpret the Bible because ultimately it's a result of our being less than fully diligent in applying ourselves to seeking the truth of God's Word. We have the assistance of the Holy Spirit, and we're called to love God with all of our minds. The person who loves God with all of his mind is not casual in how he handles the Scriptures.

There are so many different interpretations of what the Bible is saying. How do I know which one is right?

That's a problem that plagues all of us. There are some theoretical things we can say about it, but I'd rather spend time on the practical.

The Roman Catholic Church believes that one function of the church is to be the authorized interpreter of Scripture. They believe that not only do we have an infallible Bible but we also have an infallible interpretation of the Bible. That somewhat ameliorates the problem, although it doesn't eliminate it altogether. You still have those of us who have to interpret the infallible interpretations of the Bible. Sooner or later it gets down to those of us who are not infallible to sort it out. We have this dilemma because there are hosts of differences in interpretations of what the popes say and of what the church councils say, just as there are hosts of different interpretations of what the Bible says.

Some people almost despair, saying that "if the theologians can't agree on this, how am I, a simple Christian, going to be able to understand who's telling me the truth?"

We find these same differences of opinion in medicine. One doctor says you need an operation, and the other doctor says you don't. How will I find out which doctor is telling me the truth? I'm betting my life on which doctor I trust at this point. It's troublesome to have experts differ on important matters, and these matters of biblical interpretation are far more important than whether or not I need my appendix out. What do you do when you have a case like that with variant opinions rendered by physicians? You go to a third physician. You try to investigate, try to look at their credentials to see who has the best training, who's the most reliable doctor; then you listen to the case that the doctor presents for his position and judge which you are persuaded is more cogent. I'd say the same thing goes with differences of biblical interpretations.

The first thing I want to know is, Who's giving the interpretation? Is he educated? I turn on the television and see all kinds of teaching going on from television preachers who, quite frankly, simply are not trained in technical theology or biblical studies. They don't have the academic qualifications. I know that people without academic qualifications can have a sound interpretation of the Bible, but they're not as likely to be as accurate as those who have spent years and years of careful research and disciplined training in order to deal with the difficult matters of biblical interpretation.

The Bible is an open book for everybody, and everybody has a fair shot of coming up with whatever they want to find in it. We've got to see the credentials of the teachers. Not only that, but we don't want to rely on just one person's opinion. That's why when it comes to a biblical interpretation, I often counsel people to check as many sound sources as they can and then not just contemporary sources, but the great minds, the recognized minds of Christian history. It's amazing to me the tremendous amount of agreement there is among Augustine, Aquinas, Anselm, Luther, Calvin, and Edwards—the recognized titans of church history. I always consult those because they're the best. If you want to know something, go to the pros.

When I discuss biblical concepts with my friends, I'm often met with the reply "That's your interpretation." How do I respond?

That is such a common response. You labor over a passage and do your homework, then present the passage, and somebody looks at you and says, "Well, that's your interpretation."

What do they really mean when they say that? That anything you say must be wrong, and since this is your interpretation, then it must be an incorrect one? I don't think people are trying to insult us. The real issue here is whether or not there is a correct and incorrect interpretation of Scripture. When many people say, "That's your interpretation," what they really mean is, "I'll interpret it my way, and you interpret it your way. Everybody has the right to interpret the Bible however they want to. Our forefathers died for the right of what we call private interpretation: that every Christian has the right to read the Bible for themselves and to interpret it for themselves."

When interpretation became an issue in the sixteenth century at the Council of Trent, the Roman Catholic Church took a dim view of it. One of their canons at the fourth session said that nobody has the right to distort the

IMPORTANT

Scriptures by applying private interpretations to them. Insofar as that statement is recorded at Trent, I agree with it with all of my heart because it's exactly right. Though I have the right to read the Bible for myself and the responsibility to interpret it accurately, nobody ever has the right to interpret the Bible *incorrectly.*

I believe there is only one correct interpretation of the Bible. There may be a thousand different applications of one verse, but only one correct interpretation. My interpretation may not be right and yours may not be right, but if they're different, they can't both be right. That's relativism taken to its ridiculous extreme. When someone says, "Well, that's your interpretation," I would respond, "Let's try to get at the objective meaning of the text and beyond our own private prejudices."

I recently obtained a Living Bible arranged for daily Bible readings. I have found this version to be very enjoyable, and I hate for the day's reading to end. Do we need to be wary of this version?

It seems that every time a new translation of the Bible appears in the bookstores, there's a certain degree of controversy that attends its appearance. People tend to prefer some tried-and-true translation. The first translation of the Bible from the original languages into the vernacular became such a controversial matter that those who dared to translate the Bible into German or English were, in many cases, executed.

For many years the authorized version in English was the King James Version. When a more up-to-date translation took place, such as the Revised Standard Version, there was a tremendous cry of protest against it. That protest goes on even today from those who prefer the King James edition.

There are basically two reasons we have this proliferation of new translations. One is that in the twentieth century we've experienced an explosion of knowledge and data about ancient lexicography, or word meaning. We've had so many more discoveries that shed light on the precise meaning of Hebrew and Greek words that our ability to translate the original documents accurately has been sharply increased. When that happens, it calls for a new translation. When you translate a document from one language to another, you run the risk of losing some of the precision that's in the original. Whenever you have a better grasp of the original, you want to reflect that in the next edition of your translation.

Second, we've discovered many more texts of the Greek New Testament, and to be very frank, the Greek manuscripts from which the King James Version was translated were not the best Greek manuscripts. Since the King James was first introduced, we've had great progress in reconstructing the original manuscripts of the Bible, and that's another reason for an update.

There's still another reason, and that is that language changes and words that once meant one thing in a culture now mean another. *Gay* meant "happy" twenty years ago; that's not what it means now. *Cute* meant "bow-legged" two hundred years ago; that's not what it means now. Words do undergo an evolution, and that has to be reflected in new translations. There are also different types of translations. Some try to be very accurate, word for word, and others try to give more of a paraphrase. I see *The Living Bible* as an attempt to simplify and paraphrase and speak in general terms. People find it a delightful help. I wouldn't recommend it as the most strictly accurate version for careful technical study, but in simplifying the often arcane message of Scripture, I think it has done a tremendous service to the people of God.

Does the Bible claim authority over the life of a believer?

I think it does, obviously, in what the Bible says about itself. And what the Bible says about itself is very important to the modern debate about its authority in the life of the church and in the life of the individual believer.

One of the greatest debates in our age is this question of biblical authority. Even if the Bible didn't claim authority over us, the church might still recognize it as a primary source and say, "This is the original information that we have of the teachings of Jesus." Jesus obviously has a claim of authority over every believer inasmuch as he is the Lord of the church and the Lord of every believer. And we might still attribute that kind of authority to the Scriptures.

But the authority of the Bible is not proven by its claim. It is very significant, however, that it makes the claim to be the Word of God. Now anything that is the Word of God, it would seem to me, carries with it automatically nothing less than the authority of God. The great debate in our day is whether or not the Bible is inspired or infallible or inerrant. These are the kinds of controversies about which denominations are fighting in the Christian world today.

And behind all of that debate, really, is the question of the extent of the Bible's authority.

To illustrate it, let me share a brief anecdote about a friend of mine who said he had abandoned any confidence of the Bible's inspiration or of its infallibility. He said, "But I've still maintained my belief in Christ as my Lord." I said to him, point-blank, "How does Jesus exercise his lordship over you?" And he said, "What do you mean?" I replied, "A lord is somebody who has the authority to bind your conscience, to give you marching orders, to say, 'You must,' 'You ought,' 'This is required of you.' How does Jesus become your Lord? How does he speak to you? Does he speak audibly, directly, or what?" Finally he realized that the only message that we ever have from Jesus comes to us through the medium of the Scripture. *WHAT ABOUT THE HOLY SPIRIT.* *PAGE 78*

So the authority that the Bible has over me is the authority that Christ has over me, because when he sent out his apostles he said to them, "Those who receive you, receive me." And it's the authority of Christ given to his apostles that we find in Scripture. And if it comes from Christ and hence from God, then, of course, all of the authority of God stands behind it and over me.

Does the Bible claim authority over the life of an unbeliever?

We divide the Bible into two sections, what we call the Old Testament and the New Testament, or the book of the old covenant and the book of the new covenant. In one very real sense, historically, the writings of Scripture are part of the written documents of a covenant agreement between

God and certain people. In the Old Testament it is a covenant agreement between God and the Jewish people. And the new covenant is called the covenant of Christ for his people.

Insofar as the nonbeliever has not entered into a covenant relationship with God, there is a sense in which he becomes an alien to the commonwealth of Israel or to the new covenant community of Christ and therefore is not formally bound by oath to the stipulations of that covenant agreement, part of which are the writings of sacred Scripture. However, we also have to recognize that every human being is created in the image of God. By virtue of a person's humanness, he or she is inextricably bound into a covenant relationship with the Creator. So if I choose not to believe in God or not to serve God or not to be involved in religion in any way, that does not destroy God or his existence, or change the fact that I have been created by God and am accountable to God and am required by God to obey him and to worship him and to heed his voice. So coming at it from that angle, we would say that the unbeliever, in spite of his unbelief, is still responsible to heed whatever God says. And if the Scriptures are the Word of God, then they carry the authority of God. If you were to ask, "Does God have authority over the unbeliever?" I would say, "Of course he does." And anything that God says is authoritative to all people.

What can a Christian learn from the Old Testament? Is it as pertinent to my growth as the New Testament is?

The Scriptures are not a single book but a collection of books made up of sixty-six volumes in the particular

library that we call the Bible. The New Testament covers
a period of time in human history of about thirty-five
years, and all but five of those years for the most part are
covered in the first couple of chapters. So the bulk of the
New Testament covers about a five-year period in human
history. It is the most important period in human history
of God's dealing with the human race because it covers
the earthly ministry of Jesus and the expansion of the
early church.

The Old Testament, beginning around Genesis 11 and
throughout the rest of the Old Testament, covers a period
of about two thousand years of redemptive history. That is
a wealth of information of how God has acted on behalf of
his people and for the redemption of this world.

I don't think we can say that one is more pertinent than
the other. There is a widespread feeling that a Christian is
only to be concerned with the New Testament, that the
Old Testament is antiquated, no longer truly relevant. In
fact, there is more and more the feeling that there are two
different Gods. There is the God of the Old Testament and
the God of the New Testament. The God of the Old Testament is a God of anger, wrath, justice, and holiness. The
New Testament God focuses on love, mercy, and grace.
That, of course, is a radical distortion. There is a continuity between the two Testaments. We can distinguish them,
but we dare not separate them. The same God is revealed
to us both in the Old Testament and in the New Testament. Saint Augustine said, "The Old is in the New
revealed; the New is in the Old concealed."

The Old Testament is preparation for the coming of
the Messiah and the revelation that we receive in the New

Testament. It's like asking, "Is the foundation of a house important? Is it pertinent to the house?" It's essential to the house. The structure stands upon that foundation, and that's what the Old Testament does for our faith. There are many elements of Old Testament history that are not to be applied directly to the Christian life today, such as the sacrificial system, but even the dimension of the sacrificing of bulls and goats and the like that we find in the Old Testament reveals something that points to the coming of Christ and enriches our understanding of what was accomplished by Christ. About three-fourths of the information in the New Testament is either a quotation of, an allusion to, or a fulfillment of something that was already found in the Old Testament.

How does the Old Testament apply to Christians today?

One of the great weaknesses of today's church is a tendency to denigrate and neglect the Old Testament. It's a much more sizable piece of literature than the New Testament, and it covers an enormous period of history, the history of redemption from the creation of the world until the appearance of the Messiah. All of that is a revelation of God's activity on this planet, and I believe it was inspired by the Holy Spirit and given to the church for the church's instruction and for the church's edification.

I also think that one of the great problems in today's church is an abysmal ignorance of God the Father. We relate to Jesus. He's our Redeemer. He's God in the flesh, so we have a way in which we can understand Jesus. It is more difficult when we look at God the Father and also the Holy Spirit. The history of the Old Testament certainly calls forth something of the Messiah who is to come, but it is constantly revealing the character of God the Father, the one who sends Jesus into this world, the one whom Jesus calls Father, the one from whom Jesus says he has been sent, that person to whom we are being reconciled and redeemed. So how can we possibly justify neglecting such an enormous body of literature that communicates to us the character, nature, and will of our Creator and the one who has sent our Redeemer to this planet?

Saint Augustine is the one who said that the New Testament is concealed in the Old Testament and the Old Testament is revealed by the New Testament. In fact, about three-fourths of the material of the New Testament is either a quotation from or allusion to what went before it. I don't think we can really understand the New Testament until we have made a very serious study of the Old Testament.

Obviously there are things in the Old Testament that do not apply to the Christian in our day. For example, we are not to continue the ceremonies that were required of the Jewish people; those ceremonies were "types" that anticipated the once-for-all fulfillment of them in the work of Christ. So for us to offer animals as sacrifices would be an insult to the completion of Jesus' work on the cross. That doesn't mean that since that part of the Old Testament is fulfilled we are to neglect it altogether. The Old Testament is a treasure-house of knowledge for the Christian who will seek to investigate it.

What should Christians think about evolution?

There is no single view of evolution out there. We make
one distinction, for example, between macroevolution and
microevolution. Macroevolution claims that all of life
evolved fortuitously from a single cell—one little pulsating
cell of life made up of amino acids and RNA and DNA and
all of that, and then through chance, explosions, or whatever, there were mutations. First, a lower, simplistic form of
life came about, and then from that came more complex
things, and we all emerged, as it were, from the slime,
through oozing, into our present humanity. That's the
radical view of evolution that sees life occurring as sort of
a cosmic accident.

This view of evolution—the one I hear discussed publicly
so often in the secular world—is unmitigated nonsense
and will be totally rejected by the secular scientific community within the next generation. My objections to it are not
so much theological as they are rational and logical. I
mean, the doctrine of macroevolution is one of the most
unsubstantiated myths that I've ever seen perpetuated in
an academic environment.

But there are other varieties much less radical that simply indicate that there is a change, a progression involving
different directions among various species that we can
even track historically. The kind of evolution of the latter
sort is of no consequence with respect to biblical Christianity. The big issue is with the former view, and this is the
basic question: Is man in his origin the product of a pur-
posive act of divine intelligence, or is man a cosmic accident? In other words, am I a creature of dignity or a

creature of cosmic insignificance? That's a pretty heavy issue because if I just sort of popped into being or emerged from the slime and I'm destined for annihilation, I can only fantasize that somehow in between those two poles of origin and destiny I have meaning and significance and dignity. But that's wishful thinking of the worst sort. Obviously if I come from nothing and go to nothing, I *am* nothing under any objective analysis.

A Christian cannot believe that he is a cosmic accident and at the same time believe in the sovereign God and the creator God. To be a Christian is to affirm not only Christ the Redeemer but God the Creator. And we have to affirm both. Let me say, too, before we drop this question, that some of the biggest objections I have toward this more radical view of evolution are not the theological problems, as serious as they are, but rational problems. I think that it is not only bad theology, it's bad science.

All Christians, Jews, and Muslims historically have made it a central article of affirmation that this world and all the people in it are the result of a divine act of creation. As far as Christianity is concerned, if there's no creation, then there's nothing to redeem.

Does the Bible tell us how old the earth is?

What does the Bible tell us about the age of the earth? I remember once opening a Bible that was on the pulpit of a church. I opened it to the first page because I was preaching from the first chapter of Genesis, and it said, "The Book of Genesis," and then underneath "The Book of Genesis" in black boldfaced numbers was this: "4004 B.C." Right there on the first page of Scripture. I laughed.

I thought it was funny because there was a man by the name of Archbishop Usher a couple hundred years ago who, in reading the genealogies in the Bible, calculated an average lifespan of all those mentioned in the genealogy and came up with a highly speculative figure of 4004 as the date of Creation and tried to make a case that the Bible actually called for the creation of the world in 4004 B.C. What disturbed me was to see that number actually printed on the page of Holy Scripture. Now if somebody who doesn't know the origin of that kind of speculation picks up the Bible and reads on the page of Scripture "4004 B.C." and their mother or their Sunday school teacher tells them that the world was created 4000 years before Christ but the scientific evidence indicates that the universe is billions of years old, then they get all upset and think that somebody is attacking the Bible. When the fact of the matter is, the Bible doesn't give the slightest indication of when Creation occurred. So we really shouldn't be concerned about it.

As a Christian educator, what are some of your frustrations in your efforts to teach the Word?

I have lots of frustrations about teaching. But I would say my greatest frustration is that there is a tremendous anti-intellectual spirit present in contemporary Christendom. It's extremely hard to educate people who are opposed to using their minds. How else can we get educated?

There are reasons for this attitude. Evangelical Christians, for example, have seen a wholesale attack upon the sacred things that they believe and live by—the Bible and all the rest—by colleges and universities, by professors and theologians. They've come to distrust serious education. They want to keep their faith simple lest it be open to some kind of criticism or attack. I hear it constantly. "You have to take it on faith," as if seeking to understand something were evil. And how many times have you heard people say that they want to have childlike thinking?

What the Bible says, however, is that we are to be "babes in evil," that we are to be like little children in terms of being not sophisticated in our capacity for sin. But in understanding we are to be full-grown and mature. We are to put away childish things. I am very frustrated with the resistance I encounter in the Christian community against in-depth study of the things of God.

My second great frustration is that so many Christians, in order to truly learn the things of God, first have to unlearn what they've already learned. It's not by accident that the greatest threat to the integrity of Old Testament Israel and to the safety of the nation was not the opposing nations like the Philistines and the Babylonians but the enemy within—the false prophet. And the false prophet seduced the people away from the truth of God. Now that happens today, and it happens on both sides of the camp— the liberals and conservatives. And so what happens is people are educated with teaching that is not sound, and that's frustrating.

5

The Way of Salvation

I will give you a new heart and put a new spirit within you;
I will take the heart of stone out of your flesh and
give you a heart of flesh. I will put My Spirit within you
and cause you to walk in My statutes,
and you will keep My judgments and do them.

EZEKIEL 36:26-27

Questions in This Section:

Why did God save me?

When did God decide to give us eternal life?

If I'm happy with my life, why do I need Jesus?

What is true repentance, and why should it be emphasized in our lives?

Can you repent at the moment of death and still have the same salvation as someone who's been a Christian for many years?

If someone has rejected Christianity for his entire life, but then on his deathbed decides to play it safe and profess Jesus as his Savior and Lord, will that person really be accepted into heaven?

Is it possible for a Christian to lose his salvation because of sins he commits?

Is there salvation for a Christian who has turned away from Christ and does not seem to want to repent?

Does grace give us a free ride to salvation?

How can I understand God's grace and forgiveness of my sins?

How serious is it that people, upon receiving Christ, are being told only of Christ as Savior and not as Lord?

In Mark 16:16 Jesus says, "He who has believed and has been baptized shall be saved." How does baptism fit into our salvation?

What do good deeds have to do with salvation?

What role does human achievement or good works play in salvation?

In what way does God use guilt today?

Does God put a curse on us if we disobey, or does he merely withhold his blessing?

Help me understand the doctrine of election.

My understanding of the doctrine of predestination is that natural man will only accept Christ if God plants the desire in his heart. If God never plants that desire, is it fair for that man to be eternally lost?

In John 6:70 Jesus says he chose the Twelve. Does this mean Judas was one of the elect?

How has God kept his promise to Abraham that his offspring would be saved?

What is the doctrine of eternal security?

If justification is by faith alone, how can we apply James 2:24, which says a person is justified by what he does, not his faith alone?

Isn't it being narrow-minded for Christians to say Christ is the only way?

Why did God save me?

I know of no more difficult a theological question to deal with than this one. I've been studying theology for many years, and I still can't come up with any exhaustive reason to explain why God would save me, or anyone else for that matter.

Some people give a very simple answer to this question. They say that God saved you because you put your trust and faith in Christ when you answered the summons of the gospel. On the surface that's certainly a legitimate answer because we are justified through faith and we are called to make that response.

But the deeper question is, Why did you respond to the gospel when you heard it, but someone else who heard it— even the very same presentation at the same moment—did not respond to it? What was there in you that caused you to respond positively while others are caused to reject it? I ask that about my own life. I could say the reason I responded was that I was more righteous than the other fellow. God forbid that I ever say that on the Judgment Day. I might think I'm more intelligent than somebody else, but I wouldn't want to say that either. Some might say that I recognized my need more than somebody else recognized his need, but even that recognition is a mixture of at least some measure of intelligence and some measure of humility, most of which would find its ultimate roots in the grace of God. I have to say with the ancient man, there but for the grace of God go I. I can't give any reason other than God's grace for why I am saved.

The Bible says many things about why God initiates salvation of people: He loves the world; he has a benevolent attitude toward his fallen creatures. We know that. But when we get down to the specifics, the Bible speaks of God's sovereign work of redemption and uses the terms *predestination* and *election*. These are biblical words. What is behind God's predestinating grace or his election? Some say that God foresees the choices of people. I think that takes the very heart out of the biblical teaching.

When the Scripture speaks about God's electing people, God speaks of electing people in Christ; our salvation is rooted and grounded in Jesus. What that makes me think is this: You and I are saved not only because of God's concern for us but chiefly and ultimately for God's total determination to honor his obedient Son. We are the love gifts that the Father gives to the Son so that the Son, who lived a life of perfect obedience and died on the cross, will see the travail of his soul and be satisfied. That's the main reason I think God has saved you: to honor Jesus.

When did God decide to give us eternal life?

When is a time word, and the Bible uses words like that. And when the Bible speaks about the time frame in which God's decision is made in respect to our eternal life, it generally puts the decision at the foundation of the world; that is, from all eternity God has chosen us to be among the redeemed.

I think Paul emphasizes that very clearly, particularly in the first chapter of his letter to the Ephesians. We were chosen in Christ from the foundation of the world to be conformed to Christ and to be brought into a state of redemption. This, of course, touches immediately on the very difficult and controversial doctrine of predestination. I will say in passing, as we skate over the surface of it, that every church has some doctrine of predestination. There are great variances among the churches in terms of how to understand predestination, but every church historically has had to hammer out and forge some doctrine of predestination because the Bible speaks of it. So there is a certain sense in which from all eternity God has chosen his people for salvation.

Now, obviously, that gets into some very complicated side issues. On what basis does God make a decision like that from all eternity? Did God make a decision from all eternity that certain people would be damned? Does he destine people for hell? Does he destine people to fall? I think the church has shrunk from that concept and rightly so. I think God knew from all eternity that man would fall, that man would rebel against him, and he also knew that he was going to make a provision to redeem people from all eternity. God's knowledge is as ancient and his omniscience is as eternal as he is. Everything that God knows, he knows from eternity. We need to keep this idea in front of us.

I would say that God's decision to choose us was made prior to the fall of mankind but in light of the Fall. Let me say it again. He made the decision before the Fall, with the knowledge that the Fall will come and with the knowledge of its consequences. In other words, God couldn't possibly make it his choice to save persons who were in no need of salvation. Only sinners are in need of salvation, so God must have considered us as being sinners and fallen as we were considered in the divine mind for salvation. Ultimately, the decision to save us was made in eternity, according to God's divine knowledge of us.

If I'm happy with my life, why do I need Jesus?

I hear that from a lot of folks. They say to me, "I just don't feel the need for Christ." As if Christianity were something that were packaged and sold through Madison Avenue! That what we're trying to communicate to people is "Here's something that's going to make you feel good, and everybody needs a little of this in their closet or in their refrigerator," as if it were some commodity that's going to add a dash of happiness to our lives.

If the only reason a human being ever needed Jesus was to be happy and a person is already happy without Jesus, then they certainly don't need Jesus. The New Testament indicates, however, that there's another reason you or somebody else needs Jesus. There is a God who is altogether holy, who is perfectly just, and who declares that he is going to judge the world and hold every human being accountable for their life. As a perfectly holy and just God, he requires from each one of us a life of perfect obedience and of perfect justness. If there is such a God and if you have lived a life of perfect justness and obedience—that is, if you're perfect—then you certainly don't need Jesus. You don't need a Savior because only unjust people have a problem.

The problem is simply this: If God is just and requires

perfection from me and I come short of that perfection and he is going to deal with me according to justice, then I am looking at a future punishment at the hands of a holy God. If the only way I can escape punishment is through a Savior and if I want to escape that, then I need a Savior. Some people will say that we're just trying to preach Jesus as a ticket out of hell, as a way to escape eternal punishment. That's not the only reason I would commend Jesus to people, but that is one of the reasons.

I think that many people in today's culture don't really believe that God is going to hold them accountable for their lives—that God really does not require righteousness. When we take that view, we don't feel the weight of the threat of judgment. If you're not afraid to deal with God's punishment, then be happy as a clam if you want. I would be living in terrible fear and trembling at the prospect of falling into the hands of a holy God.

What is true repentance, and why should it be emphasized in our lives?

Before I define true repentance, I'll answer the second question, "Why is it important in our lives?" The reason it's of supreme importance in our lives, according to the New Testament, is because it is the indispensable requirement for entrance into the kingdom of God. I stress that point because the view is widely held in our culture that God forgives everybody of all their sins whether or not they repent. That concept simply does not come from Scripture.

If Jesus taught anything, he taught that it is absolutely essential for someone who has offended God to turn from that sin and repent. In fact, when Jesus began his public ministry, the very first words he preached were "Repent, for the kingdom of God is at hand." There's nothing more urgent and necessary than repentance if one is going to escape the wrath of God. God calls every human being to repent—it's not an option.

Paul spoke of the former days of ignorance that God overlooked; but now God calls all people everywhere to repent. Who does that include? Everybody. We all have that responsibility, and not all of us are doing it. God meant what he said. He requires repentance.

You ask what is true repentance? I don't know if you've ever heard the Roman Catholic prayer of contrition, but I think it's an excellent prayer. Virtually every Roman Catholic person knows it by heart. I don't know it by heart, but I have heard it a number of times and have some elements of it by memory. "O my God, I am heartily sorry for having offended Thee . . . not only because of loss of reward, or fear of punishment, but because I violated you."

We make a distinction in theology between what we call attrition and contrition. Attrition is turning away from your sin or from your guilt by a motivation simply to escape punishment. The child has no remorse about stealing cookies until he's caught with his hand in the cookie jar and the mother comes with the paddle. There's something suspicious about that kind of repentance. It's the repentance to avoid punishment—what we would call a ticket out of hell. True repentance goes beyond a mere fear of punishment to what we call contrition. When David's heart was broken before God and he said, "O God, a broken and contrite heart you will not despise," he felt

real sorrow, a godly sorrow. True repentance is an awareness that we have done wrong, and it brings us to a choice
to turn from our wrong.

Can you repent at the moment of death and still have the same salvation as someone who's been a Christian for many years?

That's a tricky question, but I think it's a fascinating one
and certainly one that many people are concerned about.
We talk about foxhole faith, when people cry out in desperate moments of crisis or postpone to their deathbed the
moment of committing their lives to Christ. Some people
say that it doesn't make sense for somebody who has been
a Christian all their life to be in the same state as somebody who did as they pleased all their life and waited until
the last second to get their accounts square with God.

There's a parable in the New Testament in which Jesus
speaks about those who agree to work for a certain wage,
and then at the last minute some other people are hired
and only work for a few minutes but they get the same pay.
The first group is really bent out of shape, and they say,
"What's going on here? There's no justice in this!" Does
the second group receive the same salvation? Yes and no.
They are brought into a state of salvation; that is, they
escape the punishment of hell and enter into the kingdom
if indeed that last-breath repentance is genuine. The
requirement for entrance into the kingdom of God is to
repent and believe in Christ.

The thief on the cross did it in the last minutes of his
life, and Jesus assured him that he would be with him in

paradise. There we have Exhibit A in the New Testament of somebody who actually did that and who was promised by our Lord himself that he would participate in Jesus' kingdom. Certainly it's possible for a person at the last moment of their life to repent sufficiently, believe, and be justified and enter into all of the benefits of membership of the kingdom of heaven.

However, Paul speaks of those who make it into the kingdom by the skin of their teeth. I think a "deathbed" believer would be in that category. We tend to think that all that matters is getting there because there is an unbridgeable chasm between getting into heaven or missing it altogether. Yet Jesus tells us to work and to store up treasures for ourselves in heaven because he promises emphatically that there will be rewards dispensed to his people according to their obedience and their works. You don't get into heaven by your works, but your reward in heaven will be according to those works, according to the New Testament. What that says to me is that although people can make it by the skin of their teeth by repenting in their last dying breath, nevertheless, their degree of felicity will not be nearly as great as that of those who have been serving Christ faithfully for many, many years.

If someone has rejected Christianity for his entire life, but then on his deathbed decides to play it safe and profess Jesus as his Savior and Lord, will that person really be accepted into heaven?

Absolutely not. That person has no hope of going to heaven on the basis of the action as you have described it.

First of all, let's understand that redemption does not come through a *profession* of faith but through a *possession* of faith. Those of us who have faith are called to profess that faith; however, the mere profession of it does not guarantee that the genuine article is present. This is particularly so when somebody makes this verbal profession strictly as a means of covering his bets or to play it safe and guard against the negative consequences. From a biblical standpoint, salvation requires authentic repentance. Justifying faith is a repenting faith. If there is no repentance, then that indicates that the profession of faith is fraudulent.

If we turn your question around and ask if a person could live his whole life in sin, rebellion, and disobedience and then on his deathbed truly repent and go to heaven, the answer is yes—just as the thief on the cross met the Savior in his dying moments and was guaranteed eternity with him. The New Testament speaks of those who are saved by the skin of their teeth. It's certainly not a wise course of action to postpone your repentance until the day of your departure because we don't know when that day is on the schedule. Even though making a confession simply out of fear is not enough, that fear should give pause and cause us to think seriously about our future state.

Is it possible for a Christian to lose his salvation because of sins he commits?

The question of losing one's salvation is one that is a matter of great controversy within the household of Christian faith. There are many Christians who live in mortal fear every day of losing what they have found in Christ because the Bible gives serious warnings about falling away, and Paul himself says that he has to be very careful lest he himself become a castaway. There are biblical warnings about what would happen if we turn our backs on Christ after we've come to a knowledge of him.

On the other hand, there are also many Christians who believe that we will, in fact, never fall away, and I'm numbered among that group. I'm persuaded from a study of Scripture that we can have an assurance of our salvation not only for today but for all time. But the assurance that we have, or confidence in our future estate in salvation, must be based upon the right foundations. In other words, if my confidence that I will persevere is based on my confidence that I will not sin, it's on very shaky ground. One thing the Bible makes clear to me is that even though I am a redeemed person, I will in all likelihood, and inevitably, continue to sin to some degree. If it were up to my strength to persevere to guarantee my future salvation, then I would have very little hope of persevering.

But I'm convinced that the Bible teaches that what God begins in our life, he finishes. Paul teaches, for example, in Philippians, "He who has begun a good work in you will perfect it to the end." My confidence rests in the fact that Jesus promises to intercede for me daily as my Great High Priest. My confidence for my future salvation rests in my confidence that God will keep his promise and that Christ will intercede for me and preserve me. Again, if it were left to me, I would obviously fall away. I like to look at it this way: I'm walking the Christian life with my hand in God's hand. If my perseverance depended upon my holding tightly to God's hand, I would surely fall away because at some point I would let go. But I believe that the Scriptures teach us that God is holding my hand, and because he is holding my hand, I don't have to fear that I will fall ultimately and finally.

Now that doesn't mean that Christians don't involve themselves in serious sins and what we would call in theology "serious and radical fall," but the issue we're discussing here is whether a Christian will ever fall totally and finally. In the New Testament John tells us, for example, that "those who went out from us were never really with us," and that "Christ does not lose those whom the Father has given to him." So my confidence again rests in the intercession of Christ and God's ability and promise to hold on to me. In and of myself I am capable of sinning even unto the loss of my salvation, but I'm persuaded that God in his grace will keep me from that.

Is there salvation for a Christian who has turned away from Christ and does not seem to want to repent?

I believe that once a person is authentically redeemed, is truly in Christ, that person will never be lost to Christ. That person has what we call eternal security—not because of the person's innate ability to persevere, but I believe that God promises to preserve his own and that we have the benefit of our Great High Priest who intercedes for us every day. Now, at the same time, Christians are capable of gross and heinous sin. They're capable of very serious falls away from Christ. They're capable of the worst kind of denial and betrayal of our Lord.

Consider, for example, Exhibit A—the apostle Peter, who denied Jesus with cursing. He was so emphatic that he uttered profanities to underscore the fact that he never knew Jesus. If you talk about somebody who didn't seem to want to repent and who had turned away from Jesus, Saint Peter is your classic example. Yet his fellow disciple Judas also betrayed Jesus and turned away from him, and of course, both of the betrayals were predicted by Jesus at the Last Supper. When Jesus spoke of Judas, he said, "What you have to do, do quickly. Go." And he dismissed him to his treachery. He mentioned in the Scripture that Judas was a son of perdition from the beginning. I think it's clear in Jesus' High Priestly prayer that he understood Judas was never a Christian. So Judas's betrayal was not the case of a Christian turning on Christ.

When he announced to Peter that Peter would also betray him, he said to him, "Simon, Simon, Satan has asked for you. He would have you and sift you like wheat, but I have prayed for you so that your faith should not fail; and when you turn, strengthen the brethren." And then Peter says, "Oh no, Lord, not me. I'll never betray you." Then, of course, he did. But notice that when Jesus predicted it, he said, "When you turn"—not, "If you turn" but "When you turn, strengthen the brethren." Because Jesus had prayed as he did in his High Priestly prayer, no one would be able to snatch his people out of his hand.

The New Testament promises that he who has begun a good work in you will perfect it to the end (Phil. 1:6). I know there are many Christians who believe that a true Christian can lose his or her salvation. I don't. I'd say with the apostle John, "Those who went out from us were never really with us." I think a Christian can have a gross and serious fall but not a full and final fall—that he or she will be restored even as David realized his sin, as the Prodigal Son came to himself, as Peter ultimately repented.

Does grace give us a free ride to salvation?

We can look at the concept "free ride" in many ways. Grace by definition is something that is free in the sense that we can't earn it, we can't buy it, we can't deserve it, and there's no merit in us by which God bestows his mercy upon us. Anytime God dispenses mercy or unmerited favor, which is how we define grace, he's doing something that he has no obligation to do. I'm convinced that when we receive the grace of salvation, our eternal destiny is secure. I'm convinced that once we are clothed with the righteousness of Christ and have his merit imputed to our account by God (which is an act of God's grace) and we are redeemed, then I believe we are virtually guaranteed eternal life. In other words, I don't think that a Christian can lose his salvation. I say this because I'm persuaded that God has promised he will keep us to the end. If it were up to us to persevere, to hang on, and to be faithful and obedient to the end in order to be saved, I don't think any one of us would persevere enough to merit salvation. But God promises to finish what he has begun.

Does that mean it's a free ride? So often the concept of free ride means that since God has given me grace and since God has started this work and he promises to finish it, there's nothing left for me to do. I can do whatever I want. I'm saved and I don't have to worry about a thing.

It's free from here on in, I'm on a roller coaster without any brakes, and I can do whatever I want. I can sin as I please and enjoy it the rest of my life. It's a license to sin.

However, the apostle Paul points out that where sin abounds, grace abounds much more. That is to say, the more I sin the more I see the grace of God because more grace is necessary for me to get into heaven.

Some people say that if the more you sin the more grace you get, the best thing to do is to keep sinning and that way you'll get more grace. Paul asks the question "Should we continue in sin that grace may abound?" How does he answer it? He says, "God forbid." Sinning all the more is a totally opposite response to one that is pleasing to God. As a matter of fact, the more grace we receive, the more we are to be moved toward a sense of gratitude; the more gratitude we experience, the more we should be moved to the pursuit of righteousness through obedience to the law of God. As Paul says elsewhere, "We're to work out our salvation with fear and trembling" because God promises to work within us to will and to do what is right. But along with God's grace comes the challenge for us to fight with all of our might to resist the temptations of sin and to pursue a life of righteousness and obedience. My salvation doesn't depend on my obedience, but my obedience is to be a response to that grace of God.

How can I understand God's grace and forgiveness of my sins?

It's easy for us to come up with a theological definition of grace. We say that grace is unmerited favor—to receive something positive from the hand of God that we don't deserve. But to understand the graciousness of grace in any depth I believe is a lifelong enterprise for the Christian. When I was studying theology at the doctoral level in Europe, our professor at the Free University of Amsterdam, G. C. Berkouwer, once made this statement when we were studying systematic theology: "Gentlemen, the essence of theology is grace." I think he's right. When we get to the very essence of what our study of theology is, we are studying the grace of God, because it's by God's grace that we are Christians in the first place. It's by God's grace that we even draw a breath every moment, and it's by God's grace that we receive every benefit from his hand.

I don't think we understand this when we become Christians. The Bible talks about a progression. We're supposed to move from life to life, from faith to faith, from grace to grace. From beginning to end the whole Christian life is grace, and that's why I say that the more we study grace, the more we see grace.

I've said a thousand times that it's easy to understand justification by faith alone—in the head. It's not so easy to get it in the bloodstream, to realize that the reason I can exist in the presence of a holy God is that I am a forgiven person—that forgiveness is something I couldn't possibly buy or steal or beg or borrow or earn. I have no merit before God. The only merit I ever enjoy is the merit that was won for me by Christ. I live and move and have my being by virtue of Christ's righteousness, Christ's merit, which is given to me gratuitously, graciously by God.

We talk about the doctrines of grace. What other doctrines are there but the doctrines of grace? It all calls attention to the fact that God is just and I am not just. The only way an unjust person can possibly exist in a universe governed by a just and holy God is by grace. But it's so hard to get this through because we are a stiff-necked people, just like people in the Old Testament. We harbor these feelings deep down that God owes us a better deal than we're getting or that God owes us the gifts and the blessings that we've received. We feel that somehow we have deserved them. It's only proper and appropriate that I have a better job than you or more talents than you have, or live in a better house, because that's just God's justice prevailing here in the world. Whenever things go wrong, then that's something that I get mad about. That is when we discover we haven't learned grace.

How serious is it that people, upon receiving Christ, are being told only of Christ as Savior and not as Lord?

It's inconceivable to me that such a question would ever even arise in the New Testament church—as if we could separate the saviorhood of Christ from his lordship. I mean, the very first confession of faith in the New Testament was *Iēsous kurios,* "Jesus is Lord."

But when a person receives Christ as Savior, he not only acknowledges his need and necessity of having a Savior, he comes in humble faith and repentance, trusting Christ. How can a person trust Christ to be a Savior and at the same time utterly ignore or repudiate the clear teaching of Jesus that he is not only Savior but also Lord?

I'm afraid that what we have lurking here in this dichotomy between Jesus as Savior and Jesus as Lord is a very serious distortion of the Protestant doctrine of justification by faith alone, a distortion called antinomianism. *Antinomianism* means simply anti-lawism. Some people have been so zealous to propagate the doctrine that we are saved by faith and not by works that they have concluded that the kind of faith that saves is bare, naked faith. They believe that faith doesn't ever have to have any works follow from it and that obedience is inconsequential to the Christian life. In other words, I can sin all I want without repentance and still have remission of sins because heaven's a free gift and justification is by faith, so what difference does it make whether I continue to sin?

This type of interpretation is the very reason Luther and the Protestant fathers were so careful to point out that justification by faith alone involves, not a cheap profession of faith, but an authentic faith—the kind of faith that displays its genuine character by the fruits of obedience. The works of obedience do not merit salvation for us, but if there is no fruit of obedience to the lordship of Christ, that's the clearest indication that the faith is a dead faith, the faith of which Saint James says profits nothing. So if people are saying, "You don't have to believe in the lordship of Christ in order to be saved," what I'm hearing is a false doctrine of justification. It purports that we can believe certain things but then live any way we want.

Sometimes new converts miss the significance of Christ's lordship, mainly because it isn't explained to them clearly. Particularly if they are unfamiliar with these Christian terms, and Christians around them assume that "accepting Christ as Savior" is understood to include his lordship, these new converts suffer from a serious gap in their knowledge of basic doctrines. We need to be careful and thorough as we teach new believers.

In Mark 16:16 Jesus says, "He who has believed and has been baptized shall be saved." How does baptism fit into our salvation?

This is not only a principal point of dispute between the Roman Catholic Church and general Protestantism, but it has been argued strenously even within Protestantism.

Rome, for example, teaches that baptism is the instrumental cause of one's justification. In other words, it is the instrument by which a person is given justifying grace and placed in a reconciled relationship with God. That sacrament becomes very important. That's why the Church will hurry to baptize children that are born dying or will even baptize them as they expire. Because of a text like that, Rome does not go so far as to say that it is absolutely essential for salvation because they allow for what they call the *votum baptisma,* or the desire for baptism. There may be a person who is believing and wants to be baptized, but is hindered on his way to church. For example, he's struck by a car or he dies before he can have the sacrament. He is considered baptized just like the thief on the cross, who had no opportunity to be baptized. Yet when the thief manifested his faith, Jesus promised him redemption that very day. The text doesn't say that baptism is an absolute prerequisite for salvation.

Jesus simply says that those who believe and are baptized will be saved. All who have A and B will receive C. You could say all who have faith and who repent might be saved, too.

The general Protestant view, however, is that baptism is commanded and is necessary because Christ commands every believer to be baptized. It's a serious matter and it is a means of grace, and we certainly should be diligent in availing ourselves of it.

The general Protestant notion is that justification is by faith alone; that is, the absolutely essential prerequisite for redemption is to place one's trust in Christ. The assumption is that if you do trust Christ and submit to his lordship and you understand that he commands you to be baptized, you will add baptism to that faith. It's not the baptism that causes your salvation, and baptism is not necessary for salvation.

What do our good deeds have to do with our salvation?

From one perspective our good deeds have absolutely nothing to do with our salvation; from another perspective they have everything to do with it. This is the core debate that has been raging among Christians ever since the Protestant Reformation.

I am persuaded that our good deeds never merit salvation. To merit salvation would mean to earn it or to deserve it. The deeds would have to be so good, so perfect, with no mixture of sin in them, that it would impose an obligation upon God to grant us salvation. I believe that the New Testament is abundantly clear that none of us lives a life that is good enough to earn salvation. We receive God's salvation while we are sinners (Eph. 2:1-6). That's why we need a Savior, an atonement—and why we need grace.

People often say, "Nobody's perfect." We all agree on

that. But not one person in a thousand realizes how significant that statement is. Somehow they think that God is going to grade on a curve and "as long as my life is less sinful than somebody else's, then relatively speaking it's good enough to make it into God's kingdom." We forget that God requires perfect obedience to his law, and if we fail to obey him perfectly, then we're going to have to look elsewhere for a way to get our salvation. That's where Christ comes in. Christ makes his merit available to us. When I trust him by faith, then his righteousness becomes my righteousness in the sight of God. So it's his good work that saves me and that saves you—not our good works.

Nevertheless, in a response of gratitude we are called to obey. Jesus said, "If you love me, keep my commandments." Martin Luther taught that justification is by faith alone. But he expanded the concept by saying that justification is by faith alone, but not by a faith that is alone. A person who is truly trusting Christ and resting on Christ for redemption receives the benefits of Christ's merit by faith. But if that person has true faith, that true faith will manifest itself in a life of obedience. Simply put, I get into heaven by Jesus' righteousness, but my reward in heaven will be distributed according to my obedience or the lack of it.

What role does human achievement or good works play in salvation?

Human good works play a tremendously important role. There can be no salvation whatsoever without good works, and your good works are crucial to your salvation. Now, how can a Protestant make a statement like that?

First of all, good works are absolutely crucial and are, indeed, *necessary* for salvation because God requires good works to save anybody. Those good works are supplied and provided by Christ, who in his perfect humanity earned the infinite merit of God—the reward of which is the very basis of my salvation. Without Christ's righteousness, I am in very big trouble. So my salvation, initially, is grounded upon good works—Jesus' good works.

What about my own good works? Do they have a role? Most Protestants would say no. Justification is only one part of salvation. Salvation is the big word. Salvation is the word that covers all of the process by which God fully brings us to total redemption. Justification is that point in the process when God declares me a person who is in a state of redemption. The fact is that you are already justified, and you are in a state of salvation to a degree, but there's still more of your salvation yet to come. You still haven't gone to heaven. You still haven't been perfectly sanctified. You haven't been glorified. None of those things will happen to you until you die and go to heaven. When you die and go to heaven, God will give you a reward for whatever degree of obedience you have rendered to him in your Christian life. The reward that God bestows upon you in heaven will be given *according to your works* but not because your works are so righteous and meritorious that they impose an obligation upon God to reward them. God has graciously given us the promise that he will reward whatever obedience we give him. He doesn't have to, but out of his goodness and grace, as Augustine said, he crowns his own gifts. Our entrance into heaven is strictly by the righteousness of Christ. Our reward in heaven will be granted according to the works of obedience that we render.

In what way does God use guilt today?

When we talk about God's using guilt, it sounds strange to many people in our society because there's a widespread notion that guilt is something that is intrinsically destructive to human beings and that to impose guilt on anybody is wrong. The idea then emerges that God certainly would never use such a thing as guilt to bring about his will with human beings. If he did, that would be beneath the level of purity we would prefer in our deity.

In biblical terms, guilt is something that is real and is objective, and I think it's very important that we distinguish between guilt and guilt feelings. Guilt feelings are emotions that I experience subjectively. Guilt is an objective state of affairs. We see that in our law courts. When a person goes on trial for having broken the law, the question before the jury and before the judge is not Does the accused feel guilty? but Is there a real state of affairs that we call guilt? Has a law been transgressed? So it is with God. Guilt is objective in the eyes of God whenever his law is broken. When I break his law, I incur guilt, but I may or may not have guilt feelings about my guilt.

I suspect that behind your question is a concern about how God uses the guilt feelings as well as the actual guilt itself. One of the most important works of the Holy Spirit in the life of the believer is what the New Testament calls the conviction of sin. We can be guilty and not feel guilty. David, for example, when he got involved with Bathsheba and went even so far as arranging for her husband to get killed, felt no great remorse until Nathan, the prophet, came to him and told him a parable. The parable was about a man who took for himself a little lamb that belonged to a poor man. David was furious and wanted to know who this man was so that he could be punished. Finally Nathan pointed his finger at David and said, "You are the man." With the realization of the full import of his guilt, David was broken instantly and then wrote that magnificent song of penitence, Psalm 51, in which he cried out in his conviction of sin before God.

What God does with our guilt and guilt feelings is to bring us to that state in which we are convicted of sin and of the righteousness we've fallen short of; he uses those feelings to turn us from disobedience to obedience. In that regard, guilt and guilt feelings are healthy. Just as pain is a necessary sign of the presence of disease, so guilt feelings may often be the divine way of awakening us to our need for redemption.

Does God put a curse on us if we disobey, or does he merely withhold his blessing?

What could possibly be worse for you than if God absolutely and utterly withheld all blessedness that flows from God and God alone? You would be in the worst possible situation of cursedness. So, in my opinion, to withhold his blessing is the same as cursing us.

Does God curse us when we disobey him? In the Old Testament God makes a covenant with his people, and he gives them his law. When he gives them the law, he gives along with the law what we call dual sanctions; that is, a positive sanction and a negative sanction. He says very clearly, "If you obey my law, then I will bless you." In effect,

"Blessed will you be in the city, blessed will you be in the country, blessed will you be in the living room, blessed will you be in the dining room, blessed will you be in the kitchen, blessed will you be when you get up, blessed will you be when you go home, etc." If you read those passages in Deuteronomy, for example, you will see that God promises a blessing to those who obey his commandments.

Then God says, "But if you break my law, then cursed shall you be in the country, cursed shall you be in the city, cursed shall you be when you wake up, cursed shall you be when you go down, etc." So the God of Scripture is a God who gives blessing and curses. In fact, the whole scope of redemption as the New Testament explains it is developed in terms of this motif of blessing and cursing. What is the cross of Christ all about? Paul tells us in Galatians that on the cross, when Jesus is forsaken by the Father, Jesus receives in himself the full measure of God's curse upon disobedience. We have a Savior who takes that curse for us. And the whole drama of redemption is this: Christ takes my curse upon himself and gives to me and you and all who will embrace him the blessing that God promises for those who obey.

Help me understand the doctrine of election.

To try to answer that question in this short format would almost do more damage than good. I could put in a commercial here that Tyndale House published a book I wrote titled *Chosen by God*, which devotes itself entirely to a study of this very difficult biblical doctrine of election.

When we discuss the question of election, better known

as predestination, so often that word is associated with Presbyterian theology or Calvinism. The apostle Paul tells us in Ephesians that we have been predestined in Christ to be his craftsmanship and also follows that theme very closely in the book of Romans. So as Christians we have to struggle with the concept of divine sovereign election.

I think, again, that we have to understand the basic point of election—that God considers the human race in its fallenness and he sees all of us in a state of rebellion against him. If he were to exercise his justice totally and completely toward the whole world, then all of us would certainly perish. The Scriptures tell us that in our natural, fallen state, we are in a state of moral bondage. We still have the ability to make choices, but those choices follow the desires of our hearts, and what we lack as fallen creatures is a built-in desire for God. So Jesus said, for example, "No man can come to me unless it is given to him by the Father." I think that what election is all about is that God sovereignly and graciously gives the desire for Christ to those whom he calls out of the world. The difficulty and the great mystery is that apparently he doesn't do that for everyone. He reserves the right, as he told Moses and as Paul reiterates in the New Testament, to have mercy upon whom he will have mercy—just as he chose Abraham and not Hammurabi, just as Christ appeared on the road to Damascus to Paul in a way that he didn't appear to Pontius Pilate. That is to say, God doesn't treat everyone the same. He never treats anyone unjustly. Some receive justice and some receive mercy, and God reserves the right eternally to give his executive clemency, if you will, to those whom he chooses. There's a great debate on this, as you know, but I believe that the choice God makes is not based on my righteousness or on your righteousness but is based on his grace.

My understanding of the doctrine of predestination is that natural man will only accept Christ if God plants the desire in his heart. If God never plants that desire, is it fair for that person to be eternally lost?

I would say that the natural man needs more than God planting a desire in the heart before he will come to Christ. I think God has to bring that desire to fruition before a person will ever choose Christ. It's not such that God just plants the seed. He fertilizes the seed and brings the fruit of it. Jesus made the statement that "no man can come to me unless it's given to him of the Father." What did he mean?

Certainly human beings have a will, and we have the ability to choose what we desire. I think what Jesus meant was simply that, left to themselves, people don't have the desire to come to Christ. They don't have the desire to repent, and they don't have the desire to embrace the things of God. That's what the Bible means when it says that we are in bond service to our own sin and that we are by nature dead in our sins and trespasses. Unless God makes us alive to himself, we're never going to have a desire for Christ.

Let's say that God sees a whole human race who has no desire for him whatsoever and he knows that unless he does something to intervene in their lives and to bring life out of their spiritual death, they're never going to heed his call, they're never going to respond to his invitation, because

IN THE FULL SCOPE OF THINGS THAT SOUNDS ODD

they simply don't want to. It's their very freedom that's keeping them away from Christ. They have the freedom to choose what they desire and to refuse what they don't desire, and they are steadfastly refusing to come to Christ. So God decides that for some of these people he will provide a special work of grace. He's going to change the disposition of their hearts. I think that's exactly what happens. I think that God does overcome my hostility and my lack of desire for him and does more than plant a desire for him. He gives me a desire for Christ so that what was formerly despicable and repugnant to me is now sweetness and light, and I can't wait to embrace Christ. I think that is what happens. That's the testimony of every Christian heart.

We ask about being fair. I don't think God owes it to anyone who doesn't want Christ to give them the desire to want what they need. He doesn't owe that to anybody. The problem is that if God does it for some, why doesn't he do it for all? I can only say to you that I have no idea why he doesn't do it for all. But this I do know and ask you to think about carefully: Just because he does it for some in no way requires that he do it for everybody else—because grace is never required. God spoke to Moses, and Paul reminds us that God always reserves this prerogative: "I will have mercy upon whom I will have mercy." It's not up to us to direct God's mercy.

In John 6:70 Jesus says he chose the Twelve. Does this mean Judas was one of the elect?

Election involves God choosing people, but that does not mean that everything God chooses is a matter of election.

133

When Jesus says of the Twelve, "I chose each one of you.
You didn't choose me," we can read into that statement
that Jesus is saying, "You twelve people have been elected
from all eternity to receive the grace of salvation." If that's
what Jesus meant by saying, "I chose these twelve," then it
would certainly mean that all twelve disciples, including
Judas, would be numbered among the elect and would
presumably be saved.

But the Scripture seems to take a dim view of the future
condition of Judas, who, as far as we can discern from the
New Testament, dies without being restored to fellowship
with Christ. I think what Jesus is saying there is that he has
chosen those twelve to be his disciples. He goes on to say
that he knew all along that one of them was the son of
perdition. Jesus reveals that he knew very well the state of
Judas's soul when he chose him to participate in Jesus'
rabbinic school of disciples. Remember that a disciple is
simply a learner. A disciple in the ancient Jewish community was a person who attached himself to the school of
a particular rabbi and became his student. Jesus was a
peripatetic rabbi, a rabbi whose school was not in some
building, but out-of-doors. He walked around, and his
disciples literally followed him. They took notes and
memorized the things he taught.

Jesus selected Judas to enroll in his school. Obviously the
purpose of that was to fulfill the Scriptures. Jesus indicates
that—that this man was a "son of perdition" from the
beginning so that the Scriptures might be fulfilled, that
Jesus would be delivered through a betrayal. Jesus selected
one whom he knew would betray him and whom he knew
was not in a redeemed state in his soul. I don't think

there's any conflict or contradiction there between the fact that Jesus said he had chosen Judas and the fact that the rest of the disciples were presumably not only chosen to be disciples but also chosen to be apostles. They were chosen from all eternity to be included as the pillars of the kingdom of God and therefore chosen unto eternal salvation.

How has God kept his promise to Abraham that his offspring would be saved?

The way God has fulfilled his promise to Abraham of saving Abraham's offspring is by saving Abraham's offspring. That's exactly what God promised, and that's exactly what God did in early history and is doing today. Paul explains with much effort in his letter to the Romans that not all of those who are of Israel belong to the true Israel (Rom. 9:6-13).

In the first instance the promise of salvation to the seed of Abraham is realized in the salvation that God brings to the people of Israel. That doesn't mean that every descendant of Abraham receives salvation, but a cardinal point of both the Old and New Testaments is that salvation is of the Jews and that the Jews are the descendants of Abraham. Christ himself is a descendant of Abraham. Non-Jews are not connected to Abraham by blood; nevertheless, they are adopted into the household of Israel and become in biblical terms the spiritual heirs of Abraham and are counted as children of Abraham through the principle of adoption.

Much of the difficulty in understanding how God kept his promise to Abraham is how the promise was to be understood in the first place. One of the great mistakes of Israel as a nation in the Old Testament was assuming that biological descent from Abraham, in and of itself, guaranteed salvation. I think that's reading something into the promises of God that's certainly not there. This was a great point of dispute between Jesus and the Pharisees. Jesus said to them, "If you continue in my word, then you are my disciples. You will know the truth and the truth will set you free." The Pharisees were very annoyed by those words. They asked, "What do you mean—we're going to become free? We're already free. We're in bondage to no man. We are the children of Abraham."

Jesus said, "No, you are the children of those whom you obey." This concept of sonship is consistent with Old Testament theology; it is not defined merely in terms, or even primarily in terms, of biology but in terms of obedience. So those who were disobedient were disinherited and were replaced by those whom God called from the non-Jewish world, who were adopted into the household of God as the heirs of Abraham.

What is the doctrine of eternal security?

When we speak of the doctrine of eternal security, we're using a popular description of a classical doctrine that we call the perseverance of the saints. What it means is that once a person has become quickened by the Holy Spirit, born of the Spirit, and justified through faith in Christ and therefore placed in a state of salvation, that person will, in fact, never lose his salvation. That is a very controversial point within the context of historic Christianity.

There are many Christians who do not believe that once a person is in a state of grace, he will abide in that state of grace. The Roman Catholic Church, for example, historically teaches the distinction between venial and mortal sins. Mortal sin is defined as being mortal because it has the capacity to kill or to destroy the justifying grace that is in the soul, and such a sin makes it necessary for a person to be restored to justification through the sacrament of penance. Other Christian bodies also believe that it is possible for a Christian to lose his salvation.

Advocates of eternal security say that our salvation is secure once it is wrought through faith and that nothing shall separate us from the love of Christ. It is based on some passages in Scripture, such as Paul's teaching in Philippians. It is said that, "He who has begun a good work in you will perfect it to the end." Also, the Scriptures talk about the work of the Holy Spirit in the Christian life. Not only does the Spirit regenerate us, or quicken us, starting the whole process of Christian living, but as the Bible tells us, God gives to each Christian the sealing of the Holy Spirit and the *earnest* of the Holy Spirit. That term is a little bit obscure in everyday vocabulary, although when we buy a home the real estate agent might ask us to make a little down payment that we call earnest money. That is an economic phrase we use, and it is used in Scripture in that same way. An earnest was a down payment, an absolute guarantee that the balance would, in fact, be paid. When God the Holy Spirit puts a down payment on something, he doesn't renege on the payments. God the Holy Spirit does not give you an earnest that becomes less than ear-

137

nest. He's deadly in earnest to finish what he has begun with you.

Also, the concept of being sealed by the Spirit draws from the ancient language of the signet ring of the emperor. When something was sealed and affixed with the imprimatur of the king or the owner, then it became his possession. I think we have to make this qualifier: If it were up to us, I don't think any of us would persevere, and we would have very little to be secure about. However, the concept as I understand it biblically is that God promises that no one will snatch us out of the hands of Christ, that he will preserve us.

If justification is by faith alone, how can we apply James 2:24, which says a person is justified by what he does, not his faith alone?

That question is not critical only today, but it was in the eye of the storm we call the Protestant Reformation that swept through and divided the Christian church in the sixteenth century. Martin Luther declared his position: Justification is by faith alone, our works add nothing to our justification whatsoever, and we have no merit to offer God that in any way enhances our justification. This created the worst schism in the history of Christendom.

In refusing to accept Luther's view, the Roman Catholic Church excommunicated him, then responded to the outbreak of the Protestant movement with a major church council, the Council of Trent, which was part of the so-called Counter-Reformation and took place in the middle of the sixteenth century. The sixth session of Trent, at which the canons and decrees on justification and faith were spelled out, specifically appealed to James 2:24 to rebuke the Protestants who said that they were justified by faith alone: "You see that a person is justified by what he does and not by faith alone." How could James say it any more clearly? It would seem that that text would blow Luther out of the water forever.

Of course, Martin Luther was very much aware that this verse was in the book of James. Luther was reading Romans, where Paul makes it very clear that it's not through the works of the law that any man is justified and that we are justified by faith and only through faith. What do we have here? Some scholars say we have an irreconcilable conflict between Paul and James, that James was written after Paul, and James tried to correct Paul. Others say that Paul wrote Romans after James and he was trying to correct James.

I'm convinced that we don't really have a conflict here. What James is saying is this: If a person says he has faith, but he gives no outward evidence of that faith through righteous works, his faith will not justify him. Martin Luther, John Calvin, or John Knox would absolutely agree with James. We are not saved by a profession of faith or by a claim to faith. That faith has to be genuine before the merit of Christ will be imputed to anybody. You can't just say you have faith. True faith will absolutely and necessarily yield the fruits of obedience and the works of righteousness. Luther was saying that those works don't add to that person's justification at the judgment seat of God. But they do justify his claim to faith before the eyes of man. James is saying, not that a man is justified before God by his works, but that his claim to faith is shown to be genuine as he demonstrates the evidence of that claim of faith through his works.

Isn't it being narrow-minded for Christians to say Christ is the only way?

Well, it certainly can be an expression of narrow-mindedness for a Christian to say that Christ is the only way. I'll never forget the first time somebody asked me that. I was in college, and my college professor looked me straight in the eye and said, "Mr. Sproul, do you believe that Jesus is the only way to God?" I wanted to jump out the window or find a hole to hide in because the question put me on the horns of a dilemma. It was a terribly embarrassing situation because I knew what the New Testament said. I knew that Jesus himself had said, "I am the Way, the Truth, and the Life. No man comes to the Father except by me." And other passages in the New Testament say, "There's no other name under heaven through which men may be saved."

I was aware of those passages of exclusivity that we find in the New Testament and that focus on the uniqueness of Jesus. This professor pressed me on it and asked if I thought Jesus was the only way. If I said yes, then obviously I would be understood by everybody in the class to be an unspeakably arrogant person. I certainly didn't want that kind of a label during my college career. But if I said no, then I would be guilty of denying that unique exclusiveness that Christ claimed for himself. So I kind of hedged a little bit and tried to whisper my answer and said, "Yes, I believe that Jesus is the only way." Well, the wrath of that teacher came on my head, and the teacher just began to lay me out and said, "That's the most bigoted, narrow-minded, arrogant statement I have ever heard."

When the class was over, I went up to the professor and spoke privately to her. "I know you're not enthusiastic about Christianity, but do you allow for the possibility that people who are not arrogant and people who are not narrow minded could for some reason or other actually be persuaded that Jesus Christ is at least one way to God?" The professor said, "Oh yes, I can certainly understand that intelligent people could believe that." It was the narrow-mindedness that was bothering the professor. I said, "Don't you understand that I came to the conclusion that Jesus was *a* way to God, and then I discovered that Jesus was saying that he is *the* way?"

If I believed that Jesus were the only way to God just because it happened to be my way, then the unspoken assumption would be that whatever R. C. believes must be true. This would exclude anybody who's not in touch with what R. C. Sproul believes, and this, of course, would be unspeakably arrogant. Why should there even be one way of redemption? Sometimes we act as if God hasn't done enough.

6

Sin and the Sinner

The Lord looks down from heaven upon the children of men,
To see if there are any who understand, who seek God.
They have all turned aside,
They have together become corrupt;
There is none who does good,
No, not one.

PSALM 14:2-3

Questions in This Section:

What is meant by the term <u>original sin</u>?

How is it just that all humanity is born into sin because of Adam's fall?

Are there gradations of sin?

Has original sin changed the essence of our original created humanity?

I know God has forgiven me for my sins, but how can I begin to forgive myself?

How should we deal with stubborn pockets of sin in our lives that won't seem to go away even after much prayer and an honest, heartfelt desire to change?

The Scriptures tell us that "as a man thinketh in his heart, so is he." Often my thoughts seem to be sin filled, and yet I'm a Christian. How do I deal with this?

When the Bible says we will be accountable for all of our actions, does that include sins we've already been forgiven for?

Is our "old nature" our knowledge of sin and our familiarity with it from past experiences?

James 5 says, "Whoever brings back a sinner from the error of his way will save his soul from death." Can you explain what James means by this passage?

In the Sermon on the Mount, Jesus warns us to "judge not, lest you be judged." What did he mean?

In the first chapter of Romans, God "gives sinners over to the lusts of their hearts." What does it mean for God to give someone over to sin?

Why does the earth bear the curse of the fall of humanity? What wrong did it do?

What is meant by the term <u>original sin</u>?

Original sin has to do with the fallenness of human nature.
Jonathan Edwards wrote a tremendous treatise on original
sin. He not only devoted himself to a lengthy exposition of
what the Bible teaches about man's fallen character and his
propensity toward wickedness, but he made a study from a
secular, rational perspective that addressed the philosophy
that was widespread in his day: Everyone in the world is
born innocent, in a state of moral neutrality in which they
don't have any predilection toward either the good or the
evil. It's society that corrupts these innocent natives, so to
speak. As we are exposed to sinful behavior around us, our
normal, natural innocence is eroded by the influence of
society. But that begs the question, How did society get corrupt in the first place? Society is people. Why is it that so
many people have sinned? It's almost axiomatic in our culture that nobody is perfect. And Edwards asked questions
like, Why not? If everyone were born in a state of moral
neutrality, you would expect statistically that approximately
50 percent of those people would grow up and never sin.
But that's not what we find. Everywhere we find human
beings acting against the moral precepts and standards of
the New Testament. In fact, whatever the moral standards
are of the culture in which they live, nobody keeps them
perfectly. Even the honor that's established among thieves is
violated by thieves. No matter how low the level of morality
is in a given society, people break it.

So there is something indubitable about the fallenness of our human character. All people sin.

The doctrine of original sin teaches that people sin because we are sinners. It's not that we are sinners because we sin, but rather, we sin because we are sinners; that is, since the fall of man, we have inherited a corrupted condition of sinfulness. We now have a sin nature. The New Testament says we are under sin; we have a disposition toward wickedness, so that we all do, in fact, commit sins because it is our nature to commit sins. But that's not the nature that was originally given to us by God. We were originally innocent, but now the race has been plummeted into a state of corruption.

How is it just that all humanity is born into sin because of Adam's fall?

I think the New Testament does teach that the whole world is born into the consequences of a fallen nature because of the sin of Adam and Eve. The New Testament repeats this idea frequently—"that through the disobedience of one man, death comes into the world." This has been an occasion for much theological protest. What kind of a God would punish all people with the consequences of one individual's sin? In fact, it seems to go contrary to the teaching of the prophet Ezekiel. He rebuked the people of Israel when they said that the fathers had eaten sour grapes and the children's teeth were set on edge. The prophet said that God treats every person according to his own sin. He doesn't punish me for what my father did, nor does he punish my son for what I did, although the consequences may spill out into three or four generations. That the guilt is not transferred from one person to another seems to be the message in Ezekiel.

It makes the question all the more puzzling. In protest we want to say, "No damnation without representation." We don't like to be held accountable for what somebody else did, although there are occasions in our own system of justice where we recognize a certain level of culpability for what another person does through the means of criminal conspiracy.

For example, I might hire you to kill somebody. Even though I'm far away from the scene of the crime and don't pull the trigger, I can still be tried for first-degree murder. All you did was carry out my desire. Even though I didn't pull the trigger, I'm guilty of the intent and malice of forethought that you actually exercised.

You might say that's a poor analogy of the Fall because nobody hired Adam to sin against God in my name. Obviously we didn't. He was appointed to be the representative of the whole human race. Again, we tend to find that difficult to swallow because I don't like to be held accountable for what my representative does if I don't have the opportunity to choose my representative. I certainly didn't choose Adam to represent me. That's one of the reasons we like to have the right to elect our representatives in government: The actions that they take in the political realm have tremendous consequences on our lives. We can't all be in Washington enacting legislation. We want to elect our representatives in the hope that they will accurately represent our desires and our wishes.

There is no time in human history when you were more

perfectly represented than in the Garden of Eden because
your representative was chosen infallibly by a perfectly
holy, perfectly just, omniscient God. So I cannot say that I
would have done differently than Adam did. How S.?

One last point: If we object in principle to God's allowing one person to act for another, that would be the end of
the Christian faith. Our whole redemption rests on the
same principle, that through the actions of Christ we are
redeemed.

Are there gradations of sin?

I flinch a little bit when you ask me that question because
I have in my memory not so fond recollections of having
answered that question in the past when people got very
upset with what I said. What mystifies me is that it seems
that there are a lot of Christians who hold the position that
there are no gradations of sin, that all sin is sin and there's
no difference between less serious or more serious sins.

The Roman Catholic Church historically makes a distinction between venial sin and mortal sin, meaning that some
sins are more heinous than others. Mortal sin is so called
because it's serious enough to destroy the saving grace in
the soul. It kills grace, and that's why it's called mortal.

Protestant Reformers in the sixteenth century rejected
the concept of the distinction between venial and mortal.
Calvin, for example, said that all sin is mortal in the sense
that it deserves death, but no sin is mortal, save the blasphemy of the Holy Spirit insofar as it would destroy the
salvation that Christ has achieved for us. In the Protestant
reaction to the Roman Catholic distinction between venial

and mortal sin, the Protestant Reformers did not deny gradations of sin. They still maintained a view of lesser and greater degrees of sin. What I'm saying is that in orthodox Christianity, both Roman Catholic and Protestant denominations have taken the position that there are some sins that are worse than other sins. They make these distinctions because it's so plainly taught in the Scriptures. If we look at the Old Testament law, we see that certain offenses are to be dealt with in this world through capital punishment and others through corporal punishment. Distinctions are made, for example, between murder and malice of forethought and what we would call involuntary manslaughter. There are at least twenty-five occasions where the New Testament makes a distinction between lesser and greater forms of evil. Jesus says, for example, at his own trial, "Those who have delivered me to you have greater guilt than you have."

There is abundant evidence in the Scriptures to postulate a view of the gradations of sin. Not only that, but the very simple principles of justice would indicate that. But I think that people stumble on this point for two reasons. One is Saint James's statement "He who sins against one point of the law, sins against the whole law." That sounds as if James is saying that if you tell a little white lie, it's as bad as killing somebody in cold blood. But James is actually saying that all sin is serious insofar as every sin is an offense against the lawgiver, so that in the slightest sin I'm sinning against the law of God. I have violated the whole context of that law in many ways. So all sin is serious, but it doesn't follow logically that all sin is equally serious.

People also refer to Jesus' statement that if you lust after a woman, you've violated the law against adultery. Jesus doesn't say that it is as bad to lust as it is to commit the actual act. He's simply saying that if you merely refrain from the actual act you're not totally clean; there are lesser elements of the law that you have violated.

Has original sin changed the essence of our original created humanity?

No. If it did change the essence of our created humanity, then it would be improper to call ourselves human anymore. There are vast differences of opinion among denominations and religious groups and theologians as to the extent of damage that original sin inflicted upon the human race. The debates rage over the extent of it. Most denominations, in spite of their differences regarding the degree of fallenness, make some kind of distinction between what we would call the image of God in which we were originally created in the wider sense and the image of God in the narrower sense.

We were created in our humanness in the wider sense in that certain traits make us human beings: our ability to think, the fact that we have souls, etc. Even after the Fall we still think, we still choose, we still have passions, we still walk, we still look and act like people—we're still human beings. Our humanity remains essentially intact.

However, the Fall altered the image of God, in the narrower sense, that we were created to reflect. Originally we had the unique ability to reflect the character and holiness of our Creator. That mirroring ability of which the Scriptures speak was radically clouded by sin so that the picture of God that we give to the world is now a distortion. We don't reflect God's integrity. We lost significant moral strength and righteousness, so much so that we are told in the New Testament that by nature we are children of wrath, are dead in sin and trespasses, and are by nature at enmity with and estranged from God our Creator. That is significant. It doesn't mean, however, that our humanity has been destroyed. Our humanity is intact, but it is a weakened humanity, a fallen humanity.

I believe that the Fall has penetrated the very heart, the core, of our spiritual and moral lives. It affects every part of us. It affects our minds and our bodies. Our bodies wouldn't age and die if it weren't for sin; death came as a result of sin. That really touches our humanity. It causes suffering, pain, wickedness, and all the rest. Human life has been radically affected by sin, but humanity in its essence remains.

I know God has forgiven me for my sins, but how can I begin to forgive myself?

Frequently in his epistles, the apostle Paul goes to great lengths to describe what we call Christian liberty. In these matters God allows us freedom; he doesn't set down laws prohibiting something or commanding something. The apostle warns us against being judgmental toward our brothers, giving as an example in the Corinthian community the question about eating meat offered to idols. Paul says this has nothing to do with the kingdom of God. He says, "Those of you who have scruples about it, don't judge those who don't" and vice versa. This is a case in which we just have to respect one another.

In those admonitions, Paul uses as his basis this statement: "We are not to be judging people for whom Christ died." He reminds us that "your brother or your sister belongs to Christ. God has forgiven them. Who are you to withhold forgiveness from someone whom God has forgiven?"

Let's look at it this way. If somebody sins against me and that person repents, God forgives them. If I refuse to forgive them, can you think how ghastly that is in the sight of God? God is not obligated to forgive that person. That person has sinned against God, and God has never sinned against anybody. Here I am—a person who is a sinner refusing to forgive other sinners while God, who is sinless, is willing to forgive. Have you ever stopped to think about the arrogance that's in me when I refuse to forgive somebody that God has forgiven?

Now, how could you forgive yourself after God has forgiven you? I've had people come to me and say, "R. C., I committed such and such a sin, and I asked God to forgive me. I've gone to him ten times and asked him to forgive me, but I still don't feel forgiven. What am I going to do?" I don't have any brilliant theological answer to that. I can only tell them to ask God to forgive them one more time. When they say they've done it, I tell them this time I want them to ask God to forgive them for their arrogance. "Arrogance!?" they say. "What do you mean arrogance? I'm the most humble man in America. I've confessed this sin ten times." Doesn't God say that if you confess a sin one time, he'll forgive you? Who are you to refuse the forgiveness of God, and who are you to condemn one whom God has forgiven? That's arrogance. You may not feel arrogant, you may not mean to be arrogant, you may be rolling in humility with all of your confession. But I am telling you that if God has forgiven you, it is your duty to forgive yourself. It's not an option. You must forgive those whom God forgives, including yourself.

How should we deal with stubborn pockets of sin in our lives that won't seem to go away even after much prayer and an honest, heartfelt desire to change?

One of the great Christian classics is a devotional booklet written by Saint Thomas à Kempis called *The Imitation of Christ*. In that book he talks about the struggle that so many Christians have with habits that are sinful. He says that the struggle for sanctification is often so difficult and the victories that we achieve seem to be so few and far between, that even in the lives of the greatest saints, there were few who were able to overcome habitual patterns. We're talking about people who overeat and have these kinds of temptations, not those who are enslaved to gross and heinous sin. Now Thomas à Kempis's words are not sacred Scripture, but he gives us wisdom from the life of a great saint.

The author of Hebrews says that we are called to resist the sin that so easily besets us and that we are admonished and exhorted simply to try harder to overcome these sins. You say, How do we escape these pockets of sin that we have such great struggles with, that we have an honest and heartfelt desire not to commit? If the desire not to do it is really honest and penetrates the heart, we're 90 percent home. In fact, we shouldn't be locked into something. The reason we continue with these pockets of repeated sins is because we have a heartfelt desire to continue them, not because we have a heartfelt desire to stop them. I wonder how honest our commitment is to quit. There's a tendency for us to kid ourselves about this anytime we embrace a pet sin. We need to face the fact that we commit the sin because we want to do that sin more than we want to obey Christ at that moment. That doesn't mean that we have no desire to escape from it, but the level of our desire vacillates. It's easy to go on a diet after a banquet; it's hard to stay on a diet if you haven't eaten all day. That's what happens particularly with habitual sins that involve physical or sensual appetites. The ebb and flow of the desire is augmented and diminished. It increases and fades. Our resolve to repent is great when our appetites have been satiated, but when they're not, we have a growing attraction to practice whatever the particular sins may be.

I think what we have to do is first of all be honest about the fact that we really have a conflict of interest between what we want to do and what God wants us to do. I think we have to feed our souls with the Word of God so that we can get what God wants us to do clear in our mind and then build a strong desire to obey.

The Scriptures tell us that "as a man thinketh in his heart, so is he." Often my thoughts seem to be sin filled, and yet I'm a Christian. How do I deal with this?

The verse you have quoted is a very crucial verse. There's a strange sound to it because when we speak about thinking, we usually identify thoughts and the thinking process with the head, the brain. Why does the Bible say, "As a man thinketh in his heart"? We don't think in our hearts; we think in our heads. I think the Scriptures use the term *heart* to describe what we would call the core. The very word *core* comes from the Latin word for heart. It means that which is most focused in our thinking so that the center, the core, the heart, of our thoughts is what produces what we are. In other words, what my mind focuses on determines what I become as a person.

This is a critical concept because people are always saying to me that they don't want to study theology and they don't want to study intellectual matters because all they're really concerned about are the practical dimensions of Christian living. Yet for every practice there is always a theory. Each one of us is living out some significant theory of life. We do, in fact, live according to how we think. We may not be able to articulate that theory in a technical way, but we do all have a theory by which we live out the practice of our life. That's why Jesus is telling us to get our thinking straight. What you see as important will control the practical patterns of your living.

You mentioned the frustration you have with the conflict between what you know in your mind are the things you should be thinking about and the things that actually do creep into your mind. One of the best treatments of prayer I've ever read comes from the pen of John Calvin, the French Reformation theologian, in his *Institutes*. I always used to make my students read his chapter on prayer before they read anything else so that they could become acquainted with Calvin the spiritual giant, the man who had such a passion for the heart of God. He had such a keen devotional life. Calvin laments the fact that even in the midst of prayer, his mind is invaded by sinful thoughts. This is normal to being human, and we must learn to overcome such invasive thoughts, just as we learn to deal with other aspects of our sinful nature. The apostle tells us that whatsoever things are pure, whatsoever things are true and lovely, those are the things that we should dwell on. We have an expression in the computer trade called the GIGO principle: garbage in, garbage out. If we fill our minds with garbage, our lives will begin to manifest the stench of that garbage. I think the key is to fill our minds with the things of God.

When the Bible says we will be accountable for all of our actions, does that include sins that we've already been forgiven for?

I think so. Some people will be quick to point out that the Bible says, "As far as the east is from the west, so far has God removed our transgressions from us" and that he has cast them into the sea of forgetfulness. When God forgives us of our sins, he forgets them. He remembers them no more against us. So it would seem that we could conclude from those passages that once we are forgiven of a sin, that's the absolute end of it and we never have to be held accountable for it.

When we are forgiven by God for a sin, there are two things we have to understand. First of all, when the Bible speaks of God's forgetting our sins, we have to be careful how far we push that. That does not mean that suddenly the eternal God, very God of very God, who is omniscient and immutable, suddenly undergoes a memory lapse and that that which he once knew intimately he suddenly becomes ignorant of. If we push that, it would give us a ghastly view of God. Rather, the Bible is using this kind of language to say that he doesn't hold it against us anymore. He treats us without raising the issue in terms of delivering a punishment. The just punishment for any sin would be eternal separation from God. When we are forgiven, we are relieved of all eternal guilt and punishment so that we don't have to worry about going to hell because we have sinned.

At the same time, the New Testament tells us at least twenty-five times that the distribution of rewards in heaven will be done according to our relative degree of obedience or the works that we perform. We are told frequently by Jesus that on the last day all things will be brought into the light. Those things we have done in secret will be made manifest; every idle word will come into the judgment. I don't think that means that I'm going to be punished for those sins that I've confessed and have had forgiven. Those are covered by the righteousness of Christ and by my Mediator. But I will have to stand before God for a full and complete evaluation of my obedience as a Christian.

Whether or not at that time of evaluation he will mention the complete track record or just say, "Here's the bottom line, you'll get so many rewards"—I don't know how that's going to work. But I am going to be brought into a final accounting, and certainly in God's mind every detail of my life will be there. Even though I am forgiven and I am not punished, any sin still means that I will receive less reward than if I had been obedient.

Is our "old nature" our familiarity with sin from past experiences and our knowledge of it?

When the Bible speaks of our "old nature," it is easy to assume that it refers to our memories of what transpired in our own lives, in our old behavioral patterns. I think it means much more than that. The contrast between the old and the new natures that Paul addresses frequently in the Scriptures is often stated in other terms: the old man, and the new man. The general way in which the apostle describes it is between the flesh and the spirit.

I think that when Paul speaks of the old man, he is referring to the fallen human nature that is a direct result of original sin; that is, original sin is not the first sin that was committed by Adam and Eve but is the consequence of that. The fact is that we are fallen beings and that we, by this fallen nature, are born in a state of estrangement from God. We're dead to the things of the Spirit. Paul tells us in Romans that the mind of the flesh cannot please God. We have no inclination or disposition to obey God in a spiritual sense. That's our old nature, and we're born that way. We're by nature the children of wrath; we're by nature in this state of estrangement. It's out of that nature that the New Testament describes us as being in bondage to this inclination, or bent, or disposition to sin.

This was the debate that Jesus had with the Pharisees when he told them that if they continued in his words, they would be free, and they became very indignant, saying, "We're in bondage to no man." Jesus said, "You are a slave to those whom you serve." He said to them that they were slaves of sin.

Paul states that we are under sin; that is, under the weight of it, under the burden of it, because the only disposition and inclination that we have is of the flesh. We have no natural inclination toward the things of the Spirit until we're born of the Spirit. When a person is regenerated, the Spirit of God comes and acts upon that person, and he or she is a new person. He who is in Christ is a new creation. Behold, the old has passed away and all things become new.

That doesn't mean that the old sin nature, with its disposition away from God, is annihilated. For all intents and purposes, it has been consigned to death. We know that the battle is over. Paul says that the old nature is dying daily and that in one sense it has been crucified with Christ on the cross. There's no question of its ultimate and final destruction. In the meantime we go through this daily struggle between the old man and the new man, the old nature and the new nature, the old desire for sin and the new inclination that the Spirit of God has brought to life in our hearts. Now there is a thirst and a passion for obedience that was not there before.

James 5 says, "Whoever brings back a sinner from the error of his way will save his soul from death." Can you explain what James means by this passage?

There are different possibilities for what James might have meant. This text doesn't give us enough precise information for us to be too dogmatic about it. He could have been saying that he who leads a person to Christ—who brings a person the gospel and leads him into a state of salvation—has played the role of intermediate and clearly saved that person's soul. He's not the Savior of that soul, but he has, in a sense, worked to rescue a person from his state of lostness and from eternal punishment. Perhaps that is all this passage means.

It could also mean that whoever brings to repentance a Christian brother who has erred in his way has helped save this person's soul from death. Usually when we talk about saving the soul from death, we automatically assume that the writer is speaking about heaven or hell because we think of the soul as that which survives biological death. We often overlook the fact that there are occurrences of the word *soul* in the Bible that simply refer to the whole person. We still use the word in this way. I might say, "Who came to the meeting the other night?" and you might say, "Not a single soul." The meeting wasn't for ghosts; it was for human beings. Or we'll say, "Pity that poor soul over there." We're not looking at a disembodied spirit but at a human being. The Bible does that, so it doesn't necessarily refer to the state of a person after this life. The death that it may be referring to here is physical death.

Oscar Cullman, the brilliant Swiss New Testament theologian and church historian, wrote about the passage in 1 Corinthians that deals with the institution of the Lord's Supper and the admonition not to eat or drink unworthily of the Lord's Supper. Paul says to the Corinthians, "For this reason many of you have become sick and died because you failed to discern the Lord's body." Cullman says that this is the most neglected passage in the whole Bible because here is a statement clearly telling us that people in the New Testament community became sick and died as a direct result of a violation of the Lord's Supper, and few people are aware of it.

We read the account in the New Testament of Ananias and Sapphira, who suffer biological death (Acts 5:1-11). When the Bible says that God judges people and causes them to die, that doesn't necessarily mean they're damned. It may be his capital punishment upon his own people who are still redeemed; they forfeit a measure of enjoyment of this earthly life. James may only be saying that if we get a brother out of his wicked ways, we've saved him from the premature biological death that is sometimes the manifestation of God's judgment.

In the Sermon on the Mount, Jesus warns us to "judge not, lest you be judged." What did he mean?

Jesus enlarges on this short, pithy saying. The measure by which we judge other people is the sense in which we are endangered of being judged by God. If I lack mercy and grace in dealing with other people, then I can hardly expect God to be inclined toward mercy and grace for me.

One of the parallels is in the Lord's Prayer: "Forgive us our debts as we forgive our debtors." There is to be a spirit of mercy that's characteristic of the Christian life because we exist in the kingdom of God solely and exclusively by grace alone. If any people should be avoiding a judgmental spirit, it should be those who have experienced the mercy of God.

When Jesus says, "Judge not, lest ye be judged," he uses a word that in its most technical meaning indicates the judgment of condemnation. We find an important distinction in the New Testament between what we would call the judgment of discernment or evaluation and the judgment of condemnation. The passage in which Jesus says, "Judge not, lest ye be judged" is not an absolute prohibition against being aware of what is evil as opposed to what is good or righteous. We are called to know the difference between goodness and evil, and that means that we have to make judgments all the time—judgments of truth as to whether or not my behavior or your behavior or the group's behavior is in conformity to the principles of God.

Sometimes people get very nervous if I say, "I don't think that's something we ought to do because it would be a violation of ethics." Somebody might jump up and say, "Who are you to judge? Judge not, lest ye be judged." In fact, what we're trying to do there is to make a discernment and an evaluation of the ethical import of a given situation. But what Jesus is saying is that we are not to have a condemnatory attitude toward people—what is called a judgmental spirit.

One of the best ways I know to deal with that in practice is to understand the difference between what we call a judgment of charity and a judgment that lacks charity. It's the difference between best-case and worst-case analysis. The judgment of charity is that I give you the benefit of the doubt if you do something that maybe is not obviously the right thing to do, rather than interpret your behavior in the worst of all possible light. Unfortunately most of us reserve the judgment of charity for our own actions, and we're much kinder to ourselves than we are to others. It's that spirit and attitude that Jesus is addressing there.

In the first chapter of Romans, God "gives sinners over to the lusts of their hearts." What does it mean for God to give someone over to sin? Is this giving over active or passive?

What does it mean that God gives someone over to his sin? We find this not only in the first chapter of Romans but also in the Old Testament. Jeremiah warned the people of Israel that this was exactly what their punishment would be, that God was not going to forbear with them forever but that there would come a time when he would give them up. There would be a point when he would give them over to their sin.

Early in Genesis, at the time of the Flood, we are warned that the Spirit of God does not strive endlessly with men. God is patient, but his long-suffering is designed to give us time to come to ourselves, to repent, to acknowledge him, and to be restored to fellowship with him. But at the same time, we are warned that that forbearance does not go on forever and that there can come a point in our obstinate refusal to repent and to respond to God when he will say it's too late and will abandon us to our sin, withholding from us his saving grace. That's a very terrifying thing to consider.

The idea of giving a person over to his sin is a significant part of the final chapters of the book of Revelation, in which we read of John's vision of the inner sanctum of heaven and of the last judgment. We're told that those who have responded to Christ receive marvelous benefits, but those who have obstinately endured in their refusal to repent receive judgment at the hands of God. God says,

"Let him who is wicked be wicked still." There's kind of a poetic justice here. To the people who want to be wicked and refuse to restrain themselves in their sin, God says, "I'm not going to restrain you anymore. I'm going to take the restraints away. I'll take the leash off, give you your freedom. I'll let you do exactly what you want to do. It'll be to your everlasting destruction; it'll be to your dishonor and to your ultimate dismay, but if that's what you want, I'll give you over to it."

Is this giving over active or passive? It's active in the sense that God acts to do it. God actually does give a person over to that person's own desires. It's passive in that God remains passive toward that person's self-destruction.

Why does the earth bear the curse of the fall of mankind? What wrong did it do?

That's a provocative question, and it's a question I like because the New Testament does make it clear that the whole creation is groaning together in travail, awaiting the redemption of the sons of men (Rom. 8:22). This poignant verse indicates that there is a sense in which the whole world of nature suffers as a consequence of the sinfulness of humanity.

What wrong did the earth do to become cursed along with its sinful inhabitants? The Bible clearly indicates that the earth didn't do any wrong. Frequently the prophets of Israel would call the people of God to pay attention to the animal kingdom and the elements of nature, which follow their appointed courses, set by God. When we drop a stone, it obeys the law of gravity. Nature obeys the laws of nature, which in fact are the laws of God. There's no dis-obedience. If you add water to dirt, you get mud—just as you're supposed to. We're also told to consider the ant, who is diligent where we are slothful. We're told that the ox knows his cradle and his master's crib, and we don't even know our Creator. Again and again we find these anal-ogies drawn from Scripture in which we're actually called to emulate the elements of nature in their obedience rather than practice the persistent type of disobedience for which we are known.

Why does suffering afflict innocent nature? In creation, when Adam and Eve were created as the federal head of the human race, God gave them dominion over the entire earth. The first job or task that was assigned to our original parents was to name the animals. The very act of naming was a symbolic indicator of man's authority over the ani-mal kingdom. There's a sense in which nature is described in Scripture as that which God has made to serve the needs of humanity.

In the New Testament Jesus talks about the fact that every time a sparrow lands, God notices it and his eye is on it. He is concerned about the animals in this world. Yet Jesus says, "These things are sold for a farthing," indicating that we are so much more valuable in God's sight because man alone is given the stamp of the image of God.

Unfortunately, when we sin, those who are under us suf-fer the consequences of our fallenness. They suffer inno-cently, and that's why they groan, waiting for our redemption. Just as they participate in the consequences of our fall, so nature will participate in the consequences of our renewal.

167

7

Faith and Philosophy

But sanctify the Lord God in your hearts,
and always be ready to give a defense to everyone
who asks you a reason for the hope that is in you,
with meekness and fear.

I PETER 3:15

Questions in This Section:

Is there a distinction between Christianity and religion?

What type of philosophical developments in today's society should we, as Christians, be prepared to deal with?

Are other world religions and other philosophies a threat to Christianity?

What is existentialism, and how should I respond to it?

Could you comment on some of the heresies in the New Age movement that a Christian should be aware of?

How should Christians respond to the belief in reincarnation?

What is narcissism, and what impact is it having on our society and the future of our children?

What would you recommend we do about secular humanism?

How are Christians to view the Masons and other fraternal orders?

Doesn't science disprove Christianity?

Can something happen by chance?

How can I reason with a friend about the existence of God?

How does one convince a nonbeliever that the Bible is the Word of God?

How do you explain the discrepancies in the Scriptures, such as those between the four Gospels?

Is there a distinction between Christianity and religion?

In the first chapter of Romans, the wrath of God is revealed against distortions of God that culminate in various religious practices called idolatry. God is by no means always pleased with the operations and functions that we call religion. I would say that Christianity first and foremost is not a religion, even though we use that term to describe it from a sociological perspective.

The term *religion* describes human practices—practices of worship, of cultic involvement, of belief in a god, and of obeying certain rules that come from the god or gods. There are various kinds of religions in this world.

There is a religious aspect to Christianity. We do worship, and we are involved in certain human activities, such as prayer and Bible studies and devotions. Our religious practices are similar to the practices of other religions. But Christianity is much more than a religion; it's life.

The very fact that a person is religious does not necessarily mean that he is pleasing God; the primordial sin of man is idolatry, and idolatry is the worship of something that, in fact, is not God. The worship of idols involves the practice of religion. This is exactly what Romans 1 is speaking about; God is not pleased by any and all types of religious activity. Our religious activity may at times be insulting to God. Christianity itself can degenerate into being merely a religion; that is, it can have the external formal activities and sociological practices without the substance that moti-

vates all these things—a profound love and devotion to
God himself and a profound trust in Christ's work.

**There have always been philosophical developments
infiltrating our culture, but what type of philosophical
developments should we, as Christians, be prepared to
deal with in our present society?**

At any given time in a culture, there are all kinds of philosophical developments or philosophical schools of thought
competing for domination. I once read a scholarly essay
that claimed every culture has to have something that unifies it, some kind of viewpoint that brings it together. And
if you study all of the civilizations of history, you will see
that each one had some dominant philosophical or religious idea that tied the people together. That unifying concept may be a religious one; it may be a philosophical one;
it may even be a mythology. But there has to be some idea
that ties it all together. Scholars understand that. You have
the endless chicken-and-the-egg debate: Do ideas shape
culture and events, or do events produce the idea? I think
we would be very foolish to ignore the obvious impact that
ideas have on the shaping of a culture.

I would say that right now Western civilization is up for
grabs. There is not one dominant philosophy, theology, or
religion that has produced a consensus like we had in the
Middle Ages, with the Judeo-Christian faith dominating
the people's understanding of their world. Now, with
people in great masses turning away from the Judeo-Christian understanding of man and the world, there have been
all kinds of philosophical schools fighting with each other

to try to fill the void. It's almost like the situation in the World Boxing Association, where one association has its heavyweight champion and another association has its heavyweight champion. There is no one single heavyweight champion of the world that everybody recognizes. So now we have a little pragmatism, a little hedonism, a little existentialism, competing.

I've been arguing that if there is one overarching concept in our culture, it's what I would call secularism. We hear that word bandied about in the Christian world with frankly very little understanding of what it means. The word *secularism* as an ism means simple this: This time, this world, is all there is. There is no eternal dimension. There is the world as we find it. The world in which we live is the only environment we will ever inhabit—there is no heaven, or if there is a heaven, we can't possibly know anything about it. So the emphasis is on the here and now. That, I think, is the biggest competitor for the allegiance of people.

I'm a sophomore in college now, and I'm studying different world religions and philosophies, and I'm seeing a lot of my buddies embracing these things. Not only is it frightening to me to see them taking on these lines of thought, but I'm wondering, are other world religions and other philosophies a threat to Christianity?

Let me say something that may totally offend you or violate your sensibilities. I don't want to do that, but I recognize that the world in which we live has certain values and views in which all of us have been trained. The nineteenth century was a time of unparalleled study in world religion. As the world became smaller and more cultures were rubbing up against each other, we saw that it was necessary for people of different religions to get along peacefully rather than spilling blood all over the world through religious wars and quarrels. The world had had enough of that. So the attempt in the nineteenth century was to try to study all the different world religions and to penetrate to the essence of what they had in common. This whole science of comparative religion emerged and with it the very famous mountain analogy—that God is at the top of the mountain and that there are different kinds of paths that lead up the mountain. You know, some go a direct route, others by more circuitous routes. But all of these roads ultimately get to the same place, so it really doesn't matter which road you travel. Let me just say that if that's true, then I don't think Christianity is one of those roads because Jesus says that it matters profoundly which road you're on. The New Testament is on a collision course with those who say it doesn't matter which road you're on.

God was furious with Aaron and the children of Israel for embracing the golden calf. The principle in the Old Testament was exclusive loyalty and devotion to the God of Israel, and there was to be no syncretism, no mixing of the elements of the faith of Israel with pagan religions, with those who followed Baal or the Philistine religion or whatever. But the world doesn't take the purity of religious faith very seriously. One of the traditions of Islam is that it is virtuous for a zealous Muslim to kill an infidel. That's radically different from the teaching of Jesus. I've had people come to me and say there's no real great difference between Islam and Christianity. When people say that, it indicates to me that they either don't know anything about Christianity or they don't know anything about Islam. Just a cursory examination of these religions shows that they are radically different at important points.

Am I alarmed and concerned about this pluralistic atmosphere that's prevailing in our culture? Very much so. Other philosophies certainly can be a threat to faith when they prevent people from seeing the truth clearly. But that happens when we don't believe that the content of religion is important.

What is existentialism, and how should I respond to it?

Sometimes we underestimate the power of human ideas. We tend to neglect the ivory-tower scholars who give their lives to thinking through weighty questions of philosophy, and we say, "What does that have to do with the practical world I live in?" I don't know of any philosophy in history, with the possible exception of Marxism, that has had such a radical impact, so widely and quickly, on the shaping of human culture as has the philosophy of existentialism. Existentialism contains many variations. Its general theme focuses concern on human existence. That's why its called existentialism.

This philosophy is built primarily upon the question, What does it mean to exist as a person in this world? Existentialism, in focusing on the predicament of a human being, tends to be pessimistic and atheistic, although there are religious forms of existentialism and more optimistic forms of existentialism. But the bottom line is this: Existentialism tends to see man in a mood or an atmosphere of despair.

Two of the great contributors to twentieth-century existentialism were Albert Camus and Jean-Paul Sartre. They responded to the Holocaust of World War II, and their ideas were ones of great despair. For example, they came to the conclusion that man in his existence is a useless passion and that human life ultimately is meaningless and insignificant. In this view, with respect to the things of God, the idea is that in heaven there is nobody home.

A couple of decades ago, the Greenwich Village advocate of existentialism made this quip to a reporter for *Time* magazine: "Hey, man, I looked God up in the Yellow Pages, but he wasn't listed." The idea is that there is no one home in the universe and we are left here in our existence in an atmosphere of ultimate despair.

How shall we respond to existentialism? One thing for which I'm grateful is that existentialism produces tremendously fertile ground for the preaching of Christianity because Christianity is so optimistic. We believe that human existence is meaningful and that it is ultimately meaningful because Christ has defined the significance of our existence. So, the answer to how we should respond to existentialism is simply counter it with the hope of the gospel.

Could you comment on some of the heresies in the New Age movement that a Christian should be aware of?

First of all, let me say that the New Age movement, like any broad-based movement, has various dimensions to it. I'll restrict my remarks to one element.

One of the most troublesome views of the world that we find in the New Age movement is the focus of attention on man's ability to have virtually a magical power over his own environment. Not long ago I was at the golf course, and my golf instructor asked me, "R. C., when you hit your wedge shot around the green, what are your swing keys? What are you thinking about when you hit it?" I said, "I don't have any swing keys; I don't have any mechanics that I think about in terms of where my hands and wrists are and all that. All I do is go through the same process. Before I hit the shot I visualize in my mind's eye the flight pattern that I want the ball to take, and then I sort of send that message to my body from my mind, and then try to duplicate the feeling that I've just experienced in hitting the shot."

Now, that can sound very much like New Age–type thinking—almost a mind-over-matter type of thing. Almost any heresy is one that takes a truth to an extreme, to a point of distortion. It is true that our mental attitude has a tremendous influence on how we experience life. And it is true that Jack Nicklaus experiences shots before he hits them because all he's trying to do is program his body to a good positive image of recollection from shots that he has hit in the past.

But that's not the same thing as thinking that if I think about money I'm going to get rich, or if I focus my attention on some object, I'm going to be able to move it by the power of my mind alone. We Christians have to be very careful to understand that Christianity promises the power and the presence of God the Holy Spirit, but no magic. There's a sharp line in Scripture between spiritual reality and wizardry. And in the Old Testament, all forms of magic and wizardry were capital abominations to the character of God. The New Age movement incorporates religious elements and Eastern mystical elements in a sort of blend of spiritual truth with a whole lot of magic. I've seen it invade the evangelical world to the point that I'm very much alarmed by it.

How should Christians respond to the belief in reincarnation?

There have been far more formidable advocates of reincarnation in the history of the world than Shirley MacLaine and other recent converts to this belief. For example, the philosopher Plato, after studying with the Pythagorean school of philosophers, was persuaded of the truth of what he called the "transmigration of the soul." There are Eastern religions that have a tremendous commitment to and belief in the reincarnation of the soul. This view is not part of orthodox Christian faith.

The Christian faith teaches that it is "appointed for man to die once, but after this the judgment" (Heb. 9:27). The concept of reincarnation generally carries with it some notion of justification by works; that is, you have to earn your reward to a higher level in your next incarnation before you can finally break out of that and into a spiritual world. Usually the idea is that as you work your way up the ladder, if you're good enough, you'll be free from an incarnation with a body. Christianity believes in a resurrection of the body, so we're not looking for an ultimately pure soul-like existence without a body.

What is narcissism, and what impact is it having on our society and the future of our children?

The concept of narcissism has its roots in ancient mythology. Narcissus was simply a youth, not a minor deity. He spurned Echo the nymph's love. His pining for his own image was the punishment of the gods.

This derivation of his name has now been used to describe a certain syndrome—a cultic mentality of self-love present in our nation today. We've had unprecedented numbers of books on self-improvement to treat a great concern for self-esteem and self-image. Some people are concerned that this internal introspection and preoccupation with our self-esteem is going to end in distortions of human personality whereby we become so enamored with our own images and so much in love with ourselves that we can't really develop community and relate to other people. People, seeing such pride, will say about us, "There but for the grace of God goes God."

If you look at the history of theoretical thought in Western civilization and philosophy, you will see that different subjects attracted the major concern of society's thinkers. The early philosophers were concerned about epistemology, the science of knowing. Philosophy of history was a dominant motif in the nineteenth century. But overwhelmingly the central motif of contemporary academic and speculative investigation is, What is the meaning of man? There's a reason for that. We are in a crisis because God is no longer at the center of our thinking. If it's true (as Christianity says it is) that man is created in the image of God, that means that I can't really understand who I am or what I am apart from a prior understanding of the character of God. If God is eclipsed in my thinking, then I'm left with the question Who am I? If people are telling me that I emerged from the slime and I'm destined for nothingness, then if I'm thinking at all, I'm going to have a crisis of identity, and I'm going to read every book that I can on self-esteem and dignity and all the rest. That's what people are afraid of, that this preoccupation will end in a narcissistic complex. I don't think that's our problem. I don't think people are really falling in love with themselves and their own images. I think they're feeling the weight of the loss of God in their lives.

Do you feel that secular humanism is a real threat to Christianity? How do we deal with it in regard to our public school system?

I'm not sure how much of a threat it is, but certainly it competes with Christianity for the minds and hearts of people. Secular humanism as a worldview is on a collision course with the value system and beliefs of Christianity. These two views take radically different positions concerning how God relates to the world and to us.

I'm constantly trying to remind my Christian brothers that our forefathers, in the writing of the Constitution of the United States of America, agreed to live side by side in agreeing to disagree with unbelievers about matters like this. Christian and non-Christian share the protection of the Bill of Rights. The First Amendment guarantees us as Christians the right to the free expression of our faith. It also guarantees to the non-Christian protection from those

Christians who would seek to establish Christianity as the legal religious faith of the United States of America. We agreed constitutionally not to establish a state religion.

So when we as Christians try to use the courts to insist that Christian literature be taught in the public school system, I think we're violating the First Amendment, just as we feel some of our rights are being violated on certain occasions by some of the recent practices in legislation in this country. Incidentally, for the most part, those who have sought to have Creation taught in the public school system do it on the plea that Creation is the authentic scientific explanation for the origin of the universe and not that it's uniquely Christian. Yet it's certainly perceived as an attempt to Christianize the school system.

But what about taking "offensive" textbooks out of the public school system? This question brings into sharp focus an issue we've been wrestling with in this country for the last thirty years: What philosophical position does the public school system take in its instruction?

The Supreme Court ruled that humanism is a religion, and it also said that it's wrong to teach religion in the public schools. The problem is, anything that is taught in the public schools could be construed as a religion. Many people walk around entertaining the myth that somehow you can have a neutral worldview taught in a public school system. There's never been such a thing as value-neutral education. The irony is that the bottom-line question, given the struggle we're in, is whether or not it's possible to have a public school system within the bounds of the Constitution. That's the struggle, but we need to be careful not to try to use the law to force our faith on nonbelievers.

How are Christians to view the Masons and other fraternal orders?

My father, my grandfather, my uncle, and my father-in-law were all Masons. I'm a little distressed by all of the conflict that seems to be going on now about the Masons and other fraternal organizations. The controversy calls for some explanation.

First of all, there are different kinds of fraternal organizations, some of which are strictly social. There's nothing wrong with people getting together for social reasons. We call it fellowship in the church, and we recognize that it's a very important part of our humanity. Other fraternal organizations are banded together for the express purpose of being service organizations to alleviate suffering, helping the blind and orphans, for example. They engage in humanitarian activities. How should a Christian respond to that? I think with as much cooperation as possible. I can't imagine why a Christian would object to that.

You can run into problems with some of the organizations because their historical origins have strong religious overtones, having spelled-out creeds and ceremonies. What happens when a Christian joins an organization that has a creed that isn't altogether compatible with his own Christian beliefs? Then he has obvious conflict. That conflict can be very difficult for other people to understand.

For example, in America there is this eclectic, pluralistic view that says it doesn't matter what you believe just as long as you're sincere. Some of these groups have creeds that say there's no difference ultimately between Christianity and Islam or other religions. That's offensive to a Christian because there are significant differences between these religions, the main difference being their view of Christ. We're devoted to Christ. We're convinced that he's the only begotten Son of God. So if I confess on Sunday morning that Christ is the only begotten Son of God and at a fraternal order meeting another time confess something to the contrary, I have a conflict in my religious profession of faith. People who are sensitive to that have great struggles.

To be fair to other people, some say that it's just part of the ritual and the ceremony, that it really doesn't touch on the essence of what the club is about. I think people are very sincere when they say that. Christians have to be careful to listen to that and say that the reason these people are involved in the order is not because they're trying to make it a substitute religion. These organizations have creeds, and people are required to recite them, and whether they want it to be a religious activity or not, it is still a religious activity that puts pressure on people who have a different religious persuasion.

Doesn't science disprove Christianity?

There have been obvious conflicts between the scientific community and the religious community over certain points. Of course, the most notable dispute historically was the embarrassing episode of Galileo and the whole theory of whether the earth or the sun was the center of the solar system. We know that many bishops refused to even look at the evidence of a telescope because they had already baptized another scientific tradition that wasn't biblical. This was a case, incidentally, in which the scientific community corrected theological interpretation and misinterpretation of Scripture because Scripture doesn't teach that the earth is the center of the solar system, and it took the scientific community to correct us at that point.

To go further than that and to say that sometimes science corrects erroneous ideas is one thing, but actually to disprove Christianity . . . there are very few points of the Christian faith that are vulnerable to scientific attack. If a person says, "Well, we can scientifically prove that people can't come back from the dead," for example, and if science could prove that it's impossible for the God of the universe to raise his Son from the dead, then obviously Christianity would be discredited and disproved. I don't see how a scientist could even begin to approach that. All a scientist can do is to say that, under normal conditions and standard procedures, people who die stay dead. Of course, it doesn't take a twentieth-century scientist to understand that; first-century people were well aware of the fact that when people died, they stayed dead. So unless the scientist could somehow disprove the existence of God or the resurrection of Christ, I don't see how they could in any way actually falsify the claims of the Christian faith. Just because they're not falsified doesn't mean that they're verified obviously. But I don't see how we have anything to fear at that level.

The usual point of tension, however, has to do with the origin of the universe and the origin of life. If science proves that the world was not created, I think that would destroy the Christian faith. Christianity is committed to the concept of divine creation—that there is an eternal Creator before whom we are all responsible and by whom we were all created and that all that is made has been made through him and that the universe is not eternal. If the scientist could prove that the universe were in fact eternal, that would be the end of the Christian faith. But I don't think we have the slightest need to worry about that.

Can something happen by chance?

What are the chances of something happening by chance? My answer to that question is, "Not a chance." Nothing happens by chance. If we mean by that that chance can cause things, it is utterly impossible scientifically, rationally, and theologically for anything to be caused by chance.

Why would I make a statement like that? It seems so radical and in fact even bombastic to declare that *nothing* could possibly take place by chance. The reason I say it is this: Chance is not a thing. The word *chance* is merely a word we use to describe mathematical possibilities. We say that a coin flips in the air—we don't know whether it's going to turn up heads or tails, but we say the chances are fifty-fifty that it'll turn up heads. But chance doesn't have anything to do with its turning up heads or tails. Chance has no power to influence anything—it has no power to do anything. Because chance is not a thing. It is nothing. For something to have power or influence, it must first *be* before it can *do*. But chance is not an entity. It has no power, and it can do nothing because it is nothing.

The other side of that question is, Do things that take place in this world ultimately happen accidentally? Well, we have to understand that for everything that takes place there is a cause. Some scientists are baffled by experiments of subatomic particles involving what's called in sophisticated circles the Heisenberg uncertainty principle or the indeterminacy principle. Certain studies show that we have no idea why these subatomic particles behave the way they do. Some have jumped to the conclusion that because we don't know why these particles behave the way they do, nothing is causing them to behave the way they are behaving.

How much knowledge would we have to have before we could say that nothing is producing an observable effect? We would have to exhaust every nook and cranny of the universe and then do it again to make sure we didn't miss the culprit the first time.

Assuming that I have a good relationship with a friend who really doesn't believe in God, how can I reason with him about the existence of God?

We're living in a day during which reason itself is suspect among Christians, and somehow it is more admirable simply to affirm our faith and ask people to take what we tell them strictly on blind faith. Yet the Bible tells us, "Come now, let us reason together" (Isa. 1:18), and the Scriptures enjoin us to be prepared to give a reason for the hope within us (1 Pet. 3:15).

I remember that in grade school sometimes we could have open-book tests in math class. The advantage of it was that we could flip to the back of the book, where they had the answers to the problems. If we didn't know how to get the right answer, at least we knew what the right answer was. There's sort of a "back of the book" way that we can approach our friends on the existence of God.

The apostle Paul tells us in Romans 1 that God has revealed himself to every human being and that every person knows that there is a God. The judgment of God is not that people fail to come to a knowledge of God, but rather that they refuse to acknowledge what they know to be true. If that's true, then we come into the discussion armed with the information—means by which the person already knows that there is a God, although he or she is not yet acknowledging that. Now, what can we do? Can we just say, "You're a dirty liar. Why don't you tell the truth and tell us that you really know there is a God?" That's not the approach I suggest. Sometimes this knowledge of God is so repressed or stifled that people have only a vague comprehension about the character or existence of God. And many of the questions they ask are honest questions.

It's important that we respect people's questions. The late Francis Schaeffer had a ministry at L'Abri in Switzerland, where he specialized in outreach to intellectuals who were professed atheists. He felt that it was his obligation to give honest answers to honest questions. When we discuss questions like the existence of God, we need to be prepared to explain why we are persuaded that God exists.

I don't have time right now to go over the cosmological argument for the existence of God, but I think it's valid. Briefly, if something exists now, something has always existed from all eternity or there would be nothing. Somehow, somewhere, someone or something must have the power of being within himself, and that one who has the power of being within himself we call God. That's how I would start the discussion: "How has this world come into being? How has this cup come into being? How has anything come into being?" and then focus attention there.

How does one convince a nonbeliever that the Bible is the Word of God?

Before I try to answer that question directly, let me make a distinction that is important at the outset. There's a difference between objective proof and the persuasion or conviction that follows. John Calvin argued that the Bible carries both persuasion and conviction in terms of its internal testimony—the marks of truth that could be found just by an examination of the book itself—as well as external evidences that would corroborate that substantial evidence to give solid proof for its being the Word of God.

Yet the last thing people would want is a book telling them they are in desperate need of repentance and of a changed life and of bowing in humility before Christ. We don't want that book to be the truth. Calvin claimed that there is a tremendous bias and prejudice built into the human heart that only the influence of God the Holy Spirit can overcome. Calvin distinguished between what he called the *undicia*—those objective evidences for the trustworthiness of Scripture—and what he called the internal testimony of the Holy Spirit, which is necessary to cause us to surrender to the evidence and acknowledge that it is the Word of God.

But I think this is a critical issue upon which so much of the Christian faith depends. The Bible makes the claim that it is the unvarnished Word of God, that it is the truth of God, that it comes from him. God is its ultimate author and source, though indeed he used human authors to communicate that message.

In speaking with people about this, we have to go through the laborious process of showing first of all that the Bible as a collection of historical documents is basically reliable. The same tests that we would apply to Herodotus or Suetonius or any other ancient historian would have to be applied to the biblical records. The Christian should not be afraid to apply those kinds of historical standards of credibility to the Scriptures, because they have withstood a tremendous amount of criticism from that standpoint, and their credibility remains intact. On the basis of that, we come to an idea. If the book is basically reliable, it doesn't have to be inerrent or infallible; it gives us a basically reliable portrait of Jesus of Nazareth and what he taught.

We move from there in linear fashion. If we can on the basis of general reliability come to the conclusion that Jesus Christ did the things that history claims he did, it would indicate that Jesus is more than an ordinary human being and that his testimony would be compelling. I would move first to a study of the person of Jesus and then ask the question, what did Jesus teach about Scripture? For me, in the final analysis, our doctrine of Scripture is drawn from the teaching of Jesus and from our understanding of who he is.

How do you explain discrepancies in the Scriptures—such as those between the four Gospels—in light of scriptural inerrancy?

Much of the debate on the integrity of the Scriptures focuses specifically on those problems. When you have par-

allel accounts of something, you expect them to be consistent, particularly if you're maintaining that these accounts
are inspired by God the Holy Spirit. We know that God
may use different authors to record the same or similar
events, and the authors can describe the event from their
perspective, with their respective languages and literary
styles. But still we would expect agreement in the substance of what is being taught if all accounts are speaking
under the superintendence of God the Holy Spirit.

That's why it's interesting to me that very early in church
history there were attempts to write harmonies of the Gospels. There are three synoptic Gospels—Matthew, Mark,
and Luke—which give a biographical sketch of the life and
ministry of Jesus. Many events are parallel among those
three authors, though they don't always agree in each
detail—how many angels were at the tomb on the day of
resurrection, what the sign on the cross said, what day of
the week Jesus and the disciples celebrated the Passover
celebration in the upper room, and so forth.

Those things have received a tremendous amount of
careful attention by biblical scholars, some coming to the
conclusion that there is no way to harmonize them and
that we just have to accept that there are contradictions
among the biblical writers, which would then seem to falsify any claim to divine inspiration. Others have felt that
they indeed can be reconciled. For example, one Gospel
writer tells us that there were two angels at the tomb on
the day of the Resurrection, and another mentions only
one. Now the critical word that's absent from the text is
the word "only." If one writer says there were two angels at
the tomb and the other one comes along and says there

was *only* one, there you have a bona fide contradiction between the two. If one says there were two angels at the tomb and the other says we came and saw an angel, obviously if there are two angels, there has to be one angel—there's no contradiction. There is a discrepancy; that is, they don't say exactly the same thing. The question is, Can the two accounts be harmonized—are they logically compatible with one another?

A good friend of mine in seminary was very troubled by these issues and quoted one of our professors who said, "The Bible is filled with contradiction." And I said, "Why don't you go home and I'll meet you here tomorrow at one o'clock. You come back with fifty contradictions. If the Bible's full of them, then that should be an easy task." The next day at one o'clock I met him and I said, "Do you have your fifty?" He'd been up all night and he said, "No, but I found thirty." And we went through each one of them, rigorously applying the principles of logic and symbolic logic. To his satisfaction I demonstrated to him that not one of his alleged contradictions in fact violated the law of contradiction.

Now I have to say in closing that in my judgment he could have pulled out some more difficult passages. There are some extremely difficult passages in the Scriptures, and I'm not always happy with some of the resolutions, but I think that for the most part those difficult discrepancies have been thoroughly reconciled through biblical scholarship.

8

The Power and Purpose of Prayer

Be anxious for nothing, but in everything by prayer
and supplication, with thanksgiving,
let your requests be made known to God;
and the peace of God, which surpasses all understanding,
will guard your hearts and minds through Christ Jesus.

PHILIPPIANS 4:6-7

Questions in This Section:

We've been taught that prayer changes things. In view of God's sovereignty, what is the role of prayer in a Christian's life?

The Bible says, "Ask and ye shall receive that your joy may be made full." Elsewhere it qualifies that and says you must ask according to God's will. Would you clarify when I can expect to receive what I ask for?

In Numbers 14 it appears that Moses changed the mind of God. How can you explain this?

Does God really speak to us, and if so, how does he communicate to us?

Is it proper to say "if this be your will" when we pray?

Should we as Christians be concerned about repeating prayers? In Matthew 6:7 Jesus calls vain repetitions the prayers of heathens.

Does it make a difference if I pray five minutes a day or fifty minutes or five hours, and does it make a difference if one person prays, or fifty, or five hundred?

Can Christians today be sure that Christ will pray for others if we ask him to?

Does God hear the prayers of a non-Christian?

Does God not answer the prayers of a Christian who deliberately sins, even after sincere repentance?

How can we, as Christians, have more power in our prayer lives?

We've been taught that prayer changes things. In view of God's sovereignty, what is the role of prayer in a Christian's life?

First of all, we need to establish that it is the sovereign God who not only invites us but commands us to pray. Prayer is a duty, and as we perform that duty, one thing for sure is going to be changed, and that is us. To live a life of prayer is to live a life of obedience to God.

Also, we must understand that there is more to prayer than intercession and supplication. When the disciples said to Jesus, "Lord, teach us to pray," they saw a connection between the power of Jesus and the impact of his ministry and the time he spent in prayer. Obviously, the Son of God felt that prayer was a very valuable enterprise because he gave himself to it so deeply and passionately. But I was surprised that he answered the question by saying, "Here's how you ought to pray," and gave them the Lord's Prayer. I would have expected Jesus to answer that question a different way: "You want to know how to pray? Read the Psalms," because there you see inspired prayer. The Spirit himself, who helps us to pray, inspired the prayers that are recorded in the Psalms. When I read the Psalms, I read intercession and I read supplication, but overwhelmingly what I read is a preoccupation with adoration, with thanksgiving, and with confession. Take those elements of prayer, and what happens to a person who learns how to adore God? That person is changed. What happens to a person who learns how to express his gratitude to God? That person will now become more and more aware of the hand of Providence in his life and will grow in his sense of gratitude toward God. What happens to the person who spends time confessing his sins? He keeps in front of his mind the holiness of God and the necessity of keeping short accounts with God.

But can our requests change God's sovereign plan? Of course not. When God sovereignly declares that he is going to do something, all of the prayers in the world aren't going to change God's mind. But God not only ordains ends, he also ordains means to those ends, and part of the process he uses to bring his sovereign will to pass are the prayers of his people. And so we are to pray.

The Bible says, "Ask and ye shall receive that your joy may be made full." Elsewhere it qualifies that and says you must ask according to God's will. I'm not sure whether that means his moral will or his sovereign will. Would you clarify when I can expect to receive what I ask for?

It's difficult to put together in one whole package everything that the Bible says about prayer. So much of the instruction on prayer that we find in the New Testament comes to us by way of the literary form, the *aphorism*, which is a short, pithy statement of a general principle, almost like a proverb that's generally true but is not an absolute promise.

Jesus said, "If two of you agree on anything and ask, it shall be done." That has a whole history of qualifications in the Old Testament tradition about agreeing on matters.

But just a bare, prima facie reading of that Scripture would make you think that all you have to do is find another person to agree with what you said and it would be done. How many of us would like to see a cure for cancer? or all the wars in the world ended forever? If we could find two people to agree on that, according to what Jesus said there, it would be taken care of instantly. That's obviously not what he meant. When can we categorically, absolutely be confident that we're going to get what we ask for?

I think there are times when God does give categorical statements of promises. For example, we're told that if we confess our sins, God is faithful and just to forgive us and to cleanse us from all unrighteousness. I think it's clear in Scripture that when a person repents of sin and comes in a genuine spirit of contrition before God and confesses and acknowledges that sin before him, that person can believe with absolute certainty that his prayer has been heard and has been answered.

Elsewhere when Jesus encourages us to pray, he says, "You have not because you ask not," he makes this analogy: "What parent, if the son asks him for bread, will give him a stone, or for a fish and give him a scorpion?" and that kind of thing. Jesus encourages us to bring our petitions to God, just as Paul says, "Make your petitions with thanksgiving and bring those things that are on your mind and on your heart to God." There are a number of things that God promises to give every time.

There are other things that are futile to ask for. If we know the Scriptures clearly, there are certain things we won't ask for. I remember seeing on television a man interviewed who ran a series of houses of prostitution. He said that he made an agreement with God when he entered into this business: He would give a percentage of his income to God if God would bless his business. God had blessed his business, and he was returning the favor through all the money he was giving to the church. Well, to ask God to bless something that God abhors is to pray against God's moral will.

There are many other prayer requests that fall between those things we are not to pray for and those we know for sure to pray for. Bring the request before God in humility, and then let God be God. He sometimes says yes and he sometimes says no. You bring your request, and then you let the Father decide.

In Numbers 14 it appears that Moses changed the mind of God. How can you explain this?

"To change one's mind," in the New Testament means to *repent.* When the Bible speaks of my repenting or your repenting, it means that we are called to change our minds or our dispositions with respect to sin—that we are to turn away from evil. *Repent* is loaded with these kinds of connotations, and when we talk about God's repenting, it somehow suggests that God has to turn away from doing something wicked. But that's not what is always meant when the Bible uses this word.

Using a word like *repentance* with respect to God raises some problems for us. When the Bible describes God for us, it uses human terms, because the only language God has by which to speak to us about himself is our human language. The theological term for this is *anthropomorphic language,* which is the use of human forms and structures to describe God. When the Bible talks about God's feet or the right arm of the Lord, we immediately see that as just a human way of speaking about God. But when we use more abstract terms like *repent,* then we get all befuddled about it.

There's one sense in which it seems God is changing his mind, and there's another sense in which the Bible says God never changes his mind because God is omniscient. He knows all things from the beginning, and he is immutable. He is unchanging. There's no shadow of turning within him. He knows what Moses is going to say to him before Moses even opens his mouth to plead for these people. Then after Moses has actually said it, does God suddenly changes his mind? He doesn't have any more information than he had a moment before. Nothing has changed as far as God's knowledge or his appraisal of the situation.

What in Moses' words and actions would possibly have provoked God to change his mind? I think that what we have here is the mystery of providence whereby God ordains not only the ends of things that come to pass but also the means. God sets forth principles in the Bible where he gives threats of judgment to motivate his people to repentance. Sometimes he spells out specifically, "But if you repent, I will not carry out the threat." He doesn't always add that qualifier, but it's there. I think this is one of those instances. It was tacitly understood that God threatens judgment upon these people, but if somebody pleads for them in a priestly way, he will give grace rather than justice. I think that's at the heart of that mystery.

Is God confused, stumbling through all the different options—*Should I do this? Should I not do that?* And does he decide upon one course of action and then think, *Well, maybe that's not such a good idea after all,* and change his mind? Obviously God is omniscient; God is all wise. God is eternal in his perspective and in his full knowledge of everything. So we don't change God's mind. But prayer changes things. It changes us. And there are times in which God waits for us to ask for things because his plan is that we work with him in the glorious process of bringing his will to pass here on earth.

Does God really speak to us, and if so, how does he communicate to us?

First of all, let me say that yes, there is a sense in which God speaks to us, but there is also a sense in which he does not speak to us. When people say to me, "The Lord told me to do something," I want to ask them, "What does the Lord's voice sound like? Are you telling me that you heard a voice from heaven just as audible as the voice that spoke at Jesus' baptism saying, 'This is my beloved Son, in whom I am well pleased,' or the voice that spoke to Saul on the road to Damascus?" There have been times in the Bible when God has spoken audibly to people. But even in the life of Jesus, there are only three times recorded in the New Testament at which God spoke audibly to his only begotten Son.

In the lives of the greatest saints, such incidents are exceedingly rare. Yet there's no easier way to get people's acquiescence to what I want to do, to sidestep any possible criticism, than to preface my ideas by saying, "The Lord told me to do this." I am saying, in essence, that for someone to question what I'm saying is for them to be arguing with God himself. I think that we have an obligation to each other not to accuse each other but to ask the gentle question, "How do you know that it was God who was speaking to you?" What's the difference between the inner voice of God and indigestion? God can speak to us (and he does speak to us—I want to emphasize that), but the principal way God speaks to his people is through his written Word. And sometimes we want to not have to go through all of the difficulty of studying the Word; that takes work. People may just go by hunches and intuitions and feelings and baptize those feelings and intuitions as if they were a divine mandate from heaven.

I remember a very difficult time in my own ministry and life when the school in which I was involved as a faculty member was moving and I didn't want to go where the school was moving, and so I spent six months unemployed. The heaviest question in my life at that time was, God, what do you want me to do? I was in agony over that, praying desperately for hours every day. I had five well-intentioned, deeply spiritual close friends come to me and tell me that God told them that I was supposed to do X, Y, or Z. I thought that was remarkable because the five things that the Lord told them to tell me would have had me in five different cities in five different jobs. The only thing I liked about it were the five separate salaries, but I didn't see how I was going to be in five places at the same time. Obviously, somebody didn't have the mind of Christ.

So I urge Christians to be very, very careful before saying to people, "God told me this." You may say, "I believe that maybe God is leading me in this direction." That's a much more humble way to put it.

Is it proper to say "if this be your will" when we pray?

I don't think there are many things more proper to pray
than "if it be your will." I know that some people take a
dim view of that kind of statement in prayer, saying that it's
kind of a cop-out, that we ought to pray believing that our
prayers are heard and answered before we even see the
results of them. They think that to say "if it be your will" is
an act of unbelief.

There are times when we ought not to say, "if it be your
will." At times we approach God in prayer with issues for
which he has clearly made a promise—for example, when
God says that if we confess our sins, he is faithful and just
to forgive us. So when we confess our sins to God and
repent and ask his forgiveness, it's not necessary to add,
"if it be your will."

The one absolute rule I think everybody ought to take
into their prayer closet is that whenever you talk to God,
you must remember at all times who you are and who he
is. It's certainly not an offense to the Almighty to express
the fact that you are willing to submit yourself to his will.

The best of all possible precedents for saying "if it be
your will" is recorded in the New Testament. In our Lord's
great passion, when he entered into his agony in the
Garden of Gethsemane and wrestled with his Father, he
said, "Let this cup pass from me." Jesus flinched the night
before his death. Remember, he wasn't just facing death,
he was facing the punishment of hell for the sins of all
people. It is absolutely incomprehensible for me to understand the full measure of torment Jesus would be facing
the next day. So he cried out in the garden, "Let this cup

pass from me. Nevertheless, not my will, but yours be done." That's the same thing as saying, "If it be your will, do not ask me to do this." All things being equal, the Son was saying, "I'd sure like to have this cup go somewhere else. But if that's not what you want, then you give me the cup, and I will drink it to the bitter dregs." I think that's the way we should respect God when we come into prayer.

We are encouraged by God to bring our requests with thanksgiving and with confession, and we're told that we have not because we ask not. Jesus tells us that God in some respects is like a human father, and what father would give you a stone if you asked him for bread? God wants to answer your prayers; he wants to be of assistance to you. But at the same time we are to be respectful and humble when we come into his presence. To say "if it be your will" simply expresses our respect for God's sovereignty.

Should we as Christians be concerned about repeating prayers? In Matthew 6:7 Jesus calls vain repetitions the prayers of heathens.

This is part of Jesus' teaching in the Sermon on the Mount in which he describes the difference between the kind of worship and spiritual behavior that pleases God and the kind made popular by the Pharisees—an exercise in hypocrisy and therefore displeasing to God.

Jesus singles out "vain repetitions" (KJV), the reciting of incantations and prayers over and over again in the belief that some power is to be found in the cadences or in the mere saying of the words. Jesus warns against this.

It does not follow, however, that we are never allowed to repeat a prayer. This question comes up with the practice of the church, for example, when we frequently pray the Lord's Prayer. Some have pointed out that when the disciples requested of Jesus, "Teach us to pray," Jesus said, "When you pray, pray like this," he didn't say, "Pray this." He didn't give us an explicit command to repeat that exact prayer over and over again. But I don't think the church has done anything wrong by using it in that way, as long as we're careful not to allow our practice of repeating prayers to become meaningless.

We think, for example, of Jeremiah's rebuke of the people of Israel in his famous temple speech that's recorded in Jeremiah 7:1-4, when he said, "You people come into the presence of God and you say, 'This is the temple of the Lord, the temple of the Lord, the temple of the Lord.'" They recited it three times, and Jeremiah said, "You trust in lying words, words that cannot profit." His rebuke to the people of Israel at that point was that they had put their confidence in the mere utterance of these external formulas. Just by saying the words mechanically over and over again they thought they had some kind of spiritual power.

That comes perilously close to magic, and we see it in other religions in which people think there is a magical formula or that an incantation (the recitation of the word *om*, for example) has some kind of power. Christianity sees prayer as an act of communication, a matter of personal address to God by which the words we use carry content, matters of truth. And we should be acutely conscious of what we're saying to God when we pray. Otherwise our prayers do become vain and futile repetitions.

Does it make a difference if I pray five minutes a day or fifty minutes or five hours, and further, does it make a difference if one person prays, or fifty, or five hundred people pray?

Years ago, when I was in seminary, I was somewhat distressed when one of the New Testament professors used the Lord's Prayer as a model. He said, "Here Jesus gives us a prayer. He says, 'When you pray, pray like this.'" He said that the average time it takes to pray the Lord's Prayer is eighteen seconds, and that our prayers should not be long, drawn out, and elaborate, but they should be very short and to the point. One of the purposes of the giving of the Lord's Prayer was to tell us that we didn't need to give God a blow-by-blow account of everything that was on our mind, that eighteen seconds was long enough to take up the Deity's time. One of the students immediately put his hand up and said, "But, Professor, before Jesus selected his disciples, the Scriptures tell us that he prayed all night." Then the professor replied somewhat cynically, "Well, you're not Jesus."

I don't think we can set forth a rule about how long we should be engaged in prayer at any given time. However, people who have rich prayer lives have a tendency not to make their prayers perfunctory. The testimony of the ages has been that those who pray and wrestle with God in prayer tend to spend more than eighteen seconds (and more than five minutes) on their knees. Luther used to say that when he had a busy day, he would get up an hour early to give himself to prayer, and if he had a *really* heavy day, he would get up two hours early to make sure he started with two hours of prayer. I'm not saying that Luther is the example every person should use. If we keep in mind that prayer isn't just an exercise but time spent in God's presence learning about God and about ourselves, then it would seem that any serious believer would want to spend a lot of time in prayer. A lot of time for one person, at his or her particular place of growth and calling, might be fifteen minutes; for another, it might be an entire day or longer.

Is prayer more effective when more people are praying the same thing? James 5:13-18 reminds us of the efficacy of one man. He uses Elijah as his example. The one man turned the water off for three and a half years through his ardent prayer, and he was a righteous man. There are certain people I like to have pray for me, people whom I know to be prayer warriors. One old man that used to pray for us was a retired missionary in his eighties. He was no longer physically able to continue the rigorous activities of the mission field, but he refused to retire. He gave himself every day to eight hours of prayer. Now that man knew how to pray. And I wanted him to pray for me! If I could have found five more like him, I would have added them, too. I want to have everything going for me that I can. I don't know whether God counts noses when he listens to prayers, but there is a value, obviously from the Scriptures, to corporate prayer, in which believers are praying in one mind. The disciples would gather together in the upper room and pray together, making a corporate request to God. And so I would say that just as there's wisdom in a multitude of counselors, so there is a greater efficacy when we marshal our prayers together.

In the New Testament, Jesus mentions praying for people. Can Christians today be sure that Christ will pray for them if we ask?

I think that we can say with certainty that not only can Christians be sure that Jesus will pray for people if we ask him to pray for them but that Jesus will pray for them even if we don't ask. This is his promise to us. So often this dimension of Jesus' ministry is overlooked. We get excited about Christmas, and rightly so; we get excited about the Crucifixion and the Resurrection. But we overlook the ascension of Jesus and what that means to us. After his resurrection he ascended into heaven. *Ascend* in the New Testament is a technical term that means a person goes to a place of authority. Jesus goes to be invested as the King of kings and Lord of lords. He goes to his coronation, at which God gives him all authority over heaven and earth. But this isn't the only role he plays.

As our Messiah, our Savior, he is a Priest-King. At the same time that he is the King of kings, he functions as the supreme great High Priest. The principal task of the High Priest in heaven is to make intercession for his people. This means that Jesus prays for us and takes our petitions and concerns before the throne of God. On the night of his betrayal, when Jesus celebrated the Passover with his disciples for the last time, he predicted that Judas would betray him and that Simon Peter would deny him. In Luke 22, he said, "Simon, Satan has asked to sift you like wheat. But I have prayed for you, Simon, that your faith may not fail. And when you have turned back, strengthen your brothers." Here we see an example of

Christ praying for Peter before Peter even asked him to pray. Peter didn't even realize he needed intercessory prayer. He denied that he would ever do such a thing. But Jesus had already prayed for him.

An excellent chapter to read about Christ's prayers for us is John 17. This is the longest prayer of Jesus recorded in Scripture. It is called Christ's High Priestly Prayer, and it is a magnificent prayer of intercession. And I would say to any Christian that at that very moment in history, Jesus Christ prayed for you. As he interceded for his disciples, he pled with the Father not only for their welfare but that the blessing of the Father would come on all of those who believed through their efforts—and that includes us.

Does God hear the prayers of a non-Christian?

God hears the prayers of everybody insofar as they reach his auditory nerves (although he doesn't have auditory nerves). I mean, God is acutely conscious of everything we say. In that sense, God hears every prayer. But I presume that the real question here is, Does God hear and honor the prayers of unbelievers?

There are certainly indications in Scripture that God sometimes not only hears the prayers of unbelievers but responds to them. The Bible makes it very clear that God is not at all pleased with insincere prayers. God tells us in his Word that he will not despise a broken and contrite heart (Ps. 51:17). Conversely, he hates arrogance and he hates the prayers of the proud, whether they be Christians or non-Christians. In numerous passages the Bible tells us that God is pleased by and honors only those prayers that come to him out of a truly penitent heart. When we pray as reconciled people, then we have the promise that God will hear us. Has an unbeliever ever really dealt with the Messiah that God has sent into the world? God commands all men everywhere to come to the foot of the cross for their redemption and for their reconciliation. This is not a condition we can negotiate. As Christians, we're committed to the Son of God because we believe in him and in him alone, that he is the only means of redemption God has provided for the human race. And God wants us to come through Christ if we are going to pray. Access to the Father is through the Son.

Does God not answer the prayers of a Christian who deliberately sins, even after sincere repentance?

When we refer to Christians who deliberately sin, we're talking about every Christian who ever lived, and we're talking about something that Christians do every day of their lives. We can talk about sins that are committed in ignorance and so on, but I hope we recognize that the vast majority of the sins we commit are done deliberately. We sin because we want to, because we choose to sin.

This distinction "deliberately sins" troubles me because so many people won't own up to the fact that their sin is deliberate. They say, "Oh, I didn't mean to do it." Certainly they meant to do it. What makes sin such a grievous offense against God is that we deliberately disobey him countless times in our lives. If God refused to hear the prayers of Christians who deliberately sinned against him and then repented, God would not be listening to too many prayers.

On the contrary, the Bible tells us that if we sin, deliberately or otherwise, and we confess that sin, we have the promise of God: If we truly repent, God will forgive us of those sins. He will not turn his back upon us or refuse to hear our payers if we repent.

But what if, as a Christian, I'm involved in constant willful sin with no repentance? That's a contradiction in terms. We can go for a period of impenitence, but if we go too long in an impenitent spirit, that's an indication that Christ isn't in us at all. A true Christian, when confronted by the Word of God, is going to be brought to a state of repentance sooner or later.

True Christians can have protracted periods of impenitent sin; we know that. What happens during that time? We are warned that God resists the proud and gives grace to the humble (Prov. 3:34). There is no more blatant display of pride and arrogance than when a person sins willfully against God, showing no inclination to repent, but continuing in defiant, continuous disobedience to him. When we do this, we place ourselves in a stance whereby God says he will resist us. Our prayers at that time insult him and are offensive to him. Any hypocritical prayer is offensive to God, whether it's delivered by a Christian or a non-Christian. When we sin, we need to repent and come before God humbly. When we do that, we can be sure that he will hear us.

How can we, as Christians, have more power in our prayer lives?

I am taking this question to mean, How can we have more effective results with the prayers we are bringing before the

Father? I think we get some clues from the New Testament. The first is that "we have not because we ask not" or because we ask in the wrong way (James 4:2-3). We are told that God gives grace to the humble but he resists the proud. That tells me, as Scripture expands on it in many places, that when we come before God in prayer, we have to come in the proper attitude. Prayer is one of the deepest moments of worship an individual ever experiences. I think that in order to experience the proper attitude by which we come before God, we have to remember who it is we're talking to. We have to be acutely conscious of who God is.

Martin Luther once answered a similar question. People were frustrated because they weren't receiving the answers to the prayers they wanted. They were looking to God as sort of a cosmic bellhop who was on call twenty-four hours a day to meet every desire and whim they should bring before him. And Luther in counseling his parish said, "Let God be God." That's the attitude we must have when we come before him in prayer. Remember who he is, and let him be God. He is the one who holds the power.

We must also remember who we are. When we're praying, we want to be able to come before God as our Father and to call him "Abba" as the Holy Spirit allows us to do. We are to come boldly before the throne of grace, but never, ever arrogantly. There is a sense in which modern Christians sometimes become a bit too familiar with God in the way we talk to him in prayer—as if he were a buddy. I, for one, am old-fashioned enough to appreciate the antiquated Elizabethan language—the *thees* and the *thous* that were built right into the language. We must always remember the spirit of awe and reverence by which we are to come before God. I think if we come in the right attitude, fervently seeking to be obedient to him, then we can expect to see things happen.

9

The Growing Spiritual Life

If then you were raised with Christ,
seek those things which are above,
where Christ is, sitting at the right hand of God.
Set your mind on things above, not on things on the earth.
For you died, and your life is hidden with Christ in God.
When Christ who is our life appears, then you also
will appear with Him in glory.

COLOSSIANS 3:1-4

Questions in This Section:

What concerns you most about today's Christian?

How can I put Jesus first in my life?

How can I prevent my personal Christian growth from becoming stagnant?

How do I, as a new Christian, get a well-balanced view of what the Bible says?

What do you do in your daily devotions?

Should Christians fast today, and if so, for what reason and how often?

We live in an age that is very concerned with looks and physical beauty. What does the Bible say about a person taking care of his or her body?

How can I deal with jealousy?

How should I handle my own doubts about God's presence in my life?

How do our emotions affect spiritual growth?

What is the biblical perspective on psychology?

Is man two parts: body and soul; or three parts: mind, body, and soul?

What does it mean to be righteous?

When Jesus says, "Be ye perfect as your Father in heaven is perfect," does that mean we can attain perfection, and should we?

Romans says that "those who are in the flesh cannot please God." Does this mean that if a non-Christian performs a righteous act, it does not please God?

If the Holy Spirit lives in us, why can't we live perfect lives?

Is it possible for Christians to be pure in the things they say and do?

Jesus calls Christians to be the salt of the earth and the light of the world. Would you please give us some practical ways we can do this?

How should we be in the world but not of it? What does "not of it" mean?

How can we demonstrate godliness in our lives?

How can we be bold in our faith and excited about it, enjoying our status as chosen people, without becoming proud?

If we really love God, why do we ignore his commandments?

How does a Christian strike a balance between goal setting and being led by the Spirit?

What does the Bible mean when it says we should wait upon the Lord?

How can I make goals for my life that best glorify God?

If someone wanted to read three Christian books this year, which three would you most recommend?

How can I best prolong a useful Christian life as I grow older?

What concerns you most about today's Christian?

As a theologian and an educator, I'm biased, but my greatest frustration with Christians in general is that there seem to be so few of them who are deeply concerned about learning the things of God. Some will say, "My passion is to do evangelism" or, "My passion is to work in the inner city, where there are obvious felt needs of human beings in distress," and I appreciate that.

The recent Gallup Poll of American Christianity was the most comprehensive study of religion ever done in this nation, and one of the glaring conclusions was that as we find an increase in public zeal for religious activity, we're not seeing a corresponding depth in the understanding of religious principles or in the concern for biblical truth. I would say that this concerns me more than anything else.

Now, I don't know if that's what concerns God the most. If we push the whole of the Christian experience down to its bottom line, I think that God is most concerned about how we live. Regardless of how knowledgeable we are, are we obeying God's commandments? Jesus said, "If you love me, keep my commandments—follow me, do the things that I tell you to do."

I am concerned about people's knowledge and understanding of God's Word because I'm convinced that behind every practice is a theory. That theory may be well thought out and carefully designed, or it may be something that we just sort of adopt uncritically and respond to

by way of an impression and then fly by the seat of our
pants with it. But the clearest demonstration of what our
deepest theories are is how we live. We practice certain
things because we believe that they are the things to do.

When I become a Christian, my heart is changed immediately. I now have a passion for God that I didn't have
before. But God doesn't drill a hole in my head and fill it
with new information and teach me overnight all the
things that he wants me to know about who he is and what
he wants me to do. Rather, he has given us the Scriptures
in simple doses, and sometimes in more complex doses.
The metaphor that the Bible uses is the distinction between meat and milk. He calls us first to begin with milk as
a nutrient and then to move on to the heavier matters—
to the meat. My big concern is that it seems that we are on
a diet of milk and are terrified to eat anything more substantial.

How can I put Jesus first in my life?

We have the mandate in Matthew 6:33: "Seek first the kingdom of God and His righteousness, and all these things
shall be added to you."

Incidentally, the word that Jesus uses in that commandment is the Greek word *protos,* which has a little more force
to it than the word *first* in our own language. In English
the word *first* just seems to be one number in a sequence
of consecutive numbers. There is this weighty concept of
chiefness of priority that is found in Jesus' command, and
he is telling us to make this a matter of top priority. That's

a matter of setting priorities and setting goals. That has to come first.

Now how do we go about doing this? How does a Christian grow in grace and in devotion, love, appreciation, and obedience to the things of God? In theology we speak of the means of grace: prayer, the reading of the Scriptures, fellowship with other Christians, worship in the assemblies of the saints. These are the kinds of things that help us get our priorities straightened out.

Let me get really practical about it and even psychological, if you will. We are people of different desires. We have conflicts of desires. All of us as Christians would like to be able to push a button and say, "From now on I'm going to make God first in my life." That works until something else occupies our desires, and then we don't want God first in our lives. If we had God first in our lives consistently, we'd never sin. But whenever we sin it's because at that moment we would rather do something other than obey God.

How do we become more consistent in elevating God to his proper place in our lives? Or more to the point, how do we become more obedient? I would say one of the things we need to do is recognize our frailties and our weaknesses and the fact that we do have an ongoing desire and inclination to sin, but those desires for sin and for disobedience are not constant. It's like physical appetites. There's an analogy there. I know that it's easy for me to go on a diet right after dinner. The hard time for me to go on a diet is right before dinner. My physical desires are not constant; they change according to when I have eaten last, and so on. I know that about myself, and I know that if I'm going to develop a greater consistency, maybe I have to have help. I may enter a program where I'm going to get a support system that will help me, such as Weight Watchers.

So it is with spiritual development. We know that our spiritual desires are not always constant. That's why when we are feeling up and have a desire to be obedient, we feed the new man and starve the old man by making diligent use of those means of grace that God has given us.

How can I prevent my personal Christian growth from becoming stagnant?

There's only one absolute way I know of to keep your Christian growth from becoming stagnant, and that is to die. The only time Christian growth stops altogether is at death. That's because we don't need to grow any further; we're ushered into the state of glorification. If a person is in Christ and Christ is in that person, it is impossible for the Christian not to move, to grow. It may seem at times as if our Christian growth has been totally arrested and is in a stagnant state, but I think that's merely an outward appearance.

Obviously our Christian growth can move at various speeds, and we tend to have a kind of ebb and flow. Sometimes we're moving ahead in leaps and bounds and other times at a snail's pace. When it's moving in such a laboriously slow fashion, we may think that it has become utterly stagnant. Again, if there is no evidence of growth whatsoever then I would say it's time to examine our souls and our hearts to see if we're in Christ at all because where the spirit of Christ indwells a person, he will not permit total stagnation.

If we want to increase the pace of Christian growth, I think

there are some important practical keys we need to plug in.
Christian growth, biblically, is usually described in terms of
discipleship. To be a disciple of Jesus means to be a learner
in the school of Christ. That doesn't mean simply heaping
up intellectual data or head knowledge, so to speak, but coming to an understanding of what it is that pleases God and
what it is that pleases Christ. It means learning how to imitate him in our different ways of walking before him.

The word *discipleship* is very close to the English word
discipline. To grow requires the achievement of spiritual
discipline. How do you get it? When we are trying to progress in any area, so many times that involves discipline—
whether it's mastery of piano technique, an athletic
endeavor, or learning in a public school or college. We
have to understand that discipline doesn't happen by
magic. The best way I know of becoming disciplined is by
first learning patterns of discipline under somebody else's
tutelage. If you're having trouble growing, get yourself as
fast as you can into a Christian growth group where you
are under the discipline of a pastor or a spiritual leader,
where as part of a team, you are learning the skills of personal growth together.

How do I, as a new Christian, get a well-balanced view of what the Bible says?

Anytime new Christians read the Bible for themselves, they
risk a distortion. One of the great articles of faith of the Reformation was the principle of private interpretation, that is,
every Christian was seen to have the right to read the Bible
for themselves. The Roman Catholic Church resisted that

because they recognized that an unschooled and untrained person could very easily come to serious misunderstandings and distortions of Scripture. They warned, for example, that letting the laymen read the Bible could open a floodgate of iniquity. Luther responded to that by saying, yes, a floodgate of iniquity could be opened by unskilled people. That is why God has put teachers in the church. But he also said the basic message essential for every Christian to understand was so clear, so manifest, that a child could understand it. It is so important and so worthwhile that if it risks the opening a floodgate of iniquity, Luther said, so be it.

I agree with that, but at the same time, I am also aware of the vast difficulties that attend the virgin reading of Scripture, particularly without sound tutelage.

The Bible is a big book, but it's not so big that it can't be read in its totality. It is important that we understand the individual parts of Scripture in light of the whole. Luther, careful as he was to give detailed attention to each passage and verse, still made it a part of his yearly ministry to read through the whole Bible. He kept the big picture—the total scope of Scripture—always in his mind as he was dealing with the individual pieces. It's like walking through a vast forest. He said that the first time through, all you're trying to do is get from one end of the forest to the other. After you grow in your understanding of the forest, you begin to notice separate groupings of trees, and after a while individual trees will stand out to you. Then as you examine the individual trees and maybe climb the trees, you'll examine the different branches. Bible study, he said, isn't really fun until you're out there turning over every individual leaf, enjoying and exploring that leaf for all it can be. That's what Luther loved to do as a scholar of the Bible, to look at those words and passages that are so lively. He said that to prevent getting hung up on one tiny little section of it, "let the wind of the whole blow through your mind occasionally."

I wrote one book titled *Knowing Scripture* (InterVarsity Press, 1977), in which I set forth a practical guideline for somebody who's reading through Scripture for the first time. Most people start at Genesis, and that's fun, interesting, and easy. They get to Exodus and that's full of adventure. As soon as they get into Leviticus and Numbers, they lose it and quit. There's a way to read the history of the Old Testament in which you can skip some of those difficult and strange passages and do it in a nutshell version. That way you get the feeling of the whole and can then go back to fill in the gaps.

What do you do in your daily devotions?

To be very candid, I don't have what one would call daily devotions in terms of an established routine. My pattern varies from day to day, week to week, and month to month. There is a period of time in every day that I spend in prayer. That period is longer and sometimes more intense on some occasions than others. But I am not the kind of person who functions well in a highly regimented or structured environment. Other people have a daily agenda that is much more routine that they find very helpful.

I would say that if you take the amount of time I spend in the Scriptures over the course of a week, it would probably be considered a lot of studying. But I don't distinguish between devotional reading of Scripture and studying the Scripture. For me, all studying of the Scripture is a devotional act, and devotions should be an act of serious study. There's nothing magic about ten minutes of reading in the Scripture.

I know that people suffer a lot of guilt about this because in certain Christian subcultures it's sort of expected that everybody has a set period of daily time for Bible reading and prayer. Now the Scriptures tell us to meditate on the Word of God day and night so that our attention to the Scriptures should be devout and serious and rigorous. In fact, I recommend that people spend a lot more than ten or fifteen minutes a day studying the Scriptures. But we have to be careful not to impose upon the Christian community a set pattern of Bible study or prayer. We can't set up personal systems of devotion as tests of spirituality for other people. This has done a lot of harm to people who don't function well in a highly structured approach to prayer and study.

On the other hand, some of us are so undisciplined that we don't give adequate attention to the serious matter of prayer and the study of Scripture. These are our duties as Christians, and it's also our pleasure as Christians to spend time with God. We're to be praying "without ceasing." Jesus made it a practice to take time away for devoted seasons of prayer. If prayer was something Jesus saw as necessary for himself, how much more necessary must it be for us? I would not recommend my routine for others. But remember that my work and calling and vocation is as a teacher of the Word of God, so I'm required to spend enormous amounts of time in it. Each person has to learn for him- or herself what works best for integrating prayer and Bible study into daily life.

Should Christians fast today, and if so, for what reason and how often?

I believe that fasting is one of the most neglected means of grace that God has given to his church. It has tremendous biblical background and support. Fasting was a regular practice in the household of Israel, and that tradition was carried into the New Testament church. When the disciples failed to achieve success in their attempt to exorcise some devils on one occasion, Jesus said to them, "This kind only goes out through prayer and fasting."

So Jesus himself endorsed fasting. He went through a forty-day fast during his temptation, and he sanctified the means of grace through fasting. I don't think we should continue to neglect it. In the Roman Catholic Church, fasting is a regular discipline. Even in my lifetime, there was still the tradition in the Roman Catholic Church that Catholics did not eat meat on Friday. Some of them continue that today. So the fast at that level was not a complete doing away with eating, but it was a doing away with certain elements of eating. Many Protestants objected to the Roman Catholic form of fasting because fasting was also seen as a meritorious work in the Roman Catholic Church and people thought that because they were engaged in this practice of fasting, they were earning points in terms of their quest for entrance into the kingdom of God. Protestants, being zealous for justification by faith alone, had a tendency to throw the baby out with the bathwater and did away with fasting lest it be misconstrued as a way of working oneself into the kingdom of God. But fasting is making a comeback.

How do we carry this out in a practical way? Some people agree with the concept of fasting, but it makes them ill. There are people—diabetics, for example—for whom it would be irresponsible to be in a full and total fast. They should only be in partial types of fast, and only with a physician's direction. We are responsible to be good stewards of our bodies, and our fasting should be done in an intelligent way. I remember the first time I fasted. I just decided I wasn't going to eat anything for four days, and it was a tremendous spiritual experience for me to go four days without a bite of food, but I was about dead at the end of those four days. I had all kinds of trouble. I had stomach problems because it was unhealthy for me to go without any food in my stomach for four days. And so I think the individual must work this out in his own conscience before God and not feel a compulsion to fast in a way that would damage his own body. There are several good books available on the discipline of fasting, and any Christian should be able to incorporate this discipline in some way.

We live in an age in which people are very concerned with looks and physical beauty. What does the Bible say about a person taking care of his or her body? Should Christians be concerned with matters such as being overweight?

When you ask if Christians should be concerned about being overweight, you're trampling on my toes! But that reminds me of a story of a friend of mine. He was an Episcopalian priest and a very earthy fellow, and he chain-smoked cigarettes. One of the ladies in the congregation was very upset about this priest's habit of smoking. This woman, by the way, was obviously quite overweight. She came to the priest and said, "Father, don't you know that by smoking you're staining the temple of the Holy Spirit with nicotine?" My friend looked at the woman and replied, "Yes, ma'am, I guess I am staining the temple of the Holy Spirit, and you're stretching it." I don't know what the future relationship was between the pastor and that member of his congregation after that exchange, but it illustrates that sometimes we pick and choose certain habits that are not healthy. We set one up as a test of spirituality if we don't indulge in it. The point the priest was trying to make, not too subtly of course, was that even though he was involved in a self-destructive habit, this woman was also doing damage to her body by being so obviously overweight.

We live in a culture that tends to glorify the svelte body and downgrade people who don't meet that aesthetic standard. I don't see where the Bible says to us that we are supposed to meet the aesthetic standards of a given culture and therefore that we should all look alike, patterned after the current sex symbols. The condition of our bodies really does matter, though, from a biblical perspective. We are called to take care of our bodies, to be good stewards of our physical well-being, and I think if you have a question about whether your weight is appropriate or not, it's probably something you ought to talk over with your doctor. Our physicians are becoming more and more concerned about some of the problems caused by excessive weight. The medical sciences have discovered many links between our emotional, mental, and physical well-being. I would say that poor health or condition in any area of life—including spiritual—is going to affect the whole of life, and we need to give attention to problem areas.

How can I deal with jealousy?

I'm glad you asked that question because it's the kind of question we almost never hear anyone ask in the Christian community. It's obviously a matter of great concern to God. The Bible has much to say about jealousy and similar feelings we have toward each other.

One of the things I often ask my students in seminary is this: "Suppose you had the opportunity to write a new constitution for the government of the United States of America and we were going to start all over again. Instead of having several amendments and a bill of rights, all we were allowed to have would be ten basic rules by which our nation would be governed. What would you include in those ten rules to govern a nation?"

When we ask that question, most people would include such rules as prohibition against murder, against theft and those kinds of violations of people and property that we all recognize are evil. Yet I also wonder how many people would include in the top ten a rule to honor one's parents, or a rule to protect the sanctity of the name of God. I wonder how many would include a rule against coveting the property of others.

Jealousy is not exactly the same thing as coveting, but it is very close. Jealousy involves harboring ill feelings toward another human being because of that person's possessions or achievements or something that we want for ourselves but don't have. We have feelings of ill will toward these people because we covet what they possess. I might also add that jealousy is one of the cardinal sins of which the Scriptures speak so frequently. I think one of the reasons jealousy is such a serious matter to God, though it may not be so serious to us, is that at the root of feelings of jealousy toward other people is an unspoken, assumed criticism of God. We are, in a sense, expressing our dissatisfaction with the fact that God has been pleased to allow other people to have things that we do not have or to achieve things that we haven't achieved. Instead of being grateful for the things God has provided for us—the gifts, talents, and possessions—in our jealousy we not only hurt other people, but we are silently attacking God in his sovereignty and in his mercy. I think we need to look at it in its fullness if we are going to have the impetus to overcome it.

How should I handle my own doubts about God's presence in my life?

This question brings to mind an experience I had early in my ministry. In fact, I'd only been ordained a few months and was teaching at a college. One church had a minister who was much loved by his congregation; he had served there for twenty-five years but had become critically ill. The man was at the point of death. I was supplying the pulpit for several months and helping the congregation deal with this tragedy in their midst.

On a Saturday night, before the Sunday morning service in which we were to celebrate Communion, I received an urgent call that it was possible the minister would not live to the next day. When I came to the church the next morning, I was keenly aware of the profound sense of concern that was in the congregation. I felt an enormous weight to try to have the most meaningful Communion service I could possibly lead. I agonized in prayer, saying, "God, please let me have a special anointing as I come before these people in their need." I don't think I ever mounted the pulpit in my entire ministry with a greater desire to know the presence of God than I did that Sunday morning.

I preached, and I went through the sacrament, and it was awful. It was terrible! I just felt a total absence of God, as if I'd been utterly and completely abandoned by him. My preaching was dead, and it seemed as if I were talking to myself. When I pronounced the benediction and went to the back of the church, I really wished there was a hole in the ground I could jump into so I wouldn't have to face those people. I felt so miserable for having let them down.

I stood at the back door, and as they started to file out of the church one by one, I couldn't believe what happened! These people came out, and it was like they had been hit between the eyes. They were stunned. They were in shock. One after another said that they had never been so moved by the powerful presence of God as that which they'd experienced in that worship service! One lady said to me, "The Holy Spirit's presence was so thick today we could have cut it with a knife." I just couldn't believe it. I felt like Jacob when he woke up from his dream and said, "Surely God was in this place and I knew it not." That really had an impact on me that day. I said, "Wait a minute. God promised that he would be here." I didn't feel his presence, and so I thought he wasn't there. I had become a sensuous

Christian, allowing my strength of conviction to be determined by the strength of my feelings.

I realized that I've got to live by the Word of God, not by what I feel. I think that's how you deal with doubt. You begin to focus on what God says he's going to do rather than on your feelings.

How do our emotions affect spiritual growth?

Our society is very emotion oriented; at the same time it is very suspicious of emotional expression, particularly in the arena of religion. If you scream and yell and carry on Sunday afternoon at the football stadium, you're called a fan. If you express any emotional interest in the things of God, you're called a fanatic. It seems that we're allowed to be emotional about some things, but not others.

God has created us to have the ability to think and to be involved in the cognitive process of reason, but we are also creatures who feel. When I was taking pastoral counseling courses from psychiatrists, they would say, "When you ask a person a diagnostic question, don't ask, 'What do you think about so-and-so?' but ask them, 'How do you feel?'" They were trying to teach us how to get in touch with people's feelings because people live at the feeling level. Now part of me thought that there was some insight there, but part of me recoiled from it because I'm convinced that we're living in a time in the church when there is so much emphasis on feelings that we've become very negative with respect to the whole business of thinking. I think that if we try to make Christianity purely intellectual, we distort it.

And if we try to make Christianity purely emotional, we distort it in the other direction.

What is the relationship supposed to be between feelings and thought? If someone asked me which of the two is most important, I would say that the mind is first in terms of the order of our spiritual development, but the heart is first in importance. Let me say it another way: If my theology is correct and my intellectual understanding of Christianity is correct, but my heart is removed from Christ, I'm outside the kingdom of God. If my heart is in love with Christ, but my theology is messed up, I'm in the kingdom of God. So the heart is more important than the mind, but the way God has made us is that the better we understand him with our mind, the more our heart should be inflamed with emotion in love of God.

What is the biblical perspective on psychology? Does psychology play a helpful role in Christianity?

We have to understand at the outset that there is no such thing today as a monolithic single system of psychology. There are different schools of competing theories of psychology, all of which are trying to understand the intricacies and subtle nuances of the most complex mechanism found in the universe, which is the human personality.

At best, psychology as an academic discipline and as a science is relatively young and inexact. Early in the church's history, Christian scholars were interested in understanding the intricate behavioral patterns of people. For example, Saint Augustine is often credited, even in secular universities, as being the ancient father of psychology, because he was so concerned with what we would today call introspection, trying to probe the depths of human motives and feelings and discover what forms human personality.

Now, is there such a thing as a biblical psychology? There certainly is a biblical view of man, and there certainly is a biblical view of human behavior. We can learn much from the Scriptures about behavior and personality development, about emotions and their impact on us. There is a wealth of information in the Bible that can help us as we give counsel to others. We know, for example, that guilt is one of the most prevalent issues dealt with by psychologists and psychiatrists. There has never been a book more adequate to deal with the problem of guilt than the Bible.

I happen to believe that all truth meets at the top. I believe that the Bible is infallible. I believe that the Bible gives us a view of man that comes from the Maker of man; it comes from the very mind of God. So we get an insight into human personality from the Scriptures that we will never find anywhere else.

Yet God has also given us nature as a textbook, and through the study of human behavior we can learn valid truths. So I think that a Christian should have one eye on the Scriptures and another eye on the best of what is being discovered through the scientific study, the experience, and the observations of professionals in psychology and psychiatry.

Is man two parts: body and soul; or three parts: mind, body, and soul?

This question may seem harmless on the surface, but it's been a matter of significant controversy in early church his-

tory and again in the twentieth century. It seems a strange
thing to be fighting about, but there are reasons for the
debate.

In the first place, the classic view shared by orthodox
Christians of various denominational persuasions has been
that man is what we call dichotomous; that is, he has a physical dimension, which we call his body, and a nonphysical
aspect, which we call his soul. He is both physical and nonphysical. A danger of this view is that we can fall into dualism, whereby we see body and soul as being intrinsically
incapable of unity. It's the dualistic view that has so often
pictured anything physical as completely evil, rather than
as something created good that has been affected by sin.
The early Greeks had a problem with spirit being united
with matter in any way. To the Greek world, the great scandal of the gospel was not the Resurrection but the Incarnation because they couldn't conceive of a spirit becoming
contaminated by such close union with physical things like
a human body.

In 1 Thessalonians 5:23 Paul says, "May God keep you
body, soul, and spirit." One theologian jumped on this and
said, "Oh, there are three parts to man—body, soul, and
spirit." And in the early centuries of Christianity this tripartite view developed. The theory was that the body and soul
are basically incompatible and that it is a dualistic arrange-
ment of tension between the physical and the nonphysical.
The only way they could fit together would be to have
some third substance as the cement to put these two contradictory substances together. The body and soul were
then thought to be unified by the spirit.

The church condemned as heresy this tripartite view of

man—that he's body, soul, and spirit—because of the way it had developed from a Greek dualism that the church wanted to avoid. This view made a comeback in the twentieth century, however, and has become very popular in certain Christian circles.

Where I see it, for example, is in the influence of Watchman Nee's teaching, where Watchman Nee brings along with his Christian understanding some ideas unique to Oriental thought. He sort of combines them with classical Christianity and has been very influential as a popular teacher among Christians. We've also seen this idea become very much employed in so-called neo-Pentecostal theology and in some of the movements found in the widespread influence of Campus Crusade for Christ, for example, which has had an enormous impact on American Christianity.

One of the things that is so attractive about the idea of man being divided into three parts rather than two is that it makes it possible to construct a view of two different degrees of Christians: those Christians who are born of the Holy Spirit but who do not yet have the indwelling of the Holy Spirit—the baptism of the Holy Spirit—and those who are born of the Holy Spirit and also have the indwelling of the Spirit. Those groups that place great emphasis upon the baptism of the Holy Spirit as a subsequent work of God's grace after conversion will then say that there are three kinds of people in the world. There are the people who don't have the Holy Spirit at all; then there are people who have the Holy Spirit in conversion or in rebirth but who lack this second blessing, this second indwelling or infilling of the Holy Spirit; and finally there are those who have the Spirit in conversion and in indwelling.

If you can talk about three different kinds of people, it's convenient to then see a model of that in terms of the three parts of man. Sometimes you will see it broken down this way, that those who are not Spirit-filled Christians have the Holy Spirit in their soul but not in their spirit. The distinction is then between the compartments within us in which the Spirit dwells, and that accounts for the distinction between the so-called carnal Christian and the Spirit-filled Christian.

I think this is a case where theology is dictating our understanding of Scripture; we have a view of theology, and we try to construct a view of man to accommodate it. I just think that it is not a sound way of understanding the Bible. The Bible does, on one occasion, say body, soul, and spirit, but it also talks about the mind, the bowels, and the heart.

The overall message of the Bible is that we have a physical body and we have a nonphysical existence, sometimes called the spirit and sometimes the soul, and this nonphysical part consists of our whole self—personality, emotions, mind, spirit, will, and so forth. God created us with both parts; both were affected by the Fall, and both will be redeemed by the grace and power of God.

What does it mean to be righteous?

To be righteous means to do what God tells us to do. Righteousness means obeying the law of God. Jesus calls his people to an exceedingly high standard of righteousness.

He tells us in one of the most terrifying texts in the New Testament that unless our righteousness exceeds the righteousness of the scribes and the Pharisees, we will in no way enter the kingdom of God. Some of us get off the hook easily by saying that we have the righteousness of Christ—and certainly that exceeds the righteousness of the scribes and Pharisees, and that's true. But I don't think that's what Jesus was talking about there. I think he's talking about the righteousness that we are to manifest as regenerate and justified people—that conformity to the image of God and conformity in imitation of Christ. The evidence in our lives is the kind of standard of righteousness that Jesus calls us to possess and practice. I think we have a tendency to trivialize it.

One day I received a letter from a man who was complaining about people who danced and drank and smoked, and was saying how could these people be Christians? As if those things had anything ultimately to do with the kingdom of God. Certainly they touch on ethical matters, but they're trivial. This was the great failure of the Pharisees, whose righteousness we are called to exceed. They majored in minors. They measured righteousness strictly by externals. Jesus rebuked them for missing the weightier matters of the law.

Obviously, there are greater and lesser matters we need to be aware of if we are going to pursue authentic righteousness. For example, Jesus commended the Pharisees in tithing. They were scrupulous in tithing. They paid their tithes to the dime, and today only 3 percent of evangelical Christians tithe. But Jesus even considered that a minor matter. He said at least they tithe, but they omitted the weightier matters of justice and mercy. I think that what righteousness involves ultimately is bringing forth the fruit of the spirit of Christ. A righteous person is a person whom you can trust, who has integrity, whose word means something, and who is not dishonest. Those things are spiritual, yet we tend to judge people by things more evident and visible.

When Jesus says, "Be ye perfect as your Father in heaven is perfect," does that mean we can attain perfection, and should we?

There are a couple of things we need to understand about this statement. In the first place, the word that is translated "perfect" literally means "be complete." So often, the New Testament and the Old Testament will describe people as being upright and righteous—not in the sense that they have achieved total moral perfection, but rather that they have reached a singular level of maturity in their growth in terms of spiritual integrity. However, in this statement, it's certainly legitimate to translate it using the English word *perfect*. For example, "Be ye complete as your heavenly Father is complete." Now remember that your heavenly Father is perfectly complete! So if we are to mirror God in that way, we are to mirror him in his moral excellence as well as in other ways. In fact, the basic call to a person in this world is to be a reflection of the character of God. That's what it means to be created in the image of God. Long before the Sermon on the Mount, God required the people of Israel to reflect his character when he said to them, "Be ye holy even as I am holy." He set them apart to be holy ones. The New Testament word for that is *saints.*

Now to the question of whether we can, in fact, achieve moral perfection in this world. If Jesus says to be perfect, the assumption would be that he would not require us to do something that is impossible for us to achieve. Therefore, there are Christians, many Christians, who believe that, indeed, it is possible for a person to reach a state of moral perfection in this life. That view is called perfectionism, and people develop a theology whereby there's a special work of the Holy Spirit that gives them victory over all sin or all intentional sin that renders them morally perfect in this world. The mainstream of Christianity, however, has resisted the doctrine of perfectionism chiefly because we see the record of the greatest saints in biblical history and in church history who to a person confessed the fact that they, to their dying day, struggled with ongoing sin in their lives. Not the least of which, of course, was the apostle Paul, who talked about his ongoing struggle with sin.

Can a person be perfect? Theoretically, the answer to that is yes. The New Testament tells us that with every temptation we meet, God gives us a way to escape that temptation. He always gives us enough grace to overcome sin. So sin in the Christian life, I would say, is inevitable because of our weakness and because of the multitude of opportunities we have to sin. But on a given occasion, it is never, ever necessary. So in that sense, we could theoretically be perfect, though none of us is.

Romans says that "those who are in the flesh cannot please God." Does this mean that if a non-Christian performs a righteous act it does not please God?

Paul here is describing everyone who is unregenerate, and so from a biblical perspective, anyone who is not born of the Spirit of God would be "in the flesh." You are inferring that the passage says that those who are in the flesh cannot please God. Does that mean that a righteous act done by anyone who is in the flesh would not please God? If no one in the flesh can please God, then obviously a person in the flesh would not be able to please God under any circumstances. What about if he does a righteous act? That question represents what I would call a condition contrary to fact. That's like asking if an unbeliever would be rejected if he had faith. If he had faith, he wouldn't be an unbeliever. It would be an impossible condition for an unbeliever to be a believer at the same time.

What I'm getting at is this: Can a person who is unregenerate, who has never been made alive by the Spirit of God, actually perform real righteousness? There are two ways to approach this. On the one hand, the New Testament describes righteousness and a good deed in a comprehensive way that considers both the external action and the internal motivation for the action. The Bible makes it clear that people who are still in the flesh can and do perform activities that outwardly conform to the requirements of the law of God. There are people who are not Christians who do not steal and do not kill and who show mercy. They indicate all kinds of virtuous behavior, what the

Reformers called civil righteousness—righteousness that gives an outward obedience to the law of God.

But the New Testament has a narrower view of what authentic righteousness demands. For example, the rich young ruler thought that he had kept the Ten Commandments from the time he was a child because he wasn't actually guilty of murder, theft, adultery, etc. He said to Jesus, "All these things I have kept from my youth."

At the same time the Bible says, "There is none righteous, no, not one. There is none who does good that is in the flesh," because God's demand for righteousness is not merely external obedience to the law but that the motivation for an action proceed from a heart that is genuinely desiring to please God. If I'm not moved by the Spirit of God and am merely in the flesh, I will never be motivated to do anything out of a genuine love for God. So I would have to say that a person in the flesh can never display real righteousness in the sense of behaving from an ultimately proper motivation.

If the Holy Spirit lives in us, why can't we live perfect lives?

Let me suggest to you that we can live perfect lives. Now that may sound like the most outrageous thing you have ever heard, because one of the few things you'll get both Christian and non-Christian to agree on is that nobody is perfect!

What the New Testament teaches, as I understand it, is that once the Holy Spirit comes into my life, once I'm indwelt by the Holy Spirit, I have living within me the power to obey God. The Holy Spirit gives me the power to obey the commandments of God, and the New Testament says there is no temptation that has ever befallen me that isn't common to every person, and with the temptation God always provides a way of escape. I don't think anybody does, in fact, live a perfect life. But I think that God's grace makes perfection a possibility.

I would say that I have opportunities to sin literally thousands of times a day. Every time I'm confronted with an opportunity to sin, there is a battle within my soul. The indwelling Holy Spirit is inclining me toward righteousness and obedience. But remember that the Holy Spirit is living in me, in R. C. Sproul; he's indwelling an imperfect creature, one who has not been totally cleansed of evil inclinations. So given the manifold opportunities to sin that I have and knowing that there's warfare with every one of those opportunities between what the Bible calls my flesh and the Spirit, statistically it's virtually inevitable that I'm going to sin and be far less than perfect. If we look at them one at a time, we realize that in each single circumstance the power has actually been provided by God to resist that temptation. That's why I can never stand before God and say, "God, you will have to excuse me; the devil made me do it" or, "The Holy Spirit was not powerful enough within me to have resisted that sin." So even though I believe that not even the apostle Paul ever achieved perfection in his life, it's not because of any lack of power or ability or inclination of the indwelling Spirit.

Is it possible for Christians to be pure in the things they say and do?

I don't want to be evasive or clever; I'm very serious when I ask, How pure is pure? We talk about 99.44 percent pure with respect to a certain brand of soap; we talk about various degrees of purity of silver, gold, and other precious metals. When we talk about purity in a moral or spiritual sense, I would say that it's not possible for a Christian to be 100 percent pure in anything that he does or says for this reason: When God considers an action that we do or a word that we speak, he doesn't merely consider the surface action; he also considers the motives. The motives involve an examination of the deepest inclination and disposition of our hearts. From an ideal, absolutely pure spiritual perspective, a perfect motive would proceed from a heart that is 100 percent inclined toward God—a heart that loves God fully with all of the heart, with all of the mind, and with all of the soul. I've never done an action in my life where the moment I did it I was loving God with all of my heart, with all of my soul, and with all of my mind. Any action I've ever done, any word I've ever spoken has always been tainted by some degree of blemish and personal sinfulness.

If we use the term *pure* loosely, it becomes a relative matter. I suspect there's some degree of selfish interest in almost everything we do. We can think of people who are amazingly altruistic on the surface, and I would say, relatively speaking, we do encounter true altruism in the world. But I don't think we'll ever see a perfect deed, or a perfect thought, or a perfect word until we ourselves are perfected inwardly. That's the point: God judges our actions not only externally but he's also concerned about the heart. If all he cared about were external actions, which indeed he does care about, we would see people who have no particular love for Christ whatsoever outstripping Christians in their righteous deeds and in their altruistic concerns and compassions. The full picture involves the inward disposition of the heart, and that's where we all suffer failure.

Jesus calls Christians to be the "salt of the earth" and the "light of the world." Would you please give us some practical ways in which we can be salt and light?

Salt is that which gives zest, tang, taste to life. I think Christians, of all people, should manifest a kind of zest, a kind of excitement for life—a passion for living; they should be fun to be around. Even the apostles tell us that our speech should be seasoned with salt. Now that doesn't mean that we're supposed to talk like sailors, but it does mean that there should be some wit, some color and vitality. We are people who have been blessed with new life and abundant life, the very life of Christ.

I think that to be salt of the earth is to be people who are exciting to be with, people who add to life rather than take away from it. I express that because so often we are perceived as being dull, stern, prudish, moralistic—all of those things that we are not intended to be. We are to be salt to people—to add taste and zest. Not only salt, but light. The basic meaning of *light* in the Scriptures is the enlightenment that God's truth brings. Those of us who are Christians are called to have a passion for truth. We should care about the truth, and we should care about learning the right way to do things.

So often the church is seen as an echo of the culture. We let progress be in the hands of those outside the church. I think the Bible calls the church to be on the cutting edge of life; we are supposed to be leading the culture rather than following it, and I think that's what it means to be a light—a light to show people the way to go out of darkness. When we see, for example, a labor-management arena filled with hostility and strife, we, as Christians, should be showing models of labor-management relationships in which that hostility somehow is overcome. That's what it means to be light to the world—to show the world a more excellent way.

How should we be in the world but not of it? What does "not of it" mean?

The New Testament tells us that we are not to be conformed to this world but that we are to be transformed by the renewing of our mind (Rom. 12:2).

Let's look at those two words that are crucial to that discussion in Scripture, the difference between conformity and transformation. The prefix *con-* means "with." And so to conform to this world means literally to be with it. That's one of the strongest drives and temptations that we have as Christians. Nobody wants to be out of it; we want to be "with it." We want to be up-to-date. We want to fit in. And we're often engulfed by peer pressure that wants us to imitate and participate in all of the structures and the styles of this world. The Bible says we are not to be conformed to the patterns of this world.

Now, when we hear that as Christians, so often we think that all we have to do is to become obvious noncon-formists. So if the world wears buttons and bows, we don't wear buttons and bows, or if the world wears lipstick, we don't wear lipstick. We try to show ways in which we are different from the world. But that's not what the Bible is talking about. It's not just a matter of being different from the world; we are to go beyond nonconformity to transformation. That fits with everything the Scripture tells us of being salt and light to the world. Something that is transformed is something that is changed. The prefix *trans-* means "above and beyond." We are to be above and beyond the standards of this world, not in the sense that we are to elevate ourselves in lofty status above everybody else, but that we are called to a more excellent way of life.

That doesn't mean you drop out of the world; this world is my Father's world, and this is the arena of God's redemption. The tendency has always been to flee from the world and hide in the upper room, but God the Holy Spirit won't tolerate that. He sends his people into the world. Luther said it this way: "There's a normal pattern for Christian behavior. The person who's converted out of the world spends his first days as a Christian in a tendency to completely withdraw from the world, as Paul went to Arabia, for example, or we might have a desire to be so far removed from the stains and the pollution of this world that we become monastic in our thinking—withdrawing, stepping out of the world altogether."

But Luther said a Christian doesn't reach maturity until he reenters the world and embraces the world again, not in its worldliness and its ungodly patterns but as the theater and the arena of God's redemption. That's what Jesus did; he went into the world in order to save the world. This world is the world that God has committed himself to renew and redeem, and we are to participate in that with him.

How can we demonstrate godliness in our lives?

I'm glad you used that word, "demonstrate." I don't want to play with it too long here, but I think so often we are so concerned about how visible our piety is that we begin to use artificial, external ways to make sure that people see our piety. That was one of the most serious stumbling blocks of the Pharisees, the ones who received the most severe indictment from Jesus, because they were constantly involved in public displays of their piety. In fact, Jesus said that they degenerated to such a point that the prayers that they prayed were not for the benefit of the ears of God, but for the benefit of the ears of bystanders. So Jesus said, "When you pray, go in your closet to pray. Don't pray on the street corners like the Pharisees do to be seen of men." The Pharisees would fast, and they would go around with long faces, looking like they were suffering awfully, so that everybody could say, "Look at those poor Pharisees—they are emaciated from their rigorous spiritual fasting." Jesus said, "When you fast, anoint your head, put a smile on your face, don't let anybody know that you're involved in that kind of spiritual life." So there was one sense in which Jesus was against a public demonstration.

Yet at the same time our Lord told us to let our light shine before men. While we're not supposed to make an ostentatious display of our spirituality or of our piety, we are supposed to make a visible display of our integrity. People can see how we handle criticism, how we react when somebody pushes in front of us in a line, how we react when somebody breaks a promise to us. Do we keep our promises? Do we pay our bills on time? Those are the kinds of things that are very visible. Luther said it this way: "Every Christian is called to be Christ to his neighbor." Not that we're supposed to be crucified for our neighbor, but our lives—our trustworthiness, our friendliness, our kindness, our integrity—are to demonstrate to our friends what Jesus is like. That is an awesome responsibility.

How can we be bold in our faith and be excited about it, enjoying our status as chosen people, without becoming proud?

It's significant that Paul in 1 Timothy 3:6 gives a warning that not many who are young in the faith ought to be placed in positions of leadership in the church. In fact, the very concept of eldership has its roots in the Old Testament and is linked to a certain level of maturity that comes only through time spent growing spiritually. In our spiritual youth and enthusiasm we have a tendency to get puffed up and come across to those who are outside the household of faith as being arrogant and intolerant. A lot of that is attributed to the normal sense of excitement and enthusiasm that goes with the new discovery of Christ.

The first year of my Christian life was the most exciting year of my life, and I wanted desperately for every person I knew and loved and every person I met—including total strangers—to come to a knowledge of Christ. There's a sense in which I wish I still had that kind of enthusiasm that attended the first year of my discovery of Christ. But with that enthusiasm came a certain insensitivity, I'm sure, where I not only wanted everybody to come to faith but I wanted them to come *right now*, and I felt as if I was the

one appointed by God to make sure that they came to faith
right now. I would corner people and spend time with
them when it really wasn't appropriate. In fact, there were
times when I was downright discourteous. And I can't
blame legitimate enthusiasm for all of that.
There's nothing wrong with being zealous for Christ.
We're called to be people of zeal. There should be a passion in our Christian commitment. But again, that zeal
can get very easily mixed up with our own pride, for somehow we believe that we are God's special emissary to the
world, that the world will not be redeemed except
through our efforts. Certainly both Old and New Testaments give attention to the destructive power of pride in
spiritual life. We're told in some of the more famous statements that "pride goes before destruction and a haughty
spirit before a fall." And we're told that God gives grace
to the humble, but he resists the proud. We have to be on
guard every minute, lest pride destroy the spiritual
growth we're enjoying.

If we really love God, why do we ignore his commandments?

If we ignore his commandments absolutely and totally and
completely, that would be the clearest proof that we don't
love God. As Jesus himself said, "If you love me, keep my
commandments." The keeping of the commandments is a
manifestation of our love for God, and obedience is something that flows out of a heart that is inclined toward God
and embraces God in love. But having said this, we also
have to acknowledge that in the life of the greatest saint, of

the one whose heart is palpitating with love for God, there is still a level of disobedience and of ignoring God's commandments.

Why is this so? Simply because we are not yet fully sanctified. Once we are redeemed in Christ, we are given a new life principle, the indwelling power of the Holy Spirit. We are beginning to get well, but this whole work of sanctification is a process that is gradual, that takes time, and until we go to glory, until we go to heaven, we do not reach or attain a full state of spiritual or moral perfection. (This is what the majority of Christians believe; there are those who believe that Christians can and do achieve perfection in this world.)

One of the great distortions of the Christian faith in our day (every generation and every century has its particular deviation from classical Christianity) is a seriously defective view of sanctification. We hear this or similar statements often: "Not doctrine, but life. What God is concerned about is not my theology but my behavior." Certainly God cares about our behavior. But the pattern I see emerging is the separation of these two elements of belief and behavior; they are often set against one another, as if the Christian life had nothing to do with the Christian understanding of truth. That's a false dichotomy. In the New Testament, the Holy Spirit, who is also called the Spirit of Truth, is the principal agent in our sanctification. One of the great reasons we fail to obey God is that we are ignorant of his commandments; we lack understanding of what God has revealed. Truth and practice are inseparably related in our sanctification.

How does a Christian strike a balance between goal setting and being led by the Spirit?

I think that the principal way in which the New Testament speaks of being led by the Spirit is being led into sanctification. When the Bible speaks of the Spirit's leading, it's the Spirit leading us into holiness. Now I know that in contemporary Christian jargon and in our patterns of speech, we talk about being led by the Spirit as to whether we turn left or turn right at the stop sign, and whether we live in Omaha, Nebraska, or Saint Louis, Missouri. We are constantly looking for guidance as if God were still around with a pillar of cloud or a pillar of fire to direct our every step.

There have been times in redemptive history when God led his people visibly through signs and wonders and that type of thing. We know that in the book of Acts there were times when the Spirit directly communicated his will to the apostles to lead them from one nation to another. But the principal way by which the Christian life is to be led is by the Spirit's Book. The "lamp unto our feet" is the law of God. In other words, we are to be led by the principles for our behavior that God reveals. Some of those principles involve being responsible stewards and planners of the future.

On the one hand, Jesus said, "Take no thought for tomorrow—what you should eat, what you should drink, what you should put on," and all of that. But at the same time, Jesus encourages us to put our confidence in God's care for us on the morrow and to leave our anxieties behind. Jesus does not thereby teach that we ought not to set goals. On the contrary, in his parables he says, "What general before he goes into battle doesn't first get an intelligence report on the size of the enemy and the relative strength of the enemy before he moves into combat, or what builder doesn't first count the cost of construction before he begins his building?" That involves a kind of goal setting whereby we analyze the situation. We evaluate the merits and demerits of a given course of action and plan accordingly. Responsible living involves setting goals, goals that are consistent with biblical principles. I think what the Spirit leads us to do primarily is to live and to move toward the goals that God sets for our lives.

Paul put it this way: "Forgetting those things that are behind and reaching toward that which is ahead, we press toward the mark of the high calling which is in Christ Jesus." That's talking in the language of goals. Pressing toward the mark is pressing toward the purposes God has for our lives.

What does the Bible mean when it says we should wait upon the Lord?

Often we take this admonition in Scripture to mean that we are to postpone certain activities until we get some definite guidance or a concrete sign from God. The injunction to wait upon the Lord is given to the people of God at a particular point in history—to Israel in the Old Testament and to the church in the New Testament. In the Old Testament God promised to go before his people, and they were not to move their encampment until the signal was given by God. So that admonition is not to rush headlong into some enterprise until you know that God is in it.

In the New Testament we see Jesus' admonition to the

church to wait in Jerusalem before they set out to fulfill the great commission. He tells them to wait until the Holy Spirit has been poured out upon them. Once the Holy Spirit has been given to the church, then the church has its marching orders and it is to move out. So we have historical situations in which God is clearly in charge, giving direct and immediate guidance for his people.

Today, as twentieth-century Christians, our basic guidance comes from the teaching of Scripture, and we live by the principles that are revealed in the Scriptures. I think it's very important to search the Scriptures to make sure that what we are doing and what we are endeavoring to perform fits the patterns and the principles that God sets forth for us in Scripture. That is what I think it means to wait on God—not to wait for some special sign of endorsement, not to sit inactive, but to make sure that what we're doing fits biblical principles.

The firm I work for recently went through a long-range planning retreat, establishing goals for our firm. In doing that, I started revisiting the goals I have in my life and my career, and I'm really struggling and wondering how I can develop those goals in my life that meet what God has planned for me. How can I live my life in a way that best glorifies him?

The principle of setting goals, setting a mark to strive for, is a healthy thing and has plenty of biblical precedence. People who go wandering aimlessly without any defined goals tend to spin their wheels and get blown to and fro with every wind of doctrine. The very principle of goal setting, I think, is a godly one. But we have to qualify it. Of course, James tells us that we ought not to say with too much confidence that next year I'm going to do such and such, but we should always say, *"Deo volente,"* "God willing." As Paul said, "I planned to come; I had a goal to come and visit you, but I was providentially hindered. It was not possible for me to greet you, and God had other plans." Even the apostle Paul did not always know what God's plan was for his life, and that ought to tell us something.

We spend so much time trying to probe the secret counsel of God when, for all practical purposes, it is none of our business. While there are times when we need to know whether or not a certain thing is in God's approval, we can overdo this quest for God's counsel.

The number one thing that God wills for my life is my sanctification. What God calls me to is obedience. That's my goal. Now, how do I set goals for that? I set them in light of the principles that are set forth for me in Scripture, so that when I'm setting goals for my spiritual development and for my family's, when I'm setting them for my vocation, what I have to do is ask myself, *Are these goals in line with the principles of obedience that God has already revealed in his Word?*

What is pleasing to God is not that much of a mystery: He has given us page after page of instructions as to what pleases him. And so the ultimate goal of our lives is to be faithful in serving him. There is much latitude in the many specific goals we can attain—in career, in family, in hobbies—while following the goals for a godly life as set forth in Scripture.

If someone wanted to read three Christian books this year, which three would you most recommend?

I once did an essay for a Christian magazine dealing with the whole question of Christian publishing. I expressed in that the profound concern I have of the neglect in our day of the great, great works of the Christian classics. It seems that we're caught up in an economic problem in which people want very simple literature that they can digest quickly; they don't seem to be willing to chew on more difficult material. So, many of the Christian publishers and Christian bookstores will discourage either publishing or promoting the great Christian literature of the ages. I think that is to our shame, and it is also to our great loss. I would recommend if somebody was very serious about reading three books this year, that they read things like Calvin's *Institutes,* Martin Luther's *Bondage of the Will,* and maybe Athanasius's treatment of the incarnation of Christ, or something like Augustine's *City of God* or even *The Confessions of Saint Augustine.*

There are so many teachers in this world, and it seems that we're not all that fussy about whom we check out as our teachers. I don't want my body operated on by just any doctor. I want to know that the doctor knows his medicine and cares about me. When I look for theological teaching and instruction, I want to know that whoever is teaching me knows his stuff and loves God. Those are the two things I want to find in my teachers. That's awfully hard to know about people whose writing just comes up in meteoric rise and then passes from the scene. Maybe I'm just too traditional, but I like material that has passed the test of time and giants of the faith like Augustine and Athanasius and Aquinas and Calvin and Luther and Edwards. Those are the people whose products I would most endorse.

As I said in the essay, I would be perfectly willing to have all of my books burned and buried—put in the basement of the bookstores—if they were replaced by the great teachers, because all I am is a dwarf standing on the shoulders of giants, and I know that Jim Packer and Jim Boice and Charles Colson and Chuck Swindoll and other men whose books have been widely distributed among Christians would do the same thing, would gladly get rid of their books if we could persuade people to study the great masters.

How can I best prolong a useful Christian life as I grow older?

Behind that question is the pain of all kinds of people who have reached a certain age at which society tells them they are no longer able to contribute in a useful way. We have this rule that a person is to retire at age sixty-five. Now we do have exceptions—we've had presidents of the United States older than that. But somehow our society focuses on the young and seems to patronize at best those who are senior citizens.

We do know that with age come certain infirmities, and there are occasions on which people can no longer carry out the tasks they had been accustomed to performing in their earlier years. That does not mean that their usefulness in the kingdom of God comes to an end. In the Bible there is an emphasis on giving honor to the aged because honor is due them. I get very sentimental about it. I hardly ever see a person with gray hair without having a feeling of respect well up inside me because, if for no other reason, those people have endured, and they have survived. They may not even be Christians, but they've made it through life to a certain level. I saw a man like that the other day and I thought to myself, *I wonder how many times he's been to the dentist? I wonder how many times he's been under the surgeon's knife? I wonder how many tragedies he's witnessed and experienced in his family and in his life? Yet he is still being useful in our society.*

When I was teaching at a college, there was a man in that town who was a retired missionary. He had been on the mission field for fifty years. That's a long time. For fifty years he had poured himself out, body and soul. Five of those years he spent in a prison camp away from his wife, who was incarcerated in a different prison camp. And finally, when he was no longer able to serve on the mission field, he retired, so to speak. What he did until the day he died was get up every day and put in an eight-hour day of prayer. His body could hardly function, but he said, "I can still think, I can still speak, I can still pray." So he devoted himself to a ministry of prayer—eight hours a day. It was such that those of us who lived in that town knew no higher privilege than to have that man pray for us— because he knew how to pray, and he was an authentic prayer warrior. I ask you the question, Was his ministry useful? Probably the most useful years of his life were his later years in life, when he became a warrior of prayer.

I think the key to staying useful as we grow older is to concentrate, not on what we can no longer do, but on what we still can do. You never know when God has saved some of his best gifts and abilities for you until your later years. Some people spend much of their lives learning and gathering wisdom and during their later years are given the opportunity to compile and teach life lessons, whether through actual teaching or discipling, or through writing and speaking. Some of the people best suited to spend time listening and loving others are those who are no longer weighed down with careers and bringing up families. In God's wonderful economy, there is always work to do and love to give. But sometimes that work and love are not recognized in society's skewed view of things.

10

Understanding Satan

Be sober, be vigilant; because your adversary
the devil walks about like a roaring lion,
seeking whom he may devour.
Resist him, steadfast in the faith,
knowing that the same sufferings are
experienced by your brotherhood in the world.

I PETER 5:8-9

Questions in This Section:

In Isaiah 45:7 God says, "I form light and create darkness. I make peace and create evil." Why did he create Lucifer?

The Bible says that all power is given by God. How can we explain then the power that Satan and men such as Hitler have had in the past?

Has Satan been given dominion over the earth until Jesus returns?

In light of God's sovereignty, what should be the Christian's attitude or response when he or she is subject to the attacks of Satan?

Can the devil read my mind?

Why do we speak of Satan in such comical terms as a man in a red suit with a pitchfork when he is actually the enemy of our souls?

In Isaiah 45:7 God says, "I form light and create darkness. I make peace and create evil." Why did he create Lucifer?

Let me comment first on the text. That's one of the most misunderstood texts in the Bible, part of the problem being the Elizabethan English that's found in the old King James Version. The other part of the problem is in translation from the Hebrew. The Hebrew has about seven distinctive words that can be translated by the English word *evil*. There are all different kinds of evil. There's moral evil. There's what we would call metaphysical evil—finitude, for example. Whenever the Bible speaks of God bringing evil upon people, it is evil from their perspective. When the fires fell upon Sodom and Gomorrah, the people did not look upon that as a good thing. That was bad news. But it was ultimately good because it was an expression of God's judgment upon their wickedness. It was a punishment wrought by the hand of God upon evil. That doesn't mean that God did something wrong or something morally evil by visiting them with judgment.

This Isaiah text is also written in poetic form. It uses parallelism, a pattern of poetry common to Old Testament Judaism. There are even different types of parallelism.

An example occurs in the Lord's Prayer when Jesus says, "Lead us not into temptation, but deliver us from evil." Those two thoughts are parallel and they're basically synonymous; they are saying the same thing only with different words. We find that often in the Psalms.

In Isaiah 45 we have an example of two statements next to each other that are antithetical parallelisms. The first verse is "I create the light and the darkness." Light and darkness are opposites; they're contrasts, they are an antithesis one to another. That's why it's called antithetical parallelism.

The next statement has the same kind of antithesis, but how is the wording? "I make peace, I create evil." It doesn't ring true because peace and evil in our vocabulary are not antonyms, are they? Whereas light and dark are opposites, these are not. What the text is saying is that as God brings good things to bear in this world, he also brings about calamities in his judgment. It is not speaking about the original creation. It's unfortunate that that language persists in that particular translation.

Now, why did he create Lucifer? I don't know, but Lucifer was not created evil. We have to remember that Lucifer was created as an angel—who later rebelled against heaven.

The Bible says that all power is given by God. How can we explain then the power that Satan and men such as Hitler have had in the past?

God is saying not only that he is omnipotent, all powerful in and of himself but also that he is the fountainhead of all power and all authority in this world. And so the devil himself is subordinate and dependent upon God for any power or authority that he exercises in this world.

The question you're raising is not unlike the question

the prophet Habakkuk asked when he stood in his watch-tower and complained against God because he was watching a foreign nation, known for its unspeakable wickedness, attacking and slaughtering the Jewish people—God's own people. Habakkuk reminded God that God was too pure to even behold iniquity. How could God allow this alien power, this wicked power, to be used in such a fashion? God basically said, "Wait a minute, I have not used this enemy nation as an instrument to punish Israel because Israel is more wicked than this other nation. I'm just making use of this nation to chastise my own people who so richly deserve it. But this other nation will get theirs." That's why we have to be very careful about saying that God is always on our side. He may raise up China to punish the United States as an instrument of judgment against us—because all power is in his hands.

When I was studying in Europe back in the sixties, even though it was twenty years after the end of World War II, the bookstores in Amsterdam were filled with literature about the Second World War. The memories were still very vivid and keen to these people, who suffered so much more than we in this country suffered at that time. I remember reading a book that was a result of the release of earlier classified documents from the archives that was titled *Hitler, the Scourge of Europe,* in which private documents of Hitler's were photocopied and printed. One was an early entry from his diary, in which was scribbled in Hitler's own writing: "This evening I have made a covenant with Satan." He wasn't just kidding. There was a serious effort by Adolf Hitler to engage the assistance of the prince of darkness in the programs he set forth. Obviously that was all happening under the sovereignty of God. God has his reasons for allowing that to happen for a season, but obviously he reserves that moment when his powerful judgment falls on Satan and on people like Hitler, and God's righteous power is ultimately vindicated.

Has Satan been given dominion over the earth until Jesus returns? If so, why was he given this authority?

There's only one supreme Lord over all the world, and that's God. We are told in the Old Testament that this whole concept of dominion was shared with Adam and Eve. Man was given dominion over the earth to be vice-regents for God, that is, vice kings to represent God's reign on this planet. Of course, we made a terrible mess out of it, and we were subjected more and more to the power of Satan. That power of Satan was dealt not just a significant blow but a fatal blow by Christ in his incarnation.

We're told, first of all, that God the Father gives to Jesus all authority in heaven and on earth. In his ascension, Christ is seated at the right hand of God, where he is crowned as the King of kings and the Lord of lords. That was a tremendous blow to all worldly or satanic powers, principalities, and spiritual wickedness in high places. So if you ask me who is in dominion over this world right now, I think the New Testament is perfectly clear on that. The one who is in dominion is the Lord. The Lord God omnipotent reigns, and the Lord Christ reigns over this world right now. His kingdom may not be of this world, but it certainly includes this world, and Jesus has all authority over heaven and earth.

Even at this moment, as I'm discussing this question, Satan's authority and power are limited and subordinate to the authority that is vested in Christ. Christ right now is the king of this earth. His kingdom is invisible, and not everybody acknowledges it. People are giving more allegiance to the prince of darkness than to the Prince of Peace, but that is an act of usurpation on the part of Satan. His power is restricted, limited, and temporal. What has happened briefly is this: The power and authority of Satan has been dealt a fatal blow by Christ. The Cross, the Incarnation, the Resurrection, and the Ascension tremendously weakened any power or authority that Satan enjoyed, but it didn't annihilate him. That will come later, when Christ completes his work of redemption with the consummation of his kingdom. All things will be brought into captivity to him, and every knee will bow to him, including the fallen angels, who will bow in submission to his authority.

In light of God's sovereignty, what should be the Christian's attitude or response when he or she is subject to the attacks of Satan?

One of the difficulties for the Christian is to recognize an assault from Satan when it comes. Remember that Satan is an angelic being; he's a spirit being and he's invisible. It's not always easy to discern the presence of the enemy, although the New Testament warns us that the struggle in which we're involved is not against flesh and blood but against principalities and powers and spiritual wickedness in high places, including attacks from satanic sources.

Martin Luther felt the onslaught of Satan to such a degree sometimes in his own life that it was almost tangible. On one occasion at least, he picked up an inkwell and threw it across the room, allegedly at Satan. He couldn't really see the presence of Satan, but he was sure that he was experiencing the unbridled assault and oppression of the prince of darkness, the mortal enemy of all Christians. So one of the great problems, of course, is to know when this is happening.

The Bible warns us that Satan disguises himself as an angel of light; that is, he manifests himself under the auspices of good. Satan does not go about looking like some caricatured, grotesque person in a red flannel suit with horns and a pitchfork, but rather he's much more seductive and clever than that, appearing as the Scriptures tell us as an angel of light to deceive if possible even the elect of God. So we need to be aware of the subtleties of the one who is the prince of darkness and the prince of falsehood.

Satan is described as an accuser, a liar, and a tempter. We see him lying, distorting truth, we see him involved in temptation, and we see him accusing the saints.

Now, the Holy Spirit convicts us of sin so that we will recognize it and repent of it. If we're troubled about some sin, it could be the Holy Spirit's work, or it could be Satan accusing us. How do we know the difference? Basically we know that there's something sweet and positive about the conviction of the Holy Spirit. The Spirit's goal is to bring us to our senses. He humbles us, he brings us to a contrite heart, but he doesn't annihilate us. Satan seeks to drive us to despair. Our hopelessness and destruction are his goal, and one of his primary methods toward that goal is accusation. Scripture tells us in 1 Peter 5:8 that Satan goes about as a roaring lion seeking to devour whom he will. Yet the other image we get is of him fleeing with his tail between his legs when the Scriptures tell us that if we resist him, he will depart from us. Here we need the armor of God, the Word of God, and the application of that Word through the power of the Spirit, and we have the promise that Satan will flee.

Can the devil read my mind?

I am not certain by any means, nor do I have an exhaustive knowledge of the powers of Satan. I know that Satan has more power than one would normally find among human beings. At the same time, I know that Satan is not divine; he is not God, does not have divine powers or attributes. He is a creature with the limitations that are found normally with creatureliness. He is an angel.

The Bible doesn't give us an exhaustive list of the powers of angels. They are more powerful than people but far less powerful than God. Obviously God can read your mind. God is omniscient. He knows your thoughts as you think them—"There is not a word on my tongue, but behold, O Lord, You know it altogether" (Ps. 139:4). The tendency is for Christians to think that since God is a supernatural being and can read our minds, then Satan, also a supernatural being, must be able to read minds, too. But Satan's powers are not equal to God's.

A similar question would be, Can Satan be at more than one place at a time? I would be inclined to say no. I doubt that in my lifetime I will ever have to worry about Satan reading my mind, because I will probably never meet him.

He can only be in one place at one time. He's a creature, and creatures by definition are limited spatially and temporally. So Satan cannot be at more than one place at a time. He has all his little junior assistants, and he might send one of them to harass me and to tempt you and accuse you, but he's going to save his time and energy for people of greater influence than me.

Satan focused his assaults upon Jesus in the New Testament. In the Temptation he entered into dialogue with Jesus. He knew what Jesus was thinking because of what Jesus said. But other than that, I don't see any reason to believe that he could read your mind or read mine. Again, that may not necessarily be a divine power. He may be able to do it, but I have no reason to believe that he can.

Why do we depict Satan in such comical terms as a man in a red suit with a pitchfork when he is actually the enemy of our souls?

Obviously even a cursory reading of Scriptures indicates that such a view of Satan is foreign to the Bible. The Bible does not present Satan in comical garb at all but rather describes him as one who goes about masquerading as an angel of light. There's nothing foolish or frivolous about him. Under the disguise of goodness he counterfeits the good and can seduce people not only by his cleverness but also by his apparent beauty.

I think the last way we would ever expect Satan to appear would be in red, woolen, itchy underwear with cloven hooves and horns, a tail, and a pitchfork. Where did that description come from, and why do we have that image of

Satan in such a silly appearance? In the Middle Ages the people of God were very much concerned about the influence of Satan in their lives. They were earnest about trying to preserve their souls from their archenemy, who would try to destroy them. The church dealt in great detail with rites and rituals of exorcism and protection from evil spirits. They called upon certain angels, like Saint Michael, to protect the people from the attacks of Satan. They also came up with the idea that Satan's greatest point of vulnerability, the point that caused his fall from heaven in the first place, was his pride.

The Bible gives different images of Satan. It says that he goes about as a roaring lion seeking to devour those whom he will. Jesus said to Simon Peter, "Satan would have you and sift you like wheat." You get this image of the overwhelming power of Satan. Yet the other image that the Scriptures tell us is to "resist him and he will flee from you." So in my mind's eye I see this roaring lion who gives this ferocious snarl, but when you resist him, he runs down the street with his tail between his legs.

The church thought the best way to get rid of the assaults of Satan was to make fun of him, to insult his pride. They came up with these ludicrous caricatures in order to do that. What happened was that the next generation saw the caricatures and these grotesque cartoons and said that our fathers really believed that the devil was like this. Of course they didn't—they knew very well that the devil wasn't like that—but we have received the tradition without the explanation.

II

Heaven and Hell

The city had no need of the sun or of the moon to shine in it,
for the glory of God illuminated it. . . .
And the nations of those who are saved shall walk in its light,
and the kings of the earth bring their glory and honor into it. . . .
But there shall by no means enter it anything that defiles,
or causes an abomination or a lie, but only those who are
written in the Lamb's Book of Life.

REVELATION 21:23-24, 27

Questions in This Section:

Were the Old Testament saints confident of a personal afterlife?

Did the Old Testament "believing" Jews go to heaven, or was there a "waiting room" for them until Jesus' death and resurrection?

Does the Bible tell us what heaven will be like?

If heaven is the ultimate destination for the Christian, then why is it described so little in the Bible?

Are there gradations in heaven whereby one Christian, as a result of a lifetime of good works, has a higher rank or better quality of existence than someone who just squeaks through at his last breath?

Will we recognize each other in heaven?

What happens to animals when they die?

Is a person who has committed suicide ever able to enter heaven?

When a person dies, where does his or her spirit and body go until the Second Coming?

What happens to children who die before they can accept the gospel?

What about the millions of babies aborted each year in the United States; where will they spend eternity?

King Saul went to a sorcerer who conjured up the image of Samuel. Does this mean that people today could also conjure up the image of departed ones, or was this just a onetime act of God?

How do you explain the out-of-body, tunnellike experiences many people claim to have had before being revived?

What is the first thing you want to know when you get to heaven?

Are those who have never heard of Christ going to hell?

Would you describe hell as you see it, and conversely heaven?

Were the Old Testament saints confident of a personal afterlife?

Some forms of contemporary Judaism do not include a belief in life after death. We know that in Jesus' day there was a great debate over that point between two parties of the contemporary Jewish nation, the Pharisees and the Sadducees. The Pharisees believed in life after death; the Sadducees did not. You would think that those who were leaders in the household of Israel would be agreed on a point like that if it were spelled out with obvious clarity in the Old Testament.

Of course, one of the debates between those two parties was what constituted the Old Testament. Was it just the first five books of Moses, or did it include all of what today's Christian would consider to be the Old Testament—the Prophets and the Wisdom Literature? The concept of life after death in the Old Testament (indicated often by references to Sheol) is somewhat vague and shadowy; death is depicted as a place beyond the grave where both good and bad people go. The clarity with which the New Testament proclaims life after death is not found in the same dimension in the Old Testament. I think it's there, and if you study the Major Prophets, particularly Isaiah, you will see that the teaching of life after death is clearly set forth in the Old Testament. However, I'm looking at the Old Testament with the benefit of the information coming to me through the New Testament.

Certainly there were lots of folks who read the same Old Testament material and didn't see references to afterlife so clearly. During Job's struggle with earthly trials, he asked, "If a man dies, will he live again?" We see later that Job says in a note of triumph and as an expression of confidence and faith, "I know that my Redeemer liveth, and I will see him standing on that day." Christians have looked back at that and said, "Well, if Job is that confident of a redeemer who will set him free in some distant future, then obviously this is an expression from great antiquity of confidence in life after death." But Job's word that is translated "redeemer" actually means "vindicator." Job is simply saying that he is confident he will be vindicated. Now, whether or not that included in Job's mind an ultimate vindication in heaven is again subject to some debate.

David's confidence, however, of future reunion with his child who had died is a clear indication of his confidence in an afterlife. It was not unknown among the Old Testament saints that there would be a future life. It simply is not as clear as it is in the New Testament.

Did the Old Testament "believing" Jews go to heaven, or was there a "waiting room" for them until Jesus' death and resurrection?

On the one hand, Old Testament teaching on the afterlife is somewhat vague. We hear the use of the word *Sheol*, which seems to incorporate both the negative and positive elements of life after death. We certainly find more clear references to heaven in the New Testament, but many passages in the Old Testament, including some of David's psalms and parts of the book of Isaiah, call attention to the reality of heaven.

Did faithful people of that time go to heaven or to a waiting place? The Roman Catholic Church has the doctrine of limbo we've heard about, mainly with respect to babies. The broader concept included the "limbo of the fathers"— a place where people in the Old Testament who died in faith had to go and wait until Christ accomplished his work of redemption on the cross.

There's a link between that view, which is held in many circles, and the very cryptic reference in Peter's writings about what happened to Jesus after he died—that he went and preached to the spirits in prison (1 Pet. 3:19). Some people interpret "the spirits in prison" to mean the Old Testament saints who were being held captive until the work of Christ's redemption was completed. He released them to enter into paradise with him. Jesus was the "first-born from the dead"; he went first to the place of the dead and led out the captives, bringing these people into their state of future glory.

I'm inclined to think that Old Testament saints had immediate access to paradise because heaven itself is called "the bosom of Abraham" in the New Testament. That's not a likely descriptive term for heaven if it's some place from which Abraham was absent.

Also, based theologically on our doctrine of redemption, I think that Paul teaches in Romans 3 and 4 that salvation occurs exactly the same way in the Old Testament as it does in the New Testament—through faith. The only difference is that Old Testament faith was in a future promise that had not yet been fulfilled. The people believed, and when they believed, they were justified and counted worthy to be in the presence of God. In the New Testament we look backward to a work that is accomplished. We know that the Old Testament sacrifices had no efficacy in and of themselves; they represented the future work of Jesus, who ultimately paid for all sin. Since salvation comes to us on the basis of the merits of Christ, I see nothing that would prevent God from opening the gates of heaven prior to the Cross, even though he does it in light of the Cross.

Does the Bible tell us what heaven will be like?

When I was in seminary, I studied under an extremely learned professor who I was convinced at the time knew the answer to every possible theological question. I remember I was so in awe of him that I asked him one day with stars in my eyes, "What's heaven like?" I asked him as if he had been there and could give me a firsthand report! Of course, he steered me immediately to the last two chapters of the New Testament, Revelation 21 and 22, in which we get an extensive visual image of what heaven is like. Some dismiss it as being pure symbolism, but we must remember that the symbols in the New Testament point beyond themselves to a deeper and better reality than they themselves describe. It's here that we read of the streets of gold and of the great treasuries of jewels that adorn the New Jerusalem that comes down from heaven.

In the description of the New Jerusalem, we hear that there's no sun and no moon, no stars, because the light that radiates from the presence of God and from his Anointed One is sufficient to illumine the whole place by the refulgence of their glory. We are told that there's no death, there's no pain, and God wipes away the tears of his people.

I remember as a child having that tender experience (not often accessible to adults) in which I would scrape my knee, or something would go wrong, and I would cry and come into the house, and my mother would stoop over and dry the tears from my eyes. I received great consolation from that. But of course, when my mother dried my tears, there was always the opportunity the next day for me to cry again. But in heaven when God wipes away the tears from people's eyes, that's the end of tears—there are no more tears after that. And so heaven is described as a place of utter felicity that is filled with the radiant majesty and glory of God, where God's people have become sanctified, where justice has been brought to bear, and where his people have been vindicated. There's no more death, no more disease, no more sorrow, no more sickness, no more hatred, and no more evil. And then there is an experience of healing in that place. And that's just a glimpse, but it's enough to get us started.

If heaven is the ultimate destination for the Christian, then why is it described so little in the Bible?

I'm not sure heaven is described as little as we may think. We sometimes get the feeling that there's not much in there about heaven, but if we examine the Scripture text, we'll find a wealth of material that speaks on that subject— particularly in the New Testament teachings of Jesus, as well as from the book of Revelation. Maybe there's not as

much in there about heaven as we would like to find. Since
it is the ultimate destination of the Christian, you'd think
there would be a bit more spelled out about the nature of
heaven.

As it is depicted in the Scriptures, heaven represents a
radical change from what we experience in this world. In
other words, there is a tremendous amount of discontinuity between the life I live on this earth and what awaits me
in heaven. Anytime you have discontinuity between experiences, the only way you can speak meaningfully about
them is through some sort of analogy. We've never experienced this different life that is called heaven. It's very difficult to discuss something we've never experienced. That's
why I think the Bible uses analogies. The writers will say
heaven is like this or that because they are trying to find
some meaningful reference point in this present world
that will speak to us about that which "eye has not seen,
nor ear has heard, nor has entered in the heart of man."
It is that which transcends our ability to anticipate.

Sometimes we learn about something by finding out
what it's not. For example, in Revelation the Bible tells us
that in heaven there is no crying, there's no pain, no
death, no sorrow, no darkness. On the one hand, I can't
conceive of what life would be without any of those things;
yet at the same time I have some idea of the difference
between light and darkness, peace and warfare, joy and
sorrow, and so on. I think the main reason we're not given
more information is that we are so limited in our ability to
anticipate that which is so much greater than we can even
imagine in this world.

Are there gradations in heaven whereby one Christian, as a result of a lifetime of good works, has a higher rank or better quality of existence in heaven than someone who just squeaks through at his last breath?

This may come as a surprise to many people, but I would answer that question with an emphatic yes. There are degrees of reward that are given in heaven. I'm surprised that this answer surprises so many people. I think there's a reason Christians are shocked when I say there are various levels of heaven as well as gradations of severity of punishment in hell.

We owe much of this confusion to the Protestant emphasis on the doctrine of justification by faith alone. We hammer away at that doctrine, teaching emphatically that a person does not get to heaven through his good works. Our good works give us no merit whatsoever, and the only way we can possibly enter heaven is by faith in Christ, whose merits are imputed to us. We emphasize this doctrine to the extent that people conclude good works are insignificant and have no bearing at all upon the Christian's future life.

The way historic Protestantism has spelled it out is that the only way we get into heaven is through the work of Christ, but we are promised rewards in heaven *according to our works.* Saint Augustine said that it's only by the grace of God that we ever do anything even approximating a good work, and none of our works are good enough to demand that God reward them. The fact that God has decided to grant rewards on the basis of obedience or disobedience is what Augustine called God's crowning his own works within us. If a person has been faithful in many things through many years, then he will be acknowledged by his Master, who will say to him, "Well done, thou good and faithful servant." The one who squeaks in at the last moment has precious little good works for which he can expect reward.

I think the gap between tier one and tier ten in heaven is infinitesimal compared to the gap in getting there or not getting there at all. Somebody put it this way: Everybody's cup in heaven is full, but not everybody in heaven has the same size cup. Again, it may be surprising to people, but I'd say there are at least twenty-five occasions where the New Testament clearly teaches that we will be granted rewards according to our works. Jesus frequently holds out the reward motif as the carrot in front of the horse—"great will be your reward in heaven" if you do this or that. We are called to work, to store up treasures for ourselves in heaven, even as the wicked, as Paul tells us in Romans, "treasure up wrath against the day of wrath."

Will we recognize each other in heaven?

No specific biblical reference declares explicitly that we will recognize each other. But the implicit teaching of Scripture is so overwhelming that I don't think there's really any doubt that we will be able to recognize each other in heaven. There is an element of discontinuity between this life and the life to come: We're going to be changed in the twinkling of an eye; we'll have a new body, and the old will pass away. Nevertheless, the Christian view of life after death is not like the Eastern view of annihilation, in which we lose our personal identities in some kind of a sea of forgetfulness. Even though there is this element of discontinuity, replacing the old with the new, there's a strong element of continuity in that the individual person will continue to live on into eternity.

Part of what it means to be an individual person is to be involved in personal relationships. In fact, one of the articles of the Apostles' Creed is that we say we believe in the communion of the saints. That affirmation does not apply only to the fellowship that we enjoy with each other now, but it indicates a communion that all people who are in Christ have with one another. Even now, in this world, I mystically enter into communion with Martin Luther and John Calvin and Jonathan Edwards, who are part of the whole company of saints. There's no reason to expect that this communion will cease.

When we enter into a better level of communion with Christ and with those who are in Christ, we would think that communion would naturally intensify rather than diminish.

Although you have to be careful about how much you draw out of a parable, Jesus' parable about the rich man and Lazarus does give us an inside look at the afterlife. He talks about a rich man who had everything going for him in this world and a poor man who was a beggar at the rich man's gates. The rich man ignored the pleas of the poor man. Both of them died, and the poor man, Lazarus, was carried to the bosom of Abraham, whereas the rich man was in the outer darkness. But even there this one who was presumably in hell was able to see across the unbridgeable chasm to the bosom of Abraham and see the state of felicity this beggar was now enjoying. He pleaded with Abraham, crying across the gulf, to have mercy and to let him have the power to go back to earth or to send a message back to warn his own brothers lest they fell into the judgment he had fallen into. Of course, Jesus says it's too late at that point. At least in the parable there is recognition of the persons involved and also recognition of where people are and where they aren't.

What happens to animals when they die? I know that some people get very attached to them.

I can't answer that question for sure, but I don't want you to think for a minute that it's a frivolous question. People do get very attached to their pets, particularly if the pet has been with them for a long time. In our present culture more and more pet cemeteries are appearing, and we see people going to great expense and ceremony—gravestones and all—to dispose of the bodies of their pets.

Within the Christian church there are different schools of thought on this issue. Some people believe that animals simply disintegrate; they pass into nothingness and are annihilated, which is based on the premise that animals don't have souls that can survive the grave. However, nowhere does Scripture explicitly state that animals do not have souls.

The Bible tells us that we have the image of God in a way that animals do not. Now is the "image of God" what differentiates between a soul and a nonsoul? Those who take a Greek view of the soul—that it is this substance that continues indestructibly forever—may want to restrict that to human beings. But again, there's nothing in Scripture I know of that would preclude the possibility of animals' continued existence.

The Bible does give us some reason to hope that departed animals will be restored. We read in the Bible that redemption is a cosmic matter. The whole creation is destined to be redeemed through the work of Christ (Rom. 8:21), and we see the images of what heaven will be like; beautiful passages of Scripture tell us about the lion and the lamb and other animals being at peace with one another. Whenever heaven is described, though it may be in highly imaginative language, it is a place where animals seem to be present. Whether these are animals newly created for the new heavens and the new earth, or they are the redeemed souls of our pets that have perished, we can't know for sure.

All of this is sheer speculation, but I would like to think that we will see our beloved pets again someday as they participate in the benefits of the redemption that Christ has achieved for the human race.

Is a person who has committed suicide ever able to enter heaven?

I think it is possible for a person who has committed suicide to go to heaven. I say that for several reasons. Psychiatrists have studied people who have made serious attempts to take their own lives but failed in the process. When interviewed afterwards, the vast majority of these people (90 percent, according to the psychiatrists) said that they would not have committed suicide had they waited twenty-four hours. So often the act of suicide is a surrender to an overwhelming but momentary attack of acute depression. We really don't know the last thoughts that go through a person's mind before he or she dies. Suppose a man decides to end his life and he jumps off a thirty-story building, and at the sixteenth story he's thinking, *This is a mistake; I shouldn't do this.* Obviously, there's room in the grace of God for that man's final repentance from that sin.

Even though the Scriptures are very clear that we are not to take our own lives, I know of nothing in Scripture that identifies suicide as the unforgivable sin. Now, if a person is ending his or her life in the full possession of their faculties, this act may represent a final and absolute act of unbelief, a surrender to despair and hopelessness rather than a confidence in the living God. However, I don't think we can assume that this is the mental state of everyone who actually commits suicide.

Some people who attempt suicide are not in a sober state of thinking and not culpable for their behavior at the last moment. Since the Bible is relatively silent about that, I don't like to jump to conclusions. I would prefer to rest our hope for such cases in the grace and the kindness of God.

When a person dies, where does his or her spirit and body go until the Second Coming?

Throughout its history, the church has struggled with the concept of what is called the "intermediate state"—our position between the time we die and the time Christ consummates his kingdom and fulfills the promises that we confess in the Apostles' Creed. We believe in the resurrection of the body. We believe there will be a time when God reunites our soul and our body, and that we will have a glorified body even as Christ came out of the tomb as the "firstborn from the dead." In the meantime, what happens?

The most common view has been that, at death, the soul immediately goes to be with God and there is a continuity of personal existence. There is no interruption of life at the end of this life, but we continue to be alive in our personal souls upon death.

There are those who have been influenced by a cultic view called *psychopannychia,* more famously known as soul sleep. The idea is that at death the soul goes into a state of suspended animation. It remains in slumber, in an unconscious state, until it is awakened at the time of the great resurrection. The soul is still alive, but it is unconscious, so that there is no consciousness of the passing of time. I think this conclusion is drawn improperly from the euphemistic way in which the New Testament speaks about people in death being asleep. The common Jewish expression that they are "asleep" means they are enjoying the reposed, peaceful tranquility of those who have passed beyond the struggles of this world and into the presence of God.

But the overall teaching of Scripture, even in the Old Testament, where the bosom of Abraham was seen as the place of the afterlife, there is this persistent notion of continuity. Paul put it this way: To live in this world is good; the greatest thing that can ever happen is to be participating in the final resurrection. But the intermediate state is even better. Paul said that he was caught between two things.

On the one hand, his desire was to depart and be with Christ, which is far better, and on the other hand, he had a desire to remain alive and continue his ministry on this earth. But the apostle's judgment that the passing beyond the veil of death to that intermediate state is far better than this one gives us a clue, along with a host of other passages. Jesus said to the thief on the cross, "I say to you, today you shall be with me in paradise." The image of Dives and Lazarus in the New Testament (Luke 16:19-31) indicates to me that there is a continuity of life and of consciousness in that intermediate state.

What happens to children who die before they can accept the gospel?

In my own theological tradition, we believe that those children of believers who die in infancy are numbered among the redeemed. That is to say, we hope and have a certain level of confidence that God will be particularly gracious toward those who have never had the opportunity to be exposed to the gospel, such as infants or children who are too disabled to hear and understand.

The New Testament does not teach us this explicitly. It does tell us a lot about the character of God—about his mercy and his grace—and gives us every reason to have that kind of confidence in his dealings with children. Some will make a distinction between infants in general and those who are children of believers, the reason being that when God made a covenant with Abraham, he made it not only with Abraham, but with Abraham's descendants. In fact, as soon as God entered into that relationship with

Abraham, he brought Isaac into it—when Isaac was still an infant and didn't have an understanding of what was going on. This is the reason, incidentally, that a large number of Christian bodies practice the baptism of infants; they believe that children of believers are to be incorporated into full membership in the church. We see this relationship within the family in biblical history.

We also see David's situation in the Old Testament when his infant child dies. Yet David is given the confidence that he will see that child again in heaven. That story of David and his dying child gives a tremendous consolation to parents who have lost infants to death.

Now the point that we have to make is that infants who die are given a special dispensation of the grace of God; it is not by their innocence but by God's grace that they are received into heaven. There are great controversies that hover over the doctrine of original sin. Lutherans disagree with Roman Catholics, who disagree in turn with Presbyterians, etc., on the scope and extent of what we call original sin. Original sin does not refer to the first sin that was committed, but rather to the result of that—the entrance of sin into the world so that all of us as human beings are born in a fallen state. We come into this world with a sin nature, and so the baby that dies, dies as a sinful child. And when that child is received into heaven, he is received by grace.

What about the millions of babies aborted each year in the United States; where will they spend eternity?

You are asking a question that the Christian church has been seriously divided over throughout its history for several reasons. There's little information in Scripture that speaks about it directly. The Roman Catholic Church has its traditional doctrine of limbo, and limbo is of two varieties. There is the limbo for Old Testament people who died before the coming of Christ, and then there's limbo for infants. Here, limbo is defined as sort of a lesser corridor of hell. It's not heaven, but the historic definition is that it's where the fires of judgment do not reach. The unbaptized babies are assigned to that place, where they lose the blessings of heaven but don't actually participate in the punishments of hell.

Protestant churches differ on what happens to babies that die. Some distinguish between those who are baptized and those who are not. In my denomination, we hold as an article of faith that the children of believers are given a special dispensation of grace and are taken to heaven, not because they are innocent, but because they are recipients of grace.

Are unborn children the same as babies? Again, the controversy there is whether or not these unborn fetuses are, in fact, considered by God to be human lives. Some take the position that an aborted baby is a real human person, and it would seem consistent to say that whatever you think happens to babies who die in infancy would then, therefore, apply to unborn children. My personal belief is that unborn babies who die through abortion are treated as human beings by God and that the same grace he dispenses to babies who die in infancy would apply to unborn children. That doesn't depend on whether the abortion is intentional or unintentional. The term *abortion* is also a term we use to describe a miscarriage. My wife has had four miscarriages, and we fully hope and expect to see

those unborn children in heaven with us. We assume that
we have six children and not only two, and we're looking
forward to a reunion with the children that we've never
been able to know personally.

**King Saul went to a sorcerer who conjured up the
image of Samuel. Does this mean that people today
could also conjure up the image of departed ones, or
was this just a onetime act of God?**

I don't think it was an act of God. Just recently, incidentally, I wrote a chapter in a book on that whole question of
the witch of Endor because it's such a provocative and difficult piece of Scripture to deal with. This narrative tells us
that after the death of Samuel, Saul disguised himself and
sought out a medium. Such mediums were outlawed in
Israel, and the practice of this kind of activity was a capital
offense. Not only was it a capital offense under the Mosaic
law, but Saul himself had enforced this and insisted that all
necromancers leave the land. That's why Saul disguised
himself. He went to this witch, or medium, and asked her
to conjure up Samuel. The text says that Samuel appeared
and complained about being disturbed. The woman then
realized that it was the king who had induced her to do
this, and she was terrified.

When I look at that, I have to ask this question: What
really happened there? Is the Bible speaking in phenomenological language, describing what appeared, or does the
Bible intend to say that the medium was in fact able to
bring Samuel back from the dead? Was it the clever trick of
a magician? Was it a natural ability, one that some people

may have today? Is it possible today to contact the dead, or is it a counterfeit activity of Satan himself? I'm not altogether sure which of these, if any, explain the situation.

Let me say what we know for sure. If we can contact the dead today and conjure them up as you say, we're certainly not allowed to. There's no question about that. This is a radical offense to God. We're simply not permitted to be involved in séances, in spiritualism, or in the use of mediums. That is anathema to God, and in fact, people who do that are included in the final chapter of the New Testament as those who are excluded from the kingdom of God. The warnings are severe and weighty about being involved in these kinds of activities.

But—is it possible? I don't think so. I don't think we can call forth the spirits of the dead. I believe all mediums resort to trickery to perform these feats. In the late nineteenth century, Sir Arthur Conan Doyle got enamored with the possibility, and the great Harry Houdini offered a large sum of money to any medium who could make any phenomenon occur that he couldn't duplicate with his own art of illusion. No one ever collected the money from Houdini. The best "ghost busters" are magicians themselves. It takes a thief to know a thief. I'm persuaded that the people who are practicing this are hoaxers.

How do you explain the out-of-body tunnellike experiences many people claim to have had before being revived?

I'm not sure I can explain the so-called Kübler-Ross phenomenon. There's been a significant amount of research on this.

I've heard reports saying that as many as 50 percent of those who have suffered clinical death and have been resuscitated through CPR or forms of medication report some kind of a strange experience that may be called an out-of-body experience. They report the sensation of looking down from the ceiling as their soul is leaving the body and seeing their own body lying in the bed and the doctor pronouncing them dead or a nurse not finding a pulse. Then they talk about going through this tunnel and seeing this marvelous light. The vast majority of those who have been researched have a very positive recollection, although there are some who don't see lovely lights at the end of the tunnel but very ghastly and horrendous things that gave them pause about what might be beyond the veil.

I don't know how to answer these questions. There are various possible answers. One could be that a person who is near death can have a short circuit in the electrical nervous system of their brain and can get their time sequences all messed up. They could be recalling a dream that was very vivid and intense that makes them feel as if they really lived it. All of us have some dreams that are qualitatively different from others, that become so intense that you feel as if it had actually happened. It could be the result of medication or the lack of oxygen to the brain.

To deal sufficiently with those possible explanations would require a competent physician who can talk about whether it's possible for such short circuits to take place and whether it could be explained in natural terms. I haven't ruled out the experience.

The other possible explanation is that people do, in fact, have a glimpse of something that's about to take place in transition from death to wherever we go after death. We as Christians do believe that we have a continuity of personal existence and that the cessation of physical life is not the end of actual life. Whether we're good or bad, whether we're redeemed or unredeemed, we're going to continue in a living state though not biologically alive. It shouldn't shock the Christian when people undergoing clinical death and being revived come back with certain recollections. I've tried to keep an open mind, and I hope that this interesting phenomenon will get the benefit of further research, analysis, and evaluation. Too many of these experiences have been reported for us to simply dismiss them as imaginary or hoaxes.

What is the first thing you want to know when you get to heaven?

Of course, the first thing I want to know is, What do I have to do to see Jesus? I want to see the Lord. In the past I've asked friends and family members, "Suppose that after you got the chance to see Jesus in heaven he said, 'OK, you can see any three people who are here and spend time one-on-one with those people'—who would you want to see?" The first person I would want to see would be my father. This is one of the great consolations of the Christian faith—we have the promise of reunion with those whom we love who have gone ahead of us. After seeing my father, I'd love to meet the psalmist David. I'd love to meet Jeremiah. And the list goes on.

One of the first questions I am going to ask is, "Who wrote the book of Hebrews?" I'm dying to find that out!

Another question: "Where did evil come from?" because I haven't been able to figure that one out. And, of course, I would have to know, "Are there any golf courses up here?" I'd like to study art for the first ten thousand years, music for the next ten thousand years, and literature for the next ten thousand years and just continue to soak in everything that God has made and everything he has ordained. I'd love to sit there and learn theology with the full assurance that I am never being deceived or that I'm not making any errors and that I'm no longer looking through a glass darkly, but now I am in the presence of Truth itself, in all of its purity. But I suspect that those things that I think about doing will have to wait for the sheer joy of being in the presence of God and enjoying the beatific vision—of seeing Christ face-to-face. I don't know if that would ever wear off. I'd be satisfied to just do that, I think, for eternity.

Are those who have never heard of Christ going to hell?

That's one of the most emotionally laden questions that a Christian can ever be asked. Nothing is more terrifying or more awful to contemplate than that any human being would go to hell. On the surface, when we ask a question like that, what's lurking there is, "How could God ever possibly send some person to hell who never even had the opportunity to hear of the Savior? It just doesn't seem right."

I would say the most important section of Scripture to study with respect to that question is the first chapter of Paul's letter to the Romans. The point of the book of

Romans is to declare the Good News—the marvelous story
of redemption that God has provided for humanity in
Christ, the riches and the glory of God's grace, the extent
to which God has gone to redeem us. But when Paul intro-
duces the gospel, he begins in the first chapter by declaring that the wrath of God is revealed from heaven and this
manifestation of God's anger is directed against a human
race that has become ungodly and unrighteous. So the reason for God's anger is anger against evil. God's not angry
with innocent people; he's angry with guilty people. The
specific point for which they are charged with evil is in the
rejection of God's self-disclosure.

Paul labors the point that from the very first day of creation and through the creation, God has plainly manifested his eternal power and being and character to every
human being on this planet. In other words, every human
being knows that there is a God and that he is accountable
to God. Yet every human being disobeys God. Why does
Paul start his exposition of the gospel at that point? What
he's trying to do, and what he develops in the book of
Romans, is this: Christ is sent into a world that is already
on the way to hell. Christ is sent into the world that is lost,
that is guilty of rejecting the Father whom they do know.

Now, let's go back to your original question, "Does God
send people to hell who have never heard of Jesus?" God
never punishes people for rejecting Jesus if they've never
heard of Jesus. When I say that, people breathe a sigh of
relief and say, "Then we'd better not tell anybody about
Jesus because somebody might reject him. Then they're
really in deep trouble." But again, there are other reasons
to go to hell. To reject God the Father is a very serious

thing. And no one will be able to say on the last day, "I didn't know that you existed," because God has revealed himself plainly. Now the Bible makes it clear that people desperately need Christ. God may grant his mercy unilaterally at some point, but I don't have any reason to have much hope in that. I think we have to pay serious attention to the passionate command of Christ to go to the whole world, to every living creature, and tell them of Jesus.

Would you describe hell as you see it, and conversely heaven?

I was once asked that question by a student who put it to me this way, "Do you believe that hell is a literal lake of fire, where people are burning and in torment? Do you think there's weeping and gnashing of teeth, darkness, and a place where the worm never dies?" He asked if I believed hell was literally like that, and I said no, I didn't. He breathed a heavy sigh of relief. Then I said that I thought a person who is in hell would do everything in his power to be in a lake of fire rather than to be where he is. I really have no graphic picture of hell in my mind, but I can't think of any concept more terrifying to the human consciousness than that concept. I know that it's a very unpopular concept and that even Christians shrink in horror at the very idea of a place called hell.

I've always wondered about two phenomena that we find in the New Testament. One, that Jesus speaks more of hell than he does of heaven. Two, almost everything that we know about hell in the New Testament comes from the lips of Jesus. I'm just guessing that in the economy of God, people wouldn't bear it from any other teacher. They're not going to listen if R. C. Sproul warns them of the dreadful consequences of hell or if some other person does. People don't believe in it even when Jesus teaches it. It's like we're proving the parable of the rich man and Lazarus. Dives wanted to go back and warn his brothers of the wrath that was to come. Jesus said they wouldn't believe even if somebody came back from the dead. People just don't want to pay any attention to it.

I ask myself this question: Why did Jesus, when he was teaching about the nature of hell, use the most ghastly symbols and images he could think of to describe that place? Whenever we talk about symbols or images, we use a symbol to represent a reality. The reality always exceeds in its substance what the symbol contains. If the images of the New Testament view of hell are but images and symbols, then that would mean to me that the reality is much, much worse than the literal symbols we are given.

Conversely, I would say that the good news is the marvelous images we have of heaven: streets of gold, crystal lakes, a city with buildings of precious stones. The literal fulfillment would be dazzling and wonderful, but I would think that it's going to be incomparably greater. Again, in this case, the reality will far exceed the images that the Bible uses to communicate to us, who are limited to an earthly perspective.

12

Sharing the Faith

———

Go therefore and make disciples of all the nations,
baptizing them in the name of the Father and of the Son
and of the Holy Spirit, teaching them to
observe all things that I have commanded you;
and lo, I am with you always, even to the end of the age.

MATTHEW 28:19-20

Questions in This Section:

What is faith?

Is the Christian faith really rational?

Is evangelism a necessary activity for a Christian?

What makes Christianity—and not Buddhism or Hinduism or others—the right religion?

How can you present the gospel to a friend or family member who might be an atheist?

How can I tell others about Jesus in a manner that is nonthreatening yet convincing?

My father is not a Christian, and whenever I talk to him, he doesn't listen, no matter what I talk to him about. What should I do about it?

If a non-Christian asks a question regarding morals, should we immediately and specifically refer to the Bible, or should we just give them our advice based on scriptural principles?

Is it possible for a person to be in a state of regeneration before they come to faith?

How should I respond to street preachers?

What is faith?

I think the whole concept of faith is one of the most misunderstood ideas that we have, misunderstood not only by the world but by the church itself. The very basis for our redemption, the way in which we are justified by God, is through faith. The Bible is constantly talking to us about faith, and if we misunderstand that, we're in deep trouble.

The great issue of the Protestant Reformation in the sixteenth century was, How is a person justified? Luther's controversial position was that we are justified by faith alone. When he said that, many of the godly leaders in the Roman Catholic Church were very upset. They said, "Does that mean that a person can just believe in Jesus and then live any way they want to live?" In other words, the Roman Catholic Church reacted fiercely because they were afraid that Luther's view would be understood as an easy-believism in which a person only had to believe and never had to be concerned about bringing forth the fruits of righteousness. It was crucial that those who were involved in the Protestant Reformation carefully define what they meant by saving faith. So they went back and did their studies in the New Testament, specifically on the Greek word *pistein,* which means "to believe," and they were able to isolate three distinctive aspects of biblical faith.

The first is the Latin term *notitia:* "believing in the data" or the information. It's an intellectual awareness. You can't have faith in nothing; there has to be content to the faith.

You have to believe *something* or trust *someone*. When we say
that a person is saved by faith, some people say, "It doesn't
matter what you believe, just as long as you are sincere."
That's not what the Bible teaches. It matters profoundly
what you believe. What if I believed that the devil was God?
That wouldn't save me. I must believe the right information.

The second aspect of faith is what they call *assensus,* or
intellectual assent. I must be persuaded of the truthfulness
of the content. According to James, even if I am aware of
the work of Jesus—convinced intellectually that Jesus is the
Son of God, that he died on the cross for my sins, and that
he rose from the dead—I would at that point qualify to be a
demon. The demons recognize Jesus, and the devil himself
knows the truth of Christ, but he doesn't have saving faith.

The crucial, most vital element of saving faith in the
biblical sense, is that of personal trust. The final term is
fiducia, referring to a fiduciary commitment by which I put
my life in the lap of Jesus. I trust him and him alone for my
salvation. That is the crucial element, and it includes the
intellectual and the mental. But it goes beyond it to the
heart and to the will so that the whole person is caught up
in this experience we call faith.

Is the Christian faith really rational?

By all means! It is intensely rational. Now, I've had the
question asked of me, "Is it true that you are a Christian
rationalist?" I said, "By no means! That's a contradiction in
terms. A rationalist is somebody who embraces a philosophy that sets itself over and against Christianity." And so,

while a true Christian is not a rationalist, the Christian faith is certainly rational.

Is Christianity coherent? Is it intelligible? Does it makes sense? Does it fit together in a consistent pattern of truth, or is it the opposite of rational—is it irrational? Does it indulge in superstition and embrace Christians who believe that Christianity is manifestly irrational? I think that's a great tragedy. The God of Christianity addresses people's minds. He speaks to us. We have a Book that is written for our understanding.

When I say that Christianity is rational, I do not mean that the truth of Christianity in all of its majesty can be deduced from a few logical principles by a speculative philosopher. There is much information about the nature of God that we can find only because God himself chooses to reveal it to us. He reveals these things through his prophets, through history, through the Bible, and through his only begotten Son, Jesus.

But what he reveals is intelligible; we can understand it with our intellect. He doesn't ask us to throw away our minds in order to become Christians. There are people who think that to become a Christian, one must leave one's brain somewhere in the parking lot. The only leap that the New Testament calls us to make is not into the darkness but out of the darkness into the light, into that which we can indeed understand. That is not to say that everything the Christian faith speaks of is manifestly clear with respect to rational categories. I can't understand, for example, how a person can have a divine nature and a human nature at the same time, which is what we believe about Jesus. That's a mystery—but mysterious is not the same as irrational.

Mystery doesn't apply only to religion. I don't understand the ultimate force of gravity. These things are mysterious to us, but they're not irrational. It's one thing to say, "I don't understand from my finite mind how these things work out," and it's another thing to say, "They're blatantly contradictory and irrational, but I'm going to believe them anyway." That's not what Christianity does. Christianity says that there are mysteries, but those mysteries cannot be articulated in terms of the irrational; if that were so, then we have moved away from Christian truth.

Is evangelism a necessary activity for a Christian?

Some people argue that it is every Christian's duty to do the work of an evangelist. I'm not sure. The distinctive work of an evangelist is to proclaim the gospel. Preaching and proclamation comprise one of the offices in the New Testament and one of the gifts of the Spirit, and so on. This gift is not given to everybody, and so I would say that, in the technical sense, it is not every Christian's responsibility to be an evangelist.

The New Testament does make it clear that every Christian is to be a *witness*. Some of the confusion enters at this point because in Christian jargon "witness" is often used as a synonym for "evangelist." The New Testament makes a clear distinction between the two words, a distinction between the general and the particular. "Witness" is the broad statement. To bear witness to something is to make something visible that is not readily visible, or not manifest, but invisible. The New Testament word for "witness" is *martyria,* which is the word from which we get the English word *martyr.* Those who died for the faith bore witness, or made manifest, their commitment to Christ. That was one way of doing it, but it wasn't the work of evangelism.

Evangelism is one specific form of witnessing. Every Christian is called to witness; every Christian is called to confess Jesus with their speech as well as their actions. God doesn't ordain us to be secret service Christians. But not everyone is called, in my judgment, to be an evangelist; that's a special task. I think every Christian has a responsibility to participate in the evangelistic enterprise. While not everybody is called to be a missionary, we are all called to do our part in the mission of the church. The church is given the responsibility of the great commission, and every member in the body of Christ is called to do his or her part in seeing to it that the task is done. Evangelism involves much more than evangelists. It requires people to print Bibles, for instance, and people to distribute them, people to fund certain mission trips or projects, people to minister in various ways to the missionaries and the evangelists.

So while we're all called to witness and we're all responsible to some degree for seeing that the tasks of evangelism and mission are accomplished, we're not all meant to be missionaries or evangelists.

What makes Christianity—and not Buddhism or Hinduism or others—the right religion?

That's a question every person born and reared in the United States of America needs to ask and needs to ask honestly. We can't help but wonder, *Am I a Christian because I happen to be born and raised in a Christian environment, in a country where Christianity is the dominant religion and where I've had very little exposure to Hinduism or Islam or Buddhism and other world religions?* Many people join Christian organizations or Christian churches for no other reason than that is what their parents did. That's not a good way to test the truth of the claims of any religion.

I think the only way you can satisfy yourself or your children on something like this is to do an evaluation, a serious study of the basic tenets of world religions. In the nineteenth century the study of comparative religion became a very important academic discipline because the world had become smaller and more cosmopolitan. Now we live in a world in which there is much more mixing and mingling of people from radically different backgrounds. In the nineteenth century attempts were made to reach peace among the world religions by seeking a common denominator—that basic essence that was found in all religions. Many people concluded that there was really no difference, that everybody believes in the same God and we're all going the same road, but there are just different paths to the same place. I think that's a simplistic way of looking at it.

The difficulty is that if you look at the world religions and put their basic teachings side by side, you will see them flatly contradicting each other in terms of what their highest ideals are. And a thinking person will quickly see that they cannot possibly all be true in what they claim. They can all be wrong, but they can't possibly all be right.

The New Testament makes exclusive claims about Jesus,

and that is all the more provocative for people who don't want to look closely at the issues that divide the world religions. We obviously can't set forth a case for the distinctive truth claims of Christianity in a brief format like this, but I would say the one thing Christianity has that the other religions do not have—the most obvious thing—is Christ, God incarnate, and his work of atonement.

How can you present the gospel to a friend or family member who might be an atheist?

I don't think there's ever been a Christian who didn't carry throughout his life a heavy burden for the souls of the people most dear to him, and that's usually members of the immediate family as well as your best friends. We all struggle with this. How do we share our faith and communicate that which is so precious and important to us and which we are convinced is so important to them? What is the most effective way to do it? If I knew the answer to that question, I'd bottle it and sell it because there is such a need for it.

During my spiritual infancy I was filled with zeal for the things of Christ, and I desperately wanted to see my family come to Christ. I did everything the wrong way. I came on too strong and practically beat them to death quoting Scripture at them and leaving tracts on their nightstands and that sort of thing, which they took as an expression of my personal disapproval of them. That's not what I was trying to communicate, and that's not how I felt toward them, but that's how they took it.

When I became a Christian, I was so excited I went home

and talked to my mother, and filled with enthusiasm, I said, "Mom, guess what happened to me? I became a Christian." And she was completely befuddled. She said, "What do you mean you became a Christian? You've always been a Christian." And instead of sharing in my joy in my newfound faith, she got very, very defensive because what she heard me saying to her was, "Mother, you did not raise me with the proper value system. You're not a Christian. You're not worthy of being my mother." That's what she was hearing. And so I think we have to be especially sensitive to the feelings of those who are close to us because they have so much invested in the relationship we have with them.

If there's ever a place where I must earn the right to be heard, it's with my friends. It's the place we think we least need to earn the right to be heard because we already have the friendship established. We assume that because we are friends they will take what we say seriously and thoughtfully. But when I come to them with something new that contains veiled criticism of where they are standing with respect to God and Christ, they will take that as personal rejection, or at the very least disapproval. So before I can explain Christ to them or defend the faith to them, I must prove to them that I am their friend (or that I am my father's son or my mother's son or my sister's brother) so that they don't perceive that I'm making a radical break from our relationship.

How can I tell others about Jesus in a manner that is nonthreatening but yet convincing?

A few years ago, I was involved in training the laity of a local church in the activity we call personal evangelism, and I did that over a period of sixteen weeks. Of that sixteen weeks, about three weeks required training in the content of the message we call the gospel. That was the easy part. The rest of the training was devoted to helping people learn how to communicate their faith in a way that was nonthreatening and noninsulting to people. People are extremely sensitive about how they're approached on matters of religion. Many of us who are so excited about our faith in Christ want to share it with everyone we love, and our intentions are good. We care about our friends, and we want them to participate in the joy and discovery of this wonderful thing called salvation. But when we do that, so often we come across to these people as saying, in attitude if not in words, "I'm good and you're not." People are turned off by that, and rightly so.

Somebody said once that evangelism, true evangelism, is only this—one beggar telling another beggar how to find bread. There's nothing that should make me boastful about my faith. I recognize that my faith is a result of the grace of God. And so we must understand that when we're talking to people, we're called to be gracious and kind. The fruit of the Spirit that the New Testament calls us to exhibit includes gentleness, meekness, patience, and love. That's the spirit in which we are called to communicate to people.

Even though we are gracious, kind, patient, friendly, and sensitive to people's dignity, we cannot remove altogether what the New Testament calls the offense of the gospel because the gospel does call people to repentance, and people are threatened by that. But it is important that we not add unnecessarily to the offense that is built into the message of sin and redemption. Sometimes people reject us and what we say because they're rejecting Christ—and we suffer unjustly. But many more times people get angry not because they're offended by Christ but because they're offended by our insensitivity toward them as people.

My father is not a Christian, and whenever I talk to him, he doesn't listen, no matter what I talk to him about. It's gotten to the point that I don't even try to make conversation with him. What I should do about it?

One of the deepest personal struggles any Christian faces is trying to communicate the intensity of their own faith to their best friends and family who don't share that same perspective.

When I first became a Christian, what I wanted more than anything else in the world was for my family to enjoy the benefits of what I had discovered. I'm sure that many times I made myself obnoxious to my family by my zeal in trying to communicate my concern for them because I took seriously the warnings of the New Testament about what happens to those who reject the message of Christ. I was very fortunate that, even though in the early years I saw little response to my pleadings and my excitement and my desire to communicate to my family, over the years I was able to see just about everybody in my family come to Christ. I'd like to say that it was a direct result of my sterling witness, but it wasn't. God used other people to reach my family. What that taught me was how important it is to be patient with the timing of God for those you love.

I think of the story of Saint Augustine, whose mother, Monica, was a devout Christian. As he was growing up, her son was wild and unbridled in his licentious lifestyle, and Monica was a dear saint. For years, every single night she prayed for her son and saw no visible response whatsoever. On one occasion she went to see her pastor, who was the great Bishop Ambrose of Milan, Italy. She poured out her heart to the bishop, and he raised this question to her, "Monica, can a child of so many tears possibly be lost?" What Ambrose was saying was that certainly God is not going to say no to the petitions of a mother so earnest and importunate in her prayer life on behalf of her son. I think that it was a very comforting counsel Ambrose gave to Monica, but it's not necessarily sound theology.

It is possible that somebody we love very dearly will never come to faith, but there tends to be a correlation between our patience and our faithfulness to God and God's willingness to honor and bless that. I would say to you that what you need to do is pray and be as loving a daughter as you possibly can. God has not called you to be your father's evangelist; he has called you to be your father's daughter. The more Christian a daughter you are, the more God will be inclined to use that in a positive way.

If a non-Christian asks a question regarding morals, should we immediately and specifically refer to the Bible, or should we just give them our advice based on scriptural principles?

There are two questions here, really: What is the right response? and What is the best strategic response in terms of having productive dialogue with people who don't share our belief in the Scriptures?

We are living in a culture that in many ways has had just enough exposure to Christianity to be immunized against it. It's like an inoculation whereby a small dose of the disease keeps you from getting the real thing. Christianity is not some fresh voice speaking to moral issues in the United States of America. Nothing is more offensive to non-Christians than to listen to Christians talk to them with Christian platitudes and Christian jargon.

The Scriptures instruct us to let our speech be "seasoned with salt" (Col. 4:6). Part of our problem is that we are simply inarticulate. We can't express our Christian precepts and our Christian faith without using the same hackneyed language and clichés over and over again. That becomes an irritant to people, and rightfully so, when every time they hear us speak, we're saying "praise the Lord" or "God loves you." They get tired of hearing that. We ought to be able to communicate the ideals of the Christian faith in a fresh way so that people will have an opportunity to hear what we're saying.

When discussing moral issues, certainly for the Christian, there's no higher guide than the Word of God. Since I believe the Bible is the Word of God, it's binding to Christians and non-Christians. There's nothing wrong ethically with calling people's attention to what the Bible says. People don't have to believe it's the Word of God in order to be held accountable to it. If almighty God commands something, he commands it to everybody.

But the Bible is not the only place in which God reveals his law. The Bible tells us that in addition to the written Word, God reveals many of his principles, laws, and moral precepts in nature. We should have some kind of common ground on which to discuss Christian morality or ethical issues with the unbeliever without always jumping to the text of Scripture. If they don't accept that as an authority, then at least we can say that we also see evidence for the rightness of this particular behavior from nature itself, or what we would call common grace, in the common sense of the laws of the nations. You don't have to read the Bible to know that murder is wrong. You don't have to read the Bible to know that it's wrong to steal. There are certain moral issues that God makes very clear without recourse to Scripture.

Is it possible for a person be in a state of regeneration before they come to faith?

Not only is it possible for a person to be in a state of regeneration before they come to faith, but it's absolutely necessary because the supreme prerequisite for trusting in Christ is to be made alive through the Holy Spirit. Regeneration means rebirth. The other word that the New Testament uses is *quickening,* being made alive. The Bible teaches us that our natural fallen state is one of spiritual death. Faith is a manifestation of spiritual life. Before I can ever exercise faith, I have to first be made spiritually alive. That's why I would declare with all of my might that regeneration—that is, rebirth—precedes faith. It's necessary in order for faith even to be present.

I don't think I'm saying anything different from what our Lord said to Nicodemus when they had that lengthy discussion about what it means to be reborn. Jesus said that unless a person is born again, he can't even see the kingdom of God. Jesus also said, "Unless a man is born of the water and the Spirit, he cannot enter the kingdom of God." When Paul amplifies that theme in Ephesians 2, he says, "And you hath he quickened or made alive while you were dead in your sins and trespasses." I may err by thinking that while in a state of spiritual death, I can reach out by my own faith and make myself spiritually alive. That's exactly what we cannot do. That's exactly what only God can do for us. That is why Jesus said to Nicodemus that before a person can even see the kingdom of God, let alone enter the kingdom of God, he or she has to be born of the Spirit.

There's a lot of confusion among Christians about this terminology "born again." When a person comes to Christ and goes through a dramatic conversion and experiences a new life in Christ, they will say, "I am now born again," and they will think of what it means to be born again as the whole experience of new life they now enjoy. However, in the technical sense in the New Testament, regeneration describes not the whole process by which we are enjoying a new life in Christ but simply the first step. Just as birth is the beginning of human life and the necessary beginning, so spiritual birth is simply the first step after which come faith, repentance, and all the rest.

How should I respond to street preachers?

I remember in Philadelphia a few years ago I saw a photograph in the paper of Dr. Cornelius Van Til, one of the most eminent theologians of the twentieth century, engaged in preaching in the streets of Philadelphia. I was overwhelmed with a sense of being humbled by that—that this man, with his dignity, his academic credentials, his impeccable reputation as a scholar, was willing to put up with the hostility, the mockery, and all the rest that goes with publicly preaching in that manner.

I think of the apostles, of Paul, who went to the marketplace and disputed daily, spoke with people standing around the square there at Mars Hill. I think of the bizarre things that God called some of the prophets to do—walking barefoot and naked in the public square as a witness (not that he calls us to do that!) and to do object lessons through symbolic forms of behavior that would be socially totally offensive to their contemporaries.

So on the one hand, I have a respect for people who have the boldness and the courage to preach in that manner. But I've seen other kinds of street preaching—the kind where somebody gets a megaphone and stands on the corner and preaches to people who are captive at a red light. People don't want to listen, and they're sort of bombarded by this kind of activity. Sometimes we can be impolite in the way we preach to people, and I think we have to be very careful.

Part of my struggle, though, is my own pride. I'm a Christian and I'm a preacher. And I live in a culture where preaching is acceptable in certain places and in certain ways and unacceptable socially in other places and other ways. And who decides what is acceptable and what isn't? It's not always the right parties who are making the decisions, and I don't like to suffer the fallout of embarrassment from somebody else's behavior that is socially unacceptable. I'm not sure that my negative reactions to some of these things are not rooted in my own pride and fear that I might be tarred with the same brush. I hope that's not the basic reason for my negative feelings for some of that.

I'm not particularly pleased with bumper stickers. I recognize that there are different ways to communicate at different times. At one time the gospel was communicated through pamphlets. Everything was communicated that way. And then through books and music. Forms of communication change, and people put their messages on their T-shirts and on their bumpers. So why shouldn't Christians? My concern is that we do not cheapen the proclamation of Christ through being too cute or too clever with these forms.

13

Church Life

Now, therefore, you are no longer strangers and foreigners,
but fellow citizens with the saints and members
of the household of God, having been built on the
foundation of the apostles and prophets,
Jesus Christ himself being the chief cornerstone,
in whom the whole building, being fitted together,
grows into a holy temple in the Lord,
in whom you also are being built together for a
dwelling place of God in the Spirit.

EPHESIANS 2:19-22

Questions in This Section:

Who was the first Christian?

What are the basics to church growth?

What are the essential differences in church structure?

What do we need to know about a church before we attend, and what do we need to know before we become a member?

How are we to respond to poor decisions that are made in the governing body of our churches? How can we as laypersons best make our voices heard?

What should I do if my pastor is more liberal than I am, and when is it time to leave the church?

Some churches and Christian colleges have prescribed standards of behavior for all members and students. Is this biblical?

What is the significance of baptism?

Would you encourage an adult who has just come to Christ to be baptized if he or she had already been baptized as a child?

What causes the most pressure or strain on my pastor?

Should ministers run for political office?

Should a woman hold an office in a church?

In 1 Corinthians 11, Paul deals with head coverings for women in the church. How does this apply to the Christian church today?

How can church members influence seminary education?

How are we to keep the Sabbath in today's society?

Why do so many people find worship boring?

What does it mean to worship God in truth and in spirit?

Why is it necessary to praise the Lord, and what is the scriptural basis?

Dr. James Packer is critical of Christians using the crucifix and pictures of Jesus as symbols of Christianity, saying that it breaks God's second commandment. How do you feel about this?

What do we actually receive from Jesus Christ when we partake of Communion?

Should we confess our sins to one another as it says in the book of James?

In Galatians 6, what is the difference between the admonition to "bear one another's burdens" and the statement that "each one shall bear his own load?"

Is the celebration of Christmas a pagan ritual?

Can you tell us why X is used when it replaces Christ in Christmas?

What is the most pressing need of the evangelical church today if she is to make an impact on society?

What is the most crucial issue confronting today's church?

Who was the first Christian?

It depends on how we define a Christian. In *The Church from Abel*, written back in the sixties, Roman Catholic theologian Yves Congar went back to the Old Testament passages where there was discrepancy between the offering that Abel brought before God and that of his brother, Cain. You remember Cain's offering was not acceptable to God and Cain rose up in jealousy and murdered his brother, Abel. Abel was the first martyr of the faith in that regard. Congar went on to suggest that the church actually was born with Abel's act of devotion and worship. We could push it back further than that. The first hint of a gospel is found in the promise that God gives to Adam and Eve in the Garden. After the curse is imposed upon them, there is the promise that someone will come, born of the seed of the woman, who would crush the head of the serpent while having his own heel damaged in the process. We assume, I think, that Adam and Eve both put their confidence and their trust in that promise of God for their future redemption. So we could say that the first Christians were Adam and Eve.

If we want to be more specific in terms of a personal knowledge of Jesus, then my candidate would be the mother of Jesus. The angel announced to Mary that she had been overpowered by the most high God and had conceived one who was to be born and who was to be called Jesus, who would save people from their sins—he was to be

a savior. When that announcement was made to the Virgin
Mary, she sang under the inspiration of the Holy Spirit the
Magnificat: "My soul doth magnify the Lord, and my spirit
doth rejoice in God my Savior." I think that Mary, at that
moment, was putting her confidence and trust in the child
that was about to begin growing in her own womb. So I
would say that in New Testament categories Mary was the
first Christian.

The term *Christian* was not even used until the book of
Acts; there we read that believers in Jesus were first called
Christians at Antioch. So somebody might dispute it at that
point. Obviously who is entitled to the designation of the
first is not a matter of theological dogma, but more a matter of how you look at it.

What are the basics to church growth?

The most important key is the work of the Holy Spirit. We
see in the book of Acts that it's the Lord who added to the
churches daily. But that doesn't mean that every time we
see churches bulging with memberships it's the work of
the Holy Spirit. Humanly speaking, I think there are a
couple of absolutely crucial keys.

In the United States there was a study conducted of
people who had dropped out of the church. Those
people were asked, "Why did you stop going to church?"
The number one reason was, "Church is boring." The
second biggest reason was that, in their judgment, the
church is irrelevant.

I have mused on those responses many times. When I

look at the Scriptures, I see that throughout redemptive history when people encounter God, they have different kinds of reactions. Some of them cry, some of them laugh, some of them sing, some of them shout, some of them run, some of them are scared, and some of them are angry. But I have never read in Scripture of a person meeting God and being bored. It would seem to me that if, in our churches, people were having a vital encounter with the living God, nobody would say that church is boring. And I don't think they would consider the experience irrelevant.

Now let's look at it from another perspective. If we asked people who *do* attend church why they go to church, I can tell you what the number one answer would be. People would say that they go to church to worship God. They know that this is the primary reason they are supposed to go to church. But the real reason they go to church is for the fellowship they receive there; they go to be with other people. I think that a wise pastor understands that. And so I think that two of the most important factors in the church experience are (1) the worship itself becomes an *event* whereby people are brought into the presence of the living God and (2) the church recognizes that people need fellowship and they need to be relating to other people in the context of the church. Churches that put a strong emphasis on vital worship and that are meeting the fellowship needs of people are the churches that have the best chances of growth. I also think that one of the vital ingredients of growing churches is strong, biblical, expository preaching.

What are the essential differences in church structure?

Usually, when we refer to church structure, we're talking about the way in which the church organizes itself in terms of authority. There are basically three different structures among Christian churches: the episcopalian form of government, the presbyterian, and the congregational. Most churches fall into one of these three categories or structures.

By "episcopal" I'm not referring specifically to what we call the Episcopal Church. I'm using the term in the generic sense. The word *episcopalian* comes from the New Testament Greek word *episcopos,* which is the word for bishop, or overseer, in the New Testament. In this framework the authority or pastoral leadership is vested in one person who rules over an area, in some traditions called a diocese. The Anglican, Episcopal, and Methodist denominations use this type of structure. You also find it in the Roman Catholic Church and the various other catholic churches like the Greek Orthodox Church.

The presbyterian system is more of a representative form of government, in which the authority is not rooted in one man who oversees other pastors, but in a presbytery, which is sort of like a congress. This body of elders has authority over the local churches.

In the congregational system, local congregations are not connected to one another by bishops or presbyteries except by free or voluntary association. The authority or the structure of the church is rooted within the local congregation.

All of these forms have some kind of governing authority that gives magisterial leadership to the people within their fellowship of believers. These are the principal differences among Christian bodies. Other differences in structure reflect differences in theology. For instance, is the focal point of the service the sacraments or the preaching? These are not so much structural questions as doctrinal questions that in turn affect the structure.

What do we need to know about a church before we attend, and what do we need to know before we become a member?

Before we attend a church, we should know that it is a legitimate church. Now, obviously, if the sign on the front of the church reads "Church of Satan," we know it isn't a legitimate body of Christian believers. But what about churches that are not legitimate for less obvious reasons? Some religious bodies claim to be Christian that, in my judgment and in the judgment of many Christians, are not Christian churches or are apostate bodies. Even attending their services may be a sin. We can't expect a church to be perfect. But does it hold to the essentials of the faith? Does it practice a basic, sound belief in the deity of Christ and aspects of Christ that we find outlined in the New Testament?

Now, we may be worshiping every day with people who profess to be Christians but aren't; this we can't avoid because God hasn't given us the ability to look at another person's heart and say exactly where he or she is spiritually. But we can inquire into the basic beliefs of a church body, and we want to unite ourselves in worship only with a group of people who are attempting to do what is proper in the sight of God.

Obviously that bare minimum applies before you *attend* the church. Before you *join* a church I would think you'd look more closely. You would ask questions such as, Is this a church where the gospel is being preached, where there is fidelity to the Scriptures? Is this a fellowship to which I am prepared to commit myself, my time, my money, my devotion, where I'm going to be instructed in spiritual growth, along with my family? I think those are the kinds of questions you need to look at very carefully before you make the commitment to join. In our country we often join churches in the same spirit that we join any other organization, forgetting that when we join the church, we take a sacred vow before God to do certain things—to be present in worship, to make diligent use of the means of grace, to be an active participant in that church. Before you take a vow to do something like that, you need to know what it is you're joining and then, having made that vow, be prepared to keep it.

How are we to respond to poor decisions—such as liberal stances on abortion—that are made by the governing body of our churches? How can we as laypersons best make our voices heard?

This question can only be answered according to the structure of any given denomination. Some denominations operate on a purely congregational, local-church basis. If each congregation is autonomous and able to make its own decisions, in some cases set its own policy, then it's much easier for laypeople to get their viewpoints heard. But once we find ourselves in a connectional situation, where we have church representatives or central church councils setting policy and making decisions for the denomination as a whole (as in the case of Methodists, Episcopalians, Presbyterians, and Catholics), those representing bodies don't always represent what you believe as an individual.

You're asking me for a strategy on how to overturn that. I really don't know except that wherever you have a voice, let it be heard. In most denominations, a person has one vote in a the local congregation, and that's where you have the opportunity to express your views and to note your dissent. Sometimes, just as in a governmental structure in the secular world, you have leaders—representatives—to whom you can write and let your views be known. Some groups within the church may take a different position. In most denominations there are minority report groups in which you can let your voice be heard.

Even in situations where you feel your voice has very little impact, I don't think it is appropriate to do nothing. Neither do I think that it's appropriate to simply quit the church over every disagreement that you have with its governing body. Every church is constantly searching itself, examining its positions on various issues. And I think we are called to be patient with our parent denominations and our parent church bodies on some of these matters. Some pronouncements from the general assembly level break my heart, and I'm very saddened by them. I hasten to tell people that they don't necessarily represent me at that point. But there are different levels of pronouncements. For example, when the Roman Catholic Church issues a papal decree, that's quite different from a study document being presented by a group of Roman Catholic priests; a study does not carry the same weight as a papal encyclical. A general assembly pronouncement of the Presbyterian Church is a significant thing, but it doesn't have the same weight as a credal statement in the same denomination. So I think we have to weigh those kinds of factors in as we struggle together for the solutions.

What should I do if my pastor is more liberal than I am, and when is it time to leave the church?

The terms *liberal* and *conservative* are not meaningless terms, but they are very broad labels. I don't know where you are, and when you talk about a minister who is more liberal than you, you may be a flaming conservative. You may be the lunatic fringe on the right wing, and what you consider a liberal may be pure orthodoxy!

Let's say that a conservative is a person who resists change, who's married to the status quo. As Christians, we can't allow ourselves to approach life in this way. We have never arrived at a perfect state in the life of the church or in our understanding of the things of God; it's not a good idea to conserve everything from the past. I have to always be open to Reformation and new growth and experience in matters of faith and life.

From one historical perspective, *liberal* is a marvelous term. It describes someone who has experienced freedom and is not bound simply to the traditions of men, one who is open to new horizons, new vistas, new ventures in the kingdom of God. In another sense, *liberal* is not a friendly term to Christianity. For example, there was a movement in the nineteenth-century church that adopted the term *lib-*

336

eral as a technical definition for a whole system of theology that categorically erased the supernatural from the Christian faith, denying not only the Virgin Birth but the Incarnation itself—the miracles of Jesus, the atonement of Christ, the resurrection of Jesus, the ascension of Jesus, and the return of Jesus. I don't see that school of thought as part of an intramural debate among Christians trying to sort out our beliefs. There's a lot of room for disagreement within the body of Christ. But the systematic denial of the supernatural that we found in nineteenth-century liberalism was, I would say, sub-Christian or non-Christian or actually antithetical to Christianity. Here we had people within the church denying what I would view as essentials of the Christian faith.

If your minister is a liberal in the sense that he's actually denying basic tenets of the Christian faith, then you have a serious problem on your hands. Depending upon your denomination, there are certain avenues by which you can file your grievances; most churches do have ecclesiastical courts to deal with heretics, and this kind of liberalism is heresy. *Heretic* is not a word we use every day in this enlightened generation, but true heretics do exist.

As to whether or not you leave the church, I would say that your basic attitude should be one of enormous forbearance and perseverance because the church is bigger than an individual minister or even a specific local body of believers. If you find that an entire denomination has taken a heretical position, denying the essentials of the Christian faith, then I think you must leave.

Some churches and Christian colleges have prescribed standards of behavior for all members and students. Is this biblical?

I'll try to answer this question from what I have encountered in the Christian college scene.

First of all, I think it's perfectly appropriate for a private university or college to have standards that are imposed upon its people. I think it's particularly important that if an institution calls itself a Christian institution, it be extremely careful not to impose standards or rules that go beyond what the Bible actually says. What happens is that people then look at these situations and say, "Oh, this is what a Christian does or does not do." If we are so strict and so rigid that we impose rules and regulations where God leaves people free, we are provoking God's displeasure because we are actually distorting the law of God.

I mention this because I have seen many Christian colleges which, in my judgment, have rules and regulations that go far beyond what Scripture requires of people. In fact, they enforce a kind of legalism that is a distortion of the Word of God and communicates to the students and to the world a picture of the Christian faith that is simply not accurate. The motivation behind these regulations is generally good; the people who set them up understand that young people are particularly prone to sow their wild oats and to experiment with types of behavior that are questionable from a Christian point of view. College is often the first situation in which young people are away from home and left to make important decisions on their own. They have to learn to deal with freedom they've not experienced before. So Christians become zealous to protect them from the world and from falling into dangerous sins, and they do this by tightening restrictions and adding rules. The negative effect of this is overcorrection or over-protection, which often incites students to rebel. Another negative effect is that those students who don't rebel end up further isolated from the world in which we live—the true arena of redemption.

I remember one particular Christian college that was part of a national study of guilt complexes among students. This particular Christian school ranked in the 99th percentile. In other words, there were serious problems of guilt-ridden, paralyzed students on that campus. A Christian college is one place where we should feel the release and freedom from guilt because we've tasted of the forgiveness that is ours in Christ. So I would say that there is a place and purpose for certain standards in private institutions, but the misapplication of this protection can be extremely dangerous.

What is the significance of baptism?

Just as an aside, the word *significance* has as its root the word *sign*. A sign is something that points to something beyond itself. We all recognize that whatever baptism signifies, Jesus obviously thought it was very important because he gives a command to baptize all nations in the name of the Father, the Son, and the Holy Spirit. Whatever else it is, baptism is the sign of the new covenant that God makes with his people. We do have the clear mandate in the New Testament that Christians are to be baptized.

I personally do not believe that baptism is essential for salvation. If I believed that, I would think that the thief on the cross who was promised paradise with Jesus would have been disqualified because he obviously didn't have an opportunity to get baptized. But I do believe that baptism is essential for obedience because Christ commands it. It's just the same thing as when people say, "Do you have to go to church to go to heaven?" I would say, "Obviously not." But do you have to go to church to obey Christ? Yes, you do. And if you are not inclined to obey Christ and have no inclination to follow his mandates, that may be a sign that you are not headed for heaven. So church involvement becomes a very serious matter of obedience.

I would say the same about the sacrament of baptism. It's a sign of the new covenant. It's a sign of our participation in Jesus, of being partakers in his death and resurrection, which are at the heart of the gospel. It's also a sign of our cleansing from sin and guilt by the work of Jesus and the washing of regeneration. What we do outwardly with water, the Spirit does inwardly with his grace. So it's a sign of our cleansing. It's also a sign of our sanctification. It's a sign of our baptism of the Holy Spirit. It's a sign of our being set apart from the world and given the holy task to fulfill the commission that Christ gives to his church.

So there are several things that baptism signifies. I think one of our tendencies is to reduce those to one—making it merely a cleansing rite or merely a sign of empowering by the Holy Spirit—when in fact it is a sacrament that is rich and complex with meaning and significance.

Would you encourage an adult who has just come to Christ to be baptized if he or she had already been baptized as a child?

Obviously there are a lot of people who would encourage a new convert to the Christian faith to be baptized as an adult, even if they had already been baptized as infants. The main reason is that a large number of Christians believe that it's improper to baptize infants in the first place. They don't acknowledge the validity of it, so in their minds this adult baptism is the one and only true baptism they have received.

I happen to believe that infant baptism is proper and should be practiced by the church. As you know, the church is divided almost in half on that question, but I happen to be on the half that believes in infant baptism.

The reason I wouldn't encourage a person to be baptized a second time is this: We regard baptism as a sign of God's promise to bring the full measure of redemption to those who put their trust in Christ, and it's a sign of about seven or eight specific things upon which the New Testament elaborates. It's a sign of God's promise, and the integrity and the validity of that sign does not rest on the minister or the priest who administers the sacrament, or on the integrity of the parents who bring the child for baptism, or on the faith or lack of it in the infant. The integrity of the promise ultimately belongs to the integrity of the one who makes the promise, and that's God.

Here's the scenario: A person is an infant, and he receives the sign of the covenant promise of God with all of the integrity of God backing it up. It doesn't mean a thing to the baby at the time, or perhaps not even to the priest or the parents. Maybe it's a charade for all of them. Then twenty-five years later the person comes to faith and receives all of the benefits that the promise signified. Now he comes to me, and he wants me to baptize him again. Usually they say, "It didn't mean anything to me before. I wasn't even aware of it. Now that I'm a Christian, I want to experience this sacrament of baptism." I certainly am sympathetic to that and understand a person's desire to have the experience of going under the water and having the sign and the outward seal of all these wonderful things that they've just experienced. But the reason I wouldn't encourage them is that if indeed this is the sign of God's promise that certain things would happen and if you put your trust in Christ, why would you now come before God and say, "Would you run that promise by me again?" To do so in a sense casts a shadow on the integrity of that original promise that God has just fulfilled in full magnificence. Logically, I would say the repetition of the act would be a thinly veiled insult of God's integrity, though I fully recognize that not one person in a million who undergoes a second baptism intends it to be an insult.

What causes the most pressure or strain on my pastor?

In the seminary I have a responsibility to teach not only undergraduate students but students in the doctoral program, which is open only to those who have been on the field as pastors for at least five years. When they return to the seminary for more education, we have many opportunities to discuss with a large number of pastors what they find to be the heaviest pressures. Although it varies from person to person, two stresses pop up frequently.

The biggest problem pastors deal with is trying to keep people happy. As the head of a group of people, the pastor has to deal constantly with criticism from those who are unhappy with him, some of whom are taking shots at him. When you're a leader and a spokesman for a group, criticism goes with the territory. It's similar to being the president of a company. When the president has a meeting with his staff, as soon as he leaves the room, he knows a second meeting will take place. The staff is going to talk among themselves and evaluate, analyze, moan, complain, or rejoice in terms of what he, the president, has done.

The spiritual leader of the church is the pastor. The pastor speaks every Sunday morning, and every Sunday afternoon there's roast pastor for dinner in the homes of those who heard the sermon. The people are agreeing or disagreeing, happy or unhappy. He gets the letters on Monday, he gets the cold shoulder, he gets the complaints. The biggest stress I find among pastors is dealing with personal criticism.

I think the second greatest point of stress in the life of the pastor is finances. I know that people have been saying, probably as long as there have been churches, "Well, the preacher's always asking for money" or, "They're always passing the plate." But no organization can function without finances. We understand that some people drive the finance subject into the ground. But our educators, musicians, and pastors are the most underpaid professionals in our country. In every other profession, salary is set to some degree by the market for those skills. But in the Bible God establishes the value of the ministry and requires that the people tithe to make sure the minister is paid. That's not the way it works in our country. A few ministers in megachurches do pretty well financially, but most struggle on a regular basis to make ends meet because they are not valued by their church members in the same way God values them, as stated in the Scriptures. And it's not only that it hurts them financially, but it insults their dignity. Because of the way they're paid, ministers feel that they're not appreciated.

Should ministers run for political office?

In American political history we've seen many instances of clergymen seeking and winning political office. All the way back to the Continental Congress we find that kind of representation.

But *should* ministers run for political office? In the United States we have a precious principle: separation of church and state. That means that there are two spheres of activity, one that is the responsibility of the state officials and the other that is the function of the institutional church. It is not the duty of the church to be the state, and we don't elect clergymen so that they can function as clergymen in their political offices.

But can a minister decide to leave his ecclesiastical vocation and enter the political realm? Ultimately, this is a matter between that person and God. For example, I am ordained into the ministry. I am a clergyman, and that is because I have tried to give evidence to the church that I have a call or a vocation to ministry in the life of the church. That vocation is from God; God has called me to be a minister. If God calls me to be a minister and I decide—out of my own ambition—to run for a seat in the House or Senate, or even for presidential office, and in so doing forsake the vocation that God has given me, then I'm in deep trouble with God because I am disobeying my calling.

Remember when testifying before King Agrippa (Acts 26) Paul speaks of the call he received from Christ to become an apostle? He said, "King Agrippa, I was not disobedient to that heavenly calling." Is it possible that God can call a person to the ministry for a certain period of his or her life and then give him or her a new vocation in the political arena? I don't know of any reason this couldn't happen. In the history of the church there have been situations in which the church may even have suggested to some of its clergy that they take a vacation, if you will, from their ecclesiastical duties and serve God in a different capacity—in politics or in business or other forms of employment. I do think it's possible for a vocation to change.

Should a woman hold an office in a church?

Some people view the controversy over women's leadership in church as simply a collision between two viewpoints—one that espouses women's liberation of one form or another, and the other, die-hard male chauvinism. But that's a simplistic approach to the very controversial issue of women's ordination.

In 1 Timothy 2:12, the apostle Paul sets forth the qualifications for church leadership, and he makes the statement, "I will not allow a woman to have authority over a man or to teach." Now notice, he doesn't say, "I will not allow a woman to be a pastor," nor does he say, "I will not allow a woman to be ordained to ministry." He says, "I will not allow a woman to have authority over men or to teach." Therein lies the problem. The verb Paul uses in this passage that is translated "authority" occurs only once in the entire New Testament in this particular context. Because this word is only used once in the New Testament and rarely shows up in other Greek literature of that period that survives today, we're not exactly sure what that word means. Even so, we struggle to be obedient to the guidelines and the restrictions for church government that are set forth in the New Testament.

I would say that Paul prohibits a woman from having some kind of authority. As I study the patterns of that in the New Testament, I think that what Paul is saying is that women can be involved in all kinds of functions of ministry in the church but that the role of juridical authority or of governing authority is not to be held by women. I would add that the overwhelming majority of New Testament scholars through the years have agreed with the position I have just stated. I know that in certain denominations, ordination means that a person has been given governing authority in the church. If the apostle prohibits that and if he prohibits it for all generations, then obviously the practice today or yesterday or tomorrow would be inconsistent with the apostolic authority and would therefore be inconsistent with the authority of Christ.

In 1 Corinthians 11, Paul deals with head coverings for women in the church. How does this apply to the Christian church today?

During my high school years, when I went to church on Sunday morning, I never saw a woman in that church (this was a mainline Presbyterian church) whose head wasn't covered with a hat or veil. That is one of those customs that has simply disappeared for the most part from Christian culture. If you go to my Presbyterian church this Sunday, you'll see two women wearing hats. One is a woman from Holland who is dyed-in-the-wool conservative, and the other one is my wife because we are persuaded that that biblical mandate is still in effect.

We know that in the New Testament certain rules are dictated by custom and others are dictated by principle. For example, when Jesus sent out the seventy disciples on a mission of evangelism, he told them to take no shoes with them. That does not mean that all preaching and all evangelism for all times and all places has to be done in bare feet. Billy Graham is not sinning by wearing shoes when he preaches the gospel. But there are many questions like that that are not so obvious. In that whole context of the eleventh chapter of 1 Corinthians, women are called to cover their heads with a veil as a sign of their willingness to submit to the leadership or headship of their husbands. There are three elements here: the submission of the wife to the husband as the head of the home, the covering of the head, and the covering of the head by a veil. How much is principle and how much is custom?

Many Christians believe that we should no longer tell

women to submit to the headship of their husbands. Therefore, women don't have to cover their heads. Others say that the headship principle still stands in the home, but the covering of the head was a cultural custom that does not carry over into our day, and therefore the veil would be insignificant as well.

The third view of this passage is that it is describing a principle, and that women must cover their heads and use veils to do so.

I am convinced that when Paul says the women are to cover their heads, he is basing that action on how God created male and female. It would seem to me, using a principle of interpretation of what we call hermeneutics, that if there's ever an indication of a perpetual ordinance in the church, it is that which is based on an appeal to Creation. I'm persuaded that the principle of covering the head is still in effect because it was built into creation. And even though it's not culturally accepted anymore in our society, I still believe it's principle. I don't think it matters one bit whether it's a babushka, a veil, or a hat, but I think that the symbol should remain intact as a sign of our obedience to God.

How can church members influence seminary education?

I think one of the greatest crises in our country is at the level of theological education. In the last several decades we have seen the departure of many Christian institutions—including Christian universities, colleges, and even seminaries—from orthodox Christianity. Some of our fin-

est secular institutions began as Christian seminaries—
Princeton, Harvard, and Yale, for example. Over the years,
as these institutions have come under the influence of secular scholarship, they have changed their commitments,
and in some cases they have changed them drastically.

I honestly think there is very little church members can do
to influence seminary education. This may sound pessimistic, but the academic life is a world unto itself. And different
theological institutions and seminaries have their own rules
and regulations for how policy is established. In some situations the policies and the viewpoints of the seminary are
controlled absolutely by the faculty; in other cases they are
controlled by the board of directors; in still others by the
administration. And about all we can do as private individuals
or members of the local church is to insist that the people we
call to be our pastors be men of godliness, men who have
mastered the Scriptures and who are theologically literate.

Personally, I am totally committed to the concept of an
educated clergy. One of the great benefits of the Protestant Reformation was to make the Bible available for private consumption by the individual. We now print the
Bible in the vernacular in the English language; it's not
restricted to publications in Latin and Greek and Hebrew.
But at the same time, as we read the Scriptures for ourselves, the Scriptures tell us that we need teachers. The
Scriptures are often difficult and complex, and there is
great benefit in having highly educated ministers and pastors. And their thinking—the very nature of their ministry—will be shaped by the institution that educated them.

And so about the only way in which we have a voice in
the matter as church members is in the selection of our

pastors. Not every student from every seminary totally represents the party line of the seminary, but we should know what those seminary lines are, and when we look at a potential pastor's credentials, we should consider carefully where he was educated.

How are we to keep the Sabbath in today's society?

Within the Christian church there are three leading options for answering your question.

Some Christians believe that the Sabbath was an Old Testament ordinance and has no application to the New Testament church. No less a giant than Saint Augustine took the position that the Sabbath was not carried over into the New Testament community and therefore has been fulfilled and was done away with through the work of Christ. There are Christians who feel that there is no particular significance to Sabbath keeping today, although they make up a very small minority.

For the most part, Christian people, while they may disagree as to what day *is* the Sabbath—the sixth or the seventh day and all that—and how we observe it, still maintain that the Sabbath is to be observed somehow in the Christian community. God ordained the Sabbath, not at Mt. Sinai with Moses and the people of Israel, but at Creation. The later books of the Law certainly filled out the concept of the Sabbath in terms of its specifics and how it was to be observed in Israel, but the Sabbath existed long before the Ten Commandments and other laws were given. This would indicate that as long as Creation is in effect, Sabbath is in effect. In the covenant God made with Israel he says, "This is my Sabbath unto all generations." The fact that it's a Creation ordinance is strong evidence that there is still a Sabbath observation requirement for Christians—in fact, not only for Christians, because the Sabbath was part of God's design for humanity from the beginning. That's one of the reasons states have had blue laws. Sabbath keeping was not even seen as a violation of the separation of church and state; everybody was required to have a Sabbath whether they were Christian, Jew, Muslim, or whatever.

In the New Testament the church comes together on the Lord's Day, which is the first day of the week, for corporate worship. We have a clear mandate in the New Testament not to forsake the assembling of the saints (Heb. 10:25). In other words, the New Testament's simple language says that Christians are supposed to be in corporate worship on the Lord's Day. That means we're supposed to go to church. That is usually seen as one of the ways in which the Sabbath is to be observed. All Christians I know of who believe that the Sabbath is still in effect agree that on the Sabbath we should be worshiping, and also that on one day in seven there should be rest from unnecessary commerce and labor. There are still provisions for commerce that must go on—hospital work, pharmacies, and such. But commerce just for the sake of merchandising ought to cease on the Sabbath.

This group of Christians who believe the Sabbath should be observed actually splits into two groups. One holds what we call the Continental view: Recreation is permitted on the Sabbath. The other holds the Puritan view: Recreation is forbidden on the Sabbath. I take the position that recreation is a legitimate form of rest on the Sabbath.

Why do so many people find worship boring?

Someone questioned Sam Schumaker, an Episcopalian
priest in Pittsburgh, about young people who are turned
on to Jesus through the work of paraministry organizations
like Youth for Christ, Young Life, or Campus Crusade.
They get filled with zeal for Christ and then drop out of
their home churches. The interviewer was blasting these
organizations because they were driving the kids away from
church. Sam said, "I'm not so sure whether these organizations are driving the kids away from the churches, or if the
churches are so lifeless in some instances that the kids are
bored to death." Sam used the expression "You can't put a
live chick under a dead hen." It is a sad commentary that
so many times we find worship boring.

In the Scriptures I see people of all varieties of personality and background responding to God. And they respond
in many different ways: tears, fear, flight, mourning, weeping, laughing, dancing, singing. All these different passions
and emotions are provoked by the presence of God. But
there is one thing I never find in the Bible when a person
comes into the presence of the living God: He is never
bored. If our worship services are boring, then I'm afraid
that somehow we are failing to communicate the awesome,
majestic presence of God. I think we need to take a serious
look at the style of worship that characterizes so many of
our practices these days.

I've stuck my neck out on this point many times by saying that when I look at biblical worship—for example, the
worship that God designs in the Old Testament—at the
heart of it is the proclamation of the Word of God. Not

only is the mind involved by hearing instruction, but the whole person—all five senses—is integrated into Israel's worship in the Old Testament. They had the altar of incense that stimulated worship with sweet aroma. The auditory nerves were stimulated by music. The visual sight of the magnificence of the tabernacle (and later, the temple) was designed, not to give an ostentatious display of wealth or to be a monument to human grandeur, but to show the beauty of God's holiness. Now, in Protestant worship, for the most part, we sit and listen to a sermon, which is important, but the whole person is not actively involved in worship. We must be willing to bring worship back into the biblical framework of engaging the whole person if we're going to overcome this tendency to bore people.

What does it mean to worship God in truth and in spirit?

Jesus doesn't explain in John 4:23 what he means by worshiping the Father in spirit and truth, and we can only speculate about it. On the one hand, we can think about the fact that the kind of worship God wants from us is worship that comes from deep within us, from our own spirit. We think of the Magnificat of Mary at the time of the annunciation of the coming birth of the Messiah when she sings, "My soul doth magnify the Lord and my spirit doth rejoice in God my Savior." Her expression there was one of adoration and reverence that came from deep within her soul. It was spiritual worship in the sense that it wasn't simply on the surface. She was not merely going through the motions mechanically and externally, but it came from the very depths of her being.

So maybe what Jesus was speaking about there in terms of spiritual worship is a worship that comes from the depths of our own human spirit as it addresses God.

The other possible meaning of "spirit" in this passage, particularly in the way it's linked with "truth," is the very nature of God rather than our inward spirits. In the course of Jesus' conversation with the woman, he emphasizes that God is a spirit. He links that declaration with the mandate that he is to be worshiped in spirit. I think what Jesus meant in that case was that God wants to be worshiped as he is, that he is to be honored in the fullness of his character. We are not to strip God of his attributes when we come before him in worship and in honor and in praise; we are not to turn him into an idol—our image of what we think he should be. It's not by accident that the first two commandments of the Ten Commandments circumscribe and protect the sanctity of the character of God and lay down an absolute prohibition against the worship of idols. Remember that idolatry is one of the most primordial and foundational distortions of authentic religion. We see, for example, in Paul's lengthy exposition of the first chapters of Romans his expression of God's anger that is directed against those who would reduce him to an idol. To make God a man or a cow or a totem pole or even an abstract idea is not accurate, for it changes his eternal glory into a lie, and God will not have that. He desires people to worship him as he is in the fullness of his spiritual character and in truth. God wants true worship and spiritual worship.

Why is it necessary to praise the Lord, and what is the scriptural basis?

I'm not exactly sure what you mean by necessary. It is our ethical obligation as creatures of the living God to offer to God praise and adoration for who he is. I would say that justice more than anything else demands our worship and praise of God. If we go back to the definition of the word that functioned throughout the classical world and was articulated by the Greek philosopher Aristotle, *justice* is giving to someone what is their due.

When we look at the Scriptures, we see indirectly the judgment of God upon the human race. In Romans 1, Paul tried to show that the whole world is brought before the tribunal of God and is judged guilty before him. Christ comes into a world of fallen people who are exposed to the judgment of God for the basic reason that God has revealed himself to every human being in this world, but while we know there is a God, we refuse to honor God as God. That's the number one cause of the judgment of God upon us. By our fallen nature we refuse to give the honor that is due God our Creator.

Why is honor due God? God is intrinsically honorable. He is worthy of our praise and worthy of our adoration. If God is praiseworthy, then it is our obligation to praise him. Now that's a deduction from the character of God and from the character of creatures who owe to their Creator credit and thanks for every benefit they enjoy in this world. It would go without saying that we owe him praise and thanksgiving.

In addition to these kinds of indirect references, there is

the direct command of Scripture to bring the offering of praise before God. I think of Psalm 150, which says, "Let everything that has breath praise the Lord." Repeatedly, both the Old and New Testaments say that God is a spirit and that we are to worship him in spirit and in truth. To worship God truly is to offer adoration and praise. Paul speaks about offering ourselves as a living sacrifice, which is our reasonable service. It's the just thing to do, it's the reasonable thing to do, and it is the religious thing to do.

Dr. James Packer, in his book Knowing God, criticizes the use of the crucifix and pictures of Jesus as symbols of Christianity, saying that it breaks God's second commandment. How do you feel about this?

I will preface my answer by saying that Jim Packer is a very close friend of mine and we've done a lot of work together in theological conferences. I know him to be one of the finest Christian scholars in the world today. He's an Anglican theologian and has his personal roots deep in the Protestant Reformation.

You may be aware that in the sixteenth century, one of the burning issues of conflict between the Roman Catholic Church and the Protestant reaction to it was precisely over the use of images and pictures in the church. There was the great iconoclast controversy, and even in Luther's Germany the people went so far as to break into Roman Catholic churches and destroy some of the art pieces there because they felt they were in violation of the second commandment. There is a long Protestant tradition of concern about that because the second commandment says, "You shall not make for yourself a carved image—any likeness of anything . . ." (Exod. 20:4). That's not a complete prohibition against art, as even the most ardent Reformers understood. There's a tremendous use of the various art forms in the Bible—the tabernacle and the temple of Israel being primary examples. What was prohibited were human likenesses of God.

There was clear agreement among Reformers that there should be no imagery that tried to depict the nature of God. The painting in the Sistine Chapel, for example, depicting the hand and finger of God creating Adam, would have been objectionable to the Reformers. Historically, the Roman Catholic Church has taken a very strong stand, saying that while people may serve the image, they are not to worship idols or crosses or any other such things. They have defined idolatry; the word comes from *idola latria,* which literally means "the worship of idols." They make a distinction between serving the image and worshiping it; men such as Packer say that it is a distinction without a difference. Serving idols is worshiping idols, and the Reformers weren't satisfied with the Roman Catholic answer.

Now you raise the question of a depiction of Christ and the use of the cross. There are Protestants who won't have any symbols in the church, including a cross, with or without a Christ figure on it. Packer is questioning pictures of Jesus and crosses. I have a problem with them from a practical standpoint. I can't say for sure that to depict the human nature of Jesus is a violation of the second commandment. But I'm not sure this is wise because it could communicate an image to people that is inaccurate. The

Solomon's head of Christ, as beautiful as it is, has communicated to generations of people an effeminate Jesus who is somehow less than strong. I would rather communicate nothing artistically about how Jesus looked than put wrong images in people's minds.

What do we actually receive from Jesus Christ when we partake of Communion?

The various Christian bodies and denominations differ on that profoundly. We all agree on at least one issue, and that is that we receive spiritual nourishment from Christ. As Calvin said, we feed on the risen body of Christ. We are strengthened inwardly by the grace that is offered to us by his presence in this particular capacity. Anytime we go to fellowship with other Christians or into the house of God, Christ is present. Yet there is something special about the mode of Christ's presence at the Lord's Table.

We enjoy other people's company as acquaintances and friends, but we enjoy a different dimension of fellowship when we share a meal at someone's home. There's something deeply rooted in the human personality by which we experience a certain intimacy when sharing a meal. That's no less true in the spiritual dimension when we are invited to sit down at this feast.

It's also a time for the renewal of the grace of forgiveness. We come to the Lord's Table in a spirit of careful preparation and repentance in order to experience a renewed sense of the healing and forgiveness that comes to us, flowing out of the Cross and out of Christ's intercession for us in heaven. There's another kind of renewal that's almost always overlooked; I'm convinced that every time we come to the Lord's Supper we are renewing our submission to the Holy Spirit. It was in the upper room that Jesus practiced a Jewish custom called dynastic succession. He did it in covenantal terms, by which he turned us over to the leadership of the Holy Spirit—the same Spirit he said he would pour out on the day of Pentecost. In a sense, when the church gathers together in Sacred Communion, it not only honors its King and looks forward to the future banquet feast with him, but it also submits itself afresh to the leadership of the Holy Spirit.

I would say that, far and above all of these things, the most profound benefit we enjoy in the celebration of the Lord's Supper is the immediate presence of Christ. Again, not everybody agrees as to the mode of his presence. I personally don't believe that he's physically present, but I think that he's substantively, actually present in all of his power and majesty to assist us, to feed us, to heal us, and to nurture us. We really commune with Christ at the Table.

Should we confess our sins to one another, as it says in the book of James?

If James says it, then of course we should confess our sins to one another. However, one of the great divisions among Christians has to do with the act of confessing our sins to other human beings. For example, the Roman Catholic Church has the sacrament of penance, in which the faithful within the Roman Catholic Church are required at certain intervals to go into the confessional and confess their sins audibly before a priest and go through absolution and works of satisfaction.

Most Protestant bodies, but not all, have discontinued the practice of this kind of confession. The idea behind this is that we don't need a mediary; we can confess our sins directly to God. Well, I certainly agree that we can tell our sins directly to God, and we are called to confess our sins to him even as the saints in Scripture did, as examples to us. But the Scriptures do tell us not only to confess our sins directly to Christ, who is our Supreme High Priest and Mediator, but to confess our sins one to another.

Let me say at this point that the great controversy over the Catholic sacrament of penance had nothing to do with confessing sins to a person; during the time of the Reformation, the debate had to do with the works of satisfaction (and therefore the doctrine of justification), which I won't go into here.

Speaking as a Protestant, I think that something very precious has been lost in the Protestant world in our ceasing of the confessional practice. I have yet to meet a Christian who doesn't yearn to hear somebody with authority say, "Your sins are forgiven." And I think that authority, as the Roman Catholic Church believes, was indeed given to the church. That's why even in Protestant churches we have ministers standing up and giving the assurance of pardon. People need the assurance that the sins they have confessed have in fact been forgiven. I think of Isaiah in the temple when the seraphim came with the message of God: "Behold, your sin is taken away and your sins are forgiven." How liberating that was. I've talked to psychiatrists who say that the biggest burden in terms of mental illness of people in the United States is the burden of unresolved guilt. A psychiatrist said to me, "Most people who come to see me need a priest more than they need a psychiatrist." I believe that confessing our sins can be an extremely healthy practice for us. At the same time it also can become a neurotic preoccupation if we run to each other with every detail and get carried away with it.

In Galatians 6, what is the difference between the admonition to "bear one another's burdens" and the statement that "each one shall bear his own load"?

Certainly on the surface this seems like contradictory advice. If you were looking for contradictions from the pen of the apostle, you might expect them to take place in different letters ten years apart, but you don't expect to find them in the same book or chapter, as we find here.

I think Paul is speaking about two different things. On the one hand, the call to bear one another's burdens is very central to the apostle's concept of what the church is all about. That spirit is to be present among the people of God, and the accent is on compassion. To have compassion is to enter into another person's feelings, which is a frequent motif in Paul's teaching—to laugh with those who laugh, to weep with those who weep. No individual in the body of Christ is to bear his pain or suffering alone. Each person in the body of Christ is part of a community that we celebrate and confess in the Apostles' Creed. This involves a communion of saints, the uniting together with other people so that we join in shouldering one another's burdens. If you are burdened, I am called upon to help.

In biblical terms, except for the experiment in the Jerusalem church where people tried for a short time to live by common property, the historical tradition throughout Scripture places great importance upon the individual's responsibility to do everything in his power to support himself and his family and not be an unnecessary burden on the rest of the community. As Paul said, at times sounding a little harsh, "If a man doesn't work, neither shall he eat."

Then we have the strong statement in the New Testament that if a person fails to provide for his own household, he is worse than an infidel; that is, he is worse than an unbeliever. This strong work ethic has its roots deep in the Old Testament, and it is not to be confused with the kind of "bootstrap" mentality that sees every person as self-sufficient. From the very beginning of creation there's a division of labor evident in the order God has imposed upon the world, but in that division every person has a significant role to play and responsibilities to carry out. When I as an individual am working to do what God has called me to do and I run into problems, I can look to you to help me, but that doesn't mean you do my work for me. I still have my responsibility.

Is the celebration of Christmas a pagan ritual?

That question comes up every year at Christmastime. In the first place, there's no direct biblical commandment to celebrate the birth of Jesus on December 25. There's nothing in the Bible that would even indicate that Jesus was born on December 25. In fact, there's much in the New Testament narratives that would indicate that it didn't occur during that time of year. It just so happens that on the twenty-fifth of December in the Roman Empire there was a pagan holiday that was linked to mystery religions; the pagans celebrated their festival on December 25. The Christians didn't want to participate in that, and so they said, "While everybody else is celebrating this pagan thing, we're going to have our own celebration. We're going to celebrate the thing that's most important in our lives, the incarnation of God, the birth of Jesus Christ. So this is going to be a time of joyous festivities, of celebration and worship of our God and King."

I can't think of anything more pleasing to Christ than the church celebrating his birthday every year. Keep in mind that the whole principle of annual festival and celebration is deeply rooted in ancient Jewish tradition. In the Old Testament, for example, there were times when God emphatically commanded the people to remember certain events with annual celebrations. While the New Testament doesn't require that we celebrate Christmas every year, I certainly see nothing wrong with the church's entering into this joyous time of celebrating the Incarnation, which is the dividing point of all human history. Originally, it was intended to honor, not Mithras or any of the other mystery religion cults, but the birth of our King.

Incidentally, Easter can be traced to Ishtar in the ancient world. But the Christian church coming together to celebrate the resurrection of Jesus is hardly something I think would provoke the wrath of God. I wish we had more annual festivals. The Roman Catholic Church, for example, celebrates with great joy the Feast of the Ascension every year. Some Protestant bodies do, but most do not. I wish we would celebrate that great event in the life of Christ when he was raised up into heaven to be crowned King of kings and Lord of lords. We celebrate his birth; we celebrate his death. I wish we would also celebrate his coronation.

Can you tell us why X is used when it replaces Christ in Christmas?

The simple answer to your question is that the *X* in *Christmas* is used like the *R* in R. C. My given name at birth was Robert Charles, although before I was even taken home from the hospital my parents called me by my initials, R. C., and nobody seems to be too scandalized by that.

X can mean so many things. For example, when we want to denote an unknown quantity, we use the symbol *X*. It can refer to an obscene level of films, something that is X-rated. People seem to express chagrin about seeing Christ's name dropped and replaced by this symbol for an unknown quantity *X*. Every year you see the signs and the bumper stickers saying, "Put Christ back into Christmas" as a response to this substitution of the letter *X* for the name of Christ.

First of all, you have to understand that it is not the letter *X* that is put into Christmas. We see the English letter *X* there, but actually what it involves is the first letter of the Greek name for Christ. *Christos* is the New Testament Greek for Christ. The first letter of the Greek word *Christos* is transliterated into our alphabet as an *X*. That *X* has come through church history to be a shorthand symbol for the name of Christ.

We don't see people protesting the use of the Greek letter *theta*, which is an *O* with a line across the middle. We use that as a shorthand abbreviation for God because it is the first letter of the word *Theos*, the Greek word for God. The idea of *X* as an abbreviation for the name of Christ came into use in our culture with no intent to show any disrespect for Jesus. The church has used the symbol of the fish historically because it is an acronym. *Fish* in Greek *(icthus)* involves the use of the first letters for the Greek phrase "Jesus Christ, Son of God, Savior." So the early Christians would take the first letter of those words and put those letters together to spell the Greek word for fish. That's how the symbol of the fish became the universal symbol of Christendom. There's a long and sacred history of the use of *X* to symbolize the full name of Christ, and from its origin, it has meant no disrespect.

What is the most pressing need of the evangelical church today if she is to make an impact on society?

From my perspective as an educator in the Christian world, I have a rather limited view of the problems that emerge in the church and the needs that are most pressing. We have a sinful tendency to pick our own area of specialty and make that the most important one and say that's where we really need to have the energy focused or where the changes happen. Like everybody else, that's where I am.

I happen to believe that the most urgent need right now among evangelical Christians, if they're ever going to make an impact in this world, is at the level of adult education. For Christians to grow to maturity, they have to think like

Christians. To behave in the fullness of maturity as effective, principled disciples of Christ, they need to gain an in-depth understanding of the Word of God. The Bible, I think, echoes that sentiment again and again in the numerous passages that exhort us to be mature in our understanding. At times the author of Hebrews heavily rebukes the Christian community by saying that they had spent too much time as babes in Christ; they were too content with milk and were not moving on to solid meat. If we're going to make an impact in our culture, we have to be spiritually mature.

Let me put it this way: Children don't make a lot of impact in the changing of a nation. They don't create the values and the structures of the nation in which we live. I think that has a carryover spiritually. We have to grow to adulthood as Christians before we're ever going to have any kind of significant impact on the culture.

According to the most comprehensive study/poll about religion ever conducted in the United States, we should be in the greatest revival this country has ever experienced. About 65 million people in the United States claim to be born-again Christians. And yet that same study shows little or no measurable impact by that group on the shaping of the social institutions and the structures of our nation. How is it possible that a block of people that strong does not make its influence felt more significantly in the shaping of our nation? My conclusion is that we haven't yet understood the biblical values ourselves and haven't come to that depth of understanding that provides maturity for leadership.

What is the most crucial issue confronting the church today?

I'm convinced that the most crucial issue for today's church is its own belief in the deity of Christ. This may seem like an obvious truth; after all, Christ's deity is foundational to the Christian faith. But in the history of the church, the issue of the deity of Christ has been on the center stage of conflict within the church for four centuries: the fourth century, the fifth century, the nineteenth century, and now the twentieth century.

It was very fashionable one hundred years ago, with the rise of so-called modern historical critical scholarship, to raise questions about the church's faith in its Lord, its faith in the deity of Christ himself. There was a whole school of theologians who had many good things to say about Jesus. They appreciated his ethical teaching, and they applauded his agenda for social concern. But they believed that the New Testament portrait of Jesus, which emphasized his deity and his work of cosmic redemption through giving an atonement and being raised from the dead and performing miracles, was a manifestation of prescientific, rather naive first-century people who were very much influenced by unsophisticated varieties of mythology.

In the nineteenth century there was a major crisis not only in the secular world but in the church itself that one twentieth-century theologian has called (accurately, I believe) "a crisis of unbelief." And that crisis is by no means over. In many cases the issue is underground because there is still common courtesy. People expect someone who is a church member or particularly a clergy-

man to at least give lip service to the deity of Christ. It is
still a dangerous thing for a minister to come out boldly
and publicly deny the deity of Christ. That happened a few
years ago in one mainline denomination, and overnight it
was in *Time* magazine. The secular world was astonished to
hear religious people denying the very heart of their own
religion. But if you get outside the public eye and get into
the inner machinations of the academic environment of
the Christian church, into the Christian colleges and
seminaries, then you hear issues of Christ's deity openly
debated and in many cases denied by professors. So I think
that what is at stake—the greatest issue at stake—for the
Christian church today is Christ. Do we affirm his lordship
and his deity?

14

Marriage and Family

And Adam said:

"This is now bone of my bones
And flesh of my flesh. . . ."

Therefore a man shall leave his father and mother
and be joined to his wife, and they shall become one flesh.

GENESIS 2:23-24

Questions in This Section:

What should make Christian marriages distinctive?

For those who are engaged to be married, what are the most important things to be discovering about each other?

As a minister, would you marry a believer and a nonbeliever?

Why is it important for us to take wedding vows in a formal ceremony?

Does God frown upon interracial marriages?

What should we conclude about the polygamy practiced by Old Testament heroes?

What is the biblical idea of a godly Christian marriage?

Ephesians 4:3 says, "Make it your aim to be at one in the Spirit and you will be at peace with one another." How does this translate into daily practical experience in the marriage relationship?

I need to know how to deal with my non-Christian husband. Do I go to church and leave him home?

How does a woman find dignity as a housewife and mother in today's career-minded society?

What Scriptures can a Christian wife and mother use as guidelines for her responsibilities and duties?

What does the Bible say about a mother with small children who is working outside the home?

May a Christian married couple practice birth control?

If a couple cannot conceive a child and chooses to adopt, does that indicate that the couple doesn't have enough faith that God would give them a child of their own?

As Christians, how are we to deal with the sinful lifestyles of members of our family or guests that come into our home?

My teenagers are beginning to resist going to church. Should they be forced, and if so, to what age?

How can we help our children cope with peer pressure?

Are there biblical grounds for divorce, and if so, what are they?

Under what conditions can a divorced Christian remarry?

If God's will is to keep a marriage together and all is done by one of the two people in it, can the obedience and faith of that one overcome the circumstances and actually save that failing marriage?

Why isn't physical abuse legitimate grounds for divorce?

Hypothetically, how would you counsel your daughter if her children—your grandchildren—had been sexually abused by their father, and the father was unwilling to receive counseling?

We see many problems in marriage today. What should make Christian marriages distinctive?

When we talk about the difference that being a Christian makes in life, not just in marriage, we point to the reality that as Christians we are indwelt by God the Holy Spirit, who is working within us to give us assistance to be obedient to the commandments of God. We also realize that simply because we are Christian, we are by no means exempt from sin. Christians sin. We all sin and we all continue to sin. So the fact that we are Christians is no guarantee that our marriage relationships will be what they ought to be.

I've mentioned on many occasions that I'm always distressed when I hear of pastors who are so zealous to reach people with Christianity that they make promises I don't think God ever dreamed of making to people. They will say things like, "Come to Jesus and all your problems will be solved." In my experience as a Christian and one who was suddenly and dramatically converted from a pagan lifestyle, I think that my life didn't get complicated until I became a Christian because now I'm engaged in conflict such as I never knew before. There is conflict between the desires that come out of my heart that are not righteous and what God's Word is saying I should be doing.

If there's any great advantage of being a Christian, it's the advantage of having at our disposal the wisdom of God. For any human relationship to survive disputes, disagreements, struggles, and the adjustments that all human relationships go through requires more than simple moral character. It requires great wisdom. The wisdom to handle conflict in human relationships is available to us from the Word of God. We're told, for example, something as simple as this: A soft answer turns away wrath. We're instructed by those principles of wisdom how to avoid the kind of spirit that destroys relationships. Think for a minute about the gamut of emotions we go through in our friendships and our marriages. I've always said there's no human being in the world who can make me more angry than my wife can. There's no one in the world whose criticism can hurt me more than my wife's because her opinion of me means more to me than anybody else's. I have to know how to handle my emotions in that very volatile and vulnerable relationship. The Scriptures teach me that there is a difference between hurt and grief and bitterness. I'm allowed to be hurt. I'm allowed to grieve. But I'm not allowed to be bitter. I'm allowed to be angry, but I'm not allowed to let the sun go down on my wrath. The application of those principles that God gives to us goes a long way in helping us and many other people through these rough spots in human relationships.

For those who are engaged to be married, what are the most important things to be discovering about each other?

Some statistics tell us that 70 percent of the people who get married this year will end up divorced. That's a scary thing. Obviously we're making lots of mistakes in the selection of marriage partners. Studies indicate that there are common problems arising in marriages—problems that could have been avoided if some understanding had taken place before the marriage was undertaken.

Specifically, certain items were listed as being the most cited reasons for the marriages' dissolution. The first one is sexual problems; the second one is dealing with finances; and then you get into questions of in-laws; problems of physical abuse, substance abuse, alcoholism, drug addiction, and that sort of thing. So I think it's important to know whether or not you're about to marry someone who has serious problems of addiction—that's important to find out.

I also think it's important to get to know his or her family because when you marry another person, you are taking on a family, not just an individual. It's important to develop relationships with the spouse-to-be's family and also to have some understanding of the value system he or she grew up with. One of the reasons people fight about money is that regardless of how wealthy the two people are who come into a union—they could be poverty stricken or they could be enormously wealthy—every couple has a finite amount of money. No two people on this planet have exactly the same value systems when they come together for marriage. Now let's say we have one hundred dollars to spend, and you prefer to spend it on a washing machine and I prefer to spend it on golf clubs. We have a potential conflict right now. Whatever amount of money we have, we're going to have disputes about how it should be spent. I think it's important to set up what those values are before we enter into marriage. With sexual problems ranking so high, some frank premarital counseling in that area should be high priority. The more communication is established before marriage, the better the patterns of communication will be after marriage.

As a minister, would you marry a believer and a nonbeliever; that is, an "unevenly yoked" couple?

The basis for your question obviously is the biblical text that says we ought not to be yoked unequally with unbelievers. The assumption, of course, is that this text has direct reference to marriage. The Bible doesn't explicitly say that. The Bible doesn't say that a believer is not permitted to marry an unbeliever. That metaphor of unequal yoking of oxen in pulling an ox cart is the only reference we have.

Now, I will say that in the tradition of the church the vast majority of New Testament scholars have understood that passage to mean precisely that—that it is a biblical prohibition against the marrying of a Christian to a non-Christian. This follows in the Old Testament tradition, where the children of Israel were called to seek wives from their own nation—people having the same religious persuasion. The assumption is that a person's religious commitment, if it is a genuine one, is of great importance, and if a person is united in the closest intimate relationship a human being can have with another human being and they do not share that profound passion and commitment, it can be disastrous for marriage. So the practical wisdom of the church has been, for the most part, to take a dim view of marrying believers and unbelievers because it provokes so much difficulty.

We also know that today the whole estate of marriage is under siege; we've already passed the 50 percent rate of divorce. People have enough problems in seeking a healthy and successful marriage without adding this extremely difficult point of tension to it.

But you ask me would I, as a minister, perform such a marriage. As a general rule, I do not. I don't do it because I'm convinced that God does not allow me to do it. For example, in the traditional wedding ceremony, in the service we use to solemnize weddings, the standard words go something like this: "Dearly beloved, we are gathered here today in the presence of God and of these witnesses to unite this man and this woman in the holy bonds of marriage . . ." and so on. One of the phrases of the marriage ceremony reminds us that God not only instituted marriage and ordained and sanctified marriage, but God regulates marriage by his commandments. And so I am not free to perform the marriage rite for just anybody. In fact, my own church forbids me from marrying a believer to an unbeliever except on one occasion, and that is if there's already been a physical union and a child is to be born. In those circumstances I would perform a ceremony.

Why is it important for us to take wedding vows in a formal ceremony?

You'd be surprised how many times people ask me that question. The attitude frequently expressed today, particularly among young people, is, "What difference does a piece of paper make? Why do I need to go to the church or a justice of the peace to make my marriage vows significant?" In fact, many people choose to forget about it and say they're just going to live together. "I make a promise to

her; she makes a promise to me. That's it. If we decide to
break up, then we don't have to go through all the legal
entanglement of the courts and family and church. What's
the significance of this formal ceremony? It seems to be an
act of hypocrisy anyway." There are a couple of things I
need to say about that.

In the first place, a covenant in the biblical sense is something that is done with witnesses. That's because the very
nature of a covenant is that it is an agreement between two
or more people. That agreement involves a tremendous
amount of trust among those people. It's one thing for me
to say to my wife that I will love her and cherish her and
honor her and be faithful to her privately in the backseat
of a car or on a moonlight walk along the lake. It's another
thing if I make that promise to her publicly.

Notice how the Christian ceremony starts in most traditions: "Dearly beloved, we are gathered here together in
the presence of God and of these witnesses to unite this
man and this woman in the holy bonds of matrimony."
When we go through the ceremony, there are words to this
effect: "We recognize and acknowledge that marriage is
not a human institution that somebody invented as a soci-
etal convention because they thought it was a good idea,
but as Christians we believe and we confess that God
ordained marriage and that God instituted marriage."

We recognize that marriage as a ceremony was sanctified
by Christ's presence and benediction at the wedding feast
at Cana, for example. But then we go on to say in the service that we acknowledge that God regulates marriage. He
didn't just invent it and give it to us to handle however we
want, but rather God himself remains the ultimate author-

ity over marriage. In the establishment of solemn covenants, I believe solemn assemblies is part of that regulative principle of marriage that comes to us from God and from sacred Scripture. We recognize, however, that it doesn't have to be done in a church. We recognize that marriage is instituted for all people, whether they're Christians or non-Christians, and that's why we recognize marriages performed by some civil authority or an ecclesiastical authority publicly. Without the witnesses there is no legal covenant, no legal commitment, no formal binding responsibility for me to keep my promises. This way we do it formally and publicly. We make that promise, not in the backseat of a car, but before every authority structure that means anything to us: our friends, our family, our church, and the state. If I don't take my promise seriously, or if my friends don't, or if the church doesn't, or even if the state doesn't, God certainly will. At least in our culture, even today with the loose laws of divorce, the state still takes those vows seriously.

Does God frown upon interracial marriages?

Some people insist that the Bible meant for the races to remain pure, therefore prohibiting any kind of interracial marriage. Usually two biblical texts are drawn upon to support that view. One is the fact that Noah had three sons, Shem, Ham, and Japheth. As you recall, Shem received a patriarchal blessing, and an enlargement of that was given to Japheth. Ham, because he looked upon his father's nakedness, was cursed. "Cursed be Canaan" was the malediction that Noah pronounced on Ham and his descen-

dants. Some have neatly contrived from the three sons of
Noah, three survivors of the flood, that this is the historic
basis for the three basic generic types of human beings:
the Caucasian, the Negroid, and the Mongoloid. They
claim that this is the biblical justification for there being a
curse put on the black race, and white people should have
no intermarriage with them. This was cited, for example,
in the early documents of Mormonism, which was a great
embarrassment to them when it was made public a few
years ago.

Others go back to Creation, where we read that God created everything "after its kind." People say that this is the
divine order of things in creation, that God made things
according to their kind, and his intent was that they should
stay according to their kind.

In the case of both these arguments, I would say that
that is the flimsiest evidence I can think of to support what
is ultimately a racist view of the matter. I don't see anything, even in Scripture, that would prohibit interracial
marriage other than the problems people might face in
terms of cultural prejudices. Any couple that chooses to
get married in a culture that has a high degree of racism is
asking for all kinds of tension directed against their marriage. If they are willing to do that, it doesn't mean that
they are sinning by going ahead and entering into a marriage covenant.

I think one of the strongest texts that does relate to this
is in the Old Testament, where we read that Moses (who
was the mediator of the old covenant) took to himself a
wife who was a Cushite. A Cushite was an Ethiopian. All of
the evidence that we can construct on Old Testament

history indicates that Moses' wife was black. We also read that his sister, Miriam, became very distressed by the fact that her brother married a Cushite. It was a racist reaction. Miriam got angry and rebuked Moses. Because of Miriam's response, God judged Miriam and gave her leprosy. So if anything, it would seem to me that God frowns upon those who are racists.

What should we conclude about the polygamy practiced by Old Testament heroes?

We need to look at several things with respect to the biblical record. The Bible records that these great saints of the Old Testament on many occasions not only had more than one wife but in some cases (including those of David and Solomon) had hundreds of wives or concubines, which would seem to be in flagrant disobedience to the biblical principles of marriage. Polygamy was in fact flagrant disregard of the design for marriage that God set forth in Creation. I think it's clear not only in the Old Testament record itself but in how the New Testament appeals to the Old Testament, saying that marriage was to be monogamous—one wife, one husband. That's the way it was intended for all generations.

If you look carefully at the opening chapters of Genesis, you will see that after Cain kills Abel, Adam and Eve have another son, whose name is Seth. In looking at the genealogy of these two sons of Adam and Eve, we see that the descendants of Seth are characterized by godliness and righteousness. It was out of that line that Methuselah and ultimately Noah came, as well as Enoch, who was taken directly into heaven because he walked with God.

If you look at the line of Cain, it reads like a rogues' gallery, just one rascal after another. One of the chief rascals, whose biographical sketch is included in the early chapters of Genesis, is a fellow by the name of Lamech, who is distinguished for two things. One is the ghastly sword song that he writes and sings in Genesis, which is a celebration of violence. Also he is noted for being the first polygamist. The Bible doesn't say, "He was the first polygamist and this is a bad thing." It just mentions that he was the first polygamist, but it does so in the context of describing the radical expansion of human corruption and of fallenness. The Old Testament implies that polygamy was in defiance of the law of God.

Obviously, God did not call down these Old Testament heroes for their polygamy or punish them for it. He dealt with their extreme fallenness through forbearance. This forbearance ended with the appearance of Christ and the new covenant.

I've been married for a little over four years now and recently I've come to understand my Christian faith a little more. And I want to know, What is the biblical idea of a godly Christian marriage?

Some scriptural principles apply to every marriage. One of the elements of the marriage service that we find in the traditional ceremony of marriage that crosses denominations is that when we come together for marriage we say, "Dearly beloved, we are assembled together here in the presence of God and of these witnesses," etc. We recognize the fact that marriage is something that was instituted by God, ordained of God, and given sacred approval of Christ by his presence at the wedding feast at Cana. But we have a line in the traditional marriage that is often overlooked, and that is this statement: "That marriage is regulated by God's commandments." It's not simply that God ordained and instituted marriage and gave it to us as a gift and said, "Here is the gift, now you go and use it however you want to." Rather, what God ordains and institutes, he also exercises his sovereignty over within the framework of marriage. Obviously, a marriage that is to last has to be based upon a kind of mutual trust and fidelity. That's why when we take the vows, vows meaning that I commit myself body and soul to my wife as long as we both shall live, she has a reason and a right to trust that I am going to keep my word. God holds us responsible for that kind of commitment so that at the heart of every union between two people is this principle of trust. That's why the Bible takes such a dim view of adultery, for example, because it is the supreme act of infidelity that breaks the trust and breaks the faith upon which the marriage is built.

Of course, there are guidelines in terms of how the family is supposed to be run, even though it is very unpopular in our day and age. I don't think we can escape the fact that the New Testament gives the responsibility for headship or leadership in the home to the husband. That responsibility is not a license for tyranny. It is not a license for domination or for destroying the dignity of the woman, but rather it's a burden. It's a task where the buck stops with the husband in terms of giving leadership and direction in the home. But it's still in relationship of mutual love and respect of a vital partnership in the home.

These are just a few of the guidelines. Of course, the Bible has much more to say about the patterns upon which a healthy marriage is to be established.

The Phillips translation of Ephesians 4:3 says, "Make it your aim to be at one in the Spirit, and you will be bound together in peace." How does this translate into daily practical experience in the marriage relationship?

The false prophets of Israel cried, "Peace, peace" when there was no peace! It's a lot easier to declare a peace than to achieve a peace. It's also one thing to be at peace when you're all by yourself and another to be at peace when you're in a relationship with another person. Of course, there are a lot of people who don't have peace even when they're alone.

As soon as we get into the marriage relationship, which is the closest possible union any two people can have, many things can disturb the peace of that relationship. Any kind of conflict can come along and upset the peacefulness that should be at the heart of a marriage. I am absolutely convinced that it takes work on the part of both people for peace to reign in marriage. It's not natural for two human beings to spend a long time in close proximity with each other without some conflicts emerging. No two people in this world have exactly the same agenda, value system, tastes, likes, and dislikes. There are inevitable points of conflict, and it is conflict that upsets peace. I think that when we strive for oneness in spirit, we have to work to establish peace.

We have to learn the fruit of the Spirit that promotes peace; to have a spirit within ourselves of gentleness, kindness, love, and, particularly, patience. Those things do not come automatically. They don't come by nature, because by nature we tend to be impatient. We have to work at it. And just as diplomats have an earnest desire to stop conflicts from emerging on an international level in terms of warfare, so we have to become diplomats in our home, that is, diplomats who have a concern for the feelings of our partners.

I think my wife, for example, is the most sensitive woman in the United States of America. She has to be because I'm one of the most insensitive people in the world. I get off on a cloud and get like the wacky, absent-minded professor. That can drive anybody crazy. But my wife works at maintaining peace and practicing diplomacy, and that's been an example to me. Instead of letting an annoyance be fanned into a major conflict and a fight, we begin to come to understanding. One of the great principles is this: Anytime you see anger, look for the pain behind it. It's a lot easier to deal with pain than with anger. Anger breeds conflict. Dealing with pain brings peace.

I need to know how to deal with my non-Christian husband. Do I go to church and leave him at home? How do I explain him to the children?

I think the mistake that so many women make when they are in this situation is that they feel somehow God has called them to be the husband's conscience, and they end up nagging their husbands. The most significant thing a woman can do if her husband is not a Christian is to be the most godly wife she can possibly be to that man.

I knew a teenage boy who came into my study and announced that he had assumed for himself the role of the spiritual leader of the house because his father was not a Christian. Since his father had neglected the responsibility of being the priest of the home, this young man said that he believed the mantle had fallen upon him. I said, "No, God does not call you to supplant your father's role. If your father doesn't do what God calls him to do, that is not a license for you to take his place. God called you to be a son, not the father."

And so I see wives who say, "OK, my husband is not doing his duty, so I'm going to be wife and husband. I'm going to be the priest of the family." I don't think that's what God wants you to do. What he wants you to do is be a godly wife to your husband.

It gets particularly sticky when the husband says, "I don't want you wasting time going to church." Now you have to struggle with a divided loyalty. You're trying to serve two masters, as it were. God does call you to submit to the headship of your husband. Some Christians are teaching that the wife is supposed to obey her husband no matter what that husband says. Let me stress that that is a ghastly distortion of the teaching of Scripture. No woman is ever to obey her husband if her husband commands her to do something that God clearly prohibits.

If your husband (non-Christian or otherwise) forbids you to do something God commands, you must disobey him. For example, does God command his people to be in his church? The Scripture says that we ought not to forsake the assembling together of the saints. I would say that that means you are supposed to be in church on Sunday mornings, and if your husband does not allow you, you will have to disobey him in order to obey God. But that doesn't mean God calls you to be in church seven days a week. What you do, I think, is bend over backwards to make sure that you are not defying your husband at points where God has left you free to support him.

How does a woman find dignity as a housewife and mother in today's career-minded society?

The quest for dignity is not limited to women nor to women in careers or in the home, but it's a universal quest. I've been involved in many, many seminars that focus on the quest of human dignity, and I have found that every person I have ever talked to wants to be treated with dignity and wants to be sure they have dignity. At the same time, I have discovered that giving a clear definition to the concept of dignity is a very difficult task, yet everybody knows when they have lost dignity.

The woman whose vocation is being a homemaker and a mother, and that is her career rather than working in the business community, is feeling sort of a reverse pressure that other women felt a few years ago when they went into the business world and were discriminated against for somehow abandoning their place in the home. Women today are feeling an imposed guilt for not having a career; somehow being a homemaker is considered a less-than-dignified vocation.

Obviously God clearly affirms the dignity of that role for a woman. The children will rise up and call her blessed. But when God's Word affirms the dignity or value of something, that is not always enough for us to keep our own security about it. It should be enough—if God says it, that should settle it. But it doesn't settle it with us. We're feeble, fragile in our feelings, and we can be made insecure by the culture that looks down upon this particular role.

I would say that the single most important individual in maintaining the dignity of a woman in the home is the husband in the home. If the husband demeans or ignores or puts down or treats as insignificant the labor of his wife, he becomes the principal destroyer of this woman's dignity. And so the first thing that has to be done to restore the dignity of the woman in the home is having the husband and children create an environment of appreciation and verbalize that appreciation.

Somebody once made the statement that the negative input of one criticism requires nine compliments to be overcome in our personalities. That's certainly true. One criticism of a wife in the home can devastate her self-esteem in that role, particularly when the rest of the culture is trying to tell her that homemaking and mothering are no longer significant enterprises.

What Scriptures can a Christian wife and mother use as guidelines for her responsibilities and duties?

First of all, you are a human being, and you're a person who's been claimed by Christ. You are in the kingdom, so the

Scriptures you use to learn of your responsibilities and duties before God start at Genesis 1:1 and end with the last verse in the book of Revelation. All of the Word of God is to instruct you in terms of your duties and responsibilities. It's absolutely vital that Christians learn to live by principles and that those principles come to us from the Scriptures. The basic principles of life apply to us whatever our situation is, whether it's wife or husband, mother or father, or single.

The book of Ephesians sets forth some specific responsibilities for a wife in her marital relationship and also in her parental responsibilities.

One of the most famous and controversial verses is the command that God gives through the apostle Paul for wives to be subject to their husbands. That has created quite a lot of debate and also a lot of misunderstanding. Sometimes qualifiers for general principles are given to us in other Scriptures. For example, the Bible tells us that we're all responsible to obey the civil magistrates, but there are occasions when a Christian not only may disobey but must disobey the civil magistrates, as the apostles did when the Sanhedrin forbade them to preach the gospel. The apostle asked whether we should obey man or God. Anytime a husband commands a wife to do something that God forbids or does not allow her to do something that God commands, not only may that wife refuse to be in submission to her husband but she must disobey him. She first of all has her own responsiblitiy to live her life before God. That text in Ephesians should never be used as a license for men to tyrannize their wives. We know that some men have taken that text and used it to beat women down and try to bring them into a slavish obedience to themselves, something the text never intended.

Also, Proverbs 31 gives you a great view of the entrepreneurial woman.

What does the Bible say about a mother with small children who is working outside of the home?

The Bible describes the godly woman in the classical statement in the book of Proverbs (chapter 31). If we look at that as a job description of a godly wife, I think it would be threatening to just about every woman in the world because that woman is the entrepreneur's entrepreneur. Not only is she being a wife and a mother but she is at the gate early in the morning. She is performing services, and she's involved in a business enterprise.

I think that a mother's first responsibility is to the young children in the home, particularly the infants. If the mother can take care of the children and also be involved in a career, that's something that the woman has to work out between herself, her family, and God because the Bible does not give a prohibition or an explicit commandment regarding this. There is a lot of emotion about it in the Christian world, and there are those who argue that every woman has a right to be a mother and a career person at the same time.

We are supposed not only to study these matters in terms of what God reveals to us in Scripture but to pay attention to what used to be called natural law. I happen to believe that God reveals himself not only in the Bible but also in the scientific laboratory, that all truth is God's truth, and that all truth meets at the top. I say that for this reason: One of the things that gives me an uneasy feeling about young mothers working very soon after they have children is the studies indicating that a child's dependence on the mother is extremely powerful from the time of birth until the child is five years old. In other words, the studies indicate that the single most important contributing factor to the development of a personality of a human being from birth to age five is the mother's relationship to the child. From age six to age ten it is the father's relationship to that child, and then from age eleven to age eighteen it is the child's peer relationships.

If that research is valid and accurate, then it gives me pause. I don't want to just say, "Hey, do your thing and do whatever you want to do," because caring for a child is an extremely important enterprise. I don't think that the Bible says that only the mother has the responsibility to take care of the child. The father also has this responsibility; we just tacitly assume it's OK for the father to be at work eight hours a day. Does that mean that the mother has to stay home? We need to pay attention to all the information. The Bible doesn't give us a simple formula for working out family life.

May a Christian married couple practice birth control?

I presume you mean by that artificial methods of birth control. That's one of those issues in Christian ethics where there is a seriously divided house in the history of the church. The Roman Catholic Church, as you are aware, has taken a very dim view of artificial birth control. Papal encyclicals as recently as the last decade have reinforced the Roman Catholic prohibition of artificial means of birth control on certain theological grounds.

Protestantism has allowed for various types of birth control, some allowing almost any kind of artificial birth control, others drawing a line between those that are contraceptive and those that are in fact abortive. Certain varieties of IUDs have been discovered to be not so much contraceptive as abortive inasmuch as they destroy the fertilized egg. That has created an ethical crisis among Protestants who are profoundly opposed to abortion of any type.

The basic issue between Protestantism and Roman Catholicism has focused on what is the legitimate use of sexual intercourse within marriage. Historically Rome has taken the position that the goal of sexual intercourse and the justification for the sexual act is procreation. So anything that artificially prevents the possibility of procreation changes the intended purpose of the sexual relationship, making it therefore an unnatural type of act.

Protestants on the other hand have tended to include in the legitimate use of sex between married people the simple pleasure of the enjoyment of the sexual relationship—the intimacy it brings and the fact that we are physically composed in such a way that sexual intercourse is by natural design pleasurable.

Theoretically, God could have invented sex in a way that it wasn't pleasurable but merely a biological function necessary for reproduction. So some are saying that we have the right to carry out the mandate of creation, to have dominion over the earth, and if we can plan our families through this, then it's all right. But even among certain conservative Protestants there are those who raise a question at this level: Is artificial birth control against nature? Does it violate natural law by bringing into the sexual relationship a hindrance to the full expression of it? It's for that reason that many Protestants say that this is wrong.

If a couple cannot conceive a child and chooses to adopt, does that indicate that the couple doesn't have enough faith that God would give them a child of their own?

I would say emphatically not; that would not be any necessary indication that the people didn't have enough faith. It probably is an indication that the people didn't have enough biological equipment to bear a child. It's like the man born blind that we find in the Gospel of John; was this man born blind because he didn't have enough faith? Obviously not, although he did receive his sight later on. People might point to that and say once he got the faith, then he got his eyes, and if people would just have enough faith, then they'll get the baby.

We find occasions in Scripture where people who are described as people of faith do not get the fullness of their desires completed. We know that Paul prayed for the relief from his thorn in the flesh. Whether it was physical or whatever it was, it still was something that bothered him, and he prayed. If any man ever prayed in faith, it was the apostle Paul. He prayed three times for God to remove this occasion for suffering from him, and as you know, God said no. His answer to Paul was, "My grace is sufficient for you." It wasn't a matter of a lack of faith that caused God not to alleviate this suffering for Paul.

Also in the New Testament we see that Peter is arrested and put into prison, and the disciples go into the upper room and pray as hard as they can for him. Even as they were praying, an angel opened the prison doors and Peter came to the prayer meeting. They at least had enough faith to make that request, and Peter was released.

The apostle James was also arrested, but his execution was carried to completion. The Bible doesn't say that the other apostles prayed for Peter and didn't pray for James. And I can't imagine that they didn't pray just as earnestly for James as they did for Peter. For whatever reasons, God was not pleased to say yes to that particular prayer.

We see that Paul left one of his comrades sick. Obviously he had prayed for him and did not get the answer he had hoped for any more than Jesus got his request in the Garden of Gethsemane.

You may say that these are not the same as having babies, but it's the same principle. In both Old and New Testaments we have cases of barren women being given that special gift of grace and becoming pregnant (Hannah and Elizabeth, for instance). Sarah, in her barrenness, was given a special supernatural deliverance from it, but not all of the faithful of God's people who were barren were able at one point in this world to have children. It's one of those things that you can't set up a law for. There is ample evidence throughout the history of believers everywhere that lack of certain blessings is not always—or even most of the time—the result of a lack of faith.

As Christians, how are we to deal with the sinful lifestyles of members of our family or guests that come into our home?

We are called to be gracious people. God has not called us to be the policemen of the world. I have run into this problem many times in Christian families where one member of the family is a Christian and the other members aren't Christians. Sometimes Christians become so intolerant and judgmental that they give a bad impression to the rest of the family by their negative, critical behavior. When they do that, they feel completely justified because that to which they are reacting is indeed a sinful lifestyle. We're often blind to our own intolerance at that point, forgetting who we are and where we have come from and the fact that the only way we can exist in the family of God is by grace. I think that Christians need to remember who they are.

We need to let people know that, whether we approve or disapprove of their lifestyle, we are *for them* as people. When my daughter went from junior high to senior high, she came home one night and I asked her, "Well, how do you like high school?" She said, "I don't like it at all." And I asked, "What's the matter? You loved junior high." And she replied, "When I was in junior high, I felt like our teachers were for us. They disciplined us, they gave us homework, they rebuked us and all of that, but somehow they communicated to us that they were behind us and they really cared about us. I get the feeling in this school that the teachers aren't for us." That's the critical thing in terms of these relationships because you can do more for people by

loving them than you ever will be able to do by judging
them.

Keep in mind that the principal power by which people
are brought under conviction of sin is the Holy Spirit. You
are not the Holy Spirit, and neither am I. Now that doesn't
mean that we are therefore trying so hard to get along
with them that we endorse and embrace everything they
do. We don't have to be judgmental to communicate that
we live a different way. In fact, we have to go overboard to
communicate our love.

**My teenagers are beginning to resist going to church.
Should they be forced, and if so, to what age?**

Being a parent is one of the most difficult and thrilling
experiences that any human being ever has the privilege of
going through. Exercising discipline over our children
many times requires the wisdom of Solomon. I know this
sounds like terrible theology, but sometimes I think raising
children is 10 percent skill and 90 percent luck. It's very
difficult to discern how much pressure we can apply before
we are provoking our children and making matters worse.
I've dealt with young people whose parents are so pushy
and demanding that their very harshness is the thing driving them away from the church.

The general answer to your question is that when you
have children, you have a responsibility under God to raise
them in the nurture and admonition of the Lord. In my
church we baptize infants, and when we do, as a congregation we make a promise before God to raise these children
in the nurture and admonition of the Lord. Even if you

don't practice infant baptism, that responsibility is still there. The Bible tells us that we ought never to neglect the assembling together of the saints, which is corporate worship on Sunday morning. I take that to mean that it is my obligation as a Christian, as a member of the covenant community, to be in worship on Sunday morning with my household. So it is my responsibility to see to it that my children are in church. It is also my responsibility to be sensitive and gentle and not tyrannical, so I have to somehow find that fine line of being firm but loving, gentle, and kind in that firmness. Again, I am accountable to God for their being there for the nurture and instruction of the things of God on Sunday morning. So my answer to the first part of your question is yes.

I don't like the word "force" because to some people that means baseball bats and child abuse. That's not what I'm talking about. I am talking about parental leadership whereby the authority resides in the parents and you see to it that the authority is carried out. You asked to what age: I would say as long as the children are under your roof and under your authority as part of your family unit. I would encourage you to make it a special point of concern to do everything in your power to get your kids to church and to make it an attractive time for them rather than a bad experience.

How can we help our children cope with peer pressure?

You're not asking me theology anymore—now you're asking me to do magic! I'm not sure I'm equipped to deal with that. I breathed a sigh of relief when our youngest child turned twenty-one, having survived those teenage years.

The research coming out of the scientific community has indicated some very sobering things to us. You can't absolutize these things, but as a general pattern, the single most important relationship that shapes a child's identity, from birth to age five, is that child's relationship to its mother. That doesn't mean that the other relationships are unimportant, but the mother is of supreme importance at that point. Then from age six to about twelve, the single most important relationship that child has is with the father.

But from age thirteen onward a child's most significant relationships are with his or her peers. So there is a very real sense in which our ability to continue to shape the child's attitudes and value system is severely limited once they enter those teenage years.

As a Christian and a theologian, I do not believe in luck. But 90 percent of raising children is luck! You do everything you can, and then you stand back and hope for the best—you trust them to God. You try to instill principles in your children. And one of the most important things parents can do with a teenager is to keep the lines of communication open. Sometimes that can be very difficult. When they hit thirteen, each of our kids started to live in a cave— their room. They'd come home from school, disappear into the cave, and I'd hear music coming out of there. I'd wonder whether there was any human being alive up there, and it was very difficult to get them to come out of the cave and enter into family life. Those were hard times, and we had to persevere through them. Vesta and I used to comfort each other by saying, "This is just a phase. If we can survive it, they'll survive it." But keep the lines of communication open, and particularly when they are teenagers, make sure those lines of communication run both ways.

Kids will talk, but they need the opportunity. They need to be sure they can come to their parents. Make sure your kids know that you support more than criticize them and that they can count on you when times are difficult or confusing.

Are there any biblical grounds for divorce, and if so, what are they?

A lot of the debate over divorce has to do with the way we interpret and handle Jesus' teaching on the subject. In Matthew's Gospel, for example, the Pharisees come to Jesus for a decision and they are trying to trick him into speaking against the law of Moses. They ask, "Is it lawful to put away one's wife in the case of infidelity?"

At that time we know from our own historical research that there was an ongoing debate in Israel between two major rabbinical schools, the school of Shammai, which was a very conservative school, and the school of Hillel, which took a more liberal approach to interpreting the Old Testament law. The liberal view allowed divorce on many grounds, giving a very broad interpretation to the meaning of "unclean thing" in the Old Testament legislation. The more conservative school took a very narrow view of the matter and said that only on the grounds of adultery could divorce be legitimized in Israel.

To me it seems clear that Jesus does allow divorce in the case of adultery. On the one hand, he said that if a man divorces his wife for any other reason than sexual immorality, then of course he is guilty of sin. So Jesus, at that point, says that there ought not to be divorce for grounds other than sexual impurity or immorality.

Then he goes on to say that because of the hardness of our hearts, the law was given to Moses that did make a provision for divorce in the Old Testament. He then quotes the law from Deuteronomy in which the so-called unclean thing is cited as the legitimate grounds for divorce in the Old Testament. But Jesus hastens to add this statement: "But from the beginning it was not so" (Matt. 19:8). His reference back to Creation reminds us of the sanctity of marriage. It's certainly true that the provision for divorce is given to us because of the hardness of hearts, because of sin. Because adultery is a sin, when somebody violates marriage through adultery and breaks that trust, then the sacred vow, and the innocent party in the divorce, is so violated that the provision is given to them in that context of fallenness to be engaged lawfully in divorce.

It's obvious that Jesus is rebuking the liberal view of divorce that was prevalent in his own day. I think that Jesus does remind us that the original intention of marriage did not include divorce. He acknowledges that there is a ground, and he is not criticizing God for making this allowance in the Old Testament. People are fallen, and God does condescend to the fact that people commit sins against marriage that are serious enough to be grounds for dissolving the marriage. That sin is sexual infidelity.

I think one other ground for divorce given by the apos-

tle Paul in the Corinthian correspondence is the case of
the willful and irreparable separation of the unbeliever
(1 Cor. 7:15). Those are the only two grounds I find in
Scripture.

**There seems to be a difference of opinion as to
whether a divorced Christian can ever remarry. When,
and under what conditions, is this permissible?**

It is difficult to sort out Jesus' teaching on this, partly
because, when he addressed the problem, it was in the context of settling a dispute between different rabbinical
schools of the day. The religious scholars came to Jesus
and asked about the lawfulness of divorcing—a man divorcing his wife for this cause or that cause. Jesus, in responding to that, reminded the Pharisees that Moses did give a
provision for divorce in the Old Testament, but that at the
same time the original design for marriage did not include
the concept of divorce. He acknowledged Moses' provision, but he's not rebuking Moses for doing that, for Moses
was simply an agent of God at that point. So God, in the
old covenant, did clearly give provision for divorce.

However, because Jesus speaks to that and reminds them
that the original purpose was no divorce, some have concluded that what Jesus was doing was removing the Old
Testament provision for divorce and saying that there's no
justification for divorce whatsoever.

Now how you view divorce will have tremendous bearing
on how you view the question of remarriage. If you take
the position that divorce is never legitimate, then you
would have to say that the remarriage of a divorced person

is never legitimate either. So before you can talk about the legitimacy of remarriage, you first have to settle whether or not there are any legitimate grounds for divorce.

I take the position that there are in fact legitimate grounds for divorce: Sexual infidelity is one, and the other one is separation of the unbeliever. Paul says that if an unbelieving spouse wants out and departs, the believer is then free. Now he doesn't define what free is. Does that mean free just to let him go and then live a life of celibacy and singleness? Some people take that view. I think that Paul means free from the marriage contract, from the oaths and obligations; that person is now considered single and, I would say, free to remarry.

So I take the position that an innocent party in divorce is free to remarry. Now, when we say innocent or guilty, we recognize that everybody contributes to the breakdown of a marriage. By "guilty party" I mean the one who committed the sin serious enough to dissolve the marriage. But I would also say that even the guilty party can get remarried if there is authentic repentance.

In 1 John 5:14-15 it talks about asking things according to God's will and our desires will be answered. If God's will is to keep a marriage together and all is done by one of the two, can the obedience and faith of that one overcome the circumstances and actually save that failing marriage?

The easy answer to your question is, of course the actions of one can be the springboard for the saving of the marriage. However, it doesn't necessarily follow that it absolutely will in every instance and in that way. Many times in marriage counseling one spouse is present while the other person isn't willing to be a participant. It certainly makes it a lot easier to effect reconciliation and a healthy marriage if both parties are willing to work at it, but the fact that one person changes does change the nature of the relationship. It's almost impossible that the total relationship won't change. It might get worse, but it will certainly change. When one person changes, the other partner who is living in such close proximity is also bound to move somewhat in response to the change of the first party.

Now let's relate this to the issue of the promise of 1 John, that if we pray according to the will of God and act according to the will of God, can we be sure that our desires will be met and that God will bless that marriage? I think we have to be very careful to understand that passage in light of everything the New Testament teaches about prayer and the nature of the will of God, both of which are highly complex. The Bible tells us that if any two people agree on any one thing, that it will be done for them. Is that meant in an absolute sense? Then all we would have to do is have two of us agree that we'd like to see a cure for cancer and the end of all war in the world and the return of Jesus tonight. If we agreed on that, God would have to do it to be true to his word. That's obviously not what he meant. That's a reference to the Old Testament concept of witnesses agreeing, witnesses who are informed by the Word of God and witnesses who are in touch with the revealed Word of God. It also refers to what God has spoken and what he has had recorded in sacred Scripture. When we pray according to Scripture, we're not going to pray that God is going to bring things to pass until certain other things take place first. We're simply telling him our desires rather than praying according to his explicitly revealed will.

Also, to pray according to the will of God means to pray according to the precepts of God, according to the law of God. Here's where you say God wills the fruition of a good marriage. What we mean by that is that God has commanded that our marriages be healthy and wholesome and righteous. Certainly I think we can take comfort from the verse that if we do everything in our power to obey what God has ordered in terms of our responsibilities in marriage, while praying for the salvation of marriage, we have every reason to be optimistic that that desire will be honored by God.

Why isn't physical abuse legitimate grounds for divorce?

I don't know why God has not included wife abuse or husband abuse as grounds for divorce. I only know that he hasn't. I also have to say very candidly that if I were God, I would make that a grounds for divorce because abuse within marriage is a dreadful reality. If anything is a violation of human dignity and of the sacred vows of marriage, it is physical abuse of another person. I've wondered myself many times why God doesn't include that under his list of legitimate grounds for divorce.

I do know that we have options short of divorce in these situations. Obviously, if we're talking about a Christian family (and this is something that does take place in Christian homes), this is a situation in which the discipline of the church needs to be applied fully in order to protect the person who is being abused; the restraint of ecclesiastical authority is to be used in that situation. If that fails or if people don't even have that available to them because they're outside the church, there are other avenues of safety and protection. Many people use the legal system. I've counseled women in the past to call the police. If worse comes to worse, throw the abuser in jail because assault and battery just can't be tolerated in the home or on the streets, in the school or in the church. We do have provisions in our civil law to protect people from that kind of assault.

There are grounds in a Christian community for at least temporary separation if the abusing partner refuses to mend their ways. Maybe there is no provision for divorce in these cases because God sees that this problem, as serious and severe as it is, can be overcome. In many cases, we have seen marriages redeemed after people have repented and overcome destructive patterns of behavior. But it's an extremely serious problem in our culture and one that is only beginning to come to light, just as child abuse has come to light in the past few years.

Hypothetically, how would you counsel your daughter regarding the divorce issue if her children—your grandchildren—had been sexually abused by their father, and the father was unwilling to receive counseling?

I hope that question remains always and forever a hypothetical one, but it is certainly a reality for some people. If what you just described happened to my daughter, or to any-body else's daughter, and they came to me for pastoral counsel, and the husband refused to submit to counseling, to church discipline, and all of the other avenues that you try to explore, then in all probability my counsel would be for the wife to seek a divorce. I think she would have bibli-cal grounds. The sexual abuse of the children would be a sexual violation of the marriage. I think it is a form of adul-tery. If it were done in an impenitent way, I would think that the woman would not only have the right but would have good reason to instigate proceedings for her own pro-tection as well as for the protection of the children. It would probably be wise for her to exercise her biblical option of divorce.

No two situations like this are exactly the same, and so I hesitate to give general advice about how to deal with it. Divorce is certainly not the first solution, but I do think that there are times when ministers ought to counsel in that direction (given the assumption that there are such things as legitimate grounds for divorce).

I've seen women who have been victims of repeated infi-delities by their husbands or who have known that a sexu-ally abusive situation existed in their home. But some women feel that the Word of God really doesn't give them the option of divorce. And just because we have the right to do something, it's not always wise to exercise that right. The Bible doesn't say you have to get divorced in such a situation, but I think it does say that you may. The sexual abuse of children is a heinous crime against the entire family, and it requires strong measures.

15

Career Issues

There are diversities of gifts, but the same Spirit.
There are differences of ministries, but the same Lord.
And there are diversities of activities,
but it is the same God who works all in all.

1 CORINTHIANS 12:4-6

Questions in This Section:

I became a lawyer nine years ago, before I was a Christian. I'm wondering now how I can know whether or not I should stay in a profession that was chosen years ago on the basis of personal strengths and desires, and how I can trust God for the radical change that might be involved in a midlife career change.

I've been wrestling with a career decision. What thinking processes should Christians use in decision making?

What is the biblical concept, if any, of retirement?

Is God's highest calling full-time Christian ministry, certain spiritual activities such as prayer or witnessing, and Bible study? Are they higher priorities than the everyday activities of a person in business?

What does it mean to be called into the ministry?

How should Christian values impact business ethics in the office?

What do you think of committed Christians being in partnership with nonbelievers, particularly nonbelievers who are hostile to the Lord?

Do labor unions pose ethical problems for Christians?

How can an employer show employees Christlike dignity?

I became a lawyer nine years ago, before I was a Christian. I'm wondering now how I can know whether or not I should stay in a profession that was chosen years ago on the basis of personal strengths and desires, and how I can trust God for the radical change that might be involved in a midlife career change.

The first person the Bible speaks of as being filled with the Holy Spirit was a man by the name of Bezalel who along with Oholiab was chosen of God to be an artisan and craftsman to fashion the utensils and the furniture for the building of the tabernacle. This is important for us to realize because so often we think that the only vocations or tasks that receive the benediction of God or the anointing of the Spirit are those that are associated with full-time Christian ministry.

The very term *vocation* comes from the Latin *vocare*, which means "to call." We believe that God calls people to various vocations, and he does that calling not only in a sacred environment but also in a secular one. The fact that you chose a particular career or vocation before you became a Christian does not indicate that you are necessarily out of the vocation that God would have you in now that you are a Christian. Frequently I see that when people are converted, the first question they have is, Does that mean I'm supposed to stop the enterprise I'm in now? Well, if you're in some illegitimate enterprise—if you're a thief, for instance—then of course you have to stop being a thief. But we need to remember that most likely Bezalel or

Oholiab were already gifted and given talents by God for their professions before they were filled with the Spirit. It would seem that, in his wisdom, God would call people into careers and ministries for which they have been gifted all along; sometimes we have discovered the best use of our natural gifts before we become Christians, and sometimes that comes after conversion.

There certainly are occasions on which God does lead a person into a new career—and sometimes that change is radical. Who's a better example of that than Moses? Moses was an old man before God called him to a position of leadership. He'd spent virtually his whole life as a shepherd in the wilderness before he became a statesman and a leader of a nation. I think of a couple of other men who are famous in our time. Winston Churchill and Douglas MacArthur, two of the most prominent individuals in the twentieth century, did not embark upon the things that made them famous until after they reached what we would call retirement age. I support the people who ask themselves at age thirty-five or forty, or even fifty, if it's time for a new career, a new vocation. There's nothing in the Bible that says you have to stay in one field all your life. So often, the decisions of career and vocation are made way too early, and we get locked into professions that are not at all fulfilling for us or the best use of our gifts.

I've been wrestling with a career decision. What thinking processes should Christians use in decision making?

Unfortunately, in today's Christian environment the whole idea of thinking has become suspect. It's as if using our natural abilities of intellect—particularly in areas of career—somehow represents a lack of faith. The concept is that we're supposed to entrust our career and our vocation to God, and God will do the thinking for us; God will show us through some kind of miraculous sign what he wants us to do. I think the most significant thing we're called to do when we're seeking the will of God in our lives, whether it's for our vocation or for our choice of a mate or where we're to live, is to think. Now, *how* are we to think? In what *way* are we to think? The Bible tells us that we ought to make a sober analysis of our gifts and talents. We recognize in doing so that it is God who gives us the gifts. It is God who gives us the talent, and it is God whom we are trying to serve and whom we want to please. That's why we want to discern what his will is for our vocation. How do we make a sober analysis of our gifts and talents? We have to think, and we have to think deeply and accurately. We can get some help in this process. We are encouraged by Scripture to seek the counsel of others because usually our gifts are recognized by the body of Christ. People in our church, in our family, and in our circle of friends have a tendency to call attention to the gifts we display. I also believe strongly in making use of those people who are highly skilled in helping us discern what our gifts and talents are. There are a lot of Christian vocational-counseling organizations available.

Sometimes we get forced into patterns of jobs or careers where we have the skills, we have the talents, but we really don't have the desire or the motivation to apply ourselves 100 percent. I grant that it's possible God could call us to a task we hate to perform, but God is a much better manager than that. For his jobs in this world, I think God likes to hire the people who not only have the gifts he gave them and the talent he gave them but who are motivated in those directions. Somehow, I think one of the great lies of Satan is to tell us that we are supposed to be unhappy with our labor. God has called you to be fulfilled in your labor, so it's perfectly legitimate to ask yourself, What can I do that fulfills me?

We have been programmed to a certain extent by our culture to a work ethic that ends in retirement. What is the biblical concept, if any, of retirement?

Frankly, I have mixed feelings about this issue. On the one hand, there is something noble about saying to a person, "You have done the job, you have really made a contribution, and now we're going to give you an opportunity to spend your twilight years with your avocation or doing whatever you'd like to do. We're going to give you a pension." There's some virtue in that.

On the other hand, I'm a bit skeptical about the underlying motivation for that whole process. Let me give it an analogy. We've seen all kinds of conflict in our culture between labor and management; there's an arena that I'm keenly concerned about. A lot of people are down on management, and other people are angry at unions and labor. We see the whole history of trade unionism in the United States, for example, as having an interesting, informative impact on our culture and life as we know it. If I go out in the streets and ask people, "Who is the traditional enemy of the union?" I would be willing to guess that at least 80 percent of the people would answer, "Management."

But the traditional—the original—enemy of the union was the nonunion worker, particularly in the level of the unskilled labor where if you had four people competing for a job and nobody had specified skill, and there are only two jobs available, that meant two people got jobs and two didn't. Right now approximately 25 percent of the workforce in the United States is union. So that means that when an unskilled job becomes available in a union shop, there's one person out of four who has a tremendous advantage over the other three because he has his union card.

Now you ask, what does that have to do with retirement? The fact is that the workforce, the whole labor force, is a competitive system. I'm just skeptical enough to think that maybe this whole idea of retirement was conjured up by somebody who wanted to make room for other people to get a job, and they said, "Let's just pack this guy out of here so that we can open up that slot in the organization and I can step into it." I don't know if that's really true or if that's just a jaundiced view that comes out of my experience. If you think of some of the greatest leaders and the greatest contributors to the world, you'll find that so many of them made those contributions after they would be at what, in our culture, is the mandatory retirement age. There seems to be something arbitrary about that.

There is built-in dignity of labor in the Scripture, and God calls me to labor in his vineyard until I die. It may not be at one particular job, but I have to be actively productive as long as I possibly can.

Is God's highest calling full-time Christian ministry, certain spiritual activities such as prayer or witnessing, and Bible study? Are they higher priorities than the everyday activities of a person in business?

Is full-time Christian service the highest vocation there is? I have to say yes and no. I once heard a Methodist preacher say that God only had one son and he made him a preacher. I'm very zealous to uphold the dignity of those who labor in full-time Christian service because we live in a culture, even within the church, that does not hold those people in high esteem. In fact, the simple way to measure it is to look at the economics of how ministers are paid. I know lots of people will respond to that and say, "Well, we feel it is our duty to make sure that our pastors are not in this for 'filthy lucre.' They're not in it for what they can make out of it, and so we're bound and determined to keep them humble. Therefore we won't pay our tithes and will make it necessary to keep them the lowest-paid professional group in America." I think God is very distressed by that in terms of our value system.

But to say that full-time Christian service is the highest calling is to overreact. I hold to the Reformation position, the concept of vocation in which God calls us to all different ways to serve him. A man who's making steel, a person who's farming and who's producing food, a person who makes clothes—those are all vital services that are just as important in God's view as full-time ministry. I don't think we can elevate full-time Christian service above other vocations in an absolute way.

But you're also asking about priorities for a person who

is in, say, the business world. Is it more important for him to be making a profit, or is he supposed to give a priority to prayer and Bible study, etc.? The Bible does have priorities for everybody. Jesus put it this way: "Seek first the kingdom of God and his righteousness, and all these things will be added unto you." When he said "first," the New Testament Greek word he uses is *protos,* which means not just first in a series, in a sequence, but first in terms of order of priority. So Jesus does give seeking the things of God the highest priority.

The New Testament makes it very clear that we have a responsibility to work and that there's a dignity to our labor and to earning a profit. There's nothing wrong with that. In fact, that's what makes survival possible for the human race. The way that you profit is by meeting the needs of others and providing goods and services for them. The way they profit is by meeting your needs and offering goods and services to you. We are designed by God so that we are able to meet both the responsibilities of our spiritual growth and the responsibilities of our labor.

What does it mean to be called into the ministry? Does that mean that you have certain spiritual gifts and you choose to use them full-time, or does that mean that you're called to some special appointment for full-time service in ministry?

This is a question that a lot of people struggle with, particularly those who think that maybe God is calling them to what we call full-time ministry—the ordained ministry.

They're wondering if they are running from God and being disobedient to that call.

In my church (and in most churches) we have a distinction between what we call an internal call and an external call. It's a nice distinction, but it also gets very fuzzy because the internal call is highly subjective. Within myself I have a feeling or an inclination that God is somehow moving me toward this particular course of action to seek ordination into the ministry.

I'm not a mystic by inclination, but I cannot deny that there are genuine mystical elements to the Christian faith. Certainly the apostle Paul experienced such moments and communicated them. I believe God does incline us inwardly in certain ways and at certain times, but because it is so subjective, we can easily deceive ourselves. I'm not always sure that I can distinguish between the internal leading of the Spirit and indigestion. I don't mean to be facetious, but we need to be very candid about this because some people think every hunch or every thought that pops into their mind is a direct communication from God, and that results in all kinds of problems. For example, Jim Jones was convinced that his inclinations were from God, and he led his followers to commit mass suicide.

The Bible tells us to test the spirits to see if they are of God. That's why the church has a distinction between the internal and external calls—the subjective and objective. The apostle Paul tells us that we ought not to think more highly of ourselves than we should and that we ought to think soberly. And then he goes on to talk about callings and gifts and abilities. So we are called to make a sober analysis of the gifts and talents God has given us and at the same time a sober evaluation of the needs of the church—of the kingdom of God—and consider prayerfully that God may be inclining us to use these particular gifts and talents in a full-time, ordained way for his kingdom.

The external call comes when the church (the body of Christ itself, the visible church, the institutional church, other people) recognizes those abilities and talents and actually calls me or you to pursue that task. That's why even though I had a seminary education, I couldn't get ordained until I either had a call to a church or a call to teach in a Christian college, which is the basis by which I was ordained. Even though I had given evidence of an inward call, I still had to have the outward call before I could qualify for ordination.

How should Christian values impact business ethics in the office?

I remember having a discussion a few years ago in the boardroom of one of the Fortune 500 corporations here in the United States. I was speaking to the chairman of the board, the president, and several vice presidents of this corporation on the issue of the relationship between theology, philosophy, and ethics. At the end of the discussion the chairman of the board looked at me and said, "Do I understand you to be saying that ethical issues—that is, policies that we have in our business organization—touch the whole question of ethics, and in turn those ethics touch the question of philosophy, and in turn philosophy touches theology? Are you saying to us that how we run our business ultimately has theological significance?"

I said, "Yes, that's what I'm trying to say." And it was like the lights came on in this man's head for the first time in his life. It astonished me that he thought this principle to be so obscure.

When we use the term *ethics*, we're talking about doing what is right. From a Christian perspective, we believe that the ultimate norm and ultimate standard of rightness is the character of God and his perfect righteousness. So biblical principles of ethics have great relevance for the business world. I'm talking about simple things like God telling us it's wrong to steal. You don't have to be a Christian to appreciate honesty and respect for private property in the business community.

I once talked to someone who was astonished because they gave $5,000 to an automobile salesman in Orlando, Florida, to have some work done and the guy took off with the $5,000 and never did the work. His wife was really upset, saying, "How can people do that? That's crooked business." One doesn't have to be a Christian to feel violated when a businessman steals one's money. The Bible tells us to honor contracts, to pay our bills on time. What businessman doesn't appreciate it when his customers pay him what they owe him? The Bible has much to say about false weights and measures. How do you like it if you are buying "short measure" in perfume or in ketchup? That's a business consideration. All of these are very practical, concrete principles of ethics that touch the very heart of doing business.

Honesty, industry, integrity—we know that the Christian has no corner on these particular virtues. These virtues are significant in every realm of business and, most important, how we treat people in the realm of business. Do we treat them with dignity? That is a top priority of Christian ethics, that we treat our customers, our employees, our personnel with dignity.

What do you think of committed Christians being in partnership with nonbelievers, particularly nonbelievers who are hostile to the Lord?

Let me first make a little theological correction. If I understand the New Testament, every nonbeliever is hostile to the Lord. The Bible tells us that all fallen people are by nature at enmity with God. I think this is one of the Bible's most provocative statements. Nothing makes the unbeliever angrier than to suggest that he is, in fact, at enmity with God and in a hostile relationship with God. They'll prefer to say that they're just indifferent, not hostile. God says they are hostile. I don't think there are some people who are particularly hostile and others who are not. If you're not willing to submit to the lordship of God, then that unwillingness to commit yourself to God is an act of hostility against God. Jesus was crucified for proclaiming that very same idea: If you're not for him, you're against him.

Having said that, let's get to the substance of your question. I presume that you're referring to hostility that is particularly open. We need to distinguish between an ethical issue and a prudential one. I think the Bible does make it clear that Christians are not allowed to be engaged in marriage partnerships with unbelievers. But what about a business partnership? There are many ventures and enterprises in this world, many vocations in the secular world, for example, that Christians and non-Christians are involved in that are perfectly legitimate vocations. I don't think there's anything dictating from an ethical perspective that a Christian not be in a partnership with a non-Christian. For example, two doctors performing their greatly needed services could work side by side for a common cause even though one is a Christian and one isn't. I can see two men making automobiles or programming computers, one a Christian and one not.

Obviously, the most important thing in a Christian's life is his commitment to Christ. If he is in a daily partnership with a person who is openly hostile to that, it's almost inevitable that their vastly different approaches to what's ultimately important to them will create certain points of friction in that relationship, and it may at times create friction at the point of decision making in that business. But I must say that when the friction comes up between a Christian and a non-Christian in a business partnership over ethics, it is not always the Christian who is pushing to do the ethical thing.

The difference between a Christian and a non-Christian is not that one is good and the other isn't; the difference lies in whether or not they've embraced Jesus as Savior.

Do labor unions pose ethical problems for Christians?

I'm sure there are many Christians who are troubled by certain elements of the labor movement and its history. I have all kinds of mixed feelings myself because I've been deeply involved in the whole arena of labor and management relations in an attempt to mediate difficulties and seek reconciliation between labor and management. So often in this country organized labor (in this case unions) and management have been enemies. But we've seen a swing in the last few years. People are beginning to realize that as far as the national economy is concerned, we're all in this together. There has been much more close cooperation between these two segments of our society than in times past. There's so much historical hostility on both sides that it's difficult to wade through it all.

The problem that I have with labor unions is that the traditional enemy of the union worker is not management, but the nonunion worker. Union members sometimes have an advantage in gaining a job, while a nonunion member is blocked out of the possibility of employment. That's why I think states have had to move to right-to-work laws, which I think are very healthy.

But the other side of that coin is the whole principle of collective bargaining. I'm not convinced that there's anything wrong, in principle, with collective bargaining, but we've seen grave abuses in the last few years. One person said that there have been so many strikes in America that we look more like a bowling alley than a producing nation.

The labor union has accomplished a tremendous amount of good, and I don't see anything within the concept of a union that is principally opposed to Christian ethics or that would make it impossible for a Christian to be actively engaged in a union. Even though my background is in management, I have found that I tend to have more sympathy with labor than I do with management when we actually get into mediation. I deal with these issues in the noneconomic aspects—those that deal with human dignity—not at the bargaining table where they're debating

about wages and benefits. I think that at the heart of the
issue between labor and management, people are saying,
"Even though I may not be highly skilled in my job, I am
still a human being, and I want to be treated with dignity."
If we see that as the core motivation behind trade unions,
we'll have a deeper appreciation for them.

How can an employer show employees Christlike dignity?

One of the best ways to affirm the dignity of an employee
is to set high standards for him. To set low standards and
make no demands for performance is a thinly veiled insult
to employees, and they will catch the drift. If we don't hold
a standard of excellence in front of them, we're not doing
anything for their dignity.

We need to value people as people. I was deeply involved
for many years in a movement in the labor-management
arena that is called "The Value of the person Movement"
in business and industry. We recognized that noneconomic
issues are ultimately behind the volatile hostility that exists
between labor and management, employer and employee,
and results in so many strikes and the disruption of produc-
tion and of school systems. The studies have shown again
and again that industrial sabotage and disputes over wages
and salaries have roots in a deeper level of dissatisfaction.
The only place I can fight back with somebody who is deni-
grating my dignity, the only leverage I have is at the bargaining table, where we're dealing with salaries, perks, and
that sort of thing.

But every worker in this country wants to be valued as a

person. What can I do to demonstrate value to the person? Well, let me count the ways: One thing is to recognize that they are people. Now that may seem like a simplistic answer, but when we interviewed dozens of laborers in steel mills in western Pennsylvania, I kept hearing the same response, particularly from black, unskilled laboring people, who said to me, "The thing I hate about working in this place is the foreman comes in here and he ducks his head." I said, "What do you mean 'he ducks his head'?" It took me a long time to pull out of these men what it was they were objecting to, and it was simply this: When management came onto the foundry floor and they caught the eye of somebody working in a dirty job, in an unskilled position, the manager almost imperceptibly turned his head away or dropped his eye to the ground rather than making direct eye contact with the worker. The worker got the message. It was a nonverbal message, but it came through loud and clear: You are nothing; you are not even worthy of having somebody look at you. On the other hand, if somebody goes out of their way to notice the labor of a person in a job and that person feels appreciated, then his dignity is enhanced and restored.

16

Money Matters

Give me neither poverty nor riches—
Feed me with the food allotted to me;
Lest I be full and deny You,
And say, "Who is the Lord?"
Or lest I be poor and steal,
And profane the name of my God.

PROVERBS 30:8-9

Questions in This Section:

Is God concerned with the material well-being of Christians?

How can we get a proper view of Christian economics and keep money from becoming an idol?

First Timothy 6:9 tells us that "those who want to get rich fall into a temptation and a snare, and many harmful and foolish desires which plunge men into ruin and destruction." Does that mean that the Christian should not want to get rich?

How should Christians respond to the overwhelming temptation of materialism in our culture?

What do you believe the Bible teaches about tithing as it relates to Christians today?

What does the Bible teach about our responsibility to pay taxes to the government?

What about debt? Should Christians use credit cards, borrow money for cars, homes, vacations, etc.?

Is there a clear biblical position against lotteries and casino gambling?

What should be a Christian's position on paramutual betting?

In 2 Corinthians 8:13-15, it sounds as if Paul is prescribing a sort of economic equality. How does this passage relate to Christians today?

Is God concerned with the material well-being of Christians?

The short answer to that, emphatically and definitely, is yes. Not only is God concerned about the material well-being of Christians, he's deeply and profoundly concerned for the material well-being of the whole world. God created a material world. He created man as a material creature with profound material needs. All we would have to do is go to the Sermon on the Mount to see Jesus' great expression of compassion for those who are in material want. There's a tremendous emphasis of concern in the New Testament that we as Christians have a profound care for those who are hungry, poor, naked, and homeless. That concern indicates a concern for the material welfare of people. The New Testament has a lot to say about wealth and poverty and the various causes and circumstances involving those conditions.

There are frightening warnings to the rich, for example, particularly those who would put their confidence in their wealth rather than in the benevolent concern of God. In this regard Jesus says, "Take no thought for tomorrow, what you should eat, what you should drink, what you should put on; but rather, consider the lilies of the field that they neither toil nor spin. Solomon in all his glory is not arrayed like one of these." He is saying that we can become so preoccupied with the accumulation of wealth that we miss the kingdom of God; we have a concern for the material things to the neglect of the spiritual things. Because we see the world preoccupied with material things and woefully neglecting the spiritual, we may be inclined to become extremists in the opposite direction and say, "All that God cares about are spiritual things." Again, a balanced view of Scripture will prevent us from coming to that conclusion, because there is nothing wrong with a concern for material welfare.

In another manner of speaking, God cares for people, and people are material creatures who require material things in order to survive. If God cares for people, obviously he cares for their material well-being. Health and healing from sickness are material matters, and so God's concern for our health is a concern for our material well-being.

How can we get a proper view of Christian economics and keep money from becoming an idol?

There are many people who think there is no such thing as Christian economics, that economics is neutral, just like anything else. Though I'm convinced the Bible is not a textbook in economics, it has much to say that applies to principles of property, monetary exchange, and even the use of currency.

The most important protection against the idolatry of "mammon," whereby we fall into that grave sin of worshiping material goods or the money that can purchase these things, is to have a clear understanding from a biblical perspective of what economics is. It's interesting to me that the term *economics* comes from the Greek word *oikonomia,* which is the New Testament word for stewardship.

I think the central economic principle in the Bible is that ultimately God is the owner of all things in this world, but he does in his law sanctify and protect what we would call private property. If you would look, for example, at the Ten Commandments, you would see that at least two of the commandments specifically protect the right to private property and also speak against a misuse and abuse of my property or your property. While private property is protected, there's no foundation at all in the Scriptures for any kind of communistic or even socialistic precept of economics.

With that right of private property comes the awesome responsibility of handling one's material goods according to the principles that God has set forth. God doesn't give us these things so that we can do with them as we please. There's a lot more to economics than simply the right to private property, but I stress that particular point because somewhere along the line many Christians have gotten the idea that private property itself is a sin.

I hear people misquote the Bible in saying that money is the root of all evil. What the Bible actually says is that the *love* of money is the root of all evil. When we have a passion simply for the acquisition of material goods, when that becomes our god and we serve it, then money becomes an idol. I don't think we can look at the subject of economics in a simplistic way, but we need to see the whole of what Scripture says concerning material goods. We need money and the things it provides; God gives us these things to enjoy. But we must learn the principles he has given for how possessions and money are to be used.

First Timothy 6:9 tells us that "those who want to get rich fall into a temptation and a snare, and many harmful and foolish desires which plunge men into ruin and destruction." Does that mean that the Christian should not want to get rich?

In the New Testament we find this passage, as well as other equally sober ones (some from the lips of Jesus) that warn us against setting our hearts on riches, living our lives with our principal goal being to accumulate wealth. It's not simply a moral issue, but there's much said here in terms of wisdom and prudence. I think the apostle is warning us to watch ourselves, to be very careful, because the pursuit of wealth can become a subtle and devastating trap. The desire for these riches and the power that goes with them can blind a person to things that are much more valuable and important in the sight of God. It can so distract our attention from the ultimate wealth—spiritual wealth—that we get tripped up and snared, caught in this pursuit to such a degree that we'll compromise our integrity, do almost anything to gain that power. Wealth can destroy us.

We read that other aphorism in the New Testament: "The love of money is the root of all evil." Money, in and of itself, doesn't do anything—it doesn't go out and kill people, for instance. But our passion for money and the power it gives us indicates something about our hearts. Jesus said that we are not to store up treasures on earth, but to store them up in heaven (Matt. 6:19-20). Those admonitions and warnings are very serious, and we need to search our souls to be sure that we are not caught up in a desire for wealth and prosperity to the point that we neglect the things of God.

There's nothing wrong with wanting to have clothes on your naked body, to have food in your hungry stomach, to have a comfortable house to live in. There's nothing wrong in trying to make a profit in the marketplace. Ultimately, your profit can help everybody; it can have a positive effect on the world. Without profit there's no commerce, and without commerce there's no material well-being. The desire to prosper is a legitimate one. God even promises certain elements of prosperity ultimately for his own people. But the pursuit of prosperity is always to be circumscribed by the priorities of the kingdom of God. I think the apostle is telling us that if we get a fixation for prosperity and get out of balance, we miss the kingdom.

How should Christians respond to the overwhelming temptation of materialism in our culture?

Probably the temptation a Christian has to worry about least is materialism. Why? Materialism proper is a philosophical worldview that sees ultimate truth as strictly material—there is no ultimate spiritual reality. In that sense, materialism is not a temptation to a Christian because a Christian would have to abandon his concept of God and everything spiritual in order to think like a materialist. Ultimate materialism as a philosophy has no room whatsoever for God.

Usually what we mean by materialism is not this sophisticated philosophy I've just described but rather the acquisition of goods and the gaining of wealth that become the ultimate end in life. That temptation is real for Christians because Christians like creature comforts just as much as anybody else does. We, too, can fall into the sin of greed or covetousness. Christians have to be very conversant with the New Testament warnings about setting one's heart on material pleasures and gains. At the same time, we don't want to despise them, denying that good things, material or not, come from God. We are to understand the proper place and use of the material. As Paul said, he learned how to be abased, how to abound, and he learned to be content whether or not he was prospering.

Because there's a lot of affluence in our culture, there tends to be a lot of guilt about the enjoyment of prosperity. If you read the Old Testament for ten minutes, you'll see that the Jewish people did not perceive prosperity as a crime. God was constantly promising the blessing of material well-being to people as a consequence of obedience.

The issue for Jesus is, Where's the heart? Our priority is to be the seeking of the kingdom and its righteousness. If, in the seeking of the kingdom, God is pleased to bless you with abundance and prosperity, don't feel guilty about it, but thank him for it and use it responsibly.

What do you believe the Bible teaches about tithing as it relates to Christians today?

There are many people who believe that tithing is no longer incumbent upon Christians because it's an Old Testament mandate that is not specifically repeated in the New Testament.

Even though this was part of the law of the covenant of Israel in the Old Testament, I don't think that everything God demanded of his people in the Old Testament is abrogated if the New Testament is silent about it. I would say that if the tithe were abrogated, we would expect to have an explicit teaching in the New Testament that says tithing is no longer in effect. Tithing was a responsibility central to the old-covenant economy and would be carried over, particularly when you understand that the new-covenant community was established principally among Jews, who would obviously continue that practice unless they were told that it was no longer necessary. I would say that, in the absence of any evidence of a repeal, tithing carries through into the New Testament.

When Jesus was on earth and the new covenant hadn't been established yet, he did bless the Pharisees for their tithe. He rebuked them for failing in weightier matters, but Jesus certainly congratulated them for at least being scrupulous in their tithing. They tithed their mint and their cummin, which meant that they tithed down to the smallest of things. Most of the tithes in the Old Testament were done agriculturally or with livestock—it was an agrarian society. But these Pharisees were so scrupulous about giving their ten percent to God that if they grew a little bit of parsley in the backyard, they tithed that. It would be as if you found a dime on the street and made sure a penny of it went to God. Jesus said that these men were so scrupulous they paid down to the last penny, and he complimented them for that (Luke 11:42).

When the New Testament refers to giving, it talks about giving out of our abundance and out of a spirit of gratitude. Whenever the two covenants are compared, particularly in the book of Hebrews, we are told that the New Testament is a much richer covenant. The benefits we receive as Christians far exceed the benefits that the people of the old covenant enjoyed. But it also follows that the responsibilities of New Testament people exceed the responsibilities of the Old Testament people. We're in a better situation. I would say that the tithe is not some high ultimate standard for the super-Christian, but it's the rock bottom. It's the starting point for a person who is in Christ and who understands something of the benefits he receives from God.

What does the Bible teach about our responsibility to pay taxes to the government?

On the surface it would seem that the biblical answer to the question is very simple. Our Lord said, "Render therefore to Caesar the things that are Caesar's" (Matt. 22:21). In the New Testament, the apostles teach us that we are to give honor to whom honor is due and taxes to whom taxes are due. We are to pay the tribute that is exacted from us by the civil magistrates.

There have been many Christians, particularly in recent years, who have raised some significant questions about that. Questions like, Are we to willingly submit to Caesar when Caesar transcends his realm of authority? Are we to render to Caesar those things that are *not* Caesar's? We remember that the context in which that question was raised in the New Testament was a very puzzling situation. People came to Jesus and asked him why his disciples weren't paying their taxes. Jesus doesn't really answer the question, and that bothers me. I've scratched my head and thought, *Is it true that they weren't paying all the taxes they were supposed to be paying? I mean, were the disciples guilty of tax evasion?* That's so foreign to the attitude underscored again and again in the New Testament, of honoring the civil magistrates and being responsible to our civic duties.

The other sort of loophole that some Christians are examining is the statement, "Render unto the government taxes that are due." Now, the government tells me what taxes are due them. But that word, "due," is a loaded word, at least in its historical meanings. Aristotle, for example, defined the nature of justice as giving people what is their due—not simply what they deserve, but what is due them. There are circumstances in which certain things are due another person or an institution. The unspoken presupposition is that the government is due taxes that are enacted for just causes. And so some people (among them Francis Schaeffer, before he died) raise the questions: Is it appropriate to give voluntarily taxes that are used for unjust causes? Must Christians always submit to unjust taxes? It's a taxing problem.

What about debt? Should Christians use credit cards, borrow money for cars, homes, vacations, etc.?

There's a great controversy within the Christian church about that question. Some people take the position that under no circumstances should a Christian encumber himself in financial indebtedness, quoting such passages as "Owe no one anything except to love one another" (Rom. 13:8).

There are numerous passages, particularly in the Old Testament Wisdom Literature, that warn against the folly that can befall us if we allow ourselves to be in debt in a certain way. I take those passages in the context in which they are given, as wisdom sayings that warn us against practices that are imprudent and can be destructive to our home. I don't see those as absolute prohibitions against ever being in debt. There is a responsible way to be in debt, and there are provisions for indebtedness in Old Testament society.

In today's society, throughout much of the world, monetary exchange—the whole process of trade—involves not only hard currency but paper money. We use checks and credit cards. Credit cards are used in different ways. Sometimes they are used exactly as the name suggests—as an instant line of credit that includes carrying charges if we don't pay our bill fully when it comes in. This is dangerous because it's an enticement for people to live beyond their means and to be less responsible in their purchasing habits.

I use credit cards because they provide a great convenience for me; I don't have to carry large amounts of cash when I travel. We also keep good records of our finances. It has been my personal policy and practice never to pay a carrying charge; that is, I pay those bills in full when they come in. In essence, the credit cards for me become another form of a check.

In America's economic system it has become standard practice to borrow in order to provide for major necessities, such as homes and automobiles. Very few people can pay cash for a house. The fact that we can pay for a home over thirty years has its benefits and its liabilities. We end up paying far more than the price of the property because of interest. But at the same time we are able to become home owners. Again, that to me comes down to a matter of stewardship and responsibility. I don't see any basic, scriptural prohibition against credit, but we are to be wise in using it.

Is there a clear biblical position against lotteries and casino gambling?

Is there an explicit, direct, biblical prohibition of casino gambling or lotteries? Not that I know of. However, the Christian church has consistently taken a dim view of casino gambling and the use of lotteries based on the implications of certain biblical principles. For example, in the church where I am ordained as a minister, part of our confessional position is that we are to follow not only what the Bible teaches explicitly but what can be drawn from the Scriptures by clear and necessary inference. The Bible does have clear principles that touch issues like this. The most notable, of course, is the principle of stewardship, whereby I am responsible to act as a steward of my possessions, including my wealth, and not be wasteful or irresponsible in how I spend my money.

The biggest problem I have personally with casino gambling, and particularly with lotteries, is that they tend to be very poor investments, and inevitably they exploit the poor of the society. The poor man dreams of improving his material welfare. He dreams of owning a house and a nice car. He dreams of being liberated from the endless grinding tasks of day-to-day toil with very small rewards. As a person working for a low hourly wage or depending on a government welfare check, he never has much of an opportunity to accumulate enough money to give himself a solid base or invest in the future. His only chance to get financial security and improve his situation is to hit the numbers or to hit it big in the casinos. He will take his dollar and hope to win the million-dollar jackpot. That's his dream. But he doesn't have a full understanding of how the system works and how huge the odds are against him.

We went through this struggle in the state of Pennsylvania when I was living there, and everybody was worried about organized crime and all of that. Well, organized crime was already there. When I was growing up, there was already a lottery in Pennsylvania. It wasn't state owned; it was run by the Mafia, and you could buy a number on almost any street corner in Pittsburgh. The thing that astonished me was that when the state took it over for the benefit of senior citizens, the odds for winning under the state-run system were worse than the odds under the Mafia's system. So I saw the state taking advantage of people's desire for the get-rich-quick dollar and exploiting the poor by this terrible form of investment.

What should be a Christian's position on paramutual betting?

When an ethical question deals with our culture, it's important that we try to address that ethical question from a framework of biblical principles. If you go out in the street and ask one hundred Christians, "Is gambling wrong?"

ninety-five to a hundred of them will probably respond automatically, "Yes, of course." In other words, the subcultural traditions of the Christian community have rigorously opposed gambling of almost any type for centuries.

The Bible doesn't say, "Thou shalt not gamble." So we have to be very careful before we declare to the world that God is opposed to all forms of gambling. What about investing in the stock market? What about investing in a company? What about any kind of capital investments? In all of these cases, you're taking a chance with your money; each is a form a gambling. What difference does it make whether you're investing in a horse race or stocks on the New York Stock Exchange? Some theologians make a distinction between games of chance and matters of commerce or matters of skill. It is one thing to invest money in a company that I am going to be operating myself, the success of which, to some degree, will depend upon my energy level, my industry, my wisdom and skill; it is another thing to lay down money at a paramutual betting window to see what happens in this game of luck.

I think the real issue of paramutual gambling or state lotteries from a biblical perspective focuses on the biblical principle of stewardship. God gives us certain resources, benefits, talents, and skills, and we are responsible to use them wisely. God takes a dim view of wasting money, of being careless with the goods he entrusts to us. The big problem with gambling is that it isn't very good stewardship. In a horse race or dog race or a state lottery, the odds are so stacked against you, particularly in paramutual betting, that it is poor use of one's investment capital. At that point I would say that Christians ought not to support this enterprise.

In 2 Corinthians 8:13-15, it sounds as if Paul is prescribing a sort of economic equality. How does this passage relate to Christians today?

Paul does use the word *equality* in an economic sense in this passage; he specifically says in verses 13-14: "Our desire is not that others might be relieved while you are hard pressed, but that there might be equality."

Some people have taken this simple verse to mean that Paul has given sort of a cryptic proof text for Marxism. Those who have tried to synthesize Marxism and Christianity make a lot of hay out of that particular verse, and I think they completely pull it out of its immediate context. They certainly pull it out of the context of what the rest of the Bible says about private property. The Old Testament system required that wealth be distributed not on the basis of equality but on the basis of equity. Equity is a little different from equality; that is, if a man works, he's entitled to the abundanace—he reaps what he sows. And this carries into the New Testament. In 2 Thessalonians 3:10 Paul says that if a man won't work, he shouldn't eat.

In the 2 Corinthians passage, Paul is not referring to the economic situations of individual Christians, but about charitable giving among the churches. He's talking about the responsibility of the congregations to participate equally during a crisis—in this case, in the relieving of a specific suffering congregation.

This is not the first plea from Paul to the Corinthian congregation. There had been a famine in Jerusalem. This, coupled with the extreme persecution leveled at Jewish Christians in that region, had put them in a desperate situation. A number of churches in other regions were taking up a collection. Paul's first mention of this is found in 1 Corinthians 16, where he urges them to be responsive to the Jerusalem church's needs, as other churches have responded. Now, in 2 Corinthians, he reminds them that some of the other churches have been very sacrificial in their giving.

Incidentally, some of the scholars who have studied the historical circumstances of the Jerusalem church's poverty argue that it was brought about by their experiment in communal living, which ended in disaster and economic failure. It was precisely because of their attempt at Marxism, if you will, that the rest of the church had to bail them out.

17

Life-and-Death Issues

For You formed my inward parts;
You covered me in my mother's womb.
I will praise You, for I am fearfully and wonderfully made;
Marvelous are Your works. . . .
Your eyes saw my substance, being yet unformed.
And in Your book they all were written,
The days fashioned for me,
When as yet there were none of them.

PSALM 139:13-14, 16

Questions in This Section:

What is your opinion of abortion, and are there any Scriptures that would back it up?

Are there circumstances that might ever allow a true Christian to justify abortion?

Based on the fact that God has given doctors the ability to use amniocentesis to determine defects in a fetus, do you feel that abortion should be used if the fetus proves to be abnormal?

Is a woman acting in sin when she aborts a pregnancy that is the result of rape?

Does the Bible say anything about euthanasia?

In the case of a terminally ill person, who should decide when to discontinue life-support systems—to "pull the plug"?

What should be the Christian stand on the death penalty?

What is your opinion of abortion, and are there any Scriptures that would back it up?

We are all aware of hellfire-and-damnation preachers who rave and scream about the decadence of the world. It can become tiresome to listen to all of that. I think we all respect people who can disagree with others in a spirit of charity, and as a rule, I try to abide by that as much as I can. But when it comes to this question of abortion, my tolerance dissipates. I'm convinced that the matter of abortion facing the American public right now is the greatest wickedness in our nation's history. It makes me almost ashamed to be an American. I'm ashamed of the medical profession, but I'm most deeply ashamed of the church for its failure to scream literally, "Bloody murder" about abortion.

Abortion is a monstrous evil, and if I know anything about the character of God, I am totally convinced that this is an outrage to him. From the beginning to the end of sacred Scripture, there is a premium on the sanctity of human life. Anytime we see human life cheapened—as it clearly is in the wanton destruction of unborn children— then those who have an appreciation for the value and the dignity of human life need to stand up and protest as loudly as they possibly can.

From a biblical standpoint, the issue focuses on the origin of life. It would be merely sophistry for me to accuse somebody of murder if in fact they were not killing a human life. I think the biblical evidence is manifold that life begins at conception. We see that repeatedly in the literature of the prophets in the Old Testament, in the psalms of David, and in the New Testament where at the meeting of Elizabeth and Mary, after she has conceived Jesus, John the Baptist, as yet unborn, bears witness to the presence of the Messiah, who also is not yet born. Neither one of these are born infants, and yet there is communication taking place. Jeremiah and the apostle Paul both speak of being consecrated and sanctified while they were still in their mothers' wombs. These and a host of other passages indicate clearly that life begins before birth and, I believe, at conception. I just pray that this nation will sober itself about this and do something to restore the sanctity of life.

Are there any circumstances that might ever allow a true Christian to justify abortion?

Long before *Roe v. Wade,* a movie came out entitled *The Cardinal,* starring Tom Tryon, in which the cardinal faced the excruciating ethical dilemma of being faithful to his church or faithful to the love and compassion he felt for a member of his own family. His sister was put into that very rare situation of being threatened with death in the delivery of a baby. The physicians had to make the choice: the mother or the unborn child. In this case, the cardinal was his sister's guardian, and he had to make that choice. He wanted very much to save his sister, but canon law at that time required that he take the stand for the unborn child.

The reaction of people was strong, and they were very much divided over it. When anyone faces the question of making a decision between who lives, the baby or the mother, we enter a completely different ethical sphere than when we are debating the issue that is before the American public today, that is, abortion for the sake of convenience. I think we need to distinguish clearly between the two.

So often the issues get confused when people take a position against abortion-on-demand. They say, "Does that mean you would let a woman die in a life-threatening situation or make a young girl who's been a victim of rape go through with a birth?" I think that's a completely different matter. I would prefer to separate those questions before trying to answer them. I would say that better men and more knowledgeable students of ethics than I are divided on the question of whether there ever is a justifiable time for abortion. My personal opinion (this is just R. C. Sproul, not the dogma of Christendom) is that abortion is never justifiable. This becomes a lot more iffy when it comes to an either-or situation, the mother's life or the child's, but I would not crusade against those who differ with me. However, I am militantly opposed to abortion-on-demand.

When I was pregnant with my last child, my doctor asked if I wanted to have amniocentesis to determine if the baby was normal. Based on the fact that God has given doctors the ability to use amniocentesis to do this, do you feel that abortion should be used if the fetus proves to be abnormal?

As Christians, we have to go back a step further and settle the question of when life begins. If, for example, one takes the traditional and classical Christian view that life begins at conception, then the question could have a parallel question; that is, suppose we didn't have that information prior to birth and the child was born deformed—should we then destroy the child after it's born?

Some people would say, "Well, you're confusing the issue." No, we're not, because the real issue is whether or not we have the moral right to destroy human life after it starts. If the taking of a human life after it starts is a form of murder, then it would be murder before birth or after birth. It really wouldn't make a whole lot of difference morally.

I believe that life begins at conception, so I would not accept abortion as morally justifiable if one knows through testing that the child is going to be deformed.

Most of the questions about abortion today have to do with the issue of abortion-on-demand. Most abortions are being performed for matters of convenience, not because the people involved go through this excruciatingly difficult problem of bearing a deformed child that is going to be expensive and heartbreaking.

You are really asking a question here about euthanasia. When we first were seriously debating this question of abortion, back in the middle 1960s, I didn't hear anyone— from a theological or ethical scientific perspective— advocating infanticide, and I didn't hear anybody back then advocating euthanasia for older people. That is not the case today, and I think that the prophets back then who warned that acceptance of abortion would lead to acceptance of euthanasia were correct.

Is a woman acting in sin when she aborts a pregnancy that is the result of rape?

Those who are opposed to abortion-on-demand are opposed because they are convinced that human life begins before birth. Obviously, the issue that has divided this nation so vehemently is not the question of whether or not it's legitimate to have an abortion in the case of incest or rape or when the life of the mother is threatened, but rather what we might call abortion for convenience. I point that out not to dodge the specific aspect of your question but to warn people not to get sidetracked by that "special case" issue.

Many scholars and theologians who are rigorously opposed to abortion-on-demand believe abortion in certain mitigating circumstances and situations to be ethically viable, as in the case of incest, rape, or when the life of the mother is threatened. I would say only a very small minority of theologians would argue that abortion is always wrong and is always a sin. I would have to count myself in that very small minority. I do think that we should never be involved in therapeutic abortions. Again, I recognize that there's certainly a much less clear ethical premise when you're dealing with these difficult questions. I certainly don't think that it is clearly against the law of God to have a therapeutic abortion in the case of rape and incest. The very act of rape is such a terrible outrage to the dignity of a woman. Then to ask her to bear the consequences of that outrage in a pregnancy to which she was not voluntarily acquiescing—I can certainly understand those who would want to say that it would be permissible. The reason I hesitate is that I'm convinced that it would still be a human life, and as grievous a situation as it would be for that expectant mother, I would ask her to bear that grief for the sake of saving the child's life.

Does the Bible say anything about euthanasia?

There is no explicit mention of euthanasia in the Scriptures. Certain principles set forth in Scripture do apply, however. Our generation, as never before, is feeling the intensity of that question because of the advances of technology and modern medicine. People are being kept clinically alive who, if left to nature, would die. That raises a whole set of moral questions about which many conscientious physicians are seeking clear guidance.

In principle, the question of euthanasia has been with us as long as there have been suffering people. Obviously, suffering is not a twentieth-century phenomenon; people of all generations have had to deal with pain. Scripture does not contain a statement that allows one to hasten the termination of the life of a person who is suffering. The only passages we have are ones given without comment—for example, when Saul, in the midst of humiliating defeat, asks his armor bearer to help him fall on his own sword so that he can commit suicide rather than be taken prisoner by his enemies. This is a form of euthanasia, but the Scriptures don't indicate God's response to this.

In general the Scriptures strenuously uphold the sanctity of life, and we know that one of the great struggles for the saints in Scripture was their desire to die and not to be allowed to do so. Kierkegaard wrote at length about this being one of the most miserable situations for a person of virtue to be in—to long for death and not be allowed to die.

Moses asked to die; Job asked to die; Jeremiah asked to die. And today many people ask to die. The pattern in Scripture seems to teach that we are not allowed to actively engage in the destruction of human life, even to put someone out of his or her misery. We do make distinctions between active and passive euthanasia. Is it possible to allow people to die naturally, to die with dignity? This question really requires a much more lengthy and detailed statement, but I would say that there are times when it is permissible to allow people to die—to forgo further treatment, for instance, or elect not to be kept alive artificially.

In the case of a terminally ill person, who should decide when to discontinue life-support systems—to "pull the plug"?

Last year I addressed eight hundred physicians at the University of Alabama in Birmingham. I was asked to address that precise question: How you decide when to pull the plug? I was also interested to note that the largest single specialty group present at that particular convocation was a group of neurosurgeons. It's so often cast into their hands to make that decision as to when to pull the plug because they perform the examination to see if a person is brain-dead; that is, showing no signs of activity within the brain.

The questions surrounding the pulling of the plug are not simplistic. They involve the application of not one but several principles of ethics. I hesitate to give a quick answer as to an absolute time when you pull the plug and when you don't.

Who, ultimately, should make this decision? What I recommended to that body of physicians was not dictated so much by biblical law as by prudence. Such a weighty decision ought not to be made capriciously or by someone's unilateral suggestion. It should be decided jointly. There is wisdom in much counsel, and I would say that three basic parties ought to be involved in the making of that decision. It's a decision of such tremendous import that I think the clergy ought to be involved. It takes moral courage for a clergyman to interject himself into a family situation, but families desperately need spiritual guidance at this point, and they deserve to have a pastor help them make that decision. I think that goes with the territory of our theological background and training; we should be able to help people decide such things. But the pastor should not make it unilaterally. He should be in deep consultation with the family and with the physician.

The medical aspects of life-support systems are so technical and complex that we need the input of the medical experts in order to make a sound evaluation of the situation. So these three parties—the family, the physician, and the clergy—need to be involved in the decision.

What should be the Christian stand on the death penalty?

I'm convinced that our whole criminal justice system is in serious need of reformation and restructuring because it is not working and many inequities exist within it. Christians are divided about the issue of capital punishment. First, there is the basic question of whether or not capital punishment in and of itself is a good or bad thing. I think the majority opinion of the Christian church throughout its history has been that capital punishment is a good thing. This position has been taken, not because Christians are particularly bloodthirsty, but because Christians read the Scriptures. The Word of God institutes, ordains, and commands capital punishment in Genesis 9:6.

When the state legislature of Pennsylvania voted to reintroduce capital punishment, the then governor of the state vetoed it on the grounds that the Bible said, "Thou shalt not kill." He was aware that the Bible said, "Thou shalt not kill," and he was quoting from the Ten Commandments in Exodus 20. Yet if you go to Exodus 21, 22, and 23 (the holiness code), God sets forth the provisions for those who break that commandment. For those who murder, God commands that they be executed.

Fine distinctions are made between voluntary and involuntary manslaughter, malice of forethought, and the various kinds of situations that fall within the complexity of our jurisprudence. So I'm answering this question in its broad principle.

Usually, the great objection to capital punishment is that human life is so precious and so valuable that we ought never to lift our hands to snuff it out. Also, every human being is redeemable. Another argument is that capital punishment is not a deterrent. But the institution of capital punishment was not given as a deterrent but as an act of justice. What is the biblical rationale? Capital punishment is instituted very early in the Old Testament—before

Moses, before Sinai, before the Ten Commandments, back in the days of Noah, where God says, "If by man, man's blood is shed, by man shall his blood be shed." That's not a prediction. The structure of the language there is an imperative; it is a command. The reason is given: "Because man is made in the image of God." In other words, the Bible says that human life is so sacred, so precious, so holy—human life has so much dignity—that if with malice of forethought you wantonly destroy another human being, you thereby forfeit your own right to life. God doesn't merely allow the execution of murderers; he commands it.

18

Suffering

If God is for us, who can be against us?
He who did not spare His own Son, but delivered Him up
for us all, how shall He not with Him also freely give us all things? . . .
Who shall separate us from the love of Christ?
Shall tribulation, or distress, or persecution, or famine,
or nakedness, or peril, or sword?

ROMANS 8:31-32, 35

Questions in This Section:

If God is all powerful, then why does he allow suffering?

Why would a loving and holy God allow a child to suffer through a serious illness such as cancer?

When we experience trials, how can we determine if they are the consequences of violating a scriptural principle, a test from the Lord, or an attack from Satan?

People speak of the "problem of pain." Is it not more accurate in a fallen world to speak of the "problem of pleasure"?

In Colossians 1:24 Paul says he does his share in "filling up that which is lacking in Christ's sufferings." What is meant by this phrase?

How would you counsel Christians who are suffering with illness or old age who would rather be in heaven with their Lord than here?

Can suffering in general rather than suffering for our Christian faith be counted as sharing the suffering of Christ?

What is the difference between God testing us and tempting us?

In the book of 1 Thessalonians we're called to give thanks in all circumstances. I've sometimes heard my brothers and sisters in Christ giving thanks for things such as illness or death. Should we be doing this?

As someone in the health profession, I see people suffering every day. What can Christians expect from God in regard to healing?

What does the Bible teach us about comforting one who is suffering as a result of a crime he has committed?

In James 5:14-15 the sick are told to call upon the elders of the church to anoint them with oil and lay hands on them. Do any Christians today practice this, and should we?

If God is all powerful, then why does he allow suffering?

A recent controversial book on this matter was titled *When Bad Things Happen to Good People.* A common objection to religion is, How can anybody believe in God in light of all of the suffering that we see and experience in this world?

John Stuart Mill raised this classic objection against the Christian faith: If God is omnipotent and allows all this suffering, then he is not benevolent, he is not a kind-hearted God, he is not loving. And if he's loving to the whole world and allows all this suffering, then he's certainly not omnipotent. And given the fact of evil, or the fact of suffering, we can never conclude that God is both omnipotent and benevolent. As brilliant as John Stuart Mill is, I have to demur at that point and look at what the Scriptures say about these things.

Keep in mind that from a biblical perspective, suffering is intrinsically related to the fallenness of this world. There was no suffering prior to sin. I interpret Scripture to say that suffering in this world is part of the complex of God's judgment on the world. You are asking, How can a righteous judge allow a criminal to suffer? How can a just judge allow a violent offender to be punished? The question we should ask is, How can a just judge *not* allow punishment for those who have committed acts of violence or crimes of any sort? Behind that question always stands the holiness of God and his perfect righteousness. Our understanding of God is rooted and grounded in the teaching of Scripture that he is the just Judge. The Judge of all of the earth always does right.

In the ninth chapter of John, the Pharisees say to Jesus, "Why was this man born blind? Was it because of his sin or the sins of his parents?" Jesus said, "Neither one." We can't come to the conclusion that an individual's suffering in this world is in direct proportion to that individual's sin. That was what Job's friends did when they came to him and tormented him by saying, "Boy, Job, you're really suffering a lot. This must be an indication that you're the most miserable sinner of all." But the Bible says that we can't use such a formula. The fact is, if there were no sin in the world, there would be no suffering. God allows suffering as part of his judgment, but he also uses it for our redemption—to shape our character and build up our faith.

Why would a loving and holy God allow a child to suffer through a serious illness such as cancer?

We usually associate the love of God with the benefits we receive from him and the blessings that come from his kind and merciful hand. Because his love usually manifests itself in good things that happen to us, we sometimes fall back in shock and consternation when we see a child struck by disease or some other trauma.

Before we speak to the question of why God allows children to suffer, we need to ask the bigger question: Why does God allow suffering to happen to any person, whether he's two years old, two months old, or twenty years old? The Scriptures tell us that suffering came into the world as a consequence of the fall of man and of creation; that is to say, it is because of sin that God has visited judgment upon this planet. That includes the curses of pain, disease, sorrow, and death that attend the consequences of wickedness.

How could a loving and holy God allow a baby to suffer a debilitating disease? I think the answer is partly contained in that very question. God is holy, and in his holiness he exercises judgment against the wickedness that is prevalent in human nature. When we ask the question with respect to infants, sometimes lurking behind that question is the unspoken assumption that babies are innocent. Virtually every church in the history of Christendom has had to develop some concept of what we call original sin because the Scriptures teach us so clearly that we are born in a sinful state and that the curse of the Fall attends every human life. That sounds grim and dreadful until we realize that in that judgment on fallen humanity comes also the tempering of God's wrath with mercy and grace and his whole work of redemption. We believe with great joyous anticipation that there is a special measure of grace God has reserved for those who die in infancy. Jesus said, "Suffer the little children to come unto me, for to such belongs the kingdom of God."

One warning that I have to raise at this point is that we dare not jump to the conclusion that an individual person's particular disease or affliction is a direct result of some particular sin. That may not be the case at all. As humans, all of us must participate in the broad complex of the fallenness of our humanity, which includes the tragedy of disease.

When we experience trials, how can we determine if they are the consequences of violating a scriptural principle, a test from the Lord, or an attack from Satan?

First of all, we need to recognize that any one of these possibilities exists when we enter tribulation, suffering, or trials of any sort. In fact, other things may be the cause of a trial we are called to endure. We may be the innocent victim of somebody else's unrighteous behavior, and we might ask why God allows us to be the victim of someone else's unkindness.

Sometimes trials and tribulations come to us as a direct judgment of God. It can be part of the corrective wrath to his children, or the punitive wrath to those who are obstinate in their disobedience toward him. Sometimes the Lord does send circumstances or people that will help us develop our spiritual muscles and character. It could also be that we are being besieged by the enemy, something Martin Luther frequently spoke of experiencing—what he called "the infection," the personal assault that comes from the prince of darkness.

It's not easy to discern between these causes. We need to begin by recognizing that God is sovereign over all tribulations. Whether it's a tribulation that follows as a consequence of my sin or God's putting me to a test or my being the victim of another person or the object of Satan's attack, God is sovereign over all of those things. In the midst of tribulation, instead of losing myself in trying to discern for sure what the cause is and trying to figure out why this thing is happening to me, it's important that I ask the deeper question, How am I to respond to it?

We can begin by searching our hearts to see if there are

any wicked ways in us that could be legitimate reasons for God to be correcting us. We ought to rejoice that God does this because it is an indication of his love for us. The correction of the Lord is designed to lead us to repentance and to the full restoration of fellowship. When I enter into a trial or into some type of tribulation, I should be saying, "Lord, is there something that you're trying to say to me? Is there an area of my life that needs attention or cleaning up?" Our normal posture of confession should be intensified in the midst of tribulation. It may not be, as I said, an act of God's chastisement, but he may be in a sense complimenting us by calling us to suffer for righteousness' sake so that we can participate in the trials that were so much a part of Jesus' ministry.

It's good to remember that the very baptism we receive is, among other things, a sign of our willingness to participate in the sufferings of Christ. Again, we come before God and say, "I don't know for sure why I'm suffering. But God, I want to suffer honorably in a virtuous way, in a way that will show my loyalty to you." That's the important thing when these things happen.

People speak of the "problem of pain." Is it not more accurate in a fallen world to speak of the "problem of pleasure"?

I can understand how God would allow pain to afflict people who are in radical rebellion against him and are daily involved in cosmic treason. If God is just and holy, we would ask, How would he *not* visit judgment upon them? If God is good, then, being good, he must punish that which is evil, and if he left evil unchecked and only gave happiness and pleasure to the wicked, you would begin to wonder about the integrity of God.

Why does God, in spite of my sin and my disobedience to him, allow me to participate in as much happiness as I am able in this world? Speaking on a practical level, pleasure and pain produce very different results. Sometimes the presence of pain in my life brings the practical benefit of sanctifying me. God works in me through affliction. As uncomfortable as pain may be, we do know that the Scriptures tell us again and again that tribulation is a means by which we are purified and driven to a deeper dependence upon God. There is a long-range benefit to us that we would presumably lose were it not for the pain we are called to "endure for a season." The Scriptures tell us to endure for a season because the pain we experience now can't even be compared with the glories stored up for us in the future.

Conversely, pleasure can be narcotic and seductive so that the more we enjoy it and the more we experience it, the less aware we become of our dependence on and need for God's mercy, help, and forgiveness. Pleasure can be evil disguised, designed by the devil to lead us into ultimate ruin. That's why the pursuit of pleasure can be a dangerous thing. Whether experiencing pain or pleasure, we don't want to lose sight of God and our need for him.

In Colossians 1:24 Paul says he does his share in "filling up that which is lacking in Christ's sufferings." What is meant by this phrase?"

This text has been a focal point of controversy in the history of the church, particularly in debates between Catholics and Protestants. The body of Christ is one of the principal images used in the New Testament to describe the church. One of the favorite themes of the Roman Catholic Church has been to call the church the continuing incarnation, in more than just a mystical or spiritual sense.

Part of the Catholic Church's doctrine has involved the "treasury of merits." This refers to works of the saints that, being above and beyond the call of duty, are added to the merit that was accrued by Christ through his life of perfect obedience. This excess merit is deposited into the treasury of merits and may be used by the church to help those who are in purgatory.

The idea behind that principle is the suffering of the martyrs, those who went to their deaths in faith before the gladiators of Rome. They were seen as suffering meritoriously. When Paul speaks of the suffering and affliction he's enduring as his "filling up that which is lacking" in the afflictions of Jesus, some people interpret that to mean that as an apostle and as a Christian, Paul's suffering adds to the meritorious suffering of Jesus. Jesus is the principal sacrifice offered for our sins. No one could be redeemed without his merit, but that merit is not the full measure of merit available to the church. In and of itself it is not complete. In other words, Christ left room for more merit to be added through victorious and innocent martyrdom and suffering of the saints.

Protestant doctrine finds that interpretation of the text abhorrent because one of the cardinal tenets of classical Protestantism is the sole sufficiency of the sacrifice of Christ; his suffering rendered perfect merit, and nothing can be added to it. There is no lack or deficiency in the atonement of Christ. What Paul means in this passage is that Christ calls all of his people to participate in his afflictions and in his humiliation. The phrase "filling up what is lacking" does not indicate a deficiency in Jesus, but simply means that the full measure of suffering that Christ and his church experience is part of God's redemptive plan. Suffering is designed to shape us more and more into Christlikeness, and ultimately it brings glory to God.

How would you counsel Christians suffering with illness or old age who would rather be in heaven with their Lord than here?

I would first commend them for their preference because they're in good company. We find that sentiment expressed frequently in Scripture. In the Old Testament, Job, Moses, Jeremiah, and others cursed the day of their birth, and in the midst of their suffering they begged God to allow them to die. Simeon, even after he saw the Messiah, made the same request when he said, "Now, Lord, let your servant depart in peace." Paul talked about his own ambivalence, saying that he was torn between two things, to depart and be with Christ, which was far better, or to remain here on earth, which he said was more needful for other people. He wanted to be of service to his flock, but his personal preference was to die and go to heaven.

Not long ago Billy Graham made such a statement publicly. He said he was tired and that the thing that he wanted more than anything else was to be able to go home and be with Christ. Not only is this desire simply the posi-

tive longing for your soul's fulfillment and reaching the
destiny of your spiritual pilgrimage (and all of us should
look forward to heaven), but that preference is also motivated, many times, by serious suffering and affliction. Life
has become such a burden and filled with so much pain
that a person yearns for simple relief. Sometimes statements about wanting to die are thinly veiled requests for
some sort of euthanasia. And though I would commend a
person for his or her desire to depart and be with Christ, I
would urge them not to take any steps to hasten that
moment through their own hand.

Kierkegaard wrote of the struggles involved in the Christian life and of the effects of dread in a book called *Sickness
Unto Death.* He said that one of the most difficult experiences
for any human being is to want profoundly to die and yet not
be allowed to do so. I visited with a woman not long ago who
was in that situation. She had been afflicted with tremendous
suffering and pain. She looked at me with tears rolling down
her cheeks and said, "I just don't know if I can take any
more." She just longed for the simple cessation of the pain.
I'm sure she had contemplated suicide. Although I certainly
understand a person's deep desire to be relieved from that
suffering, we believe that God is the author of life and death,
and it is not within our rights to take our own life.

**Can suffering in general rather than suffering for our
Christian faith be counted as sharing the suffering of
Christ?**

I think it can. If the suffering is done in faith—that is,
throughout that suffering we place our trust in God—then

I think we are participating in the sense that we are willing
to suffer and to trust God in the midst of suffering, even as
Jesus trusted the Father. There is a special promise given
in the Scriptures to those who are suffering for righteousness' sake as a result of being unjustly persecuted.

What if a person is suffering from an illness or some
other tragedy that is not a direct result of persecution? He
still enters into suffering that requires a measure of trust in
God, and that is a virtuous thing for people in that state. At
that point, insofar as they are imitating Christ's willingness
to suffer, I would say that they are participating at least indirectly in that whole process.

What if I'm suffering punishment because I've committed some kind of crime? I don't think we can call that particularly virtuous or say that we are participating in the
suffering of Jesus in any redemptive way. In fact, this is
directly addressed in 1 Peter 2:20.

In regard to the man born blind (John 9), the question
was asked of Jesus, "Who's sin was it, this man's or his parents', that he was afflicted with blindness?" Jesus said it
was neither. In other words, the question was a false
dilemma. And those who asked it were trying to reduce to
two options something that had more than two. There
was another option. Jesus said, "It wasn't because of his
sin or his parents' sin. This person was born blind so that
the power of God and the grace of God may be made
manifest." That person was suffering not from persecution. His suffering was used by God to bring honor and
glory to Christ.

I mention this instance because it is a clear biblical case
in which suffering has theological value—not merit, but

value—insofar that it is useful to the purposes of God. Christ himself tells us that we are going to have afflictions and suffering in this world. He certainly indicates that we are going to suffer persecution, and he gives a particular blessing to that in the Sermon on the Mount, saying that the reward will be great. He also indicates that there will be other kinds of suffering that come our way and that we are suffering in him and with him.

What is the difference between God testing us and tempting us?

The difference is between an action that is holy, legitimate, and righteous, and an action that would be beneath the character of God. As James tells us in the New Testament, "Let no one say when he is tempted that he is tempted of God." An explanation follows that temptation is something that rises from within the evil inclinations of our own hearts. We can't excuse our sin by saying that the devil made us do it or, worse, that God has provoked us or inclined us to sin.

There is some confusion on this because of the words in the Lord's Prayer, where Jesus instructs his disciples to pray, "Lead us not into temptation, but deliver us from evil." It almost suggests that, if we have to ask God not to lead us into temptation, perhaps there are occasions when he does. That concept has to do with being led into the place of testing.

The Bible does tell us that God will put his people through a trial or a test or an ordeal ultimately for their benefit, but sometimes for other reasons not always understandable to us. Adam and Eve failed their test in the Garden of Eden.

Jesus, of course, was led by the Spirit into the wilderness to be tested. God led him there to be tempted, not by God but by Satan. In that particular incident we have an example of the difference. God put Jesus in the wilderness to be tested. Satan's activity was to tempt him. To tempt someone is to entice him or her to commit an evil act. In that sense, it would be totally out of character for God to entice someone to sin. For his redemptive purposes and for our own character building he may put us in a situation where we are put on trial and are vulnerable to the attacks of the enemy—as Job was, as Christ was, and as Adam was.

Luther often spoke of the unbridled assault Satan directed against him. He was struggling against depression, but he never thought of that as an enticement at the hands of God. Satan will tempt us in the sense of trying to seduce us and persuade us to disobey God, though even in that temptation Satan is under the sovereignty of God.

In the book of 1 Thessalonians we're called to give thanks in all circumstances. I've sometimes heard my brothers and sisters in Christ giving thanks for things such as illness or death, and I think this is crazy. Should we be be doing this?

I don't think it's crazy. In these situations, people are trying to be faithful and obedient to what that passage calls us to do. But a lot of misunderstanding and confusion attends this passage. The Bible repeatedly tells us that we are to remember at all times and through all circumstances who

God is. We must remember that he's sovereign in and over all human circumstances that befall us. As Romans tells us, we are promised that "all things work together for good to those who love God" (Rom. 8:28). That's not because the things themselves are working for my benefit, but because God, who is sovereign over everything that takes place in my life, is using whatever happens in my life to my ultimate advantage. He will use the suffering and the pain, and he will triumph over the wickedness that comes into my life.

Paul illustrates the concept of rejoicing in all things when he says in Philippians 4:11-12 that he has learned to be content in whatever state he finds himself. He has had to learn how to live with a lot and how to live with little, how to deal with being honored and with being insulted and ill treated. He says in effect, "Whatever else happens to me—if I'm rich, if I'm poor, if I'm hungry, if I'm full, if people are loving me, if people are hating me—whatever those circumstances are, I know who I am and I know that God is committed to me. Because of that, there is something for me to rejoice about in that circumstance."

I don't think Paul meant by that passage that when he was shipwrecked or being beaten with rods he uttered a prayer of thanksgiving, saying, "Isn't this wonderful!" If I see circumstances that are plainly evil, I'm not to rejoice in the evil that is there, but I'm to rejoice in the God who stands over that evil and who stands over the grief and the sorrow.

The shortest verse in the Bible, "Jesus wept" (John 11:35), tells you something. Jesus goes to the home of Mary and Martha, and they are angry with Jesus. Martha comes to him and says, "Master, where have you been? Our brother died four days ago. If you had been here, it wouldn't have happened."

They are really angry with him. Did Jesus respond with, "Hey look, don't worry. I was just setting the stage for this dramatic resurrection that I'm about to perform. Relax, we're going to have a party, and I'm going to bring your brother back to life"? Jesus wept. He entered into the reality of human suffering and grief, fulfilling the Scripture that it's better to go to the house of mourning than to spend your time with fools. Then he proceeded to show the triumph of God over that situation by raising Lazarus from the dead. So I think that earnest Christians who seek to rejoice in all circumstances are motivated to give God the praise and honor, and to try to overcome the pain of their situation by that practice. But we must take care not to be flippant about it. We should not deny the reality of the pain, the tragedy, or the suffering. This isn't healthy faith.

As someone in the health profession, I see people suffering every day. What can Christians expect from God in regard to healing?

I don't know how many times I've seen on the walls of pastors' studies or in Christian homes the little sign, Expect a Miracle. If a miracle is something we can expect, like we expect the postman every morning, it ceases to be miraculous—it's no longer extraordinary, and it no longer does the job that miracles were designed to do, namely, to call attention in an astonishing way to the intervention of God. On the other hand, the New Testament tells us to bring our prayers before God, particularly for those who are sick. So I expect God to be merciful because he promises to be merciful, and I expect God to be present in times of trouble because he promises to be present in every time of trouble. I expect that God will take our prayers seriously when we pray on behalf of the sick. I do not expect that God is going to heal everybody we pray for because I don't know that God has ever promised to do that. And I have no right to expect something from God that he has not categorically promised in every situation.

In the New Testament we see that Jesus, as far as we know, had a perfect healing record. When Jesus asked the Father to heal somebody, they were healed. But even the apostles were not that consistent. There were times when they prayed for the healing of people and those people were healed, and there were times when they prayed for people and they were not healed. I think that in those situations, practically speaking, what we should do is bring our requests before God in fear and trembling, in passionate intercession, and then let God be God. We do expect the presence of his Holy Spirit.

The Bible tells us that in the world we have tribulation, the world is full of suffering, we are going to suffer, and God promises to go with us: "Yea though I walk through the valley of the shadow of death, I will fear no evil for thou art with me." I have never ceased to be amazed at how some Christians I know have testified to the overwhelming sense of the presence of Christ that comes to them in those situations. That's when we can most expect God to be with us.

What does the Bible teach us about comforting one who is suffering as a result of a crime he has committed?

The basic posture of the Scriptures regarding a matter like that is one of charity. For example, as Christians we have a clear mandate in Scripture to be engaged in the visiting of those who are in prison. Some have taken a narrow view of that, insisting that it's only those who are political prisoners or those who are being persecuted because they're believers—for righteousness' sake—and are unjustly incarcerated. Some people say that ministry to those in prison doesn't include a ministry to those who are there because they are guilty of committing certain crimes.

Certainly being incarcerated in prison is one form of suffering that is a direct consequence of one's sinful behavior. I think the church historically has taken that to mean very clearly that whether they're guilty or innocent, whatever the cause of their suffering, we are still called upon to exercise a ministry of mercy to them.

As a director of Prison Fellowship, I see the visitation of prison inmates as a very important ministry that fulfills a mandate of Christ. Our basic posture is to be a people who are bringing consolation and kindness and charity. If we see somebody hungry, we're not supposed to ask them why they're hungry or how they got to be hungry. Maybe they're hungry as a direct result of their own sinfulness, but we're supposed to feed them.

There are some boundaries to our charity. For example, the Bible takes a hard stand against people who habitually refuse to work: "If he refuses to work, neither let him eat." In the teachings of the apostles beyond the New Testament, one of the earliest documents is *The Didache*. It gives specific instructions on how long we should be charitable to people who are suffering as a direct consequence of their refusal to repent. It takes a tremendous measure of wisdom to know where the charity ends and the rebuke and admonition begin. On the other hand, admonition and rebuke are not necessarily incompatible with charity. That can be a part of love, although it's not usually considered a part of consolation. This is a particularly relevant question now with the national controversy over AIDS. I've seen many Christians taking the position that because some people suffer from AIDS as a direct result of immoral practices, Christians ought not to lift a finger to alleviate their suffering. I find that a total antithesis to the spirit of the New Testament. If these people are suffering, we're supposed to be agents of relief with a ministry of kindness and charity to them, regardless of the causes of their suffering.

In James 5:14-15, the sick are told to call upon the elders of the church to anoint them with oil and lay hands on them. Does anyone still practice this? Should Christians today practice this?

Actually, the implementation of that injunction in the book of James is very widespread in Christendom. For example, in the Roman Catholic Church it is elevated to the status of a sacrament. The last of the seven sacraments is called by the name extreme unction. We usually think of it in terms of what is called last rites; somebody will be on their deathbed and a priest is called to hear a final confession. That doctrine or sacrament began in the Roman Catholic Church in direct response to that passage in James, and it was seen primarily not as a transitory benediction for somebody about to depart this world, but as a healing rite.

In the Episcopalian church there is what is called the Order of Saint Luke, because Luke was a physician. This denomination practices and advocates the anointing of oil and the laying on of hands for those who are sick.

Certainly in the Pentecostal and Assemblies of God churches this is widely practiced. Throughout the whole charismatic movement there is a tremendous importance affixed to this verse in James.

Should people do it? I would say yes, but I think it's also important that we understand some things about the anointing with oil as it was practiced in New Testament churches.

Some historians insist that in this passage James is referring not to a religious rite so much as a medical rite. One of the medical practices was to anoint a person with oil with the belief that this oil had some medicinal value to it. With modern medicine available to us, it would no longer be necessary to do this for such therapeutic reasons.

The normal understanding of that text is that it was a symbol of the Holy Spirit and it was accompanied by the prayer that God would intervene and raise up the sick and that the actual anointing of oil would be a religious rite. Again, the Roman Catholic Church sees it as a sacrament. Others don't necessarily call it a sacrament but would see it as a significant religious observation.

When the New Testament calls us to perform an act of mercy like this, I think we should do it. I don't know of any church that doesn't pray for the sick. We still visit the sick and pray for them. This particular rite has disappeared from many churches while it's still maintained in others. I see no reason for its cessation.

19

The End Times

But you, brethren, are not in darkness,
so that this Day should overtake you as a thief. . . .
Therefore let us not sleep, as others do,
but let us watch and be sober.

1 THESSALONIANS 5:4, 6

Questions in This Section:

Are we living in the last days?

Should Christians spend their time studying the biblical prophecy of the Second Coming?

What signs do you see today of Christ's second coming?

Does the Bible tell us when Jesus will return?

In light of national and world conditions, do you feel that the kingdom of heaven is truly at hand?

What did Jesus mean when he said, "Truly I say to you, this generation will not pass until all these things be done"?

Do you believe the Antichrist will come from within the church?

Do the Scriptures say that during the last days the earth will be destroyed or that God will regenerate the substance that already exists here?

Do we stand before God in judgment upon death or later?

Will the Christian have to go through the final judgment in the same way the non-Christian will?

The Bible teaches that we will be judged by the measure in which we judge others. Is this an indication that on Judgment Day, the process of judgment will be significantly different among people?

What does Scripture teach us about the future role of Israel?

Are we living in the last days?

We have to be careful not to be guilty of what Jesus rebuked the Pharisees for—what I call the Red Sky Syndrome. If you recall, Jesus rebuked the Pharisees because they had an ability to predict the weather. They could look at the sky, and if it was red at night, they would say, "Sailor's delight." And if it was red in the morning, they would say, "Sailors take warning." But they missed the signs of the times, and they missed the first advent of Christ. They missed the coming of the Messiah right in their midst in spite of the fact that a host of biblical prophecies heralded the appearance of Jesus on the scene—and Jesus rebuked them for it.

When somebody asks me, "Are we in the last days?" I suspect what they mean by that is, "Are we near the last chapter of history prior to the coming of Jesus Christ?" I can't say yes or no. So I will say, "Yes, and I don't know." The sense in which I say yes is this: We have been in the last days since the first advent of Christ. And so the Scriptures tell us that we are to be living in the spirit of diligence and of vigilance from the time that Jesus departed this planet in clouds of glory until he returns. But when people ask me, "Are we living in the last days?" I suspect what they mean by that is, "Are we living in the last minutes of the last hour of the last day?" Do I think that the return of Jesus is close; is it on the horizon?

I hope I have learned something from other people's mistakes in the past. For example, when Luther went through all of the turbulent upheaval of the Christian church in the sixteenth century, he was convinced that the fragmentation of the church at that time was the harbinger of the return of Jesus. But Luther was wrong. Jonathan Edwards, living in the middle of the eighteenth century, shortly before this nation was formed as a republic, reflected on the way in which religion had declined from 1620 to 1750. He was convinced that the world was going to the dogs and that it was running out of time, that Jesus was going to come any minute. Edwards was wrong. So when I look at two titans of theology like Martin Luther and Jonathan Edwards and I see them making predictions and voicing their expectations of the near return of Jesus and being wrong, that gives me pause.

The only thing I can say, however, is that we're about 450 years closer to it than Luther was and 235 years closer to it than Edwards was. There's much that is going on in the world today—that tells me that these are the times when Christians should be reading the Bible in one hand and the newspaper in the other.

Should Christians spend their time studying the biblical prophecy of the Second Coming?

If God gives us information about anything, obviously he expects us to be diligent in the study of it. One biblical scholar made the statement that approximately two-thirds of the doctrinal material of the New Testament Scriptures are concerned in one way or another with the second coming of Christ. So just from the sheer volume of information in both the New and Old Testaments that focuses on the future consummation of the kingdom of God, it's obvious that this was a burning matter of importance to the early Christian church and to the teaching of Jesus himself. In the Olivet discourse (Matt. 24), Jesus gave very strong admonitions to his disciples to not be like the Pharisees, who could read the weather forecasts but failed to see the signs of the times. They missed the first coming of Jesus. Had they been cognizant of the Old Testament Scriptures that foretold the Messiah and applied them carefully to what was going on in the first century, they shouldn't have missed his presence.

Notice that the basic defense of the claims of Jesus found in the New Testament is grounded in the fulfillment of Old Testament prophesies concerning the person and work of Jesus. Of course, the New Testament also makes future prophecies because the New Testament does not finish all of the work of redemption that God has in mind for this planet. There is still another chapter to be written, as Jesus indicated, and so he tells us to watch for the signs of the times. He calls us to a position of diligence and to be alert, to be awake and not to be deceived.

The warnings come both from Jesus and from the apostle Paul that in the last days great deceptions will occur: a false Christ, false rumors, and falsehood so severe that it might even deceive the very elect of God. How are we to be able to discern between the true Christ and the Antichrist or the false messiahs who will come unless we give great heed to those prophetic passages of Scripture? They were given to the church for a reason—for our instruction.

I would say that the New Testament emphasis is on diligence and vigilance. At the same time we ought not to be preoccupied. There is a tendency among some people to focus all their attention on futuristic prophecies. This becomes almost a kind of magic or wizardry by which we're looking for the Second Coming behind every bush. I think the whole of Scripture must be taken into account, not only prophecies concerning the future. In fact, we are given instruction about the way we conduct ourselves *now* because of what the future predicts.

What signs do you see today of Christ's second coming?

Jesus taught us in the New Testament that we should pay attention to what he called the signs of the times so that when he comes, we won't be caught by surprise. In 1 Thessalonians 5, Paul writes that the day of the Lord will happen suddenly and without warning, just like a thief in the night.

Some people believe that, since we don't know when Jesus will come again, we ought not even think about the signs of the times—knowledge of such things was never intended for us. In the Olivet discourse, Jesus clearly suggests that we be vigilant and diligent and aware of what's going on around us. It was incumbent upon the people of Israel to see the signs that had been prophesied in the Old Testament for the original birth of the Messiah. As you well know, the vast majority of people missed him altogether.

The question, though, is, What are the signs? Some that Jesus mentions are things that are, for the most part, happening all the time: wars, rumors of wars, earthquakes, famines, apostasy in the church, godlessness reigning, and so on. These are the classical signs indicating that the time of Jesus' return is near. Since these are things that happen

in every generation and in every age, the only way in which
they would have any importance to us would be if they
took place in significant numbers or intensity.

It's interesting to me that in the calculus of violence, the
most bloody, militaristic, warring century in all of recorded
history is the twentieth. This has been the century of world
wars. We've also seen some of the worst natural catastrophes in our century, unprecedented in terms of their
destructive capacity.

Jesus also focuses attention on events developing around
the Jewish nation. There are Christian theologians who are
divided about the importance of contemporary Israel to
the biblical predictions of Jesus. In Luke, for example,
Jesus predicts the destruction of Jerusalem in A.D. 70 and
says the Jews will be carried off until the times of the Gentiles will be fulfilled. Romans 11 talks about the times of
the Gentiles being fulfilled at the end of the age before
God brings about the completion of his kingdom. That's
why there was so much excitement in the church in 1967
when, for the first time since A.D. 70, Jerusalem was no
longer held captive by Gentiles. I see that as potentially
very significant.

Does the Bible tell us when Jesus will return?

Certainly not specifically. Many people have attempted, by
a careful (and sometimes a not so careful) examination of
the prophetic passages of Scripture to establish a timetable. Some have even predicted months, days and years—
none of which, up to this point, have been correct.

When Martin Luther was going through the tremendous upheaval and agitation in Europe during the Protestant Reformation, he thought that the great distress coming upon the church in the sixteenth century was a clear sign of the eminent return of Jesus. Luther looked for it in his lifetime, and he was wrong by at least five centuries.

In the middle of the eighteenth century, before the Declaration of Independence was signed but more than one hundred years after the Pilgrims had settled this country, Jonathan Edwards was much inclined to think that the return of Christ was about to happen. Edwards was wrong. I mention these two men because there aren't too many men whose theological expertise I respect more than I do Luther's and Edwards's. To see that both of them were wrong makes me very careful about giving precise predictions about the day and the hour of Christ's return.

We remember that on the Mount of Olives Jesus told his disciples that even the Son did not know the day and the hour of his return; that is in the Father's hands. There is a day and an hour that God has ordained, and he just does not reveal it precisely. Yet at the same time Jesus was zealous, as were Paul and the other writers in the New Testament, to instruct the church of certain things they ought to be paying attention to—signs of the times, things that would have to happen before they could expect the return of Jesus.

Of course, there's a great dispute as to what those things are and if any of them have taken place. Some people believe that all such signs have already taken place. I don't know that this is true, but I think we have every reason to be optimistic that the day is drawing very close. I think many of the things that Jesus speaks of (and that are mentioned in other Scriptures as well) as harbingers or signs of the times have already taken place or are taking place now. There has been a tremendous renewal of interest in the return of Christ. I'm very hopeful that it will be soon, though I can conceive of its being another two or three thousand years.

In light of national and world conditions, do you feel that the kingdom of heaven is truly at hand?

I don't think that the kingdom of heaven is at hand. I think there's a very real sense in which the kingdom of heaven (or the kingdom of God, which is the way the other Gospels describe that phrase) is already here. It was once announced that the kingdom of heaven was at hand. We find that announcement early in the New Testament Gospels. The use of the term *heaven* as "kingdom of heaven" is found in Matthew's Gospel. It is the announcement given by John the Baptist, who is a forerunner for the appearance of Christ, the King of the kingdom.

This whole concept of the kingdom of heaven or the kingdom of God is the motif that unifies the Old and New Testaments. This is the big concept that ties together all of redemptive history. It has to do with the reign of God over his people and over the world. The promises in the Old Testament of the coming of the kingdom of God were made with respect to a vague, distant future time, through the lips and the writings of the prophets.

But when John the Baptist appears on the scene, there is a new sense of urgency when he makes the

announcement that the kingdom of heaven is at hand.
He speaks of the ax being laid at the root of the tree. He
uses the image of the farmer whose fan is in his hand;
that is, the moment has come in which the kingdom of
heaven in some sense is about to break through in power
and in significance. Of course, this is the announcement
that stirred up the Jewish nation and created so much
backlash against John the Baptist. He was saying that the
kingdom of heaven was at hand and they were not ready
for it. When Jesus came on the scene, there was a slight
change in the tenor of Jesus' announcement. He also
preached repentance because of the kingdom of God,
but his disciples didn't fast as did the disciples of John
the Baptist. Then he made the strange announcement:
"The kingdom of God is among you." He said, "If you see
me casting out Satan by the finger of God, then you know
the kingdom of God has come upon you." In a certain
sense, the kingdom of God broke into history and began
with the ministry of Jesus and certainly with the crucial
moment at which Jesus ascended to the right hand of
God for his coronation, where he now rules as the King
of kings and Lord of lords.

People ask me if the kingdom of God is at hand. I think
what they usually mean is, Is Jesus returning soon? I think
there's every reason to be encouraged and hopeful that the
final chapter of the kingdom of God is at hand. What I'm
trying to stress is that the kingdom of God has *already begun.*
It hasn't been finalized and it hasn't been consummated—
and that won't happen until Christ returns in glory. I think
we have every reason to expect that to be near.

What did Jesus mean when he said, "Truly I say to you, this generation will not pass until all these things be done"?

That's one of the toughest statements of Jesus in all of the New Testament. Some seminary students may recall that the famous New Testament scholar, missionary, and musician Albert Schweitzer wrote his principal work in which he confessed his difficulty with Jesus' identity precisely because of that passage and the sister passages from the other Gospels that refer to that discourse on the Mount of Olives.

Jesus was talking to his disciples, and in this particular context he was talking about the temple. He said that the time will come when not one stone will be left upon another, and he pointed to the walls of the temple of Jerusalem, saying that they would be destroyed and trampled underfoot. In that same discourse he talked presumably about the consummation of his kingdom and his glorious return at the end of the age. The disciples come to him, and they ask, "When will these things take place?" He says on one occasion that "this generation will not pass away until all of these things take place." Other statements he makes are, "You won't go over all of the cities of Israel until these things take place" and, "Some of you will not taste of death until all of these things take place."

Schweitzer looked at that and said that it's obvious that some of the hearers of Jesus died before everything that he announced in the Olivet discourse took place and that the Jewish missionaries did not go over all of the nations. They still haven't covered all of the nations of the world. He said that that generation has passed away and Jesus hasn't returned. So the conclusion was wrong, and Jesus died in disillusionment. According to Schweitzer, this represented Jesus' hope that God would bring the kingdom of God in that generation, but it didn't happen.

Radical scholars say that the second generation of Christians had to revise the teaching of Jesus in order to account for this great blunder on the part of their teacher. They said that he announced his coming well before it actually happened. Some try to squeeze the text to say that in the phrase "this generation will not pass away," Jesus is using the term *generation* not to describe an age group but a type of person. Jesus called people a wicked and adulterous generation. He was simply saying that this kind of wickedness and this kind of sinfulness will be around until he comes back. That may be what Jesus meant.

I think there's a better explanation, although there's not space for the details of it here. Technical scholars in the New Testament have given close attention to the function of the phrase "all of these things," which is two Greek words, *ponta touta*. When Jesus uses those terms, he uses specific reference to the destruction of Jerusalem, which in fact did take place in the year A.D. 70 and did take place within that generation and before many of them died.

Do you believe the Antichrist will come from within the church?

I'm not sure whether the Antichrist will come from within the church, but I hold that out as a very distinct possibility. As I'm sure you're aware, there has been a great deal of speculation in church history in attempts to identify the person of the Antichrist of whom Scripture speaks in such frightening terms and of whom Paul mentioned would manifest himself prior to the return of our Lord. Usually the candidates for that office have been people of enormous political power. Some thought it was Nero. Many identified Hitler, others even Mussolini because of the numerological formula that fit his title. That kind of speculation has gone on repeatedly.

But when Paul warns about the appearance of the man of lawlessness, who is usually identified with the Antichrist, he makes the statement that this person will be one who seeks to receive worship and that he will set himself up in the temple of God and ask to be treated as God.

Paul mentions that in the second letter to the Thessalonians. It's because of that reference to the appearance of the man of lawlessness in the temple of God that many have come to the conclusion that the Antichrist will be a religious person from within the church.

There are other factors, too. There is the prophetic teaching of Christ and of the apostles that in the last times a tremendous apostasy will exist within the church—a falling away from faithfulness to Christ. It would be very possible for the church to become a breeding ground for that which is opposed to Christ himself.

Also, we see that Satan is described in the New Testament as having a sort of metamorphic character. He is deceptive; he has the ability to transform himself, as the New Testament says, into an angel of light. In theology we say that Satan has the power to appear *sub species boni;* that is, under the auspices of the good, masquerading as a good personage. So, what better place to communicate a grand delusion than in the context of the church itself?

I have to add this qualifier to that. Though it's very possible that the Antichrist could come from the church, nevertheless all of these things could also be said of secular personages who usurp ecclesiastical authority, as in the ancient world when pagan rulers would come in and desecrate the temple of God and set themselves up to be worshiped. In that sense the spirit of the Antichrist doesn't necessarily have to be identified with the church.

Do the Scriptures say that during the last days the earth will be destroyed or that God will regenerate the substance that already exists here?

There's a great deal of controversy about how the end of the world will come. Many people are frightened by the startling images Scripture uses to describe the end times. When we're told that the heavens will roll up like a scroll and the earth will melt, and we see this conflagration that involves a tremendous intensity of heat, some see a cryptic foretelling of some kind of nuclear holocaust by which this whole planet will be utterly annihilated.

Though there are differences of opinion in this matter, the overwhelming consensus of believers throughout history has been that though there will be a catastrophic moment of judgment at the end of the age, the expression of God's wrath upon the earth will not involve the total annihilation of this planet. Rather, the classical view looks for a renovation of this world. We all agree that we look for a new heaven and a new earth, seen by John in his vision (the book of Revelation). In what we call eschatology, which is the study of the last things, there are a couple of principles that I think are important to keep in front of us when we pay attention to what the Bible says about this catastrophic moment at the end of history as we know it. For example, in Romans Paul says that "the whole creation groans together with us in travail," waiting for the redemption that God is going to bring upon his people. Man's fall brings the whole earth into pain, sorrow, travail, and tragedy.

We find in Scripture that along with the redemption of the human race will also come the redemption of the human race's environment, which is this world. God creates humanity and God redeems humanity. And so it is that he creates a world, and his plan of redemption is to redeem this world. The way I look at it, which is somewhat speculative, is that this mass of conflagration during the last days that the Scriptures speak of is a kind of purification of this world. Not utter annihilation, not utter destruction, but a purification of the old, which is then renewed, restored, and brought to life again.

Do we stand before God in judgment upon death or later?

We have to make a distinction, as I think the Bible does, between the judgment that we receive immediately upon our death, at which we are brought before Christ, and what the Bible speaks of as the last judgment. There's a reason the Bible refers to the last judgment as the last. That which is

last presupposes that there have been some kinds of judgment prior to it. The Bible says that it's appointed for man
to die once, and then the judgment. I think there's much
in the New Testament to indicate that at the moment we
die, we experience at least a preliminary judgment.

Paul, for example, said that he longed to depart and to
be with Christ, which was far better than to remain here in
this life and in the ministry he had. Historic Christianity
has almost universally, but not quite, confessed the idea
that the departed saints go immediately to be in the presence of Christ, in what is called the enjoyment of the intermediate state; that is, we are disembodied spirits, and we
await the final consummation of the kingdom of Christ,
whereby we will experience the resurrection of the body.
When, in the Apostles' Creed, we say, "I believe in the
resurrection of the body," we're not talking about Christ's
body but about our future resurrected bodies. As I say,
historic Christianity believes that there is an immediate
transference from this world into the presence of Christ,
at least in our disembodied spirit state. For that to happen,
some kind of judgment has to take place. For example,
Paul would not be ushered into the presence of Christ immediately upon his death without Christ first making an
evaluation that Paul was indeed one of his—that he was a
justified man in a state of salvation. I think there is a preliminary division of the sheep and the goats prior to the
final judgment on the last day, of which Scripture speaks.
Jesus warns repeatedly of that last judgment.

Very few people in our secular culture find a discussion
of judgment to be relevant; it is politically incorrect to
judge others or, to some extent, even ourselves—to distin-

guish between right and wrong, truth and falsehood. Yet these very same people will commend the teachings of Jesus as wise and wonderful. But if Jesus of Nazareth taught anything, he taught repeatedly and emphatically that everyone of us will in fact be brought before the judgment throne of God for a final, consummate judgment.

Will the Christian have to go through the final judgment in the same way the non-Christian will?

There's a sense in which we will not, and there's a sense in which we will. There's a lot of confusion about judgment in the Bible, partly due to a confusion between two words, *judgment* and *condemnation.* In the book of Romans, Paul makes it clear that one of the great fruits of our justification is that we have moved beyond the scope of condemnation. There is no condemnation for those who are in Christ Jesus. So those who are in Christ need not have any fear of ever having to face the punitive wrath of God in the final judgment. We have to make certain that we are in that state of grace before we have the confidence that we're not going to experience condemnation.

But we still must face what I would call the judgment of evaluation. Jesus warns again and again that everything we do, whether we're believers or nonbelievers, will be brought into the judgment. I will stand before God, and my life will be reviewed by my Father. Obviously my sins will be covered by the atonement and righteousness of Christ, and I will have the supreme advantage of standing at the judgment throne of God, where Christ is the judge and also the defense attorney for his people. That's a situation that the unbeliever doesn't have. His judge is not his defense attorney—he doesn't have a defense attorney. All he has is a prosecuting attorney accompanying him in the courtroom. So that's all the difference in the world between how the unbeliever stands in the last judgment and how the believer stands in the last judgment.

When we talk about our justification, we recognize that we are justified through the merits of Christ, through the atoning grace of Jesus. But we are still to be judged according to the level of our obedience in this world. This doctrine is held by virtually every Protestant church in the world, yet many Protestants forget that Christians will be rewarded in heaven according to their obedience. There are at least twenty-five times in the New Testament that we are told we will be rewarded according to our works. We don't get there by our works; we get there through the merit of Christ. What rewards we receive in heaven will be distributed according to the level of obedience and response we give to the mandates of Christ. So our lives will be evaluated, and some of us will get greater rewards than others as we are evaluated at the last judgment.

The Bible teaches that we will be judged by the same measure by which we judge others. Is this an indication that on Judgment Day, the process of judgment will be significantly different among people?

It would obviously follow from the statements that Jesus makes in the New Testament that whatever form of judgment we give is what we can expect to receive. But there are a couple of things we need to mention by way of clarification. First of all, we know that the final judgment of our lives as we stand before the Divine Tribunal will be at the hands of an infallible, omniscient, perfectly righteous Judge and that the judgment will be absolutely just. A truly just judge always considers mitigating circumstances. In other words, any act that I'm involved in of a moral kind, be it good or evil, is really a complex act. The degree of wickedness or virtue of my act is related, for example, to many things, one of which is my understanding of what I am doing. If I have a clear understanding that something is wrong and I go ahead and do it willfully, that makes my crime more severe than if I am confused about it. That doesn't necessarily excuse me altogether, but it is a mitigating circumstance. And a just judge considers all of those actions and activities when he makes an ultimate verdict about it.

Now what Jesus tells us is that when he takes everything into account, not only in the judgment of evaluating whether we were guilty or innocent, virtuous or wicked, he also dispenses benefits, rewards, and punishments on the last day. In the verse you cited, Jesus is warning us that if, in this life, we refuse to be merciful to people, God will take that into consideration, and as part of his just punishment for us he will withhold his mercy. If I, being a sinner and a guilty person, tend to be merciful toward others, God will take that into account when he gives his final judgment, and he will be inclined to show more mercy toward the merciful. "Blessed are the merciful, for they shall obtain mercy." There is a tremendous advantage to being merciful in this world because God will weigh that in the balance of our final judgment.

What does Scripture teach us about the future role of Israel?

Some Christians believe that the New Testament church replaces Old Testament Israel as the subject matter of Old Testament prophecies about Israel. That is to say that the church today is regarded as the new Israel. If this is so, then any prophecies in the Bible having to do with Israel now refer to the Christian church and have no specific reference to the nation of Israel.

Other Christians are convinced that the Scriptures have much to say about ethnic, national Israel and that God still has another chapter to write for the Jewish people as such. I am persuaded that God will write a new chapter for ethnic Israel, for the Jewish people who are alive in the world today. I'm persuaded of that principally because of Paul's teaching in his epistle to the church at Rome; in this letter he makes a clear distinction between the Jewish people and the Christian church (Rom. 11). In that distinction he speaks about the fact that God still has work to do with the Jewish people.

One of the most important sections of all of Scripture that teaches about future things is what we call the Olivet discourse, called such because it takes place on the Mount of Olives (Matt. 24). Here, Jesus and his disciples discuss future events. Jesus speaks about the last times and the signs of the times and those things that will transpire at the end of the age before he returns to this planet. For example, in Luke 21:5-28, Jesus predicts the imminent destruction of the city of Jerusalem and the temple. This took place in A.D. 70, when the Romans perpetrated a holocaust against the Jewish people by destroying Jerusalem, slaughtering about one million Jewish people, and tearing the temple down. The Jews, of course, then went into exile. But when Jesus made this prophecy about the destruction of Jerusalem, he said that Jerusalem would be trodden underfoot until the times of the Gentiles be fulfilled. So even our Lord talked in his prophetic utterances about a period in which that exile of the Jewish nation would end and they would return to Jerusalem, which has taken place in our own very day. Beyond that, I do not know and can't speak specifically to Israel's situation.

20

Lifestyle Ethics

But you are a chosen generation, a royal priesthood,
a holy nation, His own special people,
that you may proclaim the praises of Him
who called you out of darkness into His marvelous light.

I PETER 2:9

Questions in This Section:

Why do Christians think they know how other people should live?

Should Christians impose their ethics upon non-Christians?

How can we as Christians ascertain when God's Word was applicable to a certain culture and therefore may not be applicable to us today?

How do we uphold Christian ethics without being judgmental?

Do you feel more pressure as a public figure to live on a higher level of Christian ethics?

If things are going to get worse and worse until our Lord's coming, why should we concern ourselves with social activism and political involvement to make things better?

What is the biblical basis for human dignity?

What is our responsibility toward the poor?

Could you give an example of how Christ's teaching about turning the other cheek applies to today's life situations?

In terms of the arts, is there a difference between secular and Christian?

Should a Christian attorney defend someone he knows is guilty?

Rahab the harlot, the Hebrew midwives, and others throughout the Old Testament supposedly lied to protect others, and God, in turn, blessed them. Does this mean that Christians today may have occasion to lie with God's blessing?

The Bible calls drunkenness a sin. What are the dangers of our culture calling drunkenness a disease?

According to the Bible, is there anything wrong with using hypnosis to help people stop smoking or to overcome some other addiction or behavior pattern?

Why is the use of drugs such as crack escalating in our society?

Is it wrong for scientists to engage in genetic engineering?

Should Christians support AIDS research?

Why do Christians think they know how other people should live?

We hear the expression "holier than thou" quite often in our society, and people hate to have religion shoved down their throats. People are willing to let me practice my religion, but they don't want me hounding them to change their values. Lurking behind all this is society's tendency toward a relativistic view of ethics; the overriding idea is that every person has the right to do what is right in his or her own mind.

But if God is and if he is the Lord of the human race, the Creator of all of us, and if he holds us accountable to him, then there is an objective standard of what is right in his sight. God reveals very clearly that one of the great symptoms of our human fallenness is the idea that people have the right to do what is right in their own minds. The whole concept of the Judeo-Christian religion is that ultimate righteousness is declared, not by my personal preferences or by yours, but by God and his supreme character. If I as an individual come to an understanding of what God requires of people, then that means I am required to do certain things. I may also understand that he's requiring certain things of me as an individual and of people as members of community.

We consider Isaiah in the temple when he had a vision of the holiness of God. He disintegrated before that appearance of God's majesty and cried out, "Woe is me, for I am undone, for I am a man of unclean lips." And then he went on to say, "And I dwell in the midst of a people of unclean lips." Isaiah recognized that his sinfulness was not unique. The fact that he recognized that other people were also guilty of the same sins did not mean that he was entertaining a judgmental spirit toward those other people. He was simply recognizing the truth of the matter: God was sovereign and holy in relation not only to him but to everybody else as well. In practical terms I could say that, for instance, God not only prohibits me from adultery but he also prohibits you from adultery.

The fact that God's law extends beyond ourselves is a point that has been recognized by professors and teachers of ethics quite apart from the Christian faith. Immanuel Kant studied this question thoroughly and talked about the appearance of what he called the categorical imperative, the sense of duty that is present in every human being. Every human being has some idea of what is right and wrong. He made a statement very similar to Jesus': "So live that the ethical decisions that you make would be good if they were elevated to the level of a universal norm." He understood that no man is an island.

Should Christians impose their ethics upon non-Christians?

This question comes up every time a moral issue is debated in the legislature or some other government arena. Do Christians have the right to impose their ethics upon those who don't share the same religious perspective? Well, there are different ways to impose ethical standards upon people. When we talk about ethical authority, ultimately I would say that the only being in the universe having the intrinsic right to impose an obligation on any other being is God himself. Only God is the Lord of the human conscience. We would also have to qualify that and say that God has at the same time delegated certain authorities who have the right to impose ethical obligations on other people. He has delegated the right to parents to impose obligations upon their children. He has also established, created, and ordained governments to impose certain standards of law upon their constituents.

When we live in a free society where the democratic process is functioning, the majority of people in the society are given the right to vote. That vote involves an exercise of one's will that ultimately will become the law of the land if I am voting with the majority. One of the things that very much frightens me is that I hear very few Christians and non-Christians who seem to be aware of the weighty responsibility that is involved in casting a vote for something. When I am voting for a law, for example, what I am asking is that if that law is passed, then obviously that law must be enforced. I am voting that all of the power that is vested in the government of the United States of America—or in the state of Florida, or in the city of Orlando, wherever we are—be marshalled to enforce that law. Anytime I do that, I am imposing some kind of restraint on other people's freedom. That is a very weighty responsibility.

For Christians who have pet projects unique to Christian enterprises, to use the law and law enforcement to get their way in a public arena may be an exercise in tyranny. Of course, we have been victims of the same kind of tyranny when other people have become the majority and have used laws that are unjust to discriminate against us or other people. I think that Christians ought to be keenly protective of the First Amendment not only for ourselves but for everybody else out there. So I would be very hesitant before imposing uniquely Christian principles upon non-Christians.

How can we as Christians ascertain when God's Word was applicable only to a certain culture and therefore may not be applicable to us today?

The real question here is, Is everything that is set forth in Scripture to be applied to all people of all time and of all cultures? I don't know any biblical scholar who would argue that everything set forth in Scripture applies to all people at all times. Since Jesus sent out the seventy and he told them not to wear shoes, does that mean that evangelists today would be disobedient unless they preached in their bare feet? Obviously that is an example of something practiced in the first-century culture that has no real application in our culture today.

When we come to the matter of understanding and applying Scripture, we have two problems. First, there is understanding the historical context in which the Scripture was first given. That means we have to go back and try to get into the skins and into the minds and languages of the first-century people who wrote down the Scriptures. We have to study the ancient languages—Greek and Hebrew—so that we can, as best as we know how, reconstruct the original meaning and intent of the Word of God.

The second difficulty is that we live in the twentieth century, and words that we use every day are conditioned and shaped by how they are used in our here and now. There's a sense in which I'm tethered to the twentieth century, yet the Bible speaks to me from the first century and before. How do I bridge that gap?

I also think we need to study church history so that we can see those principles and precepts that the church has understood as applying across the centuries and speaking to Christians of all ages. It helps to have a historical perspective. You've heard the cliché that those who ignore the past are doomed to repeat it. There is much to be learned through a serious study of the history of the world and the history of the Christian faith, and how other generations and other societies have understood the Word of God and its application to their life situation. By doing that, we'll readily see elements of scriptural instruction that the church of all ages has understood not to be limited to the immediate hearers of the biblical message but to have principle application down through the ages.

We certainly don't want to relativize or historicize an eternal truth of God. My rule of thumb: We are to study to try to discern a difference between principle and custom. But if after having studied we can't discern, I would rather treat something that may be a first-century custom as an eternal principle than risk being guilty of taking an eternal principle of God and treating it as a first-century custom.

How do we uphold Christian ethics without being judgmental?

One of the principles of Christian ethics is that we are not to manifest a judgmental spirit. If we are judgmental in our attitudes and in our spirits, we've already violated the

Christian ethic. The Christian ethic has something to say about how we respond to other people's sins. We are not to whitewash other people's sins. We are called to demonstrate discernment, to be able to recognize the difference between good and evil.

I've often said that every nonbeliever in America knows one verse that's in the Bible: "Judge not lest ye be judged," and they appeal to that by saying that nobody ever has the right to say that anything they do is wrong. For a judge in a courtroom to declare an accused person guilty of a crime is not judgmental. For a Christian to recognize sinful behavior in another Christian or non-Christian as sinful is not judgmental.

To be judgmental in the sense in which it's prohibited in Scripture is to manifest a censorious attitude, a pharisaic attitude of condemning people out of hand and consigning them to utter worthlessness because of their sin without any spirit of patience, forbearance, kindness, or mercy.

That's why Jesus warns us about noticing the speck in our brother's eye when we have a log in our own eye. The person who is running around examining specks is a person who has this judgmental spirit that Jesus found absolutely abhorrent. That doesn't mean that we are to be loose on sin or to call good evil or evil good. *Judgmental* describes an attitude.

When a woman was brought to Jesus because she had been caught in the act of adultery, how did he deal with her? He didn't say that she wasn't guilty; he didn't explain away her sin, nor did he endorse or encourage her sin. He said to her, "Go and sin no more." He asked, "Where are those who condemn you?" They had all departed out of embarrassment moments before, and Jesus said, "Neither do I condemn you. Go in peace." He dealt with that woman. Though he rebuked, admonished, and corrected her, he did it gently and with a concern to heal her and not to destroy her. It is said of Jesus in the New Testament that a bruised reed he would not break. A judgmental spirit breaks people who are bruised. There is to be none of that present in the church or among the people of God.

Do you feel more pressure as a public figure to live at a higher level of Christian ethics?

Yes, I do. I realize objectively that every Christian is called to the same standard of righteousness. God doesn't grade on a curve; we all have the same law to which we are called to conform. At the same time, we recognize that the New Testament gives specific warnings to those who are in positions of leadership in the ministry or in teaching, as I am. I tremble at the New Testament warning: "Let not many become teachers, for with the teaching comes a greater judgment." That greater judgment is not due to our having a higher law but rather due to the advanced level of knowledge and understanding we are expected to have about theology (including the laws of God) and the Christian way of life.

To whom much is given, much is required. The more we understand and are aware of what God requires, the greater our culpability is when we don't maintain it.

Also, Jesus warns that it would be better for a person to have a millstone hung around his neck and to be thrown into the abyss than to lead any of the little ones astray. God takes very seriously the responsibility a teacher has to be accurate and disciplined in whatever he teaches. If I teach falsehood, for example, and use the position I have as a teacher to influence and persuade people, that means trouble for me on the Day of Judgment.

Even though there is no double standard ultimately, certainly there is culturally. We're all acutely aware of it. Whenever a minister is involved in some kind of sin, it becomes a public scandal. It brings a blemish to the whole community of God because of the office that the minister represents.

It was scandalous in the Old Testament when the priests were engaged in corrupt practices at the temple. God dealt at times very harshly with the priests who had violated their office and that sacred trust they held. It's a frightening thing to think about.

I can remember when I moved to Boston twenty-some years ago. The first night we arrived, our clothes had not yet arrived. The only thing I had to wear out to dinner was one of those clerical collars and the black vest. I didn't even have a shirt to wear underneath it. I know that when I was driving my car down Route 128 in Boston and somebody cut in front of me and I had the impulse to blow the horn, I hesitated because of that which clearly revealed that I was a clergyman. So, yes, there is that pressure. That's undeniable.

Given the great apostasy in the world, many Christians consider these to be the last days. If things are going to get worse and worse until our Lord's coming, why should we concern ourselves with social activism and political involvement to make things better?

This question assumes several things. It assumes that we are in that period that the Bible designates as the great apostasy. I'm not sure that we are in that period, though we may well be. In the last two hundred years, for example, we've seen a serious decline in the world influence of Christianity, particularly its influence on culture in the Western world. We've seen things take place that were unheard of in the past. The death of God was proclaimed not by secular philosophers or by atheists but by self-confessed Christian theologians. So we have seen serious manifestations of departure from classical Christian orthodoxy, which leads some people to conclude that we are in an age of great apostasy.

On the other hand, it could be said that we are in an age of unprecedented renewal. Those who are more sanguine about reading the signs of the times would have a more optimistic view of the present state of affairs.

I don't have an inside view of God's timetable concerning the consummation of his kingdom. I'm hoping he will bring the kingdom to pass soon. It may very well be that we're in the last hours of the last days. I certainly hold that as a very real possibility.

And if that is the case, how would that influence the agenda of the church? I'm of the opinion that even if we were in the last fifteen minutes of redemptive history and if we knew Jesus was coming in the next quarter hour, we still would have the mandate to do those things that he told us to do until he returns; that is, to be his witnesses, to manifest his kingship, to show and to illustrate what the kingdom of God is supposed to look like—and that includes giving food to the hungry, shelter to the homeless, and clothes to the naked. The church's agenda has been established by Jesus between the time of his departure and the time of his return. Regardless of how soon or how far away that return is, we are called to active involvement in the goals and the mandates of the kingdom.

Sometimes I become so discouraged by the opposition of the world structures to Christianity and the lack of influence we seem to have in the culture that I find myself falling back into a "snatching a few brands from the fire" mentality, just trying to reach an individual here and there and abandoning the larger tasks given us by Christ. I have to resist that, and I urge every Christian to resist that temptation.

What is the biblical basis for human dignity?

As a Christian I do not believe that human beings have intrinsic dignity. I am totally committed to the idea that human beings have dignity, but the question is, Is it intrinsic or extrinsic?

Dignity, by biblical definition, is tied to the biblical concept of glory. God's glory, his weightiness, his importance, his significance, is what the Bible uses to describe the fountainhead of all dignity. And only God has eternal value and intrinsic (that is, in and of himself) significance. I am a creature—I come from the dust. The dust isn't all that significant, but I become significant when God scoops up that dust and molds it into a human being and breathes into it the breath of life and says, "This creature is made in my image." God assigns eternal significance to temporal creatures. I don't have anything in me that would demand that God treat me with eternal significance. I have eternal significance and eternal worth because God gives it to me.

And not only does he give it to me but he gives it to every human being.

That's why in the Bible the great commandment not only deals with our relationship with God but our relationships with human beings. "Thou shalt love the Lord your God with all your heart, with all your might, and with all your strength . . . and your neighbor as much as you love yourself," because God has endowed every human creature with value.

What is our responsibility toward the poor?

If you do a word study of *poor* as it appears in Scripture, you will find that four categories emerge.

The first group consists of people who are poor as a direct result of indolence; that is, these people are poor because they are irresponsible. They are lazy. They refuse to work. The response of God to that particular category of the poor is one of somewhat harsh judgment and admonition. "Consider the ant, thou sluggard." Go watch the ant and learn how to live. Paul takes a strong view in the New Testament: "If anyone will not work, neither shall he eat" (2 Thess. 3:10). So the basic posture toward that group of people is one of admonition and a call to repentance.

Sometimes, however, people will oversimplify it and say that the only reason people are poor is because they are lazy. That's just not true. There are a lot of people who are poor for reasons that have nothing to do with being sinful or lazy. So we come to the second group of the poor identified in Scripture, those who are poor as a direct result of calamity, disease, accident, and that sort of thing. Scripture tells us that it is the responsibility of the church and of Christian people to pour out their hearts in compassion and to give assistance to those who are suffering through no fault of their own, as a result of natural calamity.

The third group is comprised of those who are poor as a result of unfair exploitation or tyrannization by the powerful, those who are victims of corrupt governments or are the almost incidental casualties of war. In that situation, you see God thundering from heaven, calling for justice to be given to these people, and God pours out his indignation against those who would sell the poor for a pair of shoes and who would tyrannize them through illegitimate means. In that sense, we should be advocates of the poor and defenders of the poor.

The fourth and final group of the poor that we find in the Bible are those who are poor voluntarily; that is, they are poor for what the Bible calls "righteousness' sake," willingly sacrificing any worldly gain as a personal commitment on their part to devote their time to other matters. Those people are to receive our support and our approval.

Could you give an example of how Christ's teaching about turning the other cheek applies to today's life situations?

There's much confusion about what Jesus meant in the Sermon on the Mount when he said that when somebody strikes you on the right cheek, you are to turn the other cheek to him as well. Many people have taken that to mean that Christians are to be doormats if they become victims of a violent assault; if somebody punches you in the face,

you're supposed to turn your face around and get
punched on the other side. What's interesting in the
expression is that Jesus specifically mentions the right side
of the face. The vast majority of people in the world are
right-handed, and for somebody to be smacked in the
right side of the face, either you have to hit them from
behind or you have to hit them with a left hook. If I hit you
on your right cheek, the most normal way would be if I did
it with the back of my right hand.

To the best of our knowledge of the Hebrew language,
that expression is a Jewish idiom that describes an insult, similar to the way challenges to duels in the days of King Arthur
were made by a backhand slap to the right cheek of your
opponent. It's not limited to simply a physical attack but
rather has primary reference to someone's insulting you.

The context in which Jesus speaks has to do with a
debate with the Pharisees over their understanding of the
Old Testament law, particularly that which we find in the
Mosaic code that says the punishment for crimes was to be
based on an eye for an eye and a tooth for a tooth. We
often hear that expression today as if this were an expression of a primitive, barbaric, and unusual punitive system
in the Jewish nation. But I think if we look at it unemotion-
ally, we will see that there's never been a more equitable
and just concept for punitive measures than a tooth for a
tooth and an eye for an eye; it's equal. But among the rabbis this statement had become an excuse, a justification,
for a spirit of bitter vindictiveness and cruel and harsh
treatment of those who had broken the law.

This "turn the other cheek" saying is given in the same
context as the statement "If your enemy wants you to go

one mile, go two. If he wants your coat, give him your cloak as well." Jesus is saying that we should bend over backward to not be involved in a spirit of bitter vindictiveness. The rest of Jesus' teaching indicates that it's not wrong for someone to seek justice in the law courts. If a widow is defrauded of her inheritance, that doesn't mean that she has to go out and give everything else she has to the one who stole it from her. But Jesus is talking about an ethic here that I believe calls for us to imitate the attitude of mercy and forbearance and patience that is found in God himself.

In terms of the arts, is there a difference between secular and Christian?

I think there is, although that difference at times is exceedingly difficult to articulate and to pinpoint. Abstractly I would say the great difference between Christian art and non-Christian art would be in perspective.

Art is a means of communication; wherever there is art, some content is being communicated. By "art" I refer in a general sense to music, sculpture, painting, etc. Art can be categorized in terms of form and content, but all art forms communicate something.

There was a famous phrase in the sixties taken from the title of Marshall McLuhan's book *The Medium Is the Message.* That means that the form itself conveys a message, a nonverbal message, just as the content in a work of art does. In a song, there are not only the words but also a structure, a form of the music that is being played. There are certain kinds of music that are very orderly, say, a Bach cantata. The structure of Bach's music follows a decisive pattern, and there's no attempt to be chaotic. Some modern musicians have attempted to create chaos, although it's an impossible task because you cannot intentionally be unintentional. You can't intentionally create ultimate chaos. There is still a pattern to this pretended chaos. They're trying to communicate through a very loose kind of form, whether it's in painting or in music, a statement against harmony and order and rationality, all of which have theological implications. It's part of the secular mood of despair that says there is no ultimate coherency.

In the world of the theater of the absurd, actors on stage utter nonsense words, implying that man has come to the place where even his language is meaningless. But even those nonsense syllables are a form of communication, and there is a message there, incoherent as it may seem.

At the other extreme, there's the attitude that, for art to be Christian, it must include a Bible verse or depict people with halos over their heads. I am convinced that if we look in the Scriptures we'll see that God is a God of beauty. He's the ultimate foundation of beauty, and his character is beautiful. Part of the task of man is to mirror and reflect the character of God. That means we are called to produce art and that that art be excellent.

Should a Christian attorney defend someone he knows is guilty?

Part of this question is simple to answer. Just because an attorney knows that his client is guilty does not disqualify that person from all of the rights that the nation gives him to legal counsel and a fair trial. It is the responsibility of the attorney to give the best legal defense he can for a client even if the client is guilty. The client may even enter a guilty plea. It may be the task of the attorney to argue for mitigating circumstances or to try to demonstrate through historical precedent that these mitigating circumstances should be taken into account when sentencing comes up. There are many defenses that are still significant—and legitimate—for a person who is clearly guilty.

What if the man is pleading innocent and the attorney knows that he's guilty? Can an attorney, in good conscience, support something he knows to be fraudulent? Knowing that a person has committed a crime or done certain things does not mean that we know in advance that that man would be judged guilty of a particular crime in a particular courtroom given all the circumstances of the trial. I would think that within the restraints of honesty and integrity, a lawyer could provide a legitimate defense for someone he knows to be guilty. A lawyer's actions become questionable when he becomes an accomplice in attempting to defraud the bench and to fool the jury into believing something other than what he knows the reality to be.

We see this kind of dishonesty every day in divorce courts. I've seen it happen again and again: The man is guilty of adultery and wants to get out of the marriage, so he sues his wife on grounds of cruel and unusual treatment, or something like that. The attorney knows very well that the guilty party in the breakup of the marriage is the husband, not the wife. Yet he'll continue to represent the husband and get everything he possibly can for his client. I have problems with that. In any profession—

medical, legal, and theological—there are people of great conscience and also people who are not all that scrupulous. Their whole concern is with winning or losing the case, and they operate from a foundation of expediency and from the motivation of the best financial solution. At that point we make a mockery out of any quest for truth and justice.

Rahab the harlot, the Hebrew midwives, and others throughout the Old Testament supposedly lied to protect others, and God, in turn, blessed them. Does this mean that Christians today may have occasion to lie with God's blessing?

The short answer I would give to that is yes, there may be occasions when God-fearing people are called upon to lie in the sense of speaking something that is not the truth.

There are many Christian ethicists who believe that the prohibition against lying is absolute and that there is never any justification for the so-called white lie. Others point to Rahab and the Hebrew midwives as examples; their lies are reported and later on they're included in the roll call of heroes. It doesn't explicitly say that God blessed or sanctified them for lying, but it seems to imply that there's not a word of rebuke for their blatant dishonesty in these situations.

There are other occasions in Scripture where we see people lying in ways that I think are clearly contrary to the Word of God. For example, some have tried to justify Rebekah's involvement in the deception of her husband so that Jacob could receive the blessing instead of Esau. She was involved in this conspiracy to deceive her own husband, and some have tried to defend her by saying that if God had willed that the elder should serve the younger, then it was God's plan for Jacob to receive the patriarchal blessing rather than Esau. All that Rebekah was doing was making sure the will of God came to pass. All that Judas was doing when he betrayed Jesus into the hands of his enemies was making sure the will of God came to pass—and God held him eminently responsible for his treachery. I'm sure that Rebekah, though she may have been blessed of God, was blessed in spite of her lying and not because of it. Some would place Rahab in the same category.

Over the centuries, in the Christian church, there has developed an ethic of truthfulness that is linked to justice. The Christian is always to give the truth and to speak the truth to whom the truth is due. The question now becomes, Is there such a case for the so-called just or justified lie? I would say so, and the situations falling most clearly into that category would involve war, murder, or criminal activities. If a murderer comes to your house and he wants to know if your children are upstairs in bed and you know that it's his intent to murder them, it's your moral obligation to lie to him, to deceive him as much as you possibly can to prevent those lives from being taken. I think that would also be true in cases of war. I don't think a person is required to tell the enemy where his group is concealed any more than a quarterback in a football game is required to announce to the defense what the intended play is. He can use faking and deception in order to execute that play. That's sort of a war game on the football field. Numerous Christians lied to the Nazis in order to protect Jews from capture and extermination. I think that in cases in which we know that lying will prevent such evil, it is legitimate.

The Bible calls drunkenness a sin. What are the dangers of our culture calling drunkenness a disease?

Drunkenness has been referred to as a disease partly out of the motivation to be compassionate toward people who suffer under a very debilitating and dehumanizing problem. Those who have labored through the suffering involved are tired of condemnatory attitudes, and they say, "Hey, look, let's quit screaming at these people and try to be a little bit more helpful and compassionate. Quit heaping all this blame on them as if they were just immoral people."

There is also some evidence in the literature to indicate that certain kinds of alcoholism involve genetic chemical imbalances, and so in that physiological aspect there may be some basis for recognizing that alcoholism is not merely a moral weakness. But there are dangers in calling this problem a disease. God does call it a sin. He holds us accountable for our behavior with respect to the use of alcohol. He calls us to temperance, and he tells us that we're simply not allowed to get into a pattern of drunkenness. God is saying that we do have a moral choice in the matter and that we can't simply blame our environment or somebody else for this problem.

Even beyond that clear theological difficulty, I see a psychological concern. If I say to somebody, "You have a disease" or, "You are sick," I may be motivated to say that to take them off the hook, to protect their self-esteem, which is a noble motivation. However, I may inadvertently be crushing their spirit because I'm saying, "There's nothing you can do. You're sick. It's as if you caught the flu or you've got cancer. Some kind of foreign antibodies invaded your system. The only way that you'll ever be cured is if somebody comes up with a wonder drug and cures you." In other words, we render a person hopeless by telling him that he's sick—unless at the same time we can offer a medicinal cure. I don't know anybody who's able to do that.

I think that the organization that has worked most effectively with this problem is Alcoholics Anonymous. They have that spirit of compassion and gentleness, but at the same time they hold each other accountable, and they encourage one another to work to get out of the situation.

According to the Bible, is there anything wrong with using hypnosis to help people stop smoking or to overcome some other addiction or behavior pattern?

I'm not exactly sure how to answer that question. We have seen the phenomenon of hypnosis being used in what I would call illegitimate ways as an attempt to penetrate areas of the occult. But I'm not sure we understand all of what hypnosis is or how it is or can be used.

To the degree that I understand it, hypnosis involves a kind of intense mental concentration whereby we can focus our consciousness on certain crucial ideas, feelings, or incidents. This could be useful in surgery; it is also used sometimes in therapy to help a person remember a traumatic event, for instance. I don't see anything intrinsically or inherently wrong from a moral standpoint with the use of hypnosis in appropriate settings for a person who is struggling with an addiction or something of that sort. The therapist talks to the patient and puts him into a hypnotic state. There is nothing magical about that. The therapist continues the conversation with the patient, trying to communicate a focused message, for example, "You do not need to continue the use of this substance. It is harmful for you." They repeat that over and over so that when the person returns to an awakened state of consciousness, that thought is imbedded in their mind and they will keep going back to it. It is almost like an intensified level of concentration to learn a lesson. Insofar as that's all it involves, I don't see anything wrong with it.

Why is the use of drugs such as crack escalating in our society today?

I can remember when I was in high school being scandalized when one of my favorite movie actors was arrested in Hollywood for smoking a marijuana cigarette. Not that many years ago, that kind of behavior was frowned upon not only in the church but throughout the secular culture.

But now we have gone through an explosive level of upheaval in drug use and abuse. It is even affecting the role models that come from the world of sports, as we're all sadly aware. The studies that have been done so far in child psychiatry indicate that in children between the ages of thirteen and nineteen years, the greatest single influence in the shaping of their self-image, their identity as people, is not their parents but the peer group to which they are striving to belong. So we have to say that once certain patterns of behavior become acceptable within a particular age group, we see a ripple effect whereby more young people are drawn into them.

One of the reasons for the escalation is the high visibility of drug use in the music culture. That's one of the earliest places where the use of hard drugs became acceptable. Suddenly the patterns that were taboo in earlier generations had become upbeat, the "in" thing for certain subcultures, and had spread prolifically into other elements of society.

But there are much deeper reasons for this escalation of drug use. I think there is a philosophical crisis in our culture whereby we have lost the understanding of what it means to be human. What does it mean to be a person? Historically we saw ourselves as people created in the image of God. But the modern view of man is that we are a cosmic mistake, we're grown-up germs, and we are insignificant. That's an unbearable feeling, and any release from the pain—if only for a few moments or hours—is welcome relief from that pessimistic view.

Is it wrong for scientists to engage in genetic engineering?

I feel hopelessly inadequate to answer some of the very perplexing issues that have arisen because of the explosion of modern technology. In the case of most ethical questions, theologians have had the benefit of two thousand years of careful evaluation and analysis of the moral dilemmas involved, whereas questions of biomedical ethics for the most part have exploded onto the scene in the twentieth century. We've been caught with relatively little time to think through all of the ramifications.

An awful lot is contained in the term *genetic engineering.* Are we talking about the kind of experiments that were made infamous by Mengele during World War II, trying to carry out the unbelievably diabolical plans of Hitler to create a master race through the purification of genes? That kind of thing is clearly evil.

But genetic engineering also involves serious researchers doing everything in their power by examining the genetic code to see if there are ways in which serious illnesses, diseases, and distortions can be therapeutically treated through genetic means. Now, here you're talking about science's legitimate task of having dominion over the earth and exercising mercy and compassion toward the ill and finding cures for horrible deformities and diseases. We ought not to say that all genetic engineering is evil. Some of it, I think, has a legitimate use. Individual issues under the umbrella of genetic engineering need to be considered individually as to their moral integrity. And while the engineers, the specialists, and the researchers themselves have the most information by which to make judgments, theologians and philosophers must stay in touch and make their voices known. These issues fall outside the boundaries of mere technology and need to be examined and debated in the realms of religion and ethics.

Should Christians support AIDS research?

I'm somewhat surprised at the frequency with which this question is being raised within the Christian community.

Of course Christians should support AIDS research. Why wouldn't we support AIDS research? We're committed to ministry to the sick and the alleviation of suffering. When we find someone sick, it's not our responsibility to ask them why they're sick. When we find someone hungry, it's not our responsibility to ask them why they're hungry. When we find someone homeless, it's not our responsibility to ask them why they are homeless. Our responsibility is to clothe the naked, to minister to the sick, and to visit the prisoners. We don't say that a prisoner in jail is there because he's committed some great sin, and therefore we shouldn't visit him. On the contrary, we're commanded to visit people who are in prison in spite of the fact that they are there because they've done something wrong.

The fact that AIDS is a disease that generally has its roots in immoral types of sexual behavior is no reason for the church to act as God's policeman and his executioner. We are to work always and everywhere for the alleviation of pain and suffering in this world. I might add that there are many, many people who have become victims of AIDS through no direct actions of their own. AIDS has been transmitted through blood transfusions. Children have contracted this dreadful disease through transfusions in hospitals or through dirty hypodermic needles. It's been traced to transmissions through tattoos. We can't just assume that AIDS is a badge of improper sexual conduct. I don't see any compelling reason for the church to be against research of AIDS.

I'm really trying to say two things here. One is that even if the only people in the world who had AIDS were guilty of gross and heinous sin, that in and of itself would not preclude Christian involvement in seeking a cure and alleviation of suffering for them. That's principle number one.

Principle number two is that, as a matter of fact, that's not the case with people and AIDS. There's really no reason I can think of that a Christian would or should be opposed to research. In fact, one of the great testimonies of the Christian church has been its place on the cutting edge when relief of suffering was concerned as in the cases of the hospital movement and the creation of orphanages. I think the AIDS situation is a marvelous opportunity for Christians to dedicate themselves to human service.

21

Christians and Government

Let every soul be subject to the governing authorities.
For there is no authority except from God,
and the authorities that exist are appointed by God. . . .
For rulers are not a terror to good works, but to evil.

ROMANS 13:1, 3

Questions in This Section:

Is it wrong to confront authority? And if it's not wrong, how do you do it in the right way?

What is a Christian's responsibility to government?

Should Christians work to have Christian values in public policy?

Are biblical solutions to world problems outdated?

Today we continually hear people screaming for moral rights. Do these people have a legitimate basis for these claims?

Are there certain biblical ethical standards the government should uphold?

How do you respond to a politician who says that his or other politicians' personal ethics should have no bearing on whether or not someone votes for them?

What does the Bible have to say about laws created by man?

Are we being too judgmental when we criticize the private lives of political leadership?

Both Peter and Paul call us to submit to governing authorities. In light of that, is revolution ever possible for a Christian, and if so, under what circumstances?

Even though the pursuit of happiness is an inalienable right in the U.S. Constitution, do we as created beings have this inalienable right? Many people expect happiness in life. But should that be a rightful expectation, especially for the Christian?

What is the relationship between Christian education and public education?

In the judicial courts we are required to swear an oath on the Bible before taking the stand. Since the Bible says that a person should not swear on anything, is it right for a Christian to refuse to swear on the Bible in court?

My whole life I've had the feeling that it's wrong to confront authority. Is it wrong or not? And if it's not wrong, how do you do it in the right way?

I suppose this feeling was ingrained in you very early through parental discipline and instruction. When I was a small boy, the one absolute nonnegotiable law of our household was that you didn't talk back to your parents and you don't sass your teachers or the next-door neighbor. Woe betide us if we talked back to anyone who was in a position of authority. I remember that once I took on a science teacher in class, and boy, I really got in trouble over that.

I think the Bible tells us that we are to give honor to those who are in authority over us. But I think it is perfectly legitimate for us to raise some questions: "Is this the proper way to do this?" or "Is this a legitimate use of authority?" As long as the questions are asked or the confrontation is done in a spirit of genuine humility and respect, it is legitimate.

This was a very difficult issue for me as a seminary student. I studied under some of the most radical scholars alive, people who systematically attacked the atonement of Christ or the resurrection of Christ. Inside I would be outraged by the fact that these were professors in the theological seminary and they were denying the very basic claims of the Christian faith. Yet I realized that no matter how wrong they were in that classroom, I had to respect the office they held as professors. When I studied in Europe,

I found a completely different environment from the one I encountered in this country. When we assembled in the amphitheater and the professor opened the classroom door and entered the room, every student rose and stood at attention until the professor stood at the lectern and nodded for us to sit down. Thereupon he would lecture for sixty minutes. No student was ever allowed to raise his hand and ask a question. At the end of the lecture the professor closed the book, stepped from the lectern, and we stood up again as he walked out. I appreciated that. It communicated a sense of honor.

We've lost the capacity to honor those in authority. Again, if the authority commands us to do something God forbids or if it forbids us to do something God commands, not only must we confront that authority but we must disobey.

What is a Christian's responsibility to government?

The New Testament gives us some broad principles on how we are supposed to respond to government. For example, Romans 13 elaborates on the origin and institution of government as something that God ordains.

The great theologian Augustine said that government is a necessary evil, that it is necessary *because* of evil. And most theologians in the history of the church have said that human evil is the reason even corrupt government is better than no government at all. The function of government is to restrain evil and to maintain, uphold, and protect the sanctity of life and of property. Given this function, the Christian understands that government is

ordained of God, and so Christians, first of all, are called
to respect whatever it is that God institutes and ordains.
For God's sake we are called to be model citizens. We are
told to bend over backwards to honor the king or be obedient to the civil magistrates. That doesn't mean a slavish
obedience to the civil magistrates. There are occasions on
which Christians not only may but must disobey the civil
magistrates. Anytime a civil government requires a Christian to do what God forbids or forbids them to do what
God commands, then the person must disobey. But our
basic posture toward government, according to the New
Testament, is to be submissive and obedient citizens of
the state. We are also given the duty of praying for earthly
governments that they may fulfill the tasks God has given
to them.

We have another responsibility, and this is the one that
sometimes brings us into controversial areas. I personally
believe in a separation of spheres of authority between the
church and state. I think it is a marvelous structure in the
United States of America that does not allow for the state
to rule the church or the church to rule the state. Historically that meant that the church was answerable to God
and the state was answerable to God. Separation of church
and state assumed a division of labor; the church has its
job, and the state has its job. The church is not to maintain
a standing army, and the state is not to do evangelism or to
administer the sacraments. Nevertheless, they are both
regarded as being under God.

Unfortunately, in today's culture separation of church
and state means separation of state and God, as if the state
and the government were answerable to no one but them-

selves—as if the government didn't have to respond to God. But God monitors governments; God raises them up and brings them down. Every human government is accountable to God and is accountable to maintain its affairs with justice and with righteousness. When the government is no longer acting justly and no longer protecting life—sanctioning abortions, for example—then it is the task of the church to be the prophetic voice, to call the state to task and tell the state to repent and do what God commands it to do.

Should Christians work to have Christian values in public policy?

One year I was invited to speak at the inaugural prayer breakfast for the newly elected governor of the state of Florida. On that occasion I had the opportunity to speak with men and women who were in strategic places in government. A question that's very high on their agenda: At what point are we to maintain that very careful line of separation of church and state?

In our political heritage, as well as in our Christian heritage, we understand that there is a difference between the institution of civil government (the state) and the institution of the church. It is not the church's task nor responsibility to tell the governor how to govern or to make the government establish our religious preferences. However, we also have to keep in mind that both the state and the church are under God. The state is not sovereign; the state never has the right to do wrong. The state is always under the authority of God. God institutes government, God ordains government, and God will judge government. He holds government and all other institutions in our society responsible for doing what is right.

What is right in given situations—right business practices, right labor practices, right judicial practices? Right and wrong are not uniquely decided by Christians. There are certain commandments we are to perform as Christians. For example, the Lord's Supper. We're not supposed to ask unbelievers to participate in the Lord's Supper. However, God tells me as a Christian to pay my bills on time. He tells me not to use false weights and balances in my business. I think that it's perfectly appropriate to recommend that the state have sound currency and not destroy the weights and balances of our society, to have honorable contracts and to do what is right. In other words, in those spheres of ethics that are right for all people, I believe it is a Christian's responsibility to remind the state to stand for what is right.

Are biblical solutions to world problems outdated?

Years ago, when I was teaching philosophy at a university, I participated in a symposium of professors of philosophy. One gentleman in that group reminded us that there are only about five basic issues in the whole history of philosophy. There have been five thousand different approaches to those five basic issues, but the same basic questions of philosophy are struggled with repeatedly by every generation.

I would say that in principle this is also true in the field of ethics. We are faced with new ethical issues that make application of ongoing principles difficult in a new environment. For example, previous generations didn't have to worry about when to pull the plug of a life-support system on somebody dying in a hospital. You didn't have to worry about that ethical dilemma because you didn't have the sophisticated equipment that makes that dilemma a reality. In that sense we have situations that previous generations did not have to struggle with ethically.

However, the principles we draw from sacred Scripture about the sanctity of life and the dignity of death, for example, speak eloquently to those specific problems that come to us afresh in each generation. I believe that we find in Scripture not simply the insights and opinions of primitive Hebrew seminomads. If that were the case, I would say there may be some collective wisdom here that we can get from them that may have application here or there. But I have a higher view of Scripture than that.

I believe that what we find in Scripture is transcendent truth—truth that comes to us from an eternal perspective. In philosophical terms, this truth is *sub species iternatotus*. That means that we get nothing less than the mind of the Creator, who knows and reveals to us principles of what is right, good, and beautiful, and these principles can be applied throughout the scope of human history. For me, to think that the Scriptures were no longer applicable to my society or that they were out of date or old-fashioned would be to think that God is out of date and old-fashioned and irrelevant. He is the one who is from everlasting to everlasting. The principles and the truths he reveals to us are from that eternal perspective. I cannot conceive of any point in world history where his truth would become outmoded or outdated.

Today we continually hear people screaming for moral rights. Do these people have a legitimate basis for these claims?

I think there's a lot of confusion about the very language of rights and obligations. Obligation, for instance. As Christians, part of our profession of faith is a recognition that God and God alone ultimately is Lord of our conscience. Only he has the intrinsic right to impose obligation upon his creatures. He can delegate that to say that parents can demand certain things from their children, and certain other authority structures can be set in place. Ultimately, all obligation is dictated by God, who is the source of all moral obligation. If there is no God, I would have to say there is no such thing as moral obligation. So-called moral issues would simply become matters of personal preference.

When you talk about rights, I think it's crucial to distinguish between moral rights and legal rights. A moral right is something that is granted to us as creatures from God. It's built into creation; God is the source and the author of any moral rights we have.

A legal right is a right granted by a human institution, notably the state. The states differ in terms of the rights they give. Human rights has become a worldwide issue because we witness groups of people—and individuals, as in the case of political prisoners—suffering from various types of oppression, according to the rights that the states over them protect or violate. We consider certain rights intrinsic to being human, those rights given us by God the Creator. And some states are not providing rights from a

547

legal standpoint that should be maintained on the basis of their being rights initially given by God. When we speak of a violation of human rights, we are usually referring to these rights.

On the other hand, a state may grant a legal right for a person to do something they have absolutely no moral right to do before God. For example, I personally see that as the issue in abortion. I hear people saying all the time that a woman has the right to her own body, to do with the issue of her own body what she wants. If she has conceived a child, she has the right to get rid of it through therapeutic abortion. People insist that she has the right to do that. What kind of a right? Obviously she does have the legal right to do it because the Supreme Court has granted that legal right in our country.

The issue, though, that has caused so much debate and controversy in our country is, Does she have the moral right to do it? We know what the law allows, but what does God allow? If a person were to say to me that they had the moral right to abortion, I would say, "Where did you get that moral right? Are you sure you have that moral right? Are you telling me that God Almighty has given you the right to dispose of your unborn child?" I shudder to think of anybody ever standing before God and saying that they have the right to do that. We never have the moral right to disobey God.

Are there certain ethical standards the government should uphold on a biblical basis?

In light of the contemporary concept of the separation of church and state that is so important to our own government, there are many who interpret that concept to mean that the state is not accountable to God, that it is not subordinate to divine authority. In other words, God has no jurisdiction over the affairs of government. Nothing could be more antithetical to biblical teaching. If we acknowledge (as our forefathers did) that God is the creator of the universe, then it should go without saying that God is sovereign over everything he creates. To be sure, he ordains and institutes the church for one particular task, and he ordains and institutes governments for another task. It's not the responsibility of the church to be the state or the state to be the church, *but the concept of separation of church and state does not mean the separation of state and God.*

The state, as much as the church, is under the authority of God, and every earthly authority at some point will be held accountable by God for how they exercised that authority. No state government, no earthly government, ever has the right or the authority to rule by their own preferences without being accountable to some ultimate standard of righteousness and justice. When the New Testament teaches that the government is grounded in divine mandate, as we read in Romans 13, we are told that governments are called to be ministers of God for the sake of righteousness. So it is the responsibility of the state to uphold standards of righteousness and of justice.

Obviously, states can become corrupt, and states may violate the standard of God's righteousness and those standards of justice that are rooted ultimately in the character of God himself. When they do that, they will be held accountable by God. We read throughout the history of the Old Testament that God's authority extends not only over the nation of Israel but also over those who are ruling Babylon, Persia, and all of the other nations of the world. We remember in Psalm 2 that the psalmist's complaint was that the rulers of the world were taking counsel against God, saying, "Let us cast his cords from off us and let us cast his ropes asunder"; that is, the rulers of the pagan nations were declaring their independence from God. The answer to the psalmist was, of course, that he who sits in the heavens shall laugh, but only for a moment. Then he will call them into account because God judges all other judges.

How do you respond to a politician who says that his or other politicians' personal ethics should have no bearing on whether or not someone should vote for them?

We're hearing that question quite frequently in these times because so many scandals have involved public figures and those in political offices. One common view is that people's personal ethics are their own business and what they do in private is of no import to their public ability to serve in office.

I think it is important to distinguish, as we do in theology, between personal ethics and social ethics, and I think it's possible for a person who is of disreputable character privately to function publicly in a very just and upright manner. But certainly a person's personal ethics will give rise to serious questions about how he will behave in terms of social ethics. For although we distinguish between personal and private, ultimately, they can't be separated because they are closely related.

For example, if a man has been convicted repeatedly of being a thief, you'd hardly want him to serve as the secretary of the treasury. There's no way of being absolutely certain that person would run off with national funds, but there are strategic points of integrity that are demanded of people in public office. I think the public has a right to expect a high degree of personal ethics from our leaders.

In looking at the United States' history, we can go back to the forties, when there was an epidemic rise in the divorce rate. Some sociologists point the finger at Hollywood for that. They say here we had movie stars who made a business of having five or six husbands or wives, multiple marriages and divorces that were part of the sensational grist for the media with these Hollywood stars and starlets. Somehow they were able to survive in their careers because their performance was of such a high standard in their field that people were willing to excuse or overlook their personal shortcomings. But what happens is that the role models—in Hollywood, in the athletic world, or in the political arena—begin to be imitated by the culture at large, and the population suffers negative effects. So while some public officials have found it possible to keep their personal failings from affecting their public functioning, it is still important and better overall for the country that they maintain high personal standards.

What does the Bible have to say about laws created by men?

Frederic Bastiat, the French jurist, wrote a very significant book on law in which he distinguished between what he calls "rule by men" and "rule by law." He articulated the classic European concept of *lex rex*. This European concept holds that law, not people, is to be king and that the ultimate authority that would govern a nation would not be the whims or the personal preferences of individuals but that we would be governed by law.

"Rule by men" versus "rule by law" is confusing to many people because they'll ask, "Don't men make the laws?" Of course they do. I don't think the Bible prohibits national governments from legislation; that's one of the responsibilities God gives them. In order to govern, they must make laws. They have to legislate. That's the duty of governments.

How does human legislation compare with divine law? The idea that law is king means that there is a bedrock of law that is rooted ultimately in the character of God that can be discovered through nature. That's why historically, even in the United States, we were grounded in the principle of natural law, saying that certain laws are revealed and endowed by our Creator, certain basic principles that we call the law of the nations, the common law of all people. Every nation is accountable to those laws, and whatever individual laws we enact or legislate in our own countries must be brought into conformity to that higher law that ultimately reaches to the character of God.

At the same time, the Bible takes a very dim view of people passing laws and then acting as if those laws came directly from God. That was the debate that Jesus had with the Pharisees. The Pharisees created laws and passed them off as the revealed law of God, and they confused the law of God with human traditions. Jesus roundly condemned this.

Are we being too judgmental when we criticize the private lives of political leadership?

As long as there have been public officials, not only in this country but in any country, there has been a desire on the part of the majority of their constituents that political leaders manifest a life of personal integrity.

The danger is that we can become judgmental—hypercritical and hypocritical as well—petty in our criticisms of people in public life. Serving in public office is an extremely difficult task for anyone. The average person in this country has no idea what the loss of privacy means, for instance. When we began the Ligonier Ministries back in Pennsylvania about twenty-five years ago, I was a minister and was dealing with the public frequently. And as people came to our facility demanding more and more personal attention from me, my family and I experienced the real loss of personal privacy. It was very difficult to handle. This was just a taste of what public officials go through.

Such sacrifice, though, goes with the territory of being a public figure. A person in public life will be submitted to much closer scrutiny in terms of his or her personal integrity, and I think the people have the right to expect their leaders to manifest an example of personal integrity. There's no question—in my mind, at least—that young people take their cue from the examples set by public figures as they are observed on television, in the press, and in the movies. It's important that we—especially Christians, who should be leaders in compassion and understanding—temper any evaluation of public figures with a profound sense of understanding and compassion for the difficult position in which they're placed to serve.

Both Peter and Paul call us to submit to governing authorities. In light of that, is revolution ever possible for a Christian, and if so, under what circumstances?

It certainly is clear that the New Testament puts an emphasis on the Christian's responsibility to be a model of civil obedience. In Romans 13, Paul tells us that the powers that be are ordained by God. That doesn't mean that they are sanctioned by God or that God endorses everything that civil governments do; we know better than that. But Paul is saying that it is God who brings government to pass, and we are called to submit to the rulers of the government out of respect for Christ.

Peter says that we ought to obey the civil magistrates "for the Lord's sake" (1 Pet. 2:13-17). How is Christ glorified by my submitting to the governor of the state of Florida or to the Congress of the United States of America? I think the broad issue here is the ultimate biblical struggle between competing voices of authority, the principles of Satan and of God. The issue is, Does the human person manifest a spirit of obedience to the law of God, or do we participate in a spirit of lawlessness? It's interesting that the Antichrist in the New Testament is identified with the man of lawlessness.

I think that when we are called to obey the civil magistrates, it's because the New Testament sees a hierarchical structure of authority, and that the ultimate authority in heaven and earth is God. God delegates authority to his only begotten Son: "All authority has been given to Me in heaven and on earth" (Matt. 28:18). Yet underneath the authority of the Son, who is the King of kings and the Lord of lords, are levels of earthly authority, such as government at its various levels down to the authority of employers over employees and parents over children. We see that ultimately authority finds its sanction in God's authority and sovereignty. The principle is not difficult to understand: If I am willy-nilly and careless in my obedience to authority at the lower levels, I am therefore implicitly placing myself in a posture of disobedience to the ultimate authority that stands above and behind the earthly. It is the law of God that we disobey. We apply this principle when we say that a child who doesn't learn to respect his parents will have trouble respecting anything or anyone else. By my being scrupulous in my civil obedience, bending over backwards to obey my teachers, my employers, my governors, and my police officers, I am honoring Christ, who is the ultimate model of authority and of obedience to the law.

Is it is ever justifiable to engage in revolt? Many Christians would say no. This was a crucial question at the time of the American Revolution, and Christian theologians fell on both sides of that issue. I believe that those who did justify the Revolution said the only time it's justifiable to revolt is when the government itself becomes lawless and functions in an illegal or unlawful manner. In colonial America the revolt was against the unlawful taxation that was taking place. That requires a longer history lesson than we have time for here.

Even though the pursuit of happiness is an inalienable right in the U.S. Constitution, do we as created beings have this inalienable right? Many people are frustrated because they expect happiness in life. But should that be a rightful expectation, especially for the Christian?

First we have to distinguish between the U.S. Constitution as a legal document that circumscribes the way in which people are to be treated under the law of the state and the principles operating in the kingdom of God that are set forth in God's law.

When the Constitution guarantees the inalienable right of the pursuit of happiness, it is meant to protect a free society from other people's attempts to destroy or to hinder that pursuit. Even the Constitution recognizes limits to this inalienable right. For example, it recognizes that if the thing that makes me happy is murdering other people, I don't have an inalienable constitutional right to pursue happiness in that manner. What we're saying here is that the law is set up to allow people to pursue those things that bring happiness to them. Of course, the Constitution doesn't guarantee the acquisition of happiness, only the right to pursue it, and that right to pursue happiness is subject to some limitations.

Does God give us this inalienable right? When we consider that a right gives us a legal claim, we have to say that, no, God does not grant us rights in the way a country's constitution does. The Bible nowhere gives any sinful human being (meaning *any* human being) an absolute guarantee or right of happiness. The Bible does hold out all kinds of promises concerning the attainment of happiness, but happiness is ultimately a gift from God, a manifestation of God's grace. If God were to deal with us in terms of rights, it would mean that he treated us strictly according to justice. The only way we would have an inalienable right would be to say that we are so virtuous and meritorious that if God is just, he must bestow happiness upon us. That's the very opposite of what Scripture teaches regarding our condition before God. We are guilty people before our Maker, and therefore our Maker owes us no happiness whatsoever.

In spite of the fact that God doesn't owe us happiness, he pours out joy and peace and happiness and blessedness in abundance to his people. I think it's perfectly legitimate for a Christian to pursue joy and contentment and the fulfillment of our humanity in everything that God has made us to be, which is found in our reconciliation with God. When we are reconciled to God and living according to his will and principles, happiness is often a by-product and, even at that, a result of God's grace and gifts. It is certainly not a demand that we make upon him.

What is the relationship between a Christian education and a public education?

In recent years we have seen the beginnings of sectarian schools in numbers that are unprecedented in American history—save for the manifestation of parochial schools sponsored by the Roman Catholic Church. In the case of Catholic theology and practice, the church has always seen education as an extremely important aspect of its whole program.

For the most part, Protestants have been content with the public school system. Part of the reason for that is that the Protestant church was intimately involved in establishing the systems and structures that were communicated through public coeducation years ago. There has been a growing secularism in this country and a new understanding of the concept of separation of church and state, which many people understand to mean a separation of the state from God. Classically, both were seen as being under the sovereignty of God and were committed to a basically common value system. That's no longer the case. Now the state has to walk a tightrope of human rights to make sure it doesn't do anything that will establish one religion over another in the school system.

The concept of antiestablishmentarianism historically has argued against establishing a particular Christian denomination as the state-endorsed church, as in the case of the Church of England. Now it has come to mean that Christianity has no particular benefit over Judaism or Islam or Hinduism or anything else. It tends to be the understanding of the state that public education is not to be religiously oriented in any way; it is to be neutral. This, of course, is manifestly impossible because you cannot have a curriculum of any type that is totally neutral. Every curriculum has a perspective, and that perspective is either theocentric or it is not. Either it acknowledges the ultimate sovereignty and supremacy of God or it does not. It may remain silent, but that silence is a statement.

I would say the great difference between Christian education and public education right now is in their commitment to their ultimate perspectives, whether it is God centered or not God centered. Christians have to make a decision as to whether to receive an education that's competitive in the other disciplines or to pay twice as much to get that God-centered perspective. Frankly, many Christian schools are not excellent in the academic disciplines, and so it becomes a very difficult decision to make.

In the judicial courts we are required to swear an oath on the Bible before taking the stand. Since the Bible says that a person should not swear on anything, is it right for a Christian to refuse to swear on the Bible in court?

The New Testament makes it clear that we are not to perform unlawful oaths and vows. Jesus warns in the Sermon on the Mount that we are to swear not by earth, nor by the altar, nor any of those things that are anything less than God. James reiterates that by saying "Do not swear, either by heaven or by earth. . . . But let your 'Yes' be 'Yes,' and your 'No,' 'No.'" (James 5:12).

However, there is a biblical provision for sacred vows and oaths; that is, there are lawful places and lawful kinds of vows and oaths that we take. In fact, a covenant is not a covenant without a vow, and that's what we're doing when we take vows in marriage and in other situations, such as those involving contractual agreements—we are entering into a covenant. The whole basis of our relationship to God is based on vows and oaths, oaths that God swears, because he can swear by nothing greater than himself.

There's nothing intrinsically wrong about the swearing of oaths and taking of vows, but I think what Jesus was objecting to was that the Pharisees were trying to fudge in their vows and their oaths by swearing by lesser things than God.

The swearing of an oath unto God or before God is an act of worship because in that vow we are saying, "So help me God," which is what we say in the courtroom: "I swear to tell the truth, the whole truth, and nothing but the truth, so help me God." I'm taking an oath before God. I am acknowledging at that moment that God is omniscient, he is there, he sees everything that I do, he can hear the words that I'm saying; God is sovereign over my vows, and he has authority over my vows. I'm recognizing God as God at the moment I take an oath. It's a religious act at that point.

If I say I swear by my mother's grave, I've just now committed an act of idolatry because I have presumed to think that my mother's grave has the ability to hear my vows, to judge my vows, and to be sovereign over my vows. I've attributed deity to the grave of my mother, which is a crass form of idolatry. That's what Jesus was objecting to when he said, in essence, "Don't swear by the altar. The altar can't hear you. The altar can't judge you. The altar isn't God." The only thing you can swear by that's a legitimate vow is God himself in an act of worship.

I'm not sure that it's wrong to swear an oath in the courtroom, but we're actually taking a vow to God, not to the Bible. We don't ask the Bible to bear witness to our vows. We don't ask that book to listen in on us, to be the judge of our consciences or be sovereign over us. But I just wonder where we ever got that symbolic practice of placing the hand on the Bible. I think it would be just as awesome and just as solemn, in fact even more solemn, to do it with your hand behind your back. But as long as you don't swear *to* or *by* the Bible, I think that it would be legitimate to swear on the Bible if you want to.

22

Puzzling Passages

And so we have the prophetic word confirmed,
which you do well to heed as a light that shines in a dark place,
until the day dawns and the morning star rises in your hearts;
knowing this first, that no prophecy of Scripture is of any private
interpretation, for prophecy never came by the will of man, but holy
men of God spoke as they were moved by the Holy Spirit.

2 PETER 1:19-21

Questions in This Section:

What is the order of Melchizedek?

God instructed Moses and Aaron to speak to the rock to bring forth water. Instead, Moses struck the rock. Because of this act, God punished both Moses and Aaron. Why?

Why in the Old Testament does God demand so much violence and war of the Jewish nation?

The Lord says in the Old Testament that he loved Jacob but he hated Esau, and in 1 John, John actually says that if we say we love God but hate our brothers, we're wrong. How can we reconcile these two passages?

Did Jacob really wrestle with an angel all night, or was that story a symbolic way of saying that he was struggling with an issue?

In the book of Judges it appears that a human sacrifice was performed and accepted. Please explain.

Proverbs 21:14 says, "A gift given in secret soothes anger, and a bribe concealed in a cloak pacifies great wrath." Why is this in the Bible?

"Where there is no vision, the people perish." What is meant by this?

Would you please expound on Ecclesiastes 9:10, which says, "Whatsoever thy hand findeth to do, do it with all thy might"?

What does the Apostles' Creed mean when it says that Jesus descended into hell?

In the Sermon on the Mount, Jesus says, "Don't let your right hand know what your left hand is doing," and in another passage he says, "Let your light so shine before men." This seems like a contradiction.

In Matthew 24:32-34, Christ tells the parable of the fig tree. In your opinion, just what does the fig tree represent?

Could you explain what Jesus meant when he said, "You will know the truth and the truth will set you free"?

Could you comment on Jesus' statement that we shouldn't throw our pearls before swine?

In the story of the adulterous woman, what did Jesus write in the sand?

In Acts 16 Paul encourages Timothy to be circumcised, then later condemns the practice. Was he being hypocritical?

What is the Christian view of baptism for the dead by proxy, referred to in 1 Corinthians 15?

What does the writer of Hebrews 6 mean when he writes, "It is impossible to restore again to repentance those who have once been enlightened and have become partakers of the Holy Spirit"?

Lately people have been talking to me about "curse Scriptures." Is this something Christians should be worried about? Are curses passed down?

What is the order of Melchizedek?

The book of Hebrews, of course, has as one of its central themes the high priestly work of our Lord Jesus. To communicate to the Jewish people that Jesus was the High Priest created some serious problems. In the Jewish expectation, their king was to come from the tribe of Judah. Jesus was from the tribe of Judah. But the priestly tribe, the tribe of Aaron and of his descendants, was the tribe of Levi. So if Jesus is not from the tribe of Levi, how can the New Testament say that he is a High Priest? For Jesus to be High Priest, he would be expected to be a descendant of Levi from the line of Aaron and Moses. But he clearly was not. What the author of Hebrews is doing here is reminding us that there is another priesthood in the Old Testament in addition to the priesthood that bears the name of Aaron or Levi. The author goes back into the earlier chapters of the book of Genesis where we read the story of Abraham coming back from battle and meeting a gentleman whose name is Melchizedek. Melchizedek is identified as a priest-king; he's the king of Salem, which means the king of peace, and he is a priest as well as a king. The point the author of Hebrews makes is this: Abraham paid a tithe to Melchizedek and Melchizedek blessed Abraham.

Then the author raises these questions: Does a person give a tithe to the greater or to the lesser, and who blesses whom in a situation like that? In Jewish categories, the one who gives the blessing is superior to the one who receives the blessing, and the lesser gives the tithe to the greater. In the activity that takes place in the meeting between Abraham and Melchizedek, Abraham clearly subordinates himself to this strange king Melchizedek. He pays the tithe to Melchizedek; Melchizedek blesses Abraham. So whoever this Melchizedek is, or wherever he came from and whatever he does, he's of a higher nature than Abraham.

Then the writer asks the question in Jewish terms, "If Abraham is the father of Isaac, and Isaac is the father of Jacob, and Jacob is the father of Levi, who's greater, Jacob or Levi? Jacob. Who's greater, Jacob or Isaac? Isaac. Who's greater, Abraham or Isaac? Abraham. Well, if Abraham is greater than Isaac and Isaac is greater than Jacob and Jacob is greater than Levi, who's greater, Abraham or Levi? Abraham. And if Abraham is greater than Levi and Melchizedek is greater than Abraham, who's greater, Melchizedek or Levi?" Whew! You know the answer. Melchizedek is of a higher order than Levi, so Jesus' priesthood is superior to the priesthood of Aaron. That's the point.

God instructed Moses and Aaron to speak to the rock to bring forth water. Instead Moses struck the rock. Because of this act, God punished both Moses and Aaron (Num. 20:1-13). Why? And why did he punish Aaron when Moses was the one who committed the act?

I'm very much puzzled—as are a number of Bible scholars—by that episode in the Old Testament. The Bible doesn't really give us a clear explanation as to why God was so upset by this action of Moses or why Aaron was implicated in it as well.

If we read the text carefully, as well as read between the lines, it appears that God had given Moses some instructions, but Moses got a bit presumptuous and took it upon himself to make this gesture in an inappropriate way. That's the only reason I can think of for God's response; Moses' sin was one of presumption. He did not do it in the right way—at the right time or in the right manner—that God instructed.

The fact that Aaron is included in the punishment would indicate that he must have been somehow included in the action. The fact that the Bible is silent on his involvement doesn't exonerate Aaron altogether. We have to presume here that the text doesn't say everything that took place, and we know that God does not punish the innocent. The fact that God punished Aaron is evidence enough for me that Aaron was guilty of complicity in this event and that presumably both of them, Aaron and Moses, acted in an arrogant way, doing something that was unauthorized. Because of that, they forfeited certain benefits and blessings in the kingdom. Of course, they were not excluded from fellowship with God, but they endured the censure and the rebuke of God.

The same sort of thing occurred with the census of David (1 Chron. 21). Did God ordain the census that David took, or was it instigated by Satan? In the one version it's attributed to God, in the other one, to Satan. Of course, I don't think that's ultimately a contradiction because God is sovereign over Satan, and God will allow certain things to come to pass by giving a long leash to

Satan. The Jews might say God ordained this, but he didn't sanction it. He stood sovereign over it, and perhaps that has bearing on that text as well. Ultimately, we have to trust in the character of God, that he is just, even when we don't get the whole picture.

Why in the Old Testament does God demand so much violence and war of the Jewish nation?

One of the most difficult episodes for us to handle as people who live on this side of the New Testament are the Old Testament records of what is called the *herem*. This is where God calls Israel to embark in what we could call a holy war against the Canaanites. He tells them to go in there and wipe out everyone—men, women, and children. They were forbidden to take prisoners and were to utterly destroy and put the ban, or curse, upon this land before they occupied it for themselves.

When we look at that, we shrink in horror at the degree of violence that is not only tolerated but seemingly commanded by God in that circumstance. Critical scholars in the twentieth century have pointed to that kind of story in the Old Testament as a clear example that this couldn't be the revealed Word of God. They say that this is the case where some bloodthirsty, ancient, seminomadic Hebrews tried to appeal to their deity to sanction their violent acts and that we have to reject that as not being supernaturally inspired interpretations of history.

I take a different view of it. I am satisfied that the Old Testament is the inspired Word of God and that God did in fact command the Jewish nation to institute the *herem* against the Canaanites. God does tell us in the Old Testament why he instituted that policy against the Canaanite people. It's not as though God commanded a group of bloodthirsty marauders to come in and kill innocent people. Rather, the background was that the Canaanites were deeply entrenched in unrestrained forms of paganism that involved even such things as child sacrifice. It was a time of profound inhumanity within that nation. God said to Israel, "I am using you here in this war as an instrument of my judgment upon this nation, and I'm bringing my violence upon this unbelievably wicked people, the Canaanites." And he said, "I'm going to have them destroyed" (Deut. 13:12-17). In effect, he said to the Jewish people, "I want you to understand something: I'm giving to the Canaanites their just deserts, but I'm not giving them into your hands because you're a whole lot better. I could put the same kind of judgment on your heads for your sinfulness and be perfectly justified to do it." That's basically the sense of what God communicated to the Jews.

He said, "I am calling you out of my grace to be a holy nation. I'm tearing down in order to build something new, and out of what I build new, a holy nation, I'm going to bless all of the people in the world. Therefore, I want you to be separated, and I don't want any of the influences of this pagan heritage to be mixed into my new nation that I'm establishing." That is the reason he gives. People still choke on it, but if God is, indeed, holy—as I think he is—and we are as disobedient as I know we are, I think we ought to be able to handle that.

The Lord says in the Old Testament that he loved Jacob but he hated Esau, and in 1 John, John actually says that if we say we love God but yet hate our brothers, we're wrong. How can we reconcile these two passages?

God, who created us, has the right to demand of his creatures anything he desires; he certainly has the right to demand that we love others. And how can we, who are sinners, hate other people who are sinners for doing the very same things we are doing? Loving God, others, and ourselves is the great commandment, given first by God and then echoed by Jesus in the New Testament.

But if we're commanded to love everybody, how do we deal with this statement of God: "Jacob have I loved; Esau have I hated"?

First of all, we are dealing with a Hebrew idiom. It is the Hebrew form of speech we call antithetical parallelism, whereby the Scriptures speak in terms of direct opposites. To understand it, we have to see that whatever God means by hating Esau it means the exact opposite of what it means to love Jacob.

We use the terms *love* and *hate* to express human emotions and human feelings that we have toward people, but in the context in which this particular text occurs, when the Bible says that God loves Jacob, it means that he makes Jacob a recipient of his special grace and mercy. He gives Jacob a gift that he does not give to Esau. He gives mercy to Jacob. He withholds that same mercy from Esau because he doesn't owe Esau the mercy and he reserves the right as he says back then and in the New Testament, "I will have mercy upon whom I will have mercy." He displays benevolence. He gives an advantage; he gives a blessing to one sinner that he does not choose to give to another. The Jewish person describes that differential by using contradictory terms. One receives love; one receives hate. Now again, we have to remember that the Bible is being written in human terms, the only terms we have, and we can't read into the text the idea of feelings of hostility or of wickedness toward a human being. That's not what the Bible means when it uses that kind of language for God.

When Israel wrestled with the angel all night, is this to be taken literally, or is this a symbolic way of saying that Israel wrestled with an issue?

So often when we are faced with the question of interpreting a narrative like that literally or symbolically, we have to be very careful of what governs our answer. So often how we side on a question like that is conditioned or governed by our prior view of the supernatural. There are people who would come to a text like that with the previous judgment that there is no supernatural realm and that any scriptural report of the miraculous or the supernatural must be recast into naturalistic terms and interpreted according to psychological states. This in a sense compromises the text.

I have to say that when we allow that kind of prejudicial approach to Scripture to affect our interpretation of Scripture, we have violated the text, and we have violated objective principles of literary interpretation. I have much more respect for the scholar who would say that the text clearly suggests that there was a real wrestling match going on between Jacob and this angel than for someone who tries to spiritualize or relativize the episode by calling it a symbol.

Now, there are clearly times when the Bible is using imaginative language, symbols that ought not to be interpreted in concrete historical terms. The basic principle that would apply in interpreting a text such as this (or any other text where there's a question of whether it should be interpreted literally or figuratively) is that the brunt of the matter must be decided by a careful analysis of the literary genre in which the text appears.

People ask me if I interpret the Bible literally, and I usually say of course. What other way is there to interpret? To interpret the Bible literally does not mean to impose a wooden, concrete literalism upon the Scripture. *To interpret it literally means to interpret the book as it was written.* That's a scientific approach; that is, you interpret poetry according to the rules of poetry, letters according to the rules of letters, historical narratives according to the genre of historical narratives, and so on. Otherwise you are changing the intended meaning of the author, which is simply unethical.

My governing consideration in that text would be, What is the literary style or form in which it appears? If it's historical narrative, then I think it should be interpreted as historical narrative. Incidentally, in the case of this particular story, I'm persuaded that the text does have all of the elements of historical narrative, and I think the author intended to convey that there was a real visitation of a real angel and that there was a real wrestling match.

In the book of Judges it appears that a human sacrifice was performed and accepted. Please explain.

Not only do we have that difficult question as it appears in the book of Judges, presumably with the vow of Jephthah to sacrifice his daughter (Jud. 11:29-35), but also even earlier, in the book of Genesis, chapter 22, when God tells Abraham to offer his son Isaac on the altar at Mount Moriah.

Kierkegaard wrote a book that wrestled with this issue, and he described it as the temporary suspension of the ethical. I don't think God suspends the ethical even for Abraham. The question you're wrestling with is how could God accept or command a practice that he reveals elsewhere as being utterly repugnant to him?

Abraham did not have the benefit of the first five books of the Old Testament, in which all the laws and legislations and codes of holiness of Israel were set forth. But presumably he had at least the benefit of what we would call a natural law. That is the law that God gave to man from Adam onward, the chief principle of which is the sanctity of life and the prohibition against murder. Abraham had to be confused by this command of God to offer his son on the altar. He would have to know that it was utterly inconsistent with natural law.

But at the same time, it's like a man who comes to a red light at an intersection and a policeman is standing there with a white glove, waving him through. The light says stop, but the policeman says go. The policeman always supersedes the written motor-vehicle code. You obey the policeman and not the traffic light. So perhaps Abraham was thinking that although he knew what the law said, if the author of that law told him to break it, he had better break it.

You asked specifically about the problem in the book of Judges. In the holiness code, in the legislation of the Pentateuch, child sacrifice, practiced by other ancient religions, was seen not only as something that God frowned upon but as a capital offense in Israel—an utter abomination to God. Scripture speaks in the strongest possible language prohibiting the sacrifice of human beings as a religious activity. Religion can sink no lower than when it seeks to appease the deity through human sacrifice—with the obvious exception of the perfect sacrifice that was offered once for all, where God sacrificed his own Son for our sins.

My understanding of the book of Judges is this: Just like the rest of the Bible and particularly the Old Testament, Judges records for us not only the virtues of the people of God but also their vices. Jephthah's vow was a sinful one. He should have never made that vow in the first place. God didn't command him to make it; he made that vow and then in a mistaken concept of vow keeping thought it was his moral obligation to keep it when he discovered that he'd actually promised to kill his own daughter.

In fact, we would call that an unlawful vow. Once a person makes a vow to sin, he is required *not* to keep that vow if it obligates him to sin. I think that this passage is not so difficult from a theological standpoint but is simply a record of Jephthah's sin.

In Proverbs 21:14 it says, "A gift given in secret soothes anger, and a bribe concealed in the cloak pacifies great wrath." Why is this in the Bible?

That's a tough one. I think to understand it we have to do

a couple of things. First of all, we have to understand the nature of a proverb. A proverb is not an absolute moral law. A proverb is an expression of practical wisdom that is drawn from the daily experiences of life. They are not absolutes. For example, in English we have the proverbs Look before you leap, and He who hesitates is lost. If you made both of those absolutes, they'd cancel each other out. The same would be true if we made all the proverbs in the Bible into absolutes.

What makes this so difficult is that the proverb here draws practical wisdom from human sinfulness and tells us that the bribe sort of greases the skids and puts people's wrath away. The author of Proverbs, as a matter of practical wisdom, is very much concerned about human relationships and how to get along. One of the recurring themes of the book is dealing with people who are angry: "A soft answer turneth away wrath." That makes sense. It's not just a matter of virtue but one of practicality.

I remember once when I was coming out of Pittsburgh off the Liberty Bridge through the tunnels. I saw that the light was going to turn red. I was going to have to sit there for a long time. This policeman was motioning me over into another lane, and I went right around and back into the lane I wanted. Just as I was going to get past him, the light turned red and I had to stop. The policeman ran up to my car and started pounding on the roof. I knew I was in big trouble. I just turned to him and said, "I'm very sorry, officer." That sort of defused him, and he told me to go ahead and leave. That made me think that a soft answer does turn away wrath. It works.

This verse uses a literary device called parallelism—

saying the same thing in two similar ways. It says, "A gift given in secret soothes anger." There's nothing wrong with giving a secret gift to somebody. Then we see the parallel statement: "A bribe concealed in the cloak pacifies great wrath." What's being described here is the same thing as a surprise present. A bribe will also turn somebody's anger away.

I would say that the author of Proverbs is doing very much the same thing that Jesus did when he said that we are not as wise in the Christian community or in the believing community as thieves are out there. He talks about the unjust steward and says we can learn practical ways of getting along with people by watching how the thieves do it; they know how to stop people's anger and wrath as a matter of practical wisdom. I think that's what the author had in mind.

"Where there is no vision, the people perish." What is meant by this?

I'm sure you've heard that verse quoted many times in church—anytime there is a building program or a new educational program, for example. People are told that they have to catch the vision. We've set the goal before us, and without a vision the people perish. It's translated to mean in contemporary situations that without a goal, a project, or an objective, the people will be destroyed. That may be a secondary application of the original text, but that is not what the text meant when it was written in antiquity.

The original meaning of that text, "Without a vision the people perish," had to do with a prophetic vision. In the

Old Testament, God revealed himself through the proclamations of his prophets. Sometimes they received a word from God. These prophets functioned as agents of revelation, like Jeremiah and Isaiah. They were human vehicles through whom God spoke his word to the people. What the Proverbs are saying is that without the supernatural revelation of the word of God, the world would perish.

When Jesus appears in the New Testament, the prophecy of the Old Testament "The people who walk in darkness have seen a great light" is fulfilled. So often in the Bible, the concept of divine revelation is expressed through that metaphor of light into darkness. What I hear that text saying is that without the light of God's revelation, humanity would be left in utter darkness, and we would, in fact, perish.

We know people who aren't involved at all in the Judeo-Christian faith. They have no commitment to it whatsoever. They're still alive, they're not perishing, they're doing fine. They may not be perishing now, but they may be perishing ultimately.

Aside from that consideration, there's no significant culture that we know of in this world that has not received some of the fallout of the benefits of divine revelation. There's no place in the darkest point of this world and in the darkest hour of the dark ages where the light of God's revelation has been totally snuffed out or obscured or eclipsed. In fact, we couldn't live as human beings on this planet for five minutes except by the Word of God. No wonder Jesus said that it's through the Word of God that we live.

Would you please expound on Ecclesiastes 9:10, which says, "Whatsoever thy hand findeth to do, do it with all thy might"?

Before I answer that question specifically, I think it's important to make a few basic comments about the type of literature we find in the book of Ecclesiastes. It's very similar to the book of Proverbs and comes under the category of Hebrew Wisdom Literature, in which nuggets of wisdom and practical application of godliness are set forth in very succinct statements. We can easily get confused if we try to treat these statements as if they were moral absolutes. I'm convinced that the Bible provides many moral absolutes in the law of God that is expressed therein. But what you find in the maxims of Wisdom Literature are practical guidelines for behavior.

This particular passage from Ecclesiastes is not a universal absolute that says, "Anything you do, do with all of your might." There are lots of things that we do with our hands that are ungodly, and we ought not to be doing them with any commitment. What the book is saying here is that in the labor to which we are called, in the devotion that we give to God, in those things that are just and proper and good to which we apply ourselves, we are to do these things with determination, not in a casual manner. It's somewhat similar to Jesus saying that he would rather people be cold or hot, not lukewarm. Those who are lukewarm he said he will spew out of his mouth. He seems to have more respect for a zealous hostility than for indifference, for example.

The spirit of slothfulness falls under the rebuke of the

Wisdom Literature repeatedly. God calls us to an attitude, a lifestyle, of purpose and diligence. That means we are to do the tasks that are set before us with not only diligence but a certain kind of zeal for them. That very idea and sentiment is again repeated in the New Testament and especially with respect to seeking the kingdom of God. Jesus tells us that we are to set ourselves with a decisive spirit of endurance in seeking God's kingdom.

What does the Apostles' Creed mean when it says that Jesus descended into hell?

The Apostles' Creed is used as an integral form of worship in many Christian bodies. One of the more puzzling statements in that creed is: [Jesus] descended into hell.

First of all, we have to look at the creed from a historical perspective. We know that the Apostles' Creed was not written by the apostles, but it's called the Apostles' Creed because it was the early Christian community's attempt to give a summary of apostolic teaching. This, like other creeds in the church's history, was partly a response to distorted teachings that were present in some communities; it was statement of orthodox belief. The earliest reference we can find to that "descent into hell" element of the Creed is around the middle of the third century. That doesn't mean that it wasn't in the original—we don't know when the original was written—but it seems to be a later addition and has caused no small amount of controversy ever since. The reason for it is theological as well as biblical.

We see this problem: Jesus, when he's on the cross in his dying agony, speaks to the thief next to him and assures him that "today you will be with me in paradise." Now that statement from Jesus on the cross would seem to indicate that Jesus was planning to go to paradise, which is not to be confused with hell. So in some sense Jesus goes to paradise. We know that his body goes into the tomb. His soul apparently is in paradise. When does he go to hell? Or does he go to hell?

In 1 Peter 3:19, Peter talks about "this Jesus, who by the same spirit by which he is raised from the dead goes and preaches to the lost spirits in prison." That text has been used as the principal proof text to say that Jesus, at some point after his death, generally believed to be between his death and his resurrection, went to hell. Some people say that he went into hell to experience the fullness of the magnitude of suffering—the full penalty for human sin—in order to give complete atonement for sin. That is regarded by some as a necessary element of Christ's passion.

But most churches that believe in an actual descent of Jesus into hell do not see him going to hell for further suffering because Jesus declares on the cross, "It is finished." Rather, he goes to hell to liberate those spirits who, from antiquity, have been held in prison. His task in hell then is one of triumph, liberating Old Testament saints. I personally think that the Bible is less than clear on that point because the lost spirits in prison could very well refer to lost people in this world. Peter doesn't tell us who the lost spirits in prison are or where the prison is. People are making a lot of assumptions when they consider that this is a reference to hell and that Jesus went there between his death and his resurrection.

In the Sermon on the Mount, Jesus says, "Don't let your right hand know what your left hand is doing," and in another passage he says, "Let your light so shine before men." This seems like a contradiction.

When Jesus gave this teaching, he used several different styles of communication, the most famous of which is the parable. Another style of teaching that was common among the rabbis was to give a nugget of truth in what was called an aphorism. An aphorism is simply a succinct, pithy little statement that encapsulates or crystallizes a spiritual truth. Sometimes if you push these too far, you'll find some that rub up against each other and apparently are in conflict with each other.

When Jesus says, "Don't let your right hand know what your left hand is doing," he has just gone through a very lengthy rebuke for the ostentatious public display of piety that was the favorite preoccupation of the Pharisees. They prayed and dressed in sackcloth so that everybody would know how spiritual they were. They paraded their spiritual disciplines before the watching world as a matter of personal pride rather than out of godliness. They fought with each other over who got the seats of honor at the feasts and who was more religious than the other. Jesus severely rebuked them, for they were praying not to God, but they were praying to be seen by people. He rebuked them for the obvious hypocrisy of that. He told them to go into their closets and pray to God in secret, for God would listen to them in secret.

It's in that context that Jesus says, "Don't let your left hand know what your right hand is doing." In other words, if you're going to be doing these honorable things that are really ultimately an offering to God, they don't have to be known by people. This is something we do privately, anonymously. We don't parade our offerings and our worship to God for the sake of being seen.

By the same token, we are called to make visible the invisible kingdom of God by living lives of integrity. Our outward integrity is to be so clearly on display that it will be a beacon to those who observe it.

In Matthew 24, Christ tells the parable of the fig tree. In your opinion, just what does the fig tree represent?

When Jesus taught in parables, he drew examples from the normal activities of daily life—from stone masonry, agriculture, etc. He used the fig tree to teach a lesson on more than one occasion. We remember the occasion on which he cursed the fig tree for having blossoms but not giving any fruit. The indispensable indicator for the presence of fruit for a fig tree was not what season it was but whether or not it had blossoms. If it had the blossoms, it should have had the fruit. Jesus saw a fig tree blossoming out of the normal season, which would make it a special species of fig tree. He went over to get something to eat, and there were no figs, and so he cursed the fig tree as an object lesson of hypocrisy.

Flipping that around, when he uses the parable here, he uses the fig tree's propensity for blooming and bearing fruit as a positive indication for looking to the future. Jesus had given the Olivet discourse, in which he told his disciples to be alert to the signs of the times so that when he returns at the end of the age, his coming is not a total surprise to those who are to be watching for him.

What, specifically, does the fig tree represent? It's exceedingly dangerous to interpret parables in an allegorical sense. In an allegory every element of the story has a one-to-one correlation to some figurative or symbolic representation. There are times when Jesus did use allegory, as in the parable of the sower. But in that case Jesus provided the allegorical interpretation of the parable. Other than that, the normal use of parables is to communicate through the little story one single, simple lesson. We get into big trouble if we look at all of the elements of the story and want to make each concrete element a symbol for something in particular. I don't think you can do that with the parable of the fig tree. I think it is like most other parables; there's one basic lesson that Jesus is trying to communicate to his disciples, and that is to watch and be ready. When you see the signs of the times, look up, knowing that your redemption is near. When we see the things happening that he describes in the Olivet discourse, we should be alert to the fact that our redemption is soon, and it may be that these things are harbingers of the very return of Christ himself.

Some would like to look at those particular elements like the fig tree and say that's the restoration of Israel to their homeland or the recapturing of the city of Jerusalem, but such interpretations are speculative. I would rather be more careful and just say that it's the general meaning of the text to be careful, to be vigilant, to watch for the signs of the times.

In the book of John there's the statement that "you will know the truth and the truth will set you free." Could you explain what Jesus meant by "set you free"?

At least a clue to the meaning can be found by taking a good look at the context. When Jesus made that statement, he was talking about discipleship, and he said, "If you continue in my word, then are you my disciples, and you will know the truth and the truth will set you free."

When he said that, it agitated some of the clergy who were standing nearby, the Pharisees specifically. They became very annoyed with Jesus for saying that, and they protested, saying, "Hey, we're in bondage to no man." And then they said, "We're the children of Abraham." Jesus rebuked them severely, saying, "You're the children of those whom you serve." And then he told them they were children of Satan because they were doing the will of their father, the devil.

On the one hand, Jesus identifies sonship in terms of obedience: "You are the son of whom you obey." Since the track that Jesus takes is one that emphasizes obedience, I think that's the clue. When he's speaking of freedom, he's not speaking of political freedom or financial freedom. He's speaking of spiritual freedom—freedom from bondage or slavery to wickedness. Jesus picks up on this theme more than once, as do other speakers and writers in the New Testament. When Paul, for example, describes the condition of fallen man, he talks of fallen man as being in bondage to his own evil inclinations. And conversely, the Holy Spirit is described as one who is the author of liberty: "Where the Spirit of the Lord is, there is liberty."

This touches on a major issue in theology that has to do with natural man; that is, fallen man's moral power or moral ability. Every church that I know of in the World Council of Churches has some doctrine of original sin. They don't all agree as to the exact degree to which the human race has fallen, and there are details of debate that center around original sin. But original sin is not the first sin, the sin that Adam and Eve committed. Original sin refers to the *result* of mankind's initial transgression against the law of God. Not only was guilt incurred and man exposed to punishment, but something happened to our moral constitution. There is a blemish in our very structure and makeup so that now, as human beings, we all have a tendency and a proclivity toward evil that was not put there by God in the first place. Insofar as we surrender to the wicked impulses that somehow can dictate our lives, we are in moral bondage and need to be liberated. This is one of the great messages of the New Testament gospel: Christ liberates us from the power of evil.

Could you comment on Jesus' statement that we shouldn't throw our pearls before swine?

That statement is what we call one of the hard sayings of Jesus. It's so uncharacteristic of Jesus to talk that way about people—to call people swine, particularly for a Jew to call somebody swine. Such a shoot-from-the-hip statement from Jesus startles us.

When Jesus sent the seventy disciples out to proclaim the gospel, he told them to travel light. He told them that when they came to a village, if the people refused to hear them, they were to shake the dust off their feet and go else-where. It's in that kind of a context that Jesus talked about giving pearls to swine. In reaching out to others with the gospel, we're not to give up easily (this patient attitude runs through several parables and in Scripture in general). But from the standpoint of strategy, it's ineffective to be reaching out constantly to people who are steadfastly, ada-mantly opposed to the Christian faith. We see many, many cases in which those people mellow and actually come to Christ. But to spend all of your attention on those people is not the best use of time and energy.

If people despise the things of God, we are certainly not supposed to write them off or to stop being concerned about them, but at the same time, we're not supposed to invest our best things over and over again in those people.

In the story of the adulterous woman, what did Jesus write in the sand?

We have no idea what Jesus wrote in the sand. In fact, that is the only reference that we have anywhere that Jesus ever wrote anything. I suspect he was literate and he could write, but he didn't leave any documents for us to read to this day—so we can only guess what he wrote in the sand. My guess is that he was being very specific. The text notes that these people were in a frenzy; they had taken up stones and were going to kill this woman who had been caught in the act of adultery. They tried to entrap Jesus with a theological issue concerning the law of Moses and the law of Caesar. On that occasion Jesus made the com-ment, "Let him who is without sin cast the first stone." And then he waited for the executioners to volunteer, and he stooped down and wrote in the sand. We're told that as he wrote in the sand the people, beginning with the older ones, started to leave—they put down their stones and walked away.

We can only speculate, of course, but I figure that Jesus looked one man in the eye and wrote the name of this man's mistress, and for another guy he wrote down, "extortion," and for another, "embezzlement." I think he could see the sins of these people. He started writing them down, and nobody wanted to see any more, so they put down their stones and got out of there in a hurry. This is sheer guesswork, but that, to me, is the kind of thing that Jesus would do to defuse a mob that's bent on passing judgment.

What are we to do with our brothers and sisters if we know them to be involved in sin? We get some instruction in the New Testament on these things. We are told that if we see a brother or sister engaged in a serious matter of sin, we are to go to them privately and discuss this with them. If there is no repentance, then we are to take two elders, and so on. There is a procedure to be followed (Matt. 18:15-17). Notice that, in the spirit of Jesus, the procedure bends over backwards to protect the dignity of the guilty person. And the whole purpose of this is not to accuse or to punish but to redeem. It's not an exercise of judgmental spirit. The New Testament says that there is a love that covers a multitude of sins. We are not to be confronting each other with peccadillos; we are not to be nitpickers. One of the Christian community's great weaknesses today is its pettiness. Pettiness can be very destructive to the Christian community, and we tend to oscillate between two extremes—overly severe and judgmental or letting anything go without daring to criticize. We are called to keep each other concerned about righteousness, but in a spirit of meekness.

In Acts 16 Paul encourages Timothy to be circumcised, then later condemns it. Was he being hypocritical?

I don't think the apostle was being hypocritical at all. This is a very interesting historical situation that the New Testament records for us. It does say that Paul circumcised Timothy and then refused to circumcise Titus, and this became a major controversy in the early church. Paul's reasoning behind it, I think, can be ferreted out through a study of Galatians, Corinthians, and Romans.

He talks about his concern for ethics and says that there are certain things God prohibits and certain things he commands. Then there are those things that are basically neutral in the ethical sense—those things that in and of themselves have no moral import or ethical significance. He is consistent in his approach to these things, as we read in correspondence to the Romans and Corinthians; these are areas in which Christians can exercise their liberty.

But the Judaizing party sprang up and threatened to destroy the infant Christian church by seeking to impose the absolute law of circumcision on every convert to Christianity. The counsel of Jerusalem in Acts 15 was one of those examples of the church having to respond to this. The counsel's conclusion was that it pleased the Holy Spirit not to add all of these burdens upon Gentile converts that God had required of the Jewish nation in the

Old Testament. What had happened in contemporary terms is this: Those who wanted to cling to some of the now antiquated practices were considered by Paul to be weaker brothers, and Paul said we don't do anything to cause the weaker brother to stumble. We want to be sensitive to the weaker brother.

But suddenly the weaker brothers became so strong that they wanted to tyrannize the church and make their preferences the absolute law of God. Whenever people do that, it is a representation of legalism that destroys the essence of the gospel. Paul, by the time he wrote Galatians, saw the expansion of this group of Judaizers as being such a threat to the truth of the Christian gospel that he steadfastly refused to engage in circumcision as a religious act and used the strongest language to condemn those who were trying to make a matter of personal preference the absolute law of God.

You remember the earlier debate that Jesus had with the Pharisees. Jesus was very harsh with them because he said that they had taken the traditions of men and passed them off as if they were the laws of God, something we are not permitted to do. Jesus took the Pharisees to task for doing it, and Paul did the same thing; that is, in the earlier situation in which circumcision didn't have this legal import to it, he went with the flow. He said if you want to be circumcised, fine; if you don't want to, you don't have to. So for those who wanted it, he did it. But when they tried to make it a law that he circumcise other people, he steadfastly refused to do it, in order to keep the integrity of the gospel intact.

First Corinthians 15:29 says, "Otherwise, what will those do who are baptized for the dead? If the dead are not raised at all, why then are they baptized for them?" I know it's a Mormon doctrine to believe in baptism of the dead by proxy. What is the Christian view of this?

There's not a single text in all of Scripture that gives an explicit mandate for the church to practice proxy baptism, or baptism for the dead, and yet here is a practice that has emerged in one religious body. The text cited as proof of this is 1 Corinthians 15:29. We notice that Paul does not say to his readers, "You should baptize the dead," but he asks the question, "Why is it that some of you are baptizing for the dead if in fact the dead are not raised?" The fact that Paul asks a question about it indicates that there were people practicing it. When he asks the question, there is neither an explicit or implicit rebuke for the practice. Some have looked at that and said that the apostle Paul recognized that this kind of practice was going on in the Corinthian community and he didn't denounce it, so it has a tacit apostolic approval, and perhaps we're missing something we ought to be doing.

But we don't have a mandate to do it, and I think there's much in Scripture to indicate that this practice is utterly repugnant to God because of its theological implications.

We have to understand why Paul says what he says in 1 Corinthians 15. This entire chapter is Paul's magnificent defense of the resurrection of Christ. He is responding as a theologian to a spirit of skepticism that had emerged in the Corinthian church. Word had come to him that some people in the church were denying the Resurrection. So Paul explored the implications of that. If there is no such thing as resurrection (which is what the Sadducees believed) and if there is no life after death, what are the consequences? First of all, if there is no resurrection, then Christ is not raised. So if there's no resurrection whatsoever, that eliminates the resurrection of Christ. If there is no resurrection of Christ, what are the implications of that? That means you're still in your sins. There's been no mark of divine approval on Christ's perfect sacrifice for your justification. It means you're a false witness of God because you've been running around telling everybody that, in fact, Jesus was raised and that it was God who raised him.

Paul goes on to say that if Christ is not raised, then those who have fallen asleep have perished. The dead are dead. We'll never see them again; it's all over. He goes on to give them all these options.

In this process he uses a classical form of argument, the ad hominem argument, in which you argue on the other person's grounds and show the inconsistency of their position. Paul, in essence, is saying, "I know some of you people are out there practicing baptism for the dead and at the same time saying that there's no resurrection. What in the world are you doing it for?" In other words, he's showing the folly of denying resurrection and practicing something that would depend on resurrection for it to have any meaning. But Paul is in no way endorsing the practice of baptism by proxy.

What does the writer of Hebrews 6 mean when he writes, "It is impossible to restore again to repentance those who have once been enlightened and have become partakers of the Holy Spirit"?

In the ongoing debate among Christians as to the possibility of losing our salvation, that text is certainly the one most frequently discussed and debated. Those who believe that you can fall from grace to the point of losing your salvation look at Hebrews 6 as Exhibit A to prove it. There is this solemn warning and admonition to those who had been enlightened, who had tasted the heavenly gift, that if they fall away, it's impossible to restore them again to repentance.

It's difficult to know exactly what the author of Hebrews means by this text, for several reasons. First of all, we don't know who wrote the book, and second, we don't know to whom it was written. Most important, we're not sure of the immediate issue that provoked the writing. Some look at it as a crisis of people caving in under Roman persecution and people were denying Christ publicly. Maybe that was the temptation. A more frequent view is that it was a temptation to fall into the sin of the Judaizing heresy of returning to a legalistic structure of Old Testament religion.

My position on the passage is this: There is a strong admonition here saying it's impossible to restore again to repentance those who have been enlightened, tasted the heavenly gift, and participated in the Holy Spirit. I question whether the author is describing a Christian in the first place. On the surface it would seem that he is because those descriptive terms "enlightened" and "tasted the heavenly gifts" would certainly be true of a Christian. However, in the broader context of Hebrews he talks about those who are church members, even as members of the body of Israel in the Old Testament, who had all the benefits of the church and the presence of Christ in their midst, who were never really redeemed.

There are many commentators who believe that the author of Hebrews is talking about people who are inside the community and have the benefits of hearing the Word of God. They are enlightened, they have the sacraments and all of these things, but they're not genuinely converted.

I'm not persuaded, however, that that's what the text means because he uses the phrase as you quoted, "to be restored again to repentance." Repentance in the book of Hebrews and throughout the whole New Testament is a fruit of regeneration. True repentance is only something that a Christian can do, so there had been an authentic prior repentance if he was talking about restoring them again to repentance.

I take the position that what we have here is an ad hominem argument throughout, in which the author is arguing a reasoning through the other man's position. He's saying, "OK, let's look at your position. Suppose it's the Judaizing heresy. If you reject Christ and go back to the old system and you've done away with the Cross, what possibility would you have of being saved under that system? You've just rejected the only way of salvation there is." He's not saying that it's the unforgivable sin, but you couldn't be restored as long as you were in that position. Notice he doesn't say that anybody does it. In fact, at the end of that text he says, "But I am persuaded of better things of you, that which is consistent to those of your calling." I think it's a hypothetical warning against an argument, but it doesn't teach that any true Christian does lose his salvation.

Lately people have been talking to me about "curse Scriptures." Is this something Christians should be worried about? Are curses passed down?

When we talk about curses in contemporary American culture, it sounds like something out of the dark ages or like some voodoo witch doctor who's putting a curse on somebody by sticking pins in dolls. Yet the concept of the curse is one of the most important concepts we find in Scripture because the laws of God that he delivers to Israel in the Old Testament are set before the nation in terms of two polarities. On the one hand, when God gives his law to his people and enters into a covenant with them, he says that if they keep the terms of this covenant, if they obey his laws, they will be blessed. He says, "Blessed will you be in the city and in the country, when you stand up and when you sit down, in everything you do I will bless you."

But he says, "If you break My law, disobey My commandment, and violate My covenant, then cursed shall you be in the city, cursed shall you be in the country." Then what follows are terrifying penalties and punishments that God promises to people who refuse to obey him. They are encapsulated by the word *curse*. To be cursed in the Old Testament meant ultimately to be cut off from the presence of God, to be sent out from his immediate presence, just as the scapegoat was cursed in Israel by being driven out into the wilderness, away from where the presence of

God was focused in the center of the camp. To be cursed meant to be sent into the outer darkness where the face of God did not shine and the light of his countenance did not penetrate.

As I said, it's so important because the whole idea of atonement, not only in the Old Testament but also in the New Testament, is centered on that concept of the curse. In Galatians Paul tells us that Christ on the cross became a curse for us; he was accursed—cut off from the Father, sent outside the camp, even crucified outside the city limits of Jerusalem—to make certain that the whole of God's curse promised to the evildoer would be visited upon himself so that he might bear the whole the sinner's punishment.

The Bible clearly speaks about curses, and the worst possible curse is to be outside the circle of God's benefits. He also says that there is such a thing as the visitation of the consequences of evil upon future generations. In the Ten Commandments we are told that the sins can be visited to the second or third generation. The descendants of Canaan are cursed by Noah. Ham is the one who received the curse, and he received it as a direct consequence of his father. Accursed Canaan is the one who received the consequence of the sin of his father, Ham.

I would say that the negative loss of many of God's promises to people flow down through time and space onto the next generation. It doesn't mean that God directly punishes a person for a sin somebody else committed. God says that each person is punished for their own sins. However, we still deal with the consequences that come down from previous generations and in that sense miss out on some of the benefits of God.

INDEX

A

597

G

grace *119-121*
  common *321*
Graham, Billy *66, 472*
Great High Priest *116*
guilt *128*

H
Habakkuk *269*
head coverings *347-348*
headship *348*
healing *478*
heaven *282-288, 291, 300, 303-304*
Hebrew Wisdom Literature *578*
Heisenberg uncertainty principle *188*
hell *301-304, 579*
heresy *337*
Hinduism *313*
Hitler, Adolf *268-269, 497, 533*
holiness of God *8, 14-16*
Holiness of God, The *8*
Holy Spirit *57, 359*
  and God's will *255*
  and regeneration *58, 60*
  baptism of *60-61, 63-64, 239, 340*
  blasphemy against *69-70*
  filling of *60-61*
  grieving of *68*
  in Old Testament *58, 64*
  indwelling of *62*
  leading of *67-68, 255*
  quenching of *66*
  Spirit of truth *68*
  work of *66, 68, 78, 137, 192, 245, 272*
human autonomy *27*
human dignity *520*

K

Kant, Immanuel *512*
Kempis, Thomas à *155*
Kierkegaard, Søren *456, 473*
King Saul *297*
kingdom of God *493-494*
kingdom of heaven *493*
Knowing God *356*
Knowing Scripture *227*
Knox, John *139*

L

labor unions *422*
Lamech *382*
language of the Bible *21*
last days *487, 489, 498, 518*
last rites *481*
Lazarus *478*
leadership *517*
life after death *288*
life goals *257*
life-support systems *457*
lifestyle *511-512, 553*
light of the world *248*
Ligonier Ministries *553*
limbo
    doctrine of *296*
Living Bible, The *90, 92*
Lord's Day *351*
Lord's Prayer *13, 199, 208-209*
Lord's Supper *358-359*
lotteries *441, 443*
love of God *5*
Lucifer *267*
Luther, Martin *126, 139, 215, 226, 250, 259-260, 271, 289, 309,*
    468, 488, 491
lying *527*

M

P

Packer, Dr. James   *356*
pain   *470*
parable of the fig tree   *582-583*
parables   *582*
paradise   *283, 294*
paramutual betting   *442-443*
pastors   *342-343*
peer pressure   *397*
perfection   *242*
personal evangelism   *316*
Peter   *118, 275*
Pharisees   *69, 136, 160, 241, 251, 281, 437, 487*
phenomenological language   *21*
philosophies   *174-175*
physical abuse   *404*
physical bodies   *230*
pleasure   *469*
politicians   *550*
politics   *344, 550*
polygamy   *381-382*
poor, the   *441, 521*
praise   *355-356*
prayer   *214*
   and God the Father   *202*
   and God's sovereignty   *199*
   and God's will   *206*
   and healing   *479*
   and nonbelievers   *212*
   and sin   *213*
   answers to   *200*
   practice of   *207, 209*
   unanswered   *393*
predestination   *29, 108, 132*
presbyterian church structure   *332*